T0049546

This book comes with access to more content online.
Take eight practice tests!

Register your book or ebook at
www.dummies.com/go/getaccess.

Select your product, and then follow the prompts
to validate your purchase.

You'll receive an email with your PIN and instructions.

ASVAB AFQT

4th Edition

by Angie Papple Johnston
Former U.S. Army NCO

ASVAB AFQT For Dummies®, 4th Edition

Published by: **John Wiley & Sons, Inc.**, 111 River Street, Hoboken, NJ 07030-5774, www.wiley.com

Copyright © 2024 by John Wiley & Sons, Inc., Hoboken, New Jersey

Published simultaneously in Canada

For general information on our other products and services, please contact our Customer Care Department within the U.S. at 877-762-2974, outside the U.S. at 317-572-3993, or fax 317-572-4002. For technical support, please visit https://hub.wiley.com/community/support/dummies.

Wiley publishes in a variety of print and electronic formats and by print-on-demand. Some material included with standard print versions of this book may not be included in e-books or in print-on-demand. For more information about Wiley products, visit www.wiley.com.

Library of Congress Control Number: 2023947982

ISBN 978-1-394-21636-9 (pbk); ISBN 978-1-394-21629-1 (ebk); ISBN 978-1-394-17268-4 (ebk)

SKY10058747_102723

Contents at a Glance

Table of Contents

Introduction

Because you're reading this book, there's a very good chance that you're interested in joining the U.S. military. I say that because military recruiting commands are the only people in the entire world who care about the Armed Forces Qualification Test (AFQT) score. The AFQT score is derived from four of the ten Armed Services Vocational Aptitude Battery (ASVAB) subtests. It's used to determine your overall qualification to join the military branch of your choice; a high enough score says that the military can most likely train you in a useful field.

Maybe you've read the best-selling *ASVAB For Dummies* (John Wiley & Sons, Inc.) or some other ASVAB prep book and you want more practice so you can earn the highest possible AFQT score, or maybe you took a few practice tests and didn't do very well in the math and English sections. Perhaps you've already taken the ASVAB, you want to retest for a higher AFQT score, and you're looking for an advantage. Or maybe you received this book as a gift from someone who cares about your future in the military. In any case, the right book is in your hands.

The ASVAB has two purposes:

» It's designed to tell the military whether you can cut it within its ranks.

» It's also designed to show the military where you'll shine as a servicemember. Four subtests of the ASVAB (Word Knowledge, Paragraph Comprehension, Mathematics Knowledge, and Arithmetic Reasoning) make up the AFQT. The same four subtests, plus the remaining six, are used to determine the fields in which you're eligible to work. (There's no such thing as an Army astronaut. I've checked.)

Long gone are the days when you could just walk into a recruiter's office and get into the military as long as you had a pulse. Today's all-volunteer military members are the cream of the crop — not only do you need to make it through the ASVAB to pass muster, but you also need to pass a physical qualification test and a medical exam.

Something else you may not know: The military services can't just grow to whatever size they want. Like any other government agency, they have a budget, and they have to operate within that budget. Every year, when Congress passes the annual Defense Authorization Act, it tells each military branch how many members it's allowed to have at any given time. By law, the services can't go over the size mandated by congressional leaders (who hold the military purse strings).

Did you also know that of every five people who walk into a military recruiter's office, only about one is allowed to enlist? Sure, many are disqualified because of medical history or criminal history, but some are turned away because their AFQT scores are too low, other qualified applicants have higher AFQT scores, or they can't pass the physical fitness requirements.

About This Book

Full-disclosure doctrine requires me to inform you that much of the information in this book can be found in *ASVAB For Dummies*. The AFQT is, after all, part of the ASVAB, and I wouldn't cheat you by putting part of the information in one book and part of the information in another.

So why should you spend some of your hard-earned money on this book, particularly if you've already bought *ASVAB For Dummies?* Because here you find expanded, more-detailed information about the AFQT and the four subtests that make up the AFQT score. If you're worried about your AFQT score, this book will help you get the highest score you can.

Even if you're not worried about your AFQT score, this book contains four additional practice tests for the four most important subtests of the ASVAB. That way, you can squeeze in some extra practice, which may help you boost your scores enough to land your dream job.

Foolish Assumptions

While writing this book, I made a few assumptions about you — namely, who you are and why you picked up this book. I assume the following:

» You aren't an idiot. You just want information to help you get the highest AFQT score possible.

» You're a high-school graduate, you have a high-school equivalency certificate, or you have at least some college credits. You just want to brush up on your high-school math and/or English skills as they apply to the AFQT. (If you aren't a high-school graduate or if you don't have a high-school equivalency certificate or at least some college credits, you probably need to get back to school before you can join the military. Very few applicants with a high-school equivalency certificate are allowed to enlist, and in many cases, only if they have college credits.)

» You want to join the U.S. military and want to take advantage of all the enlistment goodies that are available, such as enlistment bonuses or additional education benefits. Depending on current recruiting needs, the services often tie enlistment incentives to high AFQT scores. High AFQT scores also help you pick the job you want — and the job you want may be offering a high-dollar enlistment bonus.

Icons Used in This Book

Throughout this book you find icons — little pictures in the margins — that help you use the material in this book to your best advantage. Here's a rundown of what they mean:

TIP

The Tip icon alerts you to helpful hints regarding the subject at hand. Tips can help you save time and score higher on the AFQT.

REMEMBER

The Remember icon highlights important information you should read carefully.

WARNING

The Warning icon flags information that may prove hazardous to your plans of acing the AFQT. Often, this icon accompanies common mistakes people make when taking the test or qualifying for enlistment. Pay special attention to the Warning icon so you don't fall into a trap on the test.

EXAMPLE

The Example icon points out sample questions that appear in the review chapters.

The Technical Stuff icon points out information that's interesting, enlightening, or in-depth but that isn't necessary for you to read. You don't need this information to maximize your AFQT score, but knowing it may make you a better-informed test-taker — or at least help you impress your friends!

Beyond This Book

In addition to the book you're reading right now, be sure to check out the free online Cheat Sheet for details on the AFQT scores you need to enlist in each branch of the military and some pointers on how to achieve a high score on the two math subtests. To get this Cheat Sheet, simply go to www.dummies.com and type "ASVAB AFQT Cheat Sheet" in the Search box.

The online practice that comes free with this book includes computerized versions of the four AFQT practice tests you see in the book, plus four additional AFQT exams. The beauty of the online tests is that you can customize your online practice to focus on the areas that give you the most trouble. If you need help with Paragraph Comprehension questions or Arithmetic Reasoning problems, just select those question types online and start practicing. If you're short on time but want to get a mixed bag of a limited number of questions, you can specify the number of questions you want to practice. Whether you practice a few hundred questions in one sitting or a couple dozen, and whether you focus on a few types of questions or practice every type, the online program keeps track of the questions you get right and wrong so you can monitor your progress and spend time studying exactly what you need.

To gain access to the online practice, all you have to do is register. Just follow these simple steps:

1. **Register your book or ebook at** Dummies.com **to get your PIN. Go to** www.dummies.com/go/getaccess.

2. **Select your product from the dropdown list on that page.**

3. **Follow the prompts to validate your product, and then check your email for a confirmation message that includes your PIN and instructions for logging in.**

If you do not receive this email within two hours, please check your spam folder before contacting us through our Technical Support website at http://support.wiley.com or by phone at 877-762-2974.

Now you're ready to go! You can come back to the practice material as often as you want — simply log on with the username and password you created during your initial login. No need to enter the access code a second time.

Your registration is good for one year from the day you activate your PIN.

Where to Go from Here

You don't have to read this book from cover to cover in order to maximize your AFQT score. If you decide to skip around, look over the table of contents and choose which topics you're interested in studying.

You may already know that you'll ace the Paragraph Comprehension subtest, so you want to brush up on math word problems. If so, head to Chapters 10 and 11.

You may want to jump straight to Chapter 12 and take the first AFQT practice exam — that way, you can get an idea of which subjects you need to study more. Early on in your reading of the book, check out Chapter 1, which provides invaluable information regarding how the AFQT score is computed and how the score applies to military enlistment.

No matter where you start, you're smart enough to know that studying will help you in the long run — and your skill for keeping an eye on the big picture will serve you well during your military career.

1
Getting Started with the ASVAB AFQT

IN THIS CHAPTER

» **Examining the AFQT**

» **Checking out the advantages of a high AFQT score**

» **Crunching the numbers on AFQT scores**

» **Planning for retakes**

Chapter **1**
Taking a Closer Look at the AFQT

If you're thinking about joining the U.S. military, your Armed Forces Qualification Test (AFQT) score may well be the most important score you earn on any military test. It determines whether you even qualify for enlistment in the branch you choose. Without a qualifying AFQT score, your recruiter will tell you to go home, study, and try again in a few months. You could be a young Avenger in the making, in perfect health, and able to run 3 miles in 15 minutes, but none of that matters if you don't have a qualifying AFQT score.

The Armed Services have years and years of research to back up their policy of using the AFQT score as an enlistment qualification. Dozens of studies have shown that a person's AFQT score is one of the most significant factors in determining whether they'll make it through basic training and their first enlistment period. As of 2018, the latest year for which data is available, it cost between $55,000 and $74,000 to process a new recruit for enlistment and send that person through basic training and job-specific schooling, so you can see why the services want to maximize their chances of getting their money's worth.

Thankfully, with a little review, you should be able to score well on the AFQT. The score is, after all, composed of four areas that you studied intensely during your high-school years: basic math, math word problems, vocabulary, and reading. That's where this new edition of *ASVAB AFQT For Dummies* comes in. Other test-prep books, such as *ASVAB For Dummies* (John Wiley & Sons, Inc.), try to prepare you for the entire Armed Services Vocational Aptitude Battery (ASVAB) and may be a great addition to your review, but this book is specifically designed to help you boost the most important ASVAB score of all: the AFQT score.

Viewing the AFQT Close-Up

The military uses four of the ASVAB subtests to compute your AFQT score. This score determines whether you're qualified to join the military service of your choice. Each branch of military service has its own minimum AFQT score standards.

Here are the four subtests that make up your AFQT score:

» **Arithmetic Reasoning:** The Arithmetic Reasoning subtest consists of math word problems. The subtest is multiple-choice. On the computerized-adaptive test (the *CAT* version or *CAT-ASVAB*), which most applicants take, you get 39 minutes to correctly solve 16 questions. If you're taking the paper version, you get 36 minutes to solve as many of the 30 problems as you can. Chapter 10 leads you step-by-step through solving math word problems. Take a look at Chapter 11 for some tips on doing well on this subtest.

» **Word Knowledge:** The Word Knowledge subtest is a vocabulary test plain and simple. You have to find words that are "closest in meaning" or "most opposite in meaning" to underlined words in the question stem. You have to define 16 words in 8 minutes on the CAT-ASVAB or define 35 words in 11 minutes on the paper version. You can boost your vocabulary knowledge by following the advice in Chapter 4 and get an idea of what the subtest is all about in Chapter 5.

» **Paragraph Comprehension:** The Paragraph Comprehension subtest requires you to read a paragraph and then answer one to four questions about information contained in that paragraph. The computerized version has 11 questions in all, and you're expected to complete the subtest in 22 minutes; the paper version has 15 questions you have to power through in 13 minutes. Chapter 6 can help you sharpen your reading comprehension skills, and you can get a little practice with the Paragraph Comprehension subtest in Chapter 7. (*Note:* Many other standardized tests refer to this type of question as "reading comprehension." The military likes to do things its own way, so it refers to them as "paragraph comprehension" questions. Different name, same thing.)

» **Mathematics Knowledge:** This subtest measures your ability to solve high-school level math problems. You have to solve 16 basic math problems in 20 minutes on the CAT-ASVAB or 25 questions in 24 minutes on the paper version. Like the other subtests of the AFQT, all the questions are multiple-choice. To make sure your math skills measure up, see Chapter 8. Chapter 9 gives you an idea about the test format as well as a little extra math practice.

If you have a high AFQT score, you can expect your recruiter to be wining and dining you, offering you all kinds of enlistment incentives, and telling everyone in the office that you're a rockstar. On the other hand, if your AFQT score is below the minimum standards set by that service, you can expect your recruiter to say, "Don't call us. We'll call you." If you have a qualifying AFQT score that's mediocre, you can probably still enlist, but you'll most likely miss out on the extras, such as enlistment bonuses. (Maybe you'll get a free T-shirt.)

The AFQT isn't a stand-alone test. You can't just walk into a recruiter's office and say you want to take the AFQT. You have to take the entire ASVAB, which consists of nine separate subtests. Your AFQT score determines whether you're qualified to join the service of your choice. (Turn to the section "Scoring the AFQT" later in this chapter for more on the qualifying scores for each service.)

REMEMBER

The AFQT isn't the only qualifying standard the military uses. You have to meet all set standards in order to qualify for enlistment, including age, height and weight, number of dependents, medical history, education level, and criminal history.

Reaping the Benefits of the Highest Possible Score

The services put great stock in your AFQT score. Not only does a high AFQT score give you a greater chance of enlistment, but it also means you may have access to special incentives, such as the following:

>> **Enlistment bonuses and benefits:** Depending on current recruiting needs, individual services often tie the AFQT score to enlistment incentives, such as monetary bonuses or education benefits. For example, the Army often requires a minimum AFQT score of 50 to qualify for a bonus or to qualify for the Student Loan Repayment Program and other programs and benefits.

>> **More access to desirable jobs:** Most military jobs are tied to individual line scores derived from the entire ASVAB, but certain enlistment programs sometimes require a minimum AFQT score that is significantly higher than the minimum score needed for a regular enlistment. For example, some Navy jobs (such as those in the nuclear field) require a higher AFQT score.

>> **Education level:** You have to have a high-school diploma in order to join any of the services. The services can, however, take a limited number of applicants with high-school equivalency certificates each year. To qualify with one of these certificates, you must often score higher on the AFQT than a qualified high-school diploma holder.

>> **Quotas:** When the services are doing well meeting their recruitment goals, they run out of space before they run out of applicants. At these times, the services get to pick and choose whom they let join and whom they don't. Branches commonly raise their AFQT minimum scores temporarily to separate the best-qualified applicants from the rest. Sometimes enlistment gets so competitive that the services require a minimum score of 50 just to consider you. As of this writing, minimum scores for the services tend to rest in the 30s.

>> **Waivers:** One past study indicated that only three out of ten people who walked into a recruiter's office were qualified for enlistment. Certain factors — such as criminal history, age, education level, number of dependents, or medical history — made them ineligible. Some of these eligibility criteria can be waived (sometimes with difficulty and processing delays). However, when the military grants a waiver, it's taking a chance on an otherwise ineligible recruit. For example, if you have criminal misdeeds in your past and require a waiver to enlist, a service is much more likely to grant the waiver if you score 85 on the AFQT than it is if you score 45.

WARNING

Enlistment standards, programs, quotas, and incentives change — sometimes on a week-by-week basis — depending on the service's current recruiting needs. For the latest information, check with a military recruiter.

The AFQT is scored as a percentile. That means, for example, that if you score 70, you've scored as well as or higher than 70 percent of the people whose knowledge yours was measured against. The highest possible score on the AFQT is 99.

TIP

The AFQT isn't a one-shot deal. If you don't achieve a qualifying score, you can retest. After your first test, you have to wait at least 30 days to take a second test. After the second test, in most cases, you have to wait six months before you can test again. Keep in mind the age requirements and needs of the service. Although you can retest, getting a qualifying score upfront is the best way to keep your recruiter happy and your training and placement on schedule.

Understanding the ASVAB from 30,000 Feet

Depending on where and why you take the test, you may encounter two different versions of the ASVAB: the computerized version and the pencil-and-paper version.

The computerized version of the ASVAB (CAT-ASVAB) contains nine separately timed subtests. On the CAT-ASVAB, Auto Information and Shop Information are separated into two different tests, whereas they're combined on the paper version. In Table 1-1, I outline the nine ASVAB subtests in the order that you take them; the bolded subtests are used to calculate the AFQT score.

TABLE 1-1 **Details about the ASVAB Subtests**

Subtest	Questions/Time (CAT-ASVAB)	Questions/Time (Paper Version)	Content
General Science	15 questions, 10 minutes	25 questions, 11 minutes	General principles of biological and physical sciences
Arithmetic Reasoning	15 questions, 55 minutes	30 questions, 36 minutes	Math word problems
Word Knowledge	15 questions, 9 minutes	35 questions, 11 minutes	Correct meaning of a word and best synonym or antonym for a given word
Paragraph Comprehension	10 questions, 27 minutes	15 questions, 13 minutes	Questions based on paragraphs (usually a few hundred words) that you read
Mathematics Knowledge	15 questions, 23 minutes	25 questions, 24 minutes	High-school math
Electronics Information	15 questions, 10 minutes	20 questions, 9 minutes	Electricity and electronic principles and terminology
Auto and Shop Information	10 Auto Information questions, 7 minutes; 10 Shop Information questions, 6 minutes	25 questions, 11 minutes	Knowledge of automobiles, shop terminology, and tool use
Mechanical Comprehension	15 questions, 22 minutes	25 questions, 19 minutes	Basic mechanical and physical principles
Assembling Objects	15 questions, 17 minutes	25 questions, 15 minutes	Spatial orientation

You can't take just the four AFQT subtests of the ASVAB. You have to take all nine subtests in order to get a qualifying AFQT score. The military isn't set up to give *partial* ASVAB tests. For example, if you take the ASVAB and get line scores that qualify you for the military job you want but your AFQT score is too low to join, you have to retake the entire ASVAB — not just the four subtests that make up the AFQT — to get a higher AFQT score.

REMEMBER

During the initial enlistment process, your service branch determines your military job or enlistment program based on the minimum *line scores* it has established. Line scores are computed from the various subtests of the ASVAB. If you get an appropriate score in the appropriate areas, you can get the job you want — as long as that job is available and you meet other qualification factors.

The following sections examine the computerized ASVAB and the pencil-and-paper ASVAB and explain what you need to know.

The computerized ASVAB (CAT-ASVAB)

Nobody really cares about the AFQT score except the military — but the military cares *a lot!* Because you're reading this book, I'm willing to bet that you're interested in joining the military. And if you're interested in joining the military, you'll most likely take the computerized version of the ASVAB. That's because most people taking the ASVAB for the purpose of joining the military take it at a Military Entrance Processing Station (MEPS), and all these places use the computerized test.

REMEMBER

The computerized version of the ASVAB — called the *CAT-ASVAB* (*CAT* stands for Computerized Adaptive Testing) — has the same questions as the paper version. The main difference: The CAT-ASVAB adapts the questions it offers you based on your level of proficiency. (As you may have guessed, that's why it's called *adaptive*.) The first test question is of average difficulty. If you answer this question correctly, the next question is more difficult. If you answer the first question incorrectly, the computer gives you an easier question. (By contrast, on the pencil-and-paper ASVAB, easy, medium, and hard questions are presented randomly.) On the ASVAB, harder questions are worth more points than easier questions are, so you want to get to them sooner to maximize your score.

Pros of taking the CAT-ASVAB

Maybe it's because most people are more comfortable in front of a computer than they are with paper and pencil, but military recruiters have noted that among applicants who've taken both the paper-based version and the computerized version of the ASVAB, recruits tend to score slightly higher on the computerized version of the test.

When you take the CAT-ASVAB, the computer automatically calculates and prints your standard scores for each subtest and your line scores for each service branch. (If you're interested in line scores, which are used for military job-classification purposes, you may want to pick up a copy of *ASVAB For Dummies* [John Wiley & Sons, Inc.].) This machine is a pretty smart cookie; it also calculates your AFQT score on the spot. With the computerized version, you usually know whether you qualify for military enlistment on the same day you take the test and, if so, which jobs you qualify for.

Cons of taking the CAT-ASVAB

Unlike the pencil-and-paper version, you can't skip questions or change your answers after you enter them on the CAT-ASVAB. This restriction can make taking the test harder for some people. Instead of being able to go through and immediately answering all the questions you're sure of and then coming back to the questions that require you to do some head scratching, you have to answer each question as it comes. Also, judging how much time to spend on a difficult question before guessing and moving on can be tough. Finally, if you have a few minutes at the end of the test, you can't go back and check to make sure you marked the correct answer to each question.

Trying on tryout questions

I hate to break it to you, but if you take the computerized version of the ASVAB, you also get tryout questions. *Tryout* questions are new questions that ASVAB designers are testing to see if they're good or bad. Luckily, they don't count toward your score; unluckily, everyone who takes the computerized version of the test gets 15 extra questions in two to four of the ASVAB subtests. That means you'll answer 30 to 60 additional questions that don't count toward your score — but you do get extra time to complete each subtest that comes with tryout questions attached.

Your total time to complete each subtest that has tryout questions is as follows:

» General Science: 20 minutes

» Arithmetic Reasoning: 113 minutes

» Word Knowledge: 18 minutes

» Paragraph Comprehension: 75 minutes

» Mathematics Knowledge: 47 minutes

» Electronics Information: 21

» Auto Information: 18 minutes

» Shop Information: 17 minutes

» Mechanical Comprehension: 42 minutes

» Assembling Objects: 36 minutes

REMEMBER

Tryout questions only appear on the computerized version of the test, and they don't count toward your score. They appear on two, three, or four of your subtests, not all of them.

The pencil-and-paper test

Most people who take the pencil-and-paper version of the ASVAB do so under the *ASVAB Career Exploration Program*, a cooperative program between the Department of Education and the Department of Defense at high schools all across the United States. Although the results of this version can be used for military enlistment purposes (if taken within two years of enlistment), its primary purpose is to serve as a tool for guidance counselors to use when recommending possible careers to high-school students.

You can also take the pencil-and-paper version for purposes of enlistment through a recruiter, but that's not done very often these days. In unusual circumstances, when it's impractical for an applicant to travel to a MEPS location, recruiters can arrange for applicants to take the pencil-and-paper version at a Military Entrance Test (MET) site.

TECHNICAL STUFF

Another version of the ASVAB is the Armed Forces Classification Test (AFCT). This version is used by folks already in the military who want to improve their ASVAB scores for the purposes of retraining for a different military job. Except for the name of the exam, the AFCT is exactly the same as the other versions of the ASVAB.

Pros of taking the paper-and-pencil test

The paper-based test allows you to skip questions that you don't know the answer to and come back to them later. You can't do that on the CAT-ASVAB. This option can be a real help when you're racing against the clock and want to get as many answers right as possible. You can change an answer on the subtest you're currently working on, but you can't change an answer on a subtest after the time for that subtest has expired.

You can mark up the exam booklet as much as you want. If you skip a question, you can circle the number of the question in your booklet to remind yourself to go back to it. If you don't know the answer to a question, you can cross off the answers that seem unlikely or wrong to you and then guess based on the remaining answers.

THE MINI-AFQT

You may take a sort of "mini-AFQT" in the recruiter's office. This test is called the Computer Adaptive Screening Test (CAST). Another version in use is called the Enlistment Screening Test (EST).

The CAST and EST aren't qualification tests; they're strictly recruiting tools that recruiters may use at their discretion. The CAST and EST contain questions similar (but not identical) to questions appearing on the ASVAB. They help estimate an applicant's probability of obtaining a qualifying AFQT score. If you take one of these mini-tests and score low, you probably don't want to take the actual ASVAB until you've put in some extensive study time. In fact, many recruiters won't even schedule you for the ASVAB unless you score well on the CAST or EST.

Cons of taking the paper-and-pencil test

On the pencil-and-paper version, harder questions are intermingled with easier questions, so you may find yourself spending too much time trying to figure out the answer to a question that's too hard for you, and you may miss answering some easier questions at the end of the subtest because you ran out of time. The result: Your overall score will be lower.

The paper answer sheets are scored by an optical scanning machine. The machine has a conniption when it comes across an incompletely filled-in answer circle or stray pencil marks and will often stubbornly refuse to give you credit for these questions, even if you answered correctly.

Scoring the AFQT

The military uses some pretty complicated calculations to determine applicants' AFQT scores. Because harder questions carry more weight than easy questions do, the military can't give you a letter grade or a percentage of questions that you answered correctly; that wouldn't tell the armed forces exactly how much you know about each subject.

TECHNICAL STUFF

Lots of people (mistakenly) call the AFQT score their "ASVAB score." You commonly hear someone say, "I got a 67 on the ASVAB," or "My ASVAB score was 92." That's not correct; it implies that the AFQT is derived from all nine subtests of the ASVAB, and it's not. The AFQT score is computed from just four of the ASVAB subtests — the four subtests of the ASVAB that measure your math and vocabulary and reading skills (refer to the section "Understanding the ASVAB from 30,000 Feet" earlier in this chapter).

In this section, I explain how the AFQT is scored.

Comprehending raw scores

The military scores each subtest of the ASVAB by using a raw score. A *raw score* is the total number of points you receive on each subtest of the ASVAB. You don't see your raw scores on the printout you receive from your recruiter after completing the test. The recruiter walks you back to the waiting area and retrieves two or three copies of your scores on a printout that includes all your line scores for each branch, your AFQT percentile, and some other information.

REMEMBER

You can't use the practice tests in this book (or any other ASVAB or AFQT study guide) to calculate your probable ASVAB scores. ASVAB scores are calculated using raw scores, and raw scores aren't determined simply from the number of right or wrong answers. On the actual ASVAB, harder questions are worth more points than easier questions.

Computing the verbal expression score

The military uses the verbal expression (VE) score to measure your ability to communicate. The score goes toward computing the AFQT score as well as many of the military's line scores. The military brass (or at least their computers) determine your VE score by first adding the value of your Word Knowledge (WK) raw score to your Paragraph Comprehension (PC) raw score. The result is then converted to a scaled score ranging from 20 to 62.

Getting the AFQT score formula

To get your *AFQT raw score*, the computer doubles your VE score and then adds your Arithmetic Reasoning (AR) score and your Mathematics Knowledge (MK) score to it. Here's the formula: AFQT raw score = 2VE + AR + MK

You don't get to see what your AFQT raw score is on your ASVAB scoresheet. Instead, the computer converts it into a percentile that shows you how you stack up against a baseline testing group.

Normalizing the percentile score

Your AFQT raw score is converted to an AFQT *percentile score*, ranging from 1 to 99. How does that work? In 1997, the Department of Defense conducted a "Profile of American Youth" study, which examined the AFQT raw scores of a national sample of 18- to 23-year-olds who took the ASVAB during that year.

Your AFQT percentile score is derived by comparing your AFQT raw score to those of the people who took part in the study. For example, an AFQT percentile score of 50 means that you scored as well as or better than 50 percent of the individuals included in the 1997 study.

Making Sense of Minimum Qualifying Scores

The primary purpose of the AFQT percentile score is to determine whether you qualify for the military service of your choice. Each of the branches has its own priorities, so they all have different minimum qualifying scores.

Considering the AFQT tier categories

AFQT scores are grouped into five categories based on the percentile score ranges shown in Table 1-2. People who score in Categories I and II tend to be above average in trainability; those in Category III, average; those in Category IV, below average; and those in Category V, markedly below average.

If your AFQT percentile score falls into Category I, all the military services want you — probably very badly. They also want you if your score falls into Category II or Category IIIA.

If your score falls into Category IIIB, you may or may not be able to enlist, depending in large part on how your chosen branch is currently doing on making its recruiting goals.

TABLE 1-2 AFQT Tiers

Category	Percentile Score
I	93–99
II	65–92
IIIA	50–64
IIIB	31–49
IVA	21–30
IVB	16–20
IVC	10–15
V	0–9

REMEMBER

Congress has directed that the military can't accept Category V recruits or more than 4 percent of recruits from Category IV. If you're in Category IV, you must have a high-school diploma to be eligible for enlistment; you can't do it with a high-school equivalency certificate. Even so, if your score falls into Category IV, your chances of enlistment are very small.

Making the military cut

Each of the services has established minimum AFQT qualification scores within its respective recruiting regulations. Keep in mind that minimum scores can change instantly when the needs of the services change, so getting a high score is your best bet in order to remain competitive.

>> **Army (including Army National Guard and Army Reserves):** The Army requires a minimum AFQT score of 31 for those with a high-school diploma and a score of 50 for those with a high-school equivalency certificate. When the Army is experiencing high recruiting and reenlistment rates, it has been known to temporarily increase its qualifying AFQT score minimum to as high as 50.

>> **Air Force (including Air National Guard and Air Force Reserves):** Air Force recruits must score at least 36 points on the AFQT to qualify for enlistment. In actuality, the vast majority (over 70 percent) of those accepted for an Air Force enlistment score 50 or above. For those who have a high-school equivalency certificate rather than a high-school diploma, the minimum is 65.

WARNING

You're more likely to be struck by lightning than to enlist in the Air Force without a high-school diploma. Only about 0.5 percent of all Air Force enlistments each year hold high-school equivalency certificates.

>> **Navy:** Navy recruits must score at least 31 on the AFQT to qualify for enlistment. For those with high-school equivalency certificates, the minimum score is 50. Only between 5 and 10 percent of recruits can actually enlist with a high-school equivalency certificate, and those who do must also be at least 19 years old and show that they have a work history.

>> **Marine Corps:** Marine Corps recruits must score at least 32. Candidates with a high-school equivalency certificate must score a minimum of 50 on the AFQT to be considered. The Marine Corps limits high-school equivalency enlistments to 5 to 10 percent per year.

>> **Coast Guard:** The Coast Guard requires a minimum of 40 points on the AFQT. A waiver is possible for applicants with prior service if their ASVAB line scores qualify them for a specific job and they're willing to enlist in that job. For the very few people (less than 5 percent) who are allowed to enlist with a high-school equivalency certificate, the minimum AFQT score is 50.

REMEMBER

Meeting the minimum qualifying score for the service of your choice is no guarantee of enlistment. During good recruiting times, each branch gets more qualified applicants than it has room for... and that means the military can pick and choose which applicants to accept and which ones to turn away. Usually, rejections are based on ASVAB scores, physical fitness, and what the military calls *medical readiness* (they're not going to pick you if they'll need to patch you up before shipping you out).

Also, enlistment incentives such as enlistment bonuses and college loan repayment deals are often tied to minimum AFQT scores. As with quotas, this situation is subject to change at any time based on each service's current recruiting needs.

Retaking the Test

You can't actually "fail" the AFQT, but you can fail to achieve a high enough score to enlist in the service you want. If your AFQT score is too low, you need to work on one (or more) of four areas: Math Knowledge, Arithmetic Reasoning, Paragraph Comprehension, or Word Knowledge. The military uses your scores in these areas to calculate your AFQT score. Parts 2 and 3 of this book are specifically designed to help you improve your scores on these four subtests. When you're sure you're ready, you can apply (through your recruiter) for a retest.

ASVAB tests are valid for two years, as long as you aren't in the military. In most cases, after you join the military, your ASVAB scores remain valid as long as you're in. In other words, except in a few cases, you can use your enlistment ASVAB scores to qualify for retraining (getting a different job) years later.

After you take an initial ASVAB test (taking the ASVAB in high school doesn't count as an initial test), you can retake the test after 30 days. After the retest, you must wait at least six months before taking the ASVAB again. There's no lifetime limit on how many times you can retest as long as you still meet the other requirements and a recruiter is still willing to work with you.

REMEMBER

When you retake the ASVAB, the score on your *most recent* test is what counts. If you score lower on the retest, that's the score that's used for your military enlistment.

The bad news is that you can't retake the ASVAB on a whim or whenever you feel like it. Each of the services has its own rules.

Army

The Army allows a retest only if

>> Your previous ASVAB test has expired. (*Remember:* Test scores are valid for two years.)

>> You failed to achieve an AFQT score high enough to qualify for enlistment.

>> Unusual circumstances occur. For example, if you're called away from the test because of an emergency, you can retake the test.

Army recruiters aren't allowed to schedule a retest for the sole purpose of increasing scores so applicants can qualify for enlistment incentives, meet line score requirements for specific jobs, or qualify for special enlistment programs.

Air Force

The Air Force doesn't allow you to retest after you've enlisted in the Delayed Entry Program (DEP). Current policy allows retesting of applicants who aren't in the DEP but already have a qualifying AFQT score. Retesting is authorized when the applicant's current line scores limit the service's ability to match an Air Force skill with his or her qualifications.

TECHNICAL STUFF

These days, you can't just take the ASVAB, undergo a medical examination, and head straight out to basic training. You have to wait your turn. The military has only so many basic training slots each month, and it has to reserve a slot for you (often several months in the future). To ensure your commitment, the services enlist you in the DEP. Under this program, you're enlisted in the inactive reserves or in the ready reserves while waiting for your basic training date to arrive.

Navy

The Navy allows you to retake the test if your previous ASVAB test has expired or you've failed to achieve a qualifying AFQT score for enlistment in the Navy.

Recruits in the Navy's DEP can't retest.

Marine Corps

The Marine Corps will authorize a retest if your previous test is expired. Otherwise, recruiters can request a retest as long as the initial scores don't appear to reflect your true capability (considering your education, training, and experience).

Additionally, the retest can't be requested *solely* because your initial test scores didn't meet the standards prescribed for specific military job qualification.

Coast Guard

For Coast Guard enlistments, six months must elapse since your last test before you may retest for the sole purpose of raising scores to qualify for a particular enlistment option. The Coast Guard Recruiting Center may authorize retesting after 30 days have passed since an initial ASVAB test if substantial reason exists to believe that your initial AFQT score or subtest scores don't reflect your education, training, or experience.

IN THE BEGINNING, THERE WAS NO AFQT

When you start basic training, you learn about military history. Why not start a little sooner and find out where this whole testing thing came from?

The Army began general testing of draftees during World War I. In order to provide a method for classifying these soldiers, the Army developed the Army Alpha Test, which consisted of 212 multiple-choice and true/false questions, including common-sense questions and vocabulary and arithmetic problems. But many of the draftees couldn't read or write, so the Army developed the Army Beta Test, which required little word knowledge and relied on pictures and diagrams. Nearly 2 million soldiers took one of these tests during World War I.

(continued)

(continued)

During World War II, the Army General Classification Test (AGCT) replaced the Alpha and Beta tests. The new test had 150 questions — mostly vocabulary and arithmetic. The AGCT was used by the Army and Marine Corps to assign recruits to military jobs. Of the 9 million soldiers and Marines who took this test during World War II, just over 60 percent could read and write above a third-grade level. During this time, a completely separate aptitude test was given to Navy recruits; it was called the Navy General Classification Test (NGCT). (The Air Force didn't have a test because the United States technically didn't have an Air Force as you know it today; the Air Force was part of the Army back then.)

In 1948, Congress required the Department of Defense to develop a uniform screening test to be used by all the services. In 1950, the Department of Defense came up with the Armed Forces Qualification Test (AFQT). This test consisted of 100 multiple-choice questions in areas such as math, vocabulary, spatial relations, and mechanical ability. The military used this test until the mid-1970s. In addition to the AFQT, service-specific tests classified prospective recruits into jobs. The Army Classification Battery, the Navy Basic Test Battery, and the Airman Qualification Examination (to name a few) were used for classification purposes from the late 1950s to the mid-1970s.

In the 1960s, as military jobs became more diverse and technical, the Department of Defense decided to develop a standardized military selection and classification test and administer it in high schools. That's where the ASVAB entered the picture. The first ASVAB test was given in 1968, but the military didn't use it for recruiting purposes for several years. In 1973, the draft ended and the nation entered the contemporary period, in which all military recruits are volunteers. That year, the Air Force began using the ASVAB; the Marine Corps followed in 1974. From 1973 to 1975, the Navy and Army used their own test batteries for selection and classification. In 1976, the ASVAB became the official military job-classification test used by all services, and the AFQT score became the official entry standard.

Chapter **2**

Arming Yourself with a Study Plan

One of the easiest parts of prepping for the ASVAB's Armed Forces Qualification Test is done: You bought this book. Now comes the hard part: studying to get the best possible score.

REMEMBER

What the military really wants to know isn't how much knowledge you already have stashed in your head (although it does use that information). Instead, the military's big question is "Is this person trainable?" Everything in the military is set up to train a beginner, which you'll see if you end up choosing a job that you know nothing about; even if you think you know a bit about it, each branch of the military has its own TTPs (that stands for *tactics, techniques, and procedures*) that you'll have to learn from scratch.

The line scores the military uses to calculate your AFQT score will show them (and you) whether you'll be a good fit for your chosen branch. Combine your AFQT scores with the scores you get on the other subtests, and the military can tell exactly *where* you'll fit in. (You're like a puzzle piece, and the entire test battery shows whether you're part of the kitten's face or the flowers in the top-left corner.) That's why passing the Word Knowledge, Mathematics Knowledge, Arithmetic Reasoning, and Paragraph Comprehension subtests with flying colors is so important.

This chapter gives you a study plan you can customize based on how much time you have before you head to MEPS with your recruiter. After you have a timeline to follow for studying, read Chapter 3, which explains different study strategies that you can use to your advantage.

Establishing a Study Program

If you're not planning to make a study plan, you should plan again. A study plan is essential if you want to score well on the AFQT, so check out the guidelines, which I discuss in the section "Planning Your Study Strategy" later in this chapter. You can adjust the schedule based on how much time you have left before you take the ASVAB.

I can't give you one best way to prepare a study plan. Each person has their own learning preferences; what works for you might not work for your best friend. Some people learn better by hearing information, while others like a visual approach — and still others need to put their hands on learning materials to get a good mental grasp on the information.

When you're studying for the ASVAB, you most likely won't put too much emphasis on learning new information. It's more of a review of what you already know, which means you have the freedom to find study techniques that help you remember best — until you've taken the test and left MEPS with your shiny new enlistment contract, that is.

Try to figure out what type of learner you are before developing a plan of study. Chapter 3 can help with this process and give you some tips about what to include in your study plan based on your learning style.

WARNING

Most people don't look forward to sitting down for a study session. Because of that, they try to make studying more enjoyable by spending time on the subjects they already know. After all, studying familiar information is much easier than learning something new. Try not to fall into this trap! If you're already an avid reader, you probably don't need to spend much of your time improving your reading comprehension skills. You're already going to ace that portion of the AFQT, right? Instead, spend most of your time boning up on the areas where you need improvement, such as math and math word problems.

TIP

Try to dedicate one to two hours per day to your AFQT studies. Pick a time and place where nobody will interrupt you. Having your dad yell at you to cut the grass probably won't be beneficial to your study session. Also, turn off your phone. Is that call as important as your future military career? You won't be allowed to use your phone in basic training anyway, so this is a good time to get into the habit of letting it go for a while.

Figuring Out Whether You Have Enough Time

Your recruiter is going to schedule an appointment for you to take the ASVAB, but if it's too soon, don't be shy. Explain to your recruiter that you don't want to postpone your enlistment by failing the test (or that you want to get the best score possible), so you need more time to study (see Chapter 1 to find out how long you have to wait to retest if you don't meet the ASVAB's minimum scores for enlistment). You can't settle for an all-night cram session the night before you take the test — that'll leave you frazzled and frustrated, and your scores will probably be lower than they would've been if you hadn't studied at all.

Planning Your Study Strategy

Which areas are most important to you right now? If you often walk around with your nose in a book, you may not need to spend much time on Word Knowledge or Paragraph Comprehension. If you solve complex mathematical formulas for fun, it's probably safe to say that you can do without studying for Mathematics Knowledge and Arithmetic Reasoning.

This study plan assumes that you have about two months to prepare for the ASVAB, but you can adjust it by shaving off a week or two — or stretching out — each section so it reflects the right timeline.

If you're studying for other subtests of the ASVAB, you can blend them into your study plan to replace the AFQT portions of the test where you already have strong skills. If you're struggling with each of the AFQT subtests, I suggest you get a good understanding of them before moving on to other subtests because the AFQT determines whether you're even qualified for enlistment.

8 weeks out: Figure out what you need most

Take the first practice exam in Chapter 12 so you can see exactly where you need to focus your time. You may be a little better at math than you think you are, or you may need some practice figuring out the main idea of passages you've read.

When you take your first practice exam (and every practice exam after it, for that matter), make sure you're in a quiet place without distractions. Keep some scratch paper handy and put away your calculator because you won't be able to use it when you take the ASVAB, so using it now will hurt you on test day.

Stick to the time limits given for each subtest — they're printed on each one. The subtests in this book are designed to simulate the real ASVAB test, so the listed times are what you'll be up against on test day. Flip to Chapter 1 for a refresher on how much time you'll have for each subtest, whether you're taking the standard CAT-ASVAB, or you're among the minority taking the pencil-and-paper version. Take the time limits seriously now because the test proctors (and the computers) will take them seriously on test day!

Score each subtest according to the answers in Chapter 13. If you do very well, that's great... but it doesn't mean you can put away this book until the day before the test. Practicing the types of questions you see in Chapters 12, 14, 16, and 18 as well as in the four additional tests online, will help ensure that you score even *better* on test day.

If your scores aren't so hot in one or more areas, now you know where you need to focus. A great way to start: Make flashcards that help you remember important information. Read the sections in this book that explain the areas you need to improve, and then work out the practice questions that show up in the "Subtest" chapters. Review the answer explanations as you check your work to understand how to arrive at the correct answer (even if you got the answer right). Once you join the military, you'll hear more than a few people say, "Even a busted watch is right twice a day," and that applies here, too — it's not enough to land on the right answer. You need to know how to get there.

6 weeks out: Take another test

Take one of the online practice tests. The online tests are designed to give you a feel for what you'll experience when you take the computerized ASVAB at MEPS.

The test bank will automatically score your test, and your results will show you which topics you need to spend the next couple of weeks studying. Compare your scores to what you earned on the first practice test to see how far you've come and see whether you're ready to focus on another area.

Give it a week, and then take the practice test in Chapter 14. Score that based on the answers in Chapter 15 and do the same thing you did after the online test: Choose the subject you want to improve in and focus on it for another week.

If you're struggling in one area, call your recruiter and see whether they can set up a study session with you and other recruits. You can also enlist the help of a friend or family member who's stronger in those areas than you are.

4 weeks out: Surprise! Time for another test

The tests in this book and online serve a few purposes — and one of them is to show you how much progress you've made since the last time you took one. You're only a month out from taking the ASVAB, so now it's time to zero in on the area where you need to make the most improvement. Take the practice test in Chapter 16 and score it with the answers in Chapter 17. In a week, take another online practice test, too.

Which area was the worst? Don't forget to consider whether you're struggling to find the right answers or spending too much time on one type of question. That's what you need to focus on for the next week.

When you take the next online practice test, you can reevaluate your needs and figure out where to go next (or whether you should keep plugging away at your archenemy on the AFQT, whether it's English or math). If you're working on two subjects, alternate so you don't wear yourself out. There's nothing wrong with taking a break from one and switching to another!

2 weeks out: Five tests down (and three to go)

Take the practice test in Chapter 18 and score it with the answers in Chapter 19. You've been studying pretty intensely, and by now you should have a good idea of how well you'll score on the AFQT portion of the test. If you're looking for a specific job (you can find out what you need to score for your dream job by checking out the appendix in this book), now is the time to hit harder if you don't have a firm grasp on one of the AFQT subjects.

If you haven't already, review the online Cheat Sheet for this book (go to www.dummies.com and search for "ASVAB AFQT Cheat Sheet") to check out the qualifying AFQT scores for each branch and to look over some of the basic concepts that'll help you on the test. Information about minimum AFQT qualification scores for each branch is also in Chapter 1.

1 week out: Crunch time

You're a week out from taking the actual ASVAB, so take one of the two remaining online practice tests to simulate what it's really going to be like. Focus on each question and keep an eye on the clock. The military always says, "Train as you fight," which means you need to put yourself in a realistic situation while you're practicing for the real deal. By focusing on the online practice tests, you're doing exactly that.

You should see some big improvements at this point (go back and check your scores from the first practice test you took!). Rank your scores on each section so you can choose which two subjects to focus on this week. Revisit the flashcards you made (or make new ones), call your recruiter or your study buddy, and ask everyone you know to quiz you.

Wait a couple of days, and then take the final online practice test. Try to take it a few days before you go to MEPS — you'll need that time to review everything you need to remember.

The day before the test: Last-minute prep

Before your final study session, gather everything your recruiter has told you to bring to MEPS on test day (see Chapter 3). That way, you can use the afternoon and evening to relax (*yeah, right!*) and mentally prepare yourself for the big day.

When you do settle in to studying, review all the notes you've taken and flip through this book to refresh your memory. Don't be hard on yourself, though. You're as prepared as you'll ever be! Also review the last few pages of Chapter 3, which explain what to expect on test day, how to go in prepared, and what to do as you take the ASVAB.

The day before the test is important for more than just studying, too. You'll perform best on the ASVAB if you drink plenty of water, enjoy your day, and get at least eight hours of sleep.

Using the Practice Exams to Your Advantage

This book includes four full-length AFQT practice exams with questions that are very similar to those you see on the ASVAB subtests — the ones that make up your AFQT score. The practice exams included in this book (and their online counterparts) can help increase your confidence and ensure that you're ready to take the actual ASVAB, but you have to use them correctly.

I'll let you in on a little not-so-secret secret: No ASVAB or AFQT preparation book includes the exact same questions as what you'll find on the actual test. Not only would that be unethical, but it would probably also result in several federal law-enforcement agents knocking on the author's door — not my idea of a good time. Actual ASVAB test questions are controlled items; that means that the military keeps them to itself, and people can get into heaps of trouble for sharing them. If you see any questions on the actual ASVAB or AFQT that are the same as the ones you find in this book (or any other preparation guide), it's pure coincidence.

TIP

Just because the practice exams don't include the same questions you see on the AFQT doesn't mean that the practice exams aren't valuable — just use them the way they were designed to be used according to your study plan.

Sometimes recruiters try to rush people into taking the ASVAB so they can get you signed up quickly. Recruiters live and die by their recruiting goals. Make sure you don't let your recruiter schedule your exam until you're sure you're ready for it; *your* career is riding on it, not theirs.

TIP

The mini-AFQT computerized test (see Chapter 1) that recruiters have in their offices is a pretty good indicator of whether you're ready for the real test. Usually, people's AFQT scores are within five or six points of what the mini-AFQT predicts.

REMEMBER

Although you can't equate scores on the practice exam with actual AFQT scores (because of the method of scoring the AFQT; see Chapter 1), shoot for a minimum of 80 percent on each subtest, keeping in mind that the practice exams in this book mimic the paper version of the test. When you're taking the practice tests in this book, here's what you need to make a B grade:

>> **Arithmetic Reasoning:** You need to answer 24 of the 30 Arithmetic Reasoning questions correctly to hit the 80 percent threshold. If you don't, dedicate more study time to solving math word problems.

>> **Word Knowledge:** The Word Knowledge subtest has 35 questions, so focus on this section if you miss more than 7 of them.

>> **Paragraph Comprehension:** If you miss more than 3 of the 15 questions on the Paragraph Comprehension subtest, dedicate more study time to your reading skills.

>> **Mathematics Knowledge:** Missing more than 3 of the 16 Mathematics Knowledge questions puts you below 80 percent, so you need further study.

Chapter **3**

Mastering the Art of Studying and Test-Taking

A military career is all about taking tests. You take tests to enter the military, you take tests in basic training, you take tests when learning your new military job, you take tests when you go to military schools to further your career, and in some branches, you even take tests to earn promotions.

Lots of people think they can't take tests, but realistically, that's just not true. If you couldn't take tests, you never would've made it through high school or gotten a high-school equivalency cer-tificate, and one of the two is required in order to join the military. The truth is that when people get out of a school environment, they sometimes lose the motivation and skills to study properly. Lack of success in test-taking has more to do with ineffective study skills and techniques than it does with intellectual ability.

REMEMBER

Effective studying doesn't happen overnight. Studying requires time and patience, so use the plan in Chapter 2 as an outline for your own strategy. Getting the highest possible AFQT score is very much an individual affair; no one path will always produce the best results for everyone. Studying is a process that you learn through trial and error. You have to discover a strategy that works for you.

By incorporating the reading rules, study strategies, and test-taking techniques covered in this chapter, you should increase your chances of achieving the study and test-taking goals you set for yourself.

Reading for Study

I know what you're thinking: "Wait a minute. You talk about reading comprehension in Chapter 6. Why am I reading about reading here?" Reading for the purposes of study is a different kind of reading. *Reading comprehension* just requires you to place information into short-term memory long enough to answer a question about it a few seconds later. To read for the purposes of study, you need to commit important information to your long-term memory — at least long enough to take the ASVAB.

Checking out the survey, question, read, recall, and review method

This method is affectionately known as the SQR[3] method by those who make a living teaching students how to study. It helps you separate the important information from the stuff that doesn't matter. Here's how it works:

1. Survey.

The first step is to survey the material to get the big picture. This quick preview allows you to focus your attention on the main ideas and to identify the sections you want to read in detail. The purpose is to determine which portions of the text are most applicable to your task. Read the table of contents, introduction, section headings, subheadings, summaries, and the bibliography. Skim the text in between. Be sure to look at any figures, diagrams, charts, and highlighted areas.

2. Question.

After you've gained a feel for the substance of the material, compose questions about the subject you want answered. First, ask yourself what you already know about the topic and then generate your questions.

3. Read.

Now go back and read those sections you identified during your survey and search for answers to your questions. Look for the ideas behind words. While you're at it, skim the other sections again.

4. Recall.

To help you retain the material, make it a point to summarize the information at appropriate intervals, such as at the ends of paragraphs, sections, and chapters. Your goal isn't to remember *everything* you've read — just the important points. Recite these points silently or aloud. Reciting the points helps you improve your concentration. You can also jot down any important or useful points.

Finally, determine what information you still need to obtain.

5. Review.

This last step involves reviewing the information you've read. Skim a section or chapter immediately after you finish reading it and take a peek at any notes you made. Go back over all the questions you posed and see whether you can answer them.

Taking and reviewing notes

Reading something once isn't enough to really learn it. That's why note-taking is so important. Clearly written, accurate notes help to capture information for later study and review. Taking notes also helps you to focus and learn during your study time.

Here are some note-taking and note-studying tips:

>> **Organize the information.** Arrange data or ideas into small groups that make sense to you. Smaller groups make remembering the information easier.

>> **Make the information relevant.** Connect the new information with the information you already know. Recalling the information you already know about a subject helps you recall the new stuff more easily.

>> **Use all your senses during review.** Don't just speak aloud when reviewing your notes; get your entire body into the act. Get up and move around as if you're practicing for a speech.

>> **To commit information to your long-term memory, review the material several times.** Take advantage of your ability to remember best what you read last by changing the order of the information you recite during your review.

>> **Use spaced repetition.** This approach requires you to review information after increasingly long breaks. Review the material again the next day, then again in a week. Keep spacing out the intervals of your reviews to get the most out of the spaced repetition method, which also lets you practice retrieving information from the dustiest corners of your brain.

Putting Study Strategies to Work for You

Knowing how to study is like knowing how to fish: It's a set of learning skills that lasts a lifetime and brings many rewards. Just as there are many ways to fish, there are many ways to study (the following sections examine a few). The key is finding the techniques that work best for you.

Working with your own learning style

Individuals learn best in individual ways. Some people may learn more quickly by hearing something. For others, seeing something may be the way. Still others may learn best by doing something. No one style of learning is better than another. However, by identifying your most effective learning style, you can adjust your study techniques to your individual learning abilities. The point is that it doesn't matter what learning style you're most comfortable with as long as it works for you.

Auditory learners

Auditory learners use hearing to process information. When given a choice, strong auditory learners sit where they can easily hear the speaker and where outside sounds won't interfere. Some auditory learners sit to one side (on the side of their strongest ear). Many times, auditory learners have an easier time understanding the words from songs on the radio and announcements on public address systems than other people do.

Here are some characteristics of auditory learners:

>> They prefer to hear information.

>> They have difficulty following written directions.

>> They have difficulty with reading and writing.

>> They may not look the speaker in the eye; instead, they may turn their eyes away so they can focus more on listening.

TIP

If you're an auditory learner, keep in mind the following study suggestions:

>> Listen to readings and lectures on online.

>> Participate in discussions, ask questions, and repeat given information.

>> Summarize or paraphrase written material and record the information.

>> Discuss the material with someone else.

Visual learners

Visual learners need to see the big picture. They may choose a seat where they can see the whole stage or screen. They may like the back seat so everything is out in front and they can see it all. Visual learners survey the scene, like to sightsee, and can see the forest despite the trees.

Visual learners share the following characteristics:

>> They need to see it to learn it; they must have a mental picture.

>> They have artistic ability.

>> They have difficulty with spoken directions.

>> They find sounds distracting.

>> They have trouble following lectures.

>> They may misinterpret words.

TIP

If you're a visual learner, follow these suggestions:

>> Use visuals (graphics, films, slides, illustrations, doodles, charts, notes, and flashcards) to reinforce learning.

>> Use multicolored highlighters or pens to organize your notes.

>> Write down directions.

>> Visualize words, phrases, and sentences to be memorized.

>> Write everything down and review often.

Tactile learners

Tactile learners need to touch and feel things. They want to feel or experience the lesson themselves. Given a choice, strong tactile learners are right in the middle of the action. They tear things apart to see how they work and put them back together without the directions. Tactile learners immediately adjust the seat, mirror, radio, and temperature when they get in the car.

Here are some characteristics of tactile learners:

>> They prefer hands-on learning or training.

>> They can often put objects together without the directions.

>> They have difficulty sitting still.

>> They learn better when they can get involved.

>> They may be coordinated and have athletic ability.

TIP

If you're a tactile learner, try the following strategies:

>> Make a model, do lab work, role-play, "be the ball."

>> Take frequent breaks.

>> Copy letters and words to learn how to spell and remember facts.

>> Use a computer to study as much as possible.

>> Write facts and figures over and over.

>> Read and walk, talk and walk, repeat and walk.

Getting the most out of your study time

Whether you're studying for the ASVAB, the AFQT, military promotion tests, or a college course, proper study techniques can help you attain your goals.

Staying motivated

Studying and learning can take you far in life, but getting down to those tasks can be hard. Whether you're studying for college or to advance your career, studying can be one of the most important things you should be doing. Modern life — whether commercials, the Internet, friends, or TV — continually demands your attention, and all these things can feel easier to attend to than study. So what can you do to stay motivated?

>> **Give your study the attention it deserves.** If you were totally isolated, you'd study every aspect of your subject until you were completely versed in it because nothing else would be there to distract you. Imagine being in a cell with no TV or cellphone and nothing except *ASVAB AFQT For Dummies.* You'd certainly read it cover to cover — maybe many times! You'd know this book inside out because it's all you'd have to do. Having too much choice over what you pay attention to means you need to exert willpower now more than ever to stay motivated.

>> **Think about your goals.** Consider why you're studying and what you're studying for, because presumably it connects to what you want your life to be. All kinds of things may distract you when you're not studying, so focus on the big picture: You want to join the military because you believe it's the right choice for you. Keep your eye on your goal, which is a passing AFQT score (and, if you're up for it, high enough scores on the other subtests that you can choose from all the best jobs).

>> **Feed and develop your mind.** Your mind needs the rigor of study as well as the relaxation of entertainment. The more you exercise your brain, the better you'll perform in nearly all other areas of your life.

Managing your time

Procrastination is a problem for many people studying for the ASVAB or AFQT. The following tips can help you deal with this issue:

>> **Clear your schedule.** Recognize that your obligations and the resulting stress are as important as other people's needs. Set limits around being interrupted or rescheduling your work time to accommodate others. Omit or reschedule some of your other obligations. You want to give full concentration to your studies without feeling guilty about what you're *not* doing.

>> **Create a work area that's free from distractions and commit to staying there for at least one to two hours.** If you get sidetracked, remind yourself how this activity will help you meet your goals.

>> **Prioritize.** What has to be done first? What's worth more in terms of your AFQT score? (Chapter 1 can help you with this decision.) What's worth more in terms of your personal, educational, or career goals?

>> **Use a daily to-do list.** This list helps you reach your goals and prioritize your daily tasks. As soon as you've completed a task, check it off your list. There are dozens of apps you can use to keep a to-do list, and your phone probably even came with one. (My favorite is Google Keep: https://keep.google.com.)

>> **Break down your study into chunks.** Estimate how much time you need to complete the task. Don't try to do it all at once. Break it down so it's doable and not so overwhelming. Stay up-to-date to avoid overload.

>> **Recognize that you don't have to be perfect.** Some people are so afraid they won't perform perfectly that they don't do anything at all. Make sure you understand your goals. Then evaluate how important your study is and what level of performance is acceptable to you. Then just do it!

If you score better than the 50th percentile on the AFQT, you become a very attractive candidate to the military. You don't need a perfect score to get recruiters to chase you all over town.

REMEMBER

>> **Make study enjoyable.** Work on studying first, while you have more energy. Reward yourself when you check tasks off your daily to-do list.

REMEMBER

You're only human, so you probably gravitate toward studying the subject areas that you have an interest in or that you're good at. If you're an avid reader, don't spend too much of your time studying reading comprehension. (You're already likely to sail through that part of the test.) If you had a hard time in math in high school, you'll want to spend extra time brushing up on your arithmetic skills.

Finding the right place to study

After you find time to study, commit to a time and place that meets your needs. Ask yourself whether the environment in which you're studying will distract you or help you focus. Here are some aspects of the study environment you may need to consider:

>> **Time of day:** Whenever possible, schedule your most challenging courses and most intense study sessions during the time of day when you're most alert. Some people are at their best in the morning; others don't get rolling until late afternoon. You know how you work, so plan to study when you can give it your best.

>> **Posture and mobility:** Recognizing your posture and mobility needs helps you plan where and when you should study. Some people prefer to sit at a table or desk (in a formal posture) in order to concentrate and study effectively. Others are able to learn more easily while sitting comfortably on a sofa or lying on the floor (in an informal posture). Still others need to move about in order to learn; reading while walking on a treadmill may be appropriate for them. Some people can sit and study for long periods of time (they have high persistence), while others need to take frequent breaks (they have low persistence).

>> **Sound:** Contrary to popular belief, not everyone needs to study in a perfectly quiet environment. If you do choose to study to music, choose Baroque classical music, such as compositions by Johann Sebastian Bach and Antonio Vivaldi. The tempo and instrumentation of this music seem to be most compatible with study and learning.

>> **Lighting:** Light does make a difference, so study in the environment that best matches your learning preferences. Studies have shown that some people become depressed because of light deprivation during the winter months. If you're one of those people, try to study and spend as much time as possible in highly lit places.

Other studies have shown reading ability can be affected by the light contrast between print and paper color. Black letters printed on white paper create a high contrast. Some people find they have a better time reading black print on blue or gray paper, which has less contrast and is easier on their eyes. (You can't always choose the paper your study material is printed on, but you can choose it for note-taking and reviewing purposes.)

» **Temperature:** You may not be able to control the temperature of the room you're in, but you should be aware of your preference for either a cool or warm environment. Dress in layers so you can adjust to differences in room temperatures. Study in the environments in which you feel most comfortable.

Setting goals

Setting goals is a good way to accomplish a particularly difficult task. Developing study skills is one such task that takes time and effort to master. By setting SMART goals related to an area of your study skills that needs improvement, you'll be studying like a pro in no time!

SMART goals are as follows:

» **Specific:** After you decide what you want to work on, narrow it down to one thing. Be as specific as possible. Working out one problem at a time makes reaching your goal without spreading yourself too thin much easier. "I want to be a better reader" is too broad. Be more specific; for example, you may say, "I want to improve my reading speed." Write down this specific goal.

» **Measurable:** Goals are only achievable if you can measure them in some way. For example, rather than "I want to improve my reading speed," a measurable goal would be "I want to improve my reading speed by ten words per minute."

» **Actionable:** This step is where you decide how you're going to achieve your goal. Write this part as an "I will" statement. Following the example I give in the preceding bullet, your goal would now look something like "I want to improve my reading speed by ten words a minute. I will do this by skimming over words like *the* and *an.*"

» **Realistic:** Make sure your goals are within reach. "I will improve my reading speed by memorizing every word in the dictionary" isn't reasonable for most people. Everyone has limits due to time, resources, or ability. Don't ignore these restraints, or you'll be setting yourself up to fail.

» **Time sensitive:** Set a date to accomplish the goal. Make sure this date is both specific and realistic for you. "I will meet this goal sometime over the summer" is vague. Try something more like "I will meet this goal by the first day of school next fall." This wording gives you a definite time to shoot for and helps keep you working toward the goal. Goals can take only a few days to achieve; they may take months or years. Just be sure to make the timeline realistic for you and your lifestyle.

Taking the Test: Putting Your Best Foot Forward

Sooner or later, the time for you to actually sit down and take the ASVAB will arrive. It may get here before you think you're ready. Or you may think that test day can't get here fast enough. Regardless of which group you fall into, you can improve your test-taking ability by understanding test-taking techniques, keeping a positive attitude, and overcoming your fears.

TIP

Approach the big test as you'd approach a giant jigsaw puzzle. It may be tough, but you can do it! A positive attitude goes a long way toward success. Use the practice tests in Part 4 and online to familiarize yourself with the test structure and to build your confidence in the subject matter. Although the questions aren't the exact questions you'll see on the ASVAB, they're very, very similar. If you score well on the practice tests, you'll likely score well on the AFQT.

REMEMBER

Some of the tricky problems can knock you off balance. However, if you prepare a plan of attack for what to do if you get stuck, you won't get worried or frustrated. In each of the chapters where I describe the individual tests (Chapters 5, 7, 9, and 11), I give you tips about what to do when things start to look bleak. Go over these individual techniques before the test and make sure you have them down pat.

The day before

On the afternoon or evening before the test, get some exercise. Exercise can help you remain mentally sharp.

Cramming doesn't work. If you've followed the study plan in Chapter 2, the night before the test you should do a quick review and get to bed early. *Remember:* Your brain and body need sleep to function well, so don't stay up late! The night before the test isn't the best time to go out for a few beers with your friends. Hangovers and the ASVAB don't work well together.

Test day

The military has a saying: "If you're ten minutes early, you're five minutes late." You hear this tenet more than once in basic training. If you're taking the ASVAB for the purposes of joining the military (and chances of that are pretty good, if you're reading this book), then you're likely taking the test at a Military Entrance Processing Station (MEPS) and your recruiter has probably arranged your transportation.

TIP

At some stations, they conduct the ASVAB test in the afternoon and then set you up with a hotel room (depending on your travel site) to continue processing (medical examination, job selection, security clearance interview, and so on) early the next morning. At others, it's a one-day whirlwind; you stay in a hotel the night before, get up early for the medical exams and the ASVAB, have lunch at MEPS, and pick your job in the afternoon.

Arrive prepared

Your recruiter should brief you about what to expect and, in many cases, will even drive you to MEPS. In other cases, depending on how far you live from the closest MEPS (and whether you have a car), you may be provided with public transportation. In any case, you want to make sure you're on time and ready:

>> **Eat a light meal before the test (breakfast or lunch, depending on the test time).** You'll be better able to think when you have some food in your stomach. However, don't eat too much. You don't want to be drowsy during the test. Also, don't drink too much water. The test proctors will allow you to use the restroom if you need to, but with certain rules. If you leave to use the restroom during the paper version of the test, you can't come back until the next subtest begins. You can't leave to use the restroom during the computer version unless you're between subtests, and you can only be absent for up to five minutes.

>> **If possible, arrange to arrive at the test site a little early.** Find a quiet place (such as your recruiter's car) and do a ten-minute power-study to get your brain turned on and tuned up.

>> **Bring only the paperwork your recruiter gave you and a photo ID.** Don't bring a calculator, a backpack, or a sack full of munchies to the testing site. You won't be allowed to have them with you. The same goes for your cellphone, although you can ask your recruiter to hold it for you.

>> **Keep in mind that MEPS is owned and operated by the military, so it doesn't have much of a sense of humor when it comes to dress codes.** Dress conservatively. Don't wear clothes with holes in them or profanity written on them. The only people at MEPS who should see your underwear are the doctors during the physical exam. Leave your hat at home because, under the military civilian dress code, you can't wear hats indoors.

Read the directions

Although this instruction may seem obvious, you can sometimes *misread* the directions when you're in a hurry, and that won't help you get the right answer. Each subtest has a paragraph or two describing what the subtest covers and giving instructions on how to answer the questions.

Understand the questions

Take special care to read the questions correctly. Most questions ask something like, "Which of the following equals 6?" But sometimes a question may ask, "Which of the following does *not* equal 6?" You can easily skip right over the *not* when you're reading and get the question wrong.

You also have to understand the terms being used. When a math problem asks you to find the product of two numbers, be sure you know what *finding the product* means. (It means you have to multiply the two numbers.) If you add the two numbers together, you arrive at the wrong answer (and that wrong answer, which happens to be the sum in this case, will likely be one of the answer choices).

Review all the answer options

Often, people read a question, decide on the answer, glance at the answer options, choose the option that agrees with their answer, mark the answer, and then move on.

Although this approach usually works, it can lead you astray. On the ASVAB, you're usually supposed to choose the answer that's "most correct." Sometimes several answers are reasonably correct for the question at hand, but only one of them is "most correct." If you don't stop to read and review all the answers, you may not choose the one that's "most correct." Or, after reviewing all the answer options, you may realize that you hastily decided upon an incorrect answer because you misread it.

When in doubt, guess. On the paper ASVAB, guessing is okay. If you choose the correct answer, that's the equivalent of +1 (or more, depending on how the question is weighted). If you don't answer a question, that's the equivalent of 0. If you guess on a question and get the question wrong, that's also the equivalent of 0, not −1. (No penalties here!) But if you guess correctly, that's +1 (or more).

WARNING

If you're taking the CAT-ASVAB, keep in mind that choosing answers randomly toward the end of your subtests increases the likelihood of a penalty. If time is running short, try to read and legitimately answer the questions instead of making random guesses for the remaining items. The CAT-ASVAB applies a relatively large penalty when you provide several incorrect answers toward the end of a subtest.

In each of the chapters on a particular subtest (Chapters 5, 7, 9, and 11), I give you hints for making educated guesses that are specific to that topic. But here are some general rules:

>> Often, an answer that includes *always, all, everyone, never, none,* or *no one* is incorrect.

>> If two choices are very similar in meaning, *neither of them* is probably the correct choice.

>> If two answer options contradict each other, *one of them* is usually correct.

>> The longer the answer, the better the chances that it's the correct answer. The test makers have to get all those qualifiers in there to make sure it's the correct answer and you can't find an example to contradict it. If you see phrases like *in many cases* or *frequently,* that's usually a clue that the test makers are trying to make the answer "most correct."

>> Don't eliminate an answer based on how frequently it appears. For example, if Choice (B) has been the correct answer for the last five questions, don't assume that it must be the wrong answer for the question you're on just because that would make it six in a row.

>> If all else fails, trust your instincts. Often, your first instinct is the correct answer.

TIP

The Air Force Senior NCO Academy conducted an in-depth study of several Air Force multiple-choice test results taken over several years. It found that when students changed answers on their answer sheets, they changed from a right answer to a wrong answer more than 72 percent of the time! The students' first instinct was usually the correct one.

Guessing Smart

All the questions on the ASVAB are multiple-choice with four possible answers. That means that if you narrow down the possible correct answers by eliminating at least one *incorrect* answer, you boost your chances at scoring higher on the test.

Of course, you can increase these odds immensely by studying. But the chances are good that no matter how much time you put into advanced study, you'll come across at least one question on the test that leaves you scratching your head.

TIP

You can improve your odds of guessing correctly by guessing smart. Flip to Chapter 5 for tips on intelligent guessing for the Word Knowledge subtest, to Chapter 7 for techniques you can use on the Paragraph Comprehension subtest, to Chapter 9 for Mathematics Knowledge subtest guessing plans, and to Chapter 11 to discover how to make intelligent guesses on the Arithmetic Reasoning subtest.

2

Expressing Yourself and Understanding Others

Chapter **4**

Developing a Solid Vocabulary

T he military is in love with words. Military personnel write almost everything down in memos, manuals, regulations, standard operating procedures, and policy letters. They should hire a few *For Dummies* authors to write these items, because the current writers seem to love fancy words. A little shovel isn't a shovel in the military; it's an "entrenching tool." The person overseeing your duty section isn't "the boss" or even "the supervisor"; they're the "noncommissioned officer-in-charge" (NCOIC for short).

If you're going to be successful in the military, you have to have a solid vocabulary, and that's why the military includes the Word Knowledge subtest as part of the AFQT score. How can you obey a regulation if you don't know what the words mean? You can't — but failing to do what you're told is a big problem in the military, so each branch tries to only admit those who are likely to understand the rules, instructions, directives, and regulations.

Your score on the Word Knowledge subtest, along with your score on the Paragraph Comprehension subtest (see Chapters 6 and 7), is used to compute what the military calls a *verbal expression* (VE) score. The VE score is then combined with your Arithmetic Reasoning score (see Chapters 10 and 11) and your Mathematics Knowledge score (see Chapters 8 and 9) to compute your AFQT score. (For more information on how these scores combine, turn to Chapter 1.)

The VE score is also used to determine whether you're qualified for many military jobs. If you're interested in which military jobs require a good VE score, you may want to consider picking up a copy of the best-selling book *ASVAB For Dummies,* which is also published by John Wiley & Sons, Inc.

The good news is that you can improve your vocabulary. You've been learning new words and their meanings since you first learned to talk. In this chapter, I give you some hints, tips, and techniques you can use to speed up the process.

Growing Your Vocabulary

Your vocabulary naturally grows throughout your life. Even professional writers learn new words pretty frequently. But if the ASVAB is staring you in the face, you may not want to wait for life's natural process. In the following sections, I help you explore some great ways to improve your vocabulary.

Reading more to learn more

People who read a lot have larger vocabularies than people who don't read much. That sounds kind of obvious, but I'm sure the government has spent some of your tax dollars funding studies to confirm this.

It doesn't matter much what you read, as long as you make it a regular, daily practice. You don't have to read William Shakespeare or Jane Austen. Your reading choices may be action-adventure or romance books for enjoyment, the daily newspaper, magazines, Internet articles and blogs, or manga or comic books.

TIP

When reading online, get into the habit of keeping an extra browser tab open and pointed to an online dictionary site, such as www.dictionary.com. That way, if you run into a word you don't know, you can quickly copy and paste it to the online dictionary. Most browsers let you highlight a word and right-click it to search for it online, too.

Talking to people

Other people have vocabularies that differ from yours. If you speak to a variety of people, and you do it often, you're exposed to a variety of cultures and occupations, all of which expose you to new words.

TIP

When you hear a new word, look it up on your phone. Create a note on your phone or scribble it down on a piece of paper so you can look it up later.

Adding words to your vocabulary

Make a goal to learn at least one new word per day. A great way to meet that target is to visit or subscribe to one of the many Internet word-of-the-day websites or download an app. Here are a few suggestions:

>> **Dictionary.com:** You can visit the site daily or subscribe to the word of the day via email. Visit https://dictionary.reference.com/wordoftheday.

>> **Merriam-Webster Online:** A new vocabulary word appears every single day. Point your browser to www.merriam-webster.com/word-of-the-day. You can also download M-W's app to your smartphone; you'll always have a dictionary at your fingertips, and you can check out the word of the day when you have a spare 30 seconds.

>> *The New York Times* **Word of the Day:** *The New York Times* offers a new word every day, along with an example of how the word was used in recent *New York Times* stories. Visit http://learning.blogs.nytimes.com/category/word-of-the-day.

A CROSSWORD SUCCESS STORY

My Grandma Emily never found a crossword puzzle she couldn't solve. She had a tremendous vocabulary . . . but she didn't pick it all up in school. In fact, my grandma dropped out of high school (that wasn't unusual in the 1940s, particularly when kids had to help their families by working) and didn't go back to finish until 1971, after her oldest daughter graduated. Instead, she expanded her vocabulary one crossword clue at a time. She always had a big paperback book of crosswords on her kitchen table, and she could complete difficult puzzles with a pen — something that impresses me to this day!

>> *The Oxford English Dictionary:* If you want more than just a word and definition, try the *Oxford English Dictionary* word of the day. In addition to definitions, the page provides pronunciation, spelling, etymology, and a date chart that shows when the word was first used. The word of the day is also available by email subscription and RSS feed. Check out www.oed.com and explore the site's homepage to find it.

Try to use your new word in conversation a couple of times to help you remember it. Writing a few example sentences can help you remember the new words in context.

Using puzzles and games to improve your vocabulary

A fun way to increase your word knowledge is to do crossword puzzles or play word games. Scrabble and Mad Libs, for example, are great ways to reinforce new vocabulary words. There are dozens of word game apps, too, such as Word Streak and Words with Friends. You can improve your vocabulary while having fun! It's a win-win.

You're on my list: Working with word lists

Learning a new word doesn't do you much good if you forget it a week later. Learning often requires repetition, and that's especially true when it comes to memorizing new words.

TIP

Keep a list of all the new words you learn and go over that list at least two or three times a week until you're sure the new words have become part of your vocabulary.

Just to get you started, I give you 50 words in Table 4-1.

TABLE 4-1   **Fifty Vocabulary Words**

Word	Part of Speech	Meaning
Abrupt	Adjective	Beginning, ending, or changing suddenly
Acrid	Adjective	Harshly pungent or bitter
Becalm	Verb	To make quiet
Buffoon	Noun	A clown
Chaos	Noun	Utter disorder and confusion
Cognizant	Adjective	Taking notice of something

(continued)

TABLE 4-1 *(continued)*

Word	Part of Speech	Meaning
Defer	Verb	To put off or delay to a later time
Derision	Noun	The act of ridiculing or making fun of something
Effulgence	Noun	Great brightness
Enmity	Noun	Hatred
Famish	Verb	To cause extreme hunger or thirst
Fealty	Noun	Loyalty
Generalize	Verb	To draw general inferences
Grotto	Noun	A small cavern
Habitual	Adjective	According to usual practice
Hideous	Adjective	Extremely ugly or appalling
Ichthyic	Adjective	Fishlike
Icon	Noun	An image or likeness
Illusion	Noun	An unreal image
Irritate	Verb	To excite ill temper or impatience in something
Jovial	Adjective	Merry
Juxtapose	Verb	To place close together
Kernel	Noun	A grain or seed
Kinsfolk	Noun	Relatives
Laggard	Adjective or noun	Falling behind; one who lags behind
Laud	Verb	To praise
Maize	Noun	Corn
Malevolence	Noun	Ill will
Nestle	Verb	To adjust cozily in snug quarters
Novice	Noun	Beginner
Obese	Adjective	Exceedingly fat
Obtrude	Verb	To push or thrust oneself into undue prominence
Pare	Verb	To cut, shave, or remove the outside from anything
Pedagogue	Noun	Teacher; one who is fussily academic
Quadrate	Verb	To make square; to make conform or agree with
Quiescence	Noun	Quietness
Rancor	Noun	Malice
Raucous	Adjective	Loud and rowdy
Sanguine	Adjective	Cheerfully optimistic; having the color of blood
Sepulcher	Noun	A burial place
Teem	Verb	To be full to overflowing

Word	Part of Speech	Meaning
Tenacious	Adjective	Unyielding
Umbrage	Noun	Injury or offense
Vacillate	Verb	To waver
Valid	Adjective	Founded on truth
Velocity	Noun	Speed
Wile	Noun	An act or a means of cunning deception
Wizen	Verb	To become or cause to become withered or dry
Yokel	Noun	Country bumpkin
Zealot	Noun	One who is enthusiastic to an extreme or excessive degree

Getting flashes of memory with flashcards

Flashcards have been around for a long time. They're still in wide use in these days of electronics and computers because they work. And they work especially well for subjects that just require simple memorization.

You can make flashcards from any stiff paper material, like index cards, construction paper, or card stock. Write the words from your list on flashcards — words on the front and a short definition on the back. Use only one word per card.

TIP

As far back as 1885, a psychologist named Hermann Ebbinghaus, who specialized in memory research, published a study that detailed the effective use of flashcards. According to his rules, you should follow these steps:

1. **Review all the cards in the set, looking at each front and back.**

   Go through the set several times.

2. **Test and sort.**

   Read the front of the card. Try to say what's written on the back. If you're wrong, put the card in a "wrong" pile. Do the same for each card until the cards are sorted into "right" and "wrong" piles.

3. **Review the "wrong" pile.**

   Read each card in the "wrong" pile, front and back. Go through the "wrong" pile several times.

4. **Test and sort with the "wrong" pile.**

   Go through the cards of the "wrong" pile, testing yourself with them and sorting them into "right" and "wrong" piles just as you did with all the cards in Step 2. Keep working with the cards of the "wrong" pile until they're all in the "right" pile.

Building a Word from Scratch

Many English words are created from building blocks called roots, prefixes, and suffixes. Not every word has all three, but many have at least one. The *prefix* is the part that comes at the front of a word, the *suffix* is the part that comes at the end of a word, and the *root* is the part that comes in the middle of a word. Think of roots as the base of the word and prefixes and suffixes as word parts that are attached to the base.

If you don't know the meaning of a word, you can often break it down into smaller parts and analyze those parts. For instance, *introspect* is made up from the root *spect*, which means to look, and the prefix *intro*, which means within. Taken together, *introspect* means "to look within." Wasn't that fun?

If you memorize some of these word parts, you'll have a better chance of figuring out the meaning of an unfamiliar word when you see it on the Word Knowledge subtest — and that's a good thing. Figuring out the meaning of unfamiliar words is how people with large vocabularies make them even larger. (They look up words in the dictionary, too.)

Rooting around for roots

A root is a word part that serves as the base of a word. If you recognize a root, you can generally get an idea of what the word means, even if you're not familiar with it. As Mr. Miyagi said in *The Karate Kid*, "Root strong, tree grow strong." All right, Daniel-san, in terms of your vocabulary, think of it this way: If your knowledge of word roots is strong, your vocabulary will be much stronger.

In Table 4-2, I list some common roots. Memorize them. When you sit down to take the ASVAB, you'll be glad you did.

TABLE 4-2 **Roots**

Root	Meaning	Sample Word
anthro or anthrop	relating to humans	anthropology
bibli or biblio	relating to books	bibliography
brev	short	abbreviate
cede or ceed	go, yield	recede
chrom	color	monochrome
circum	around	circumnavigate
cogn or cogno	know	cognizant
corp	body	corporate
dic or dict	speak	diction
domin	rule	dominate
flu or flux	flow	influx
form	shape	formulate
frac or frag	break	fragment
graph	writing	biography
junct	join	juncture
liber	free	liberate
lum	light	illuminate
oper	work	cooperate
pat or path	suffer	pathology

Root	Meaning	Sample Word
port	carry	portable
press	squeeze	repress
scrib or script	write	describe
sens or sent	think, feel	sentient
tract	pull	traction
voc or vok	call	revoke

Attaching prefixes and suffixes

A prefix is a group of letters added before a word or base to alter the base's meaning and form a new word. In contrast, a suffix is a group of letters added after a word or base. Prefixes and suffixes are called *affixes* because they're attached to a root.

Tables 4-3 and 4-4 list some common prefixes and suffixes. Each list has the word part, its meaning, and one word that uses each word part. Writing down additional words that you know for each word part can help you memorize the lists.

TABLE 4-3 **Prefixes**

Prefix	Meaning	Sample Word
a-	no, not	atheist
ab- or abs-	away, from	absent
anti-	against	antibody
bi-	two	bilateral
contra-	against	contradict
de-	away from	depart
dec-	ten	decathlon
extra-	outside, beyond	extracurricular
fore-	in front of	foreman
geo-	earth	geology
hyper-	excess, over	hyperactive
il-	not	illogical
mal- or male-	wrong, bad	malnutrition
multi-	many	multifamily
non-	not	nonfat
omni-	all	omnivore
ped-	foot	pedestrian
que-, quer-, or ques-	ask	question

(continued)

TABLE 4-3 *(continued)*

Prefix	Meaning	Sample Word
re-	back, again	replay
semi-	half	semisweet
super-	over, more	superior
tele-	far	telephone
trans-	across	transplant
un-	not	uninformed

TABLE 4-4 Suffixes

Suffix	Meaning	Sample Word
-able or -ible	capable of	agreeable
-age	action, result	breakage
-al	characterized by	functional
-ance	instance of an action	performance
-ation	action, process	liberation
-en	made of	silken
-ful	full of	helpful
-ic	consisting of	acidic
-ical	possessing a quality of	statistical
-ion	result of act or process	legislation
-ish	relating to	childish
-ism	act, practice	Buddhism
-ist	characteristic of	elitist
-ity	quality of	specificity
-less	not having	childless
-let	small one	booklet
-man	relating to humans, manlike	gentleman
-ment	action, process	establishment
-ness	possessing a quality	goodness
-or	one who does something	orator
-ous	having	dangerous
-y	quality of	tasty

A Word by Any Other Name: Surveying Synonyms and Antonyms

English is a complicated language. You could probably learn Spanish, German, or even Korean from scratch more easily than you could English.

In the English language, you usually have more than one way to say the same thing, even by swapping just one word. These different words with the same meaning are called *synonyms*. Synonyms are different words that have the same or very similar meanings. *Funny, amusing,* and *comical* are synonyms; they all mean the same thing.

In fact, that's what the Word Knowledge subtest on the ASVAB really does: It tests your ability to select synonyms for the underlined words contained in the question stem. Look at the following example.

EXAMPLE

<u>Perform</u> most nearly means

(A) eat.

(B) dance.

(C) execute.

(D) sing.

The correct answer is Choice (C). *Execute* (to carry out something) is a synonym of *perform*, which means the same thing. Although you can perform a dance or perform a song, *dance* and *sing* don't actually mean the same thing as *perform*.

TIP

When you look up a new word in the dictionary (see the section "Adding words to your vocabulary" earlier in this chapter) and add it to your word list (refer to the section "You're on my list: Working with word lists" earlier in this chapter), you should include synonyms because you're very likely to see them on the Word Knowledge subtest.

An *antonym* is a word that has the opposite or nearly opposite meaning of another word. *Smile* and *frown* are antonyms of one another. The test makers often use antonyms as wrong answers on the Word Knowledge subtest. Knowing antonyms for words not only improves your chances of narrowing your answer choices. It also beefs up your vocabulary. For example, if you know that *fast* is an antonym of *slow* and you know what *slow* means, you also know what *fast* means.

TIP

How can you find the synonym of a word (or the antonym, for that matter)? A good place to start is the dictionary. Many dictionary entries include the abbreviation *syn.*, which means *synonym*. The words that follow this abbreviation are synonyms of the entry word. You may also see the abbreviation *ant.* in an entry. This abbreviation stands for *antonym*, and the word or words that follow it mean the opposite of the entry word.

Thesauruses are special dictionaries of synonyms and antonyms. We writers use them all the time to make us look smarter. Here are a couple of online thesauruses you can use to look up synonyms for words on your word list:

>> **Thesaurus.com:** www.thesaurus.com

>> **Merriam-Webster Online:** www.merriam-webster.com/thesaurus

Getting Homogeneous with Homonyms

Some words in the English language are spelled the same but have two or more meanings. For example, a *fluke* can mean a fish, the end parts of an anchor, the fins on a whale's tail, or a stroke of luck.

Some words are spelled the same but have different meanings and are often pronounced differently. The word *bow*, meaning a special kind of knot, is pronounced differently from *bow*, meaning to bend at the waist. *Bow*, meaning the front of a boat, is pronounced the same as *bow* (bend at the waist), but *bow*, meaning a weapon, is pronounced the same as *bow* (a special knot). See why people trying to learn English get frustrated?

Other words are pronounced the same but are spelled differently and mean something different. *To, too,* and *two* and *there, their,* and *they're* are examples. All these types of words are collectively known as *homonyms* or *homophones.*

The last type of homonym is especially important when it comes to the Word Knowledge subtest of the ASVAB. The test makers won't try to trick you by having two homonym answers for words that are spelled the same but have multiple meanings, but they may use homonyms that are spelled differently and have different meanings.

EXAMPLE

Flue most nearly means

(A) sickness.

(B) fly.

(C) chimney.

(D) None of the above.

You may be tempted to choose Choice (A), but that would be correct if *flu* were the test word. The past tense of *fly* is *flew*. The word *flue* means a chimney pipe.

Table 4-5 shows you a few more examples of common homonyms.

TIP

You can see an extensive list of homonyms on Enchanted Learning at www.enchantedlearning.com/english/homonyms.

TABLE 4-5 **Common Homonyms**

Word	Definition	Example Sentence
Allowed	Permitted	He <u>allowed</u> the audience to participate.
Aloud	Normal volume of speaking	They couldn't speak <u>aloud</u> in the library.
Cent	A penny	I couldn't believe I got the comic book for just one <u>cent</u>.
Scent	Aroma	The <u>scent</u> coming from the kitchen made my mouth water.
Sent	Past tense of *send*	He <u>sent</u> the letter Monday.
Cue	Stimulus to action	A door slamming was his <u>cue</u> to exit the stage.
Queue	Line	There was a large <u>queue</u> of cars waiting to park.
Die	To cease living	The flowers <u>die</u> when the weather gets cold.
Dye	To color or stain	She wants to <u>dye</u> her hair red.

Word	Definition	Example Sentence
Elicit	To draw or bring out	He vowed to <u>elicit</u> the truth from his friend.
Illicit	Unlawful	He used <u>illicit</u> means to avoid paying taxes.
Fairy	Supernatural being	The <u>fairy</u> was dancing in the night.
Ferry	A boat for crossing rivers or other small bodies of water	The <u>ferry</u> took us quickly across the river.
Gorilla	Large ape	I threw the <u>gorilla</u> a banana.
Guerrilla	Irregular soldier	The band of <u>guerrillas</u> attacked the convoy.
Hangar	Building for airplanes	Jack pulled the aircraft into the <u>hangar</u>.
Hanger	A device for hanging things	Mom said to put the shirt on a <u>hanger</u>.
It's	Contraction of *it is*	<u>It's</u> a very hot day.
Its	Belonging to *it*	The bank said <u>its</u> savings accounts were the best.
Know	To possess knowledge	I <u>know</u> you went to the store.
No	Zero or negative	I told John there was <u>no</u> way we would travel together.
Lessen	To make less	We gave him medicine to <u>lessen</u> his pain.
Lesson	Something to be learned	We must never forget the <u>lessons</u> of the past.
Mail	Postal delivery	I expected the check to be in the <u>mail</u>.
Male	A gender	The teacher asked all <u>males</u> to go to one room and all females to go to another.
Naval	Pertaining to ships	He wanted to become a <u>naval</u> officer.
Navel	Belly button	Mom always said not to play with my <u>navel</u>.
Ordinance	Decree or local law	Spitting on the sidewalk was against the town <u>ordinance</u>.
Ordnance	Military ammunition	We were running low, so we asked the sergeant for more <u>ordnance</u>.
Patience	The ability to suppress restlessness	I couldn't believe her <u>patience</u> with the students.
Patients	People under medical care	The nurse treated all her <u>patients</u> with respect.
Reek	Bad smell	The <u>reek</u> of the skunk invaded the living room.
Wreak	Inflict	Jack continued to <u>wreak</u> havoc every time he got upset.
Sleight	Dexterity	The magician's <u>sleight</u> of hand was amazing.
Slight	Small amount	There was only a <u>slight</u> increase in salaries this year.
Threw	Propelled by hand	He <u>threw</u> the ball to first base.
Through	In one side and out the other	Dad drove <u>through</u> the tunnel.
Vary	Change	The interest rate continues to <u>vary</u> up and down.
Very	Extreme	I am <u>very</u> happy with *ASVAB AFQT For Dummies*.
Weak	Not strong	After his illness, Paul was very <u>weak</u>.
Week	Seven days	It'll take at least a <u>week</u> to finish this report.
Your	Belonging to you	<u>Your</u> new car is really cool.
You're	Contraction of *you are*	<u>You're</u> going to be in trouble when Dad gets home.

Flex Your Lexicon: Vocabulary Exercises

The best way to improve your vocabulary? Practice, practice, and more practice. The vocabulary exercises in this section will give you a little face-time with the nuts and bolts of the questions you'll find in the Word Knowledge subtest of the ASVAB.

Practicing synonyms? It's all the same to me

Activity 1 is a matching game (See? I told you playing word games to grow your vocabulary would be fun!). Match the word on the left with the word that has the most similar meaning — its synonym — on the right; you'll find the correct answers at the end of this chapter.

ACTIVITY 1 ## Synonym Practice

Answer	Vocabulary Word	Synonym
1.	1. consider	A. uncommon
2.	2. evident	B. capsize
3.	3. scarce	C. fail
4.	4. vain	D. flounder
5.	5. render	E. go-between
6.	6. gadget	F. deliberate
7.	7. backfire	G. give
8.	8. wallow	H. descend
9.	9. habits	I. arrogant
10.	10. fabricate	J. within
11.	11. pressured	K. compelled
12.	12. keel	L. assemble
13.	13. plunge	M. obvious
14.	14. intermediary	N. customs
15.	15. internal	O. apparatus

Antithetic antonyms: The opposite of synonyms

Activity 2 has 15 vocabulary words and their opposites. Your mission, should you choose to accept it, is to match the vocabulary word with the word it is the most opposite of. The correct answers are at the end of this chapter.

Antonym Practice

Answer	Vocabulary Word	Antonym
1.	1. contrary	A. concern
2.	2. disregard	B. innocent
3.	3. protest	C. inept
4.	4. endorse	D. admire
5.	5. guilty	E. freeze
6.	6. ill	F. fabrication
7.	7. melt	G. individual
8.	8. actual	H. clumsiness
9.	9. abstain	I. agreeable
10.	10. despise	J. disapprove
11.	11. faultless	K. imperfect
12.	12. clan	L. counterfeit
13.	13. resourceful	M. continue
14.	14. fact	N. healthy
15.	15. agility	O. concur

Digging around word roots

Activity 3 gives you a word with a common root. It's your job to find the root, guess what the word means, and look it up in the dictionary (or flip to the end of this chapter, where I've written out the definition for you). It's often helpful to think of words you already know that sound similar to words you don't know; that can help you guess the right answers.

ACTIVITY 3 **Word Root Practice**

Word	Root	Your Definition
1. hemorrhage		
2. magnify		
3. alleviate		
4. verbalize		
5. dismal		
6. marine		
7. affirm		
8. admonish		
9. autograph		
10. hydrate		

(continued)

Word	Root	Your Definition
11. convene		
12. relapse		
13. liberate		
14. pathetic		
15. unanimous		

Parsing prefixes: Defining the beginnings of words

Activity 4 has 15 vocabulary words that have prefixes attached. Tap into your existing vocabulary to figure out what each word means based on its prefix. Write the prefix in the column beside the word, and then write what you think the word means. Then, when you're done, check your answers at the end of this chapter.

ACTIVITY 4 **Prefix Practice**

Word	Prefix	Your Definition
1. apolitical		
2. predetermined		
3. devalue		
4. coaxial		
5. extraordinary		
6. miniature		
7. undesirable		
8. forerunner		
9. byproduct		
10. overreact		
11. uplift		
12. midway		
13. intergalactic		
14. omnipotent		
15. substrate		

Suffering through suffixes: The ends of words

Activity 5 contains 15 vocabulary words with suffixes tacked on their back ends. Separate the suffix from the word (and write it down), jot down what the word probably means, and then check your answers in the dictionary or at the end of this chapter.

Word	Suffix	Your Definition
1. postage		
2. annoyance		
3. disciplinarian		
4. wisdom		
5. clemency		
6. artful		
7. celestial		
8. zanily		
9. completion		
10. placement		
11. authorship		
12. fascination		
13. fortitude		
14. circular		
15. audible		

Defining words from their context

You find 15 sentences in Activity 6. Try to define the underlined word based on the context of the sentence that it's in and write your definition in the "Your Definition" column. Then look up the word in the dictionary or flip to the end of this chapter to find out whether you were right (or pretty close). Write the official definition in the final column so you can better boost your vocabulary.

ACTIVITY 6 **Context Practice**

Sentence	Your Definition	Dictionary Definition
1. Smoking has deleterious effects on your health.		
2. The topic was too serious for her to be so facetious.		
3. The English lexicon contains hundreds of thousands of words.		
4. Sadie told him not to plagiarize, but he copied the text anyway.		
5. The commander didn't want to capitulate, but the general told him to surrender.		
6. Jeff's sunny disposition and sanguine attitude made everyone like him.		
7. Nobody wanted a dictator or a totalitarian regime.		

(continued)

Sentence	Your Definition	Dictionary Definition
8. David <u>vehemently</u> denied the accusations because he was not guilty.		
9. Cheryl never saw a structure as <u>colossal</u> as the Great Pyramid of Giza.		
10. Jesse's <u>bizarre</u> hairstyle often got him attention from the girls at school.		
11. The teens participated in the <u>boycott</u> by refusing to buy coffee.		
12. The <u>embargo</u> on car sales made it impossible to get a new model.		
13. The idea that black cats are unlucky is a <u>fallacy</u>.		
14. The artist made the <u>mosaic</u> with pieces of colored glass.		
15. The dog's constant barking was a nuisance.		

Answers and Explanations

Check your answers for each of the exercises here and take some time to review the explanations if you're not sure where you went wrong.

Activity 1: Synonyms

Answer	Vocabulary Word	Synonym
1. F	consider	deliberate
2. M	evident	obvious
3. A	scarce	uncommon
4. I	vain	arrogant
5. G	render	give
6. O	gadget	apparatus
7. C	backfire	fail
8. D	wallow	flounder
9. N	habits	customs
10. L	fabricate	assemble
11. K	pressured	compelled
12. B	keel	capsize
13. H	plunge	descend
14. E	intermediary	go-between
15. J	internal	within

Activity 2: Antonyms

Answer	Vocabulary Word	Antonym
1. I	contrary	agreeable
2. A	disregard	concern
3. O	protest	concur
4. J	endorse	disapprove
5. B	guilty	innocent
6. N	ill	healthy
7. E	melt	freeze
8. L	actual	counterfeit
9. M	abstain	continue
10. D	despise	admire
11. K	faultless	imperfect

Answer	Vocabulary Word	Antonym
12. G	clan	individual
13. C	resourceful	inept
14. F	fact	fabrication
15. H	agility	clumsiness

Activity 3: Word Roots

1. *Hemorrhage* is a noun that refers to an escape of blood from a ruptured blood vessel. (It's also a verb that means to bleed profusely.) If you guessed that it had something to do with blood because of the root *hemo*, you were on the right track. Other words using *hemo* include *hemoglobin*, *hemophilia*, and *hemorrhoids*.

2. *Magnify* is a verb that means to make something appear larger than it is. The root, *magn*, means great or large. Other words that use *magn* include *magnitude* and *magnificent*.

3. *Alleviate* is a verb that means to make suffering or a problem less severe. Its root is *lev*, which means to lift or raise, and you see this root used in the words *levitate*, *levity*, and *elevate*.

4. *Verbalize* is a verb that means to express ideas or feelings in words. The root of this word, *verb*, literally means word. Other words that contain *verb* include *proverb*, *reverberate*, and *verbiage*.

5. *Dismal* is an adjective that means depressing or dreary. Its root is *mal*, which means bad or wretched. *Mal* is also part of words such as *malevolent*, *malfunction*, and *malady*.

6. *Marine* is an adjective that refers to something that's of, found in, or produced by the sea. (It's a noun referring to a member of the U.S. Marine Corps, a seascape, and seagoing ships, too.) Its root, *mar*, means sea, and you find it in words such as *marina*, *maritime*, and *submarine*.

7. *Affirm* is a verb that means to state something as a fact. Its root, *firm*, means firm or strong. You also see *firm* in *confirm*, *firmament*, and *firmly*.

8. *Admonish* is a verb that means to warn or reprimand someone firmly. The root, *mon*, means warn, and it serves as the root in the words *monitor* and *premonition*.

9. *Autograph* is a noun that means a signature (especially that of a celebrity). Its root, *graph*, means to write or draw. You also see *graph* in words such as *biography*, *cartography*, and *graphic*.

10. *Hydrate* is a verb that means to cause to absorb water. *Hydr*, its root, means water. You see it in *hydrant*, *hydroponics*, and *hydrogenated*.

11. *Convene* is a verb that means to come or bring together for a meeting or activity. Its root is *ven*, which means come, just as in the words *event*, *venue*, and *intervene*.

12. *Relapse* is a verb that means to suffer deterioration after a period of improvement. (It's a noun, too, that means the return of a disease or illness after a partial recovery.) Its root is *laps*, which means to slide or slip. Other words that use *laps* include *collapse*, *elapse*, and *prolapse*.

13. *Liberate* is a verb that means to set someone free from a situation, such as imprisonment or slavery, in which their liberty is severely restricted. Its root, *liber*, means free; you also see it in *liberal* and *libertarian*.

14. *Pathetic* is an adjective that means arousing pity, particularly through sadness or vulnerability. Its root is *path*, which means feeling or disease, just like you see in *apathetic*, *pathologist*, and *sociopath*.

15. *Unanimous* is an adjective that refers to two or more people being fully in agreement about something. Its root is *un* (but don't get it confused with the prefix *un-*, which means not). You also see this root in *unity*, *union*, and *reunification*.

Activity 4: Prefixes

1. *Apolitical*'s prefix is *a-*, which means not or without. *Apolitical* is an adjective that means not involved or interested in politics. Other words with the prefix *a-* are *atheist*, *asexual*, and *apathy*.

2. *Predetermined,* which is a verb that means established or decided in advance, uses *pre-* as its prefix. *Pre-* means before, and you see it in the words *prefix*, *pregame*, and *prevent*.

3. *Devalue* is a verb that means to reduce the worth or importance of something. Its prefix, *de-*, means off, down, or away from. You see it in words such as *defrost*, *demotivate*, and *devolve*.

4. *Coaxial* is an adjective that means having a common axis (like a coaxial cable). Its prefix, *co-*, means with. *Co-* is also seen in words like *cooperate*, *co-locate*, and *coworker*.

5. *Extraordinary* is an adjective that means very unusual or remarkable. Its prefix is *extra-*, and it means outside or beyond. *Extra-* is also part of the words *extracurricular*, *extraterrestrial*, and *extrajudicial*.

6. *Miniature* is a noun that means a representation or image of something on a reduced or small scale. (It's also an adjective that refers to something that's represented on a small or reduced scale.) As a prefix, *mini-* means small; you also see it in words like *minivan*, *minimal*, and *miniseries*.

7. *Undesirable* is an adjective that means not wanted due to harmfulness or unpleasantness. The prefix, *un-*, means not or against. *Un-* also appears in words such as *unnecessary*, *unhappy*, and *unfazed*.

8. *Forerunner* is a noun that refers to a person or thing that precedes someone or something else. The prefix in this word is *fore-*, and it means before. You also see it in words like *foreman*, *foresee*, and *forego*.

9. *Byproduct* is a noun that refers to an incidental or secondary product made while making something else. Its prefix, *by-*, means near or next to. This prefix also appears in the words *byway* and *bypass*.

10. *Overreact* is a verb that means to respond more emotionally or forcibly than fits the situation. Its prefix is *over-*, which means excessive or above, and you see it in words like *overbearing*, *overjoyed*, and *overuse*.

11. *Uplift* is a verb that means to lift or raise something. It's also a noun that describes the act of raising something. Its prefix, *up-*, means greater, higher, or better, so you see it in *upgrade*, *upright*, and *upsweep*.

12. *Midway* is an adjective and adverb that means in or toward the middle of something. (It's also a noun that refers to the hotspot in an amusement park, carnival, or fair where all the concessions, games, and sideshows are located.) *Mid-* is its prefix, which means middle, so it also shows up in the words *midtown*, *midday*, and *midst*.

13. *Intergalactic* is an adjective that refers to something relating to or situated between two or more galaxies. Its prefix, *inter-*, means among or between. You find it in *international*, *Internet*, and *interim*.

14. *Omnipotent* is an adjective that means having unlimited power or able to do anything. *Omni-* is its prefix, and it means all. You also see it in *omnivore*, *omnibus*, and *omniscient*.

15. *Substrate* is a noun that means a substance or layer that underlies something. *Sub-*, its prefix, means under, so you also see it in *subway*, *submarine*, and *subsystem*.

Activity 5: Suffixes

1. *Postage* is a noun that refers to the charge for sending a letter or other matter by mail. Its suffix is *-age*, which means action or process. It also appears in *passage*, *pilgrimage*, and *voyage*.

2. *Annoyance* is a noun that means nuisance or a person or thing that annoys. Its suffix, *-ance*, means state or quality of, so you see it in words like *defiance*, *brilliance*, and *compliance*.

3. *Disciplinarian* is a noun that means a person who enforces or advocates discipline, and its suffix is *-arian*, which means a person who does something. This suffix appears in *vegetarian*, *librarian*, and *egalitarian*.

4. *Wisdom* is a noun that means scholarly knowledge or learning, or the state of being wise. Its suffix is *-dom*, which means condition of, state, or realm, so it also shows up in words like *boredom*, *freedom*, and *kingdom*.

5. *Clemency* is a noun that means a disposition to show compassion or forgiveness, leniency, or mercy. Its suffix is *-ency*, which means condition or quality. You find it in *dependency*, *efficiency*, and *complacency*.

6. *Artful* is an adjective that means crafty, cunning, skillful, or clever. Its suffix, *-ful*, means full of, so you see it in words like *helpful*, *cheerful*, and *thankful* as well.

7. *Celestial* is an adjective that means pertaining to the sky or to the universe beyond the atmosphere. Its suffix is *-ial*, which means relating to. It also makes an appearance in words like *editorial*, *martial*, and *racial*.

8. *Zanily* is an adverb that means comically or clownishly, and its suffix is *-ily*, which means in a certain manner. You see it in *sloppily*, *steadily*, and *breezily*.

9. *Completion* is a noun that means conclusion or fulfillment. Its suffix is *-ion*, which means action or process, and it appears in *celebration*, *navigation*, and *abduction*.

10. *Placement* is a noun that means location or arrangement or that indicates the act of placing. Its suffix is *-ent*, which means action or result. You see *-ent* in words like *movement*, *shipment*, and *abolishment*.

11. *Authorship* is a noun that means origin with reference to an author, creator, or producer of a work. Its suffix is *-ship*, which means skill of or state or condition of, and it shows up in words like *citizenship*, *friendship*, and *governorship*.

12. *Fascination* is a noun that means the state or instance of being fascinated, and its suffix is *-tion*. The suffix *-tion* means state or quality, so you also see it in *frustration*, *attention*, and *dejection*.

13. *Fortitude* is a noun that means mental and emotional strength during difficulty, adversity, or danger. Its suffix, *-tude*, means state, condition, or quality, and it shows up in words like *gratitude*, *magnitude*, and *servitude*.

14. *Circular* is an adjective that means having the form of a circle or being roundabout or indirect. Its suffix is *-ular*, which means relating to or resembling. You find it in *cellular*, *muscular*, and *regular*, too.

15. *Audible* is an adjective that means capable of being heard, and its suffix is *-ible*, which means able to be. You see it in words like *plausible*, *legible*, and *visible*.

Activity 6: Context

1. *Deleterious* is an adjective that means causing harm or damage.

2. *Facetious* is an adjective that means treating serious issues with deliberately inappropriate humor.

3. *Lexicon* is a noun that means the vocabulary of a person, language, or branch of knowledge.

4. *Plagiarize* is a verb that means to take someone else's work or idea and pass it off as one's own.

5. *Capitulate* is a verb that means to cease to resist or to surrender.

6. *Sanguine* is an adjective that means optimistic or positive, especially in a difficult or bad situation.

7. *Totalitarian* is an adjective that means relating to a system of centralized, dictatorial government that requires complete subservience to the state.

8. *Vehemently* is an adverb that means in a forceful, passionate, or intense manner.

9. *Colossal* is an adjective that means extremely large.

10. *Bizarre* is an adjective that means very strange or unusual, especially in a way that causes interest or amusement.

11. *Boycott* is a verb that means to withdraw from commercial or social relations as a punishment or protest.

12. *Embargo* is a noun that means an official ban on trade or other commercial activity with a particular country.

13. *Fallacy* is a noun that refers to a mistaken belief, especially if it's based on an unsound argument.

14. *Mosaic* is a noun that refers to a picture or pattern made by arranging small colored pieces of a hard material.

15. *Nuisance* is a noun that means a person, thing, or circumstance causing inconvenience or annoyance.

Chapter 5

The Word Knowledge Subtest

A decent vocabulary is essential in the military if you want to get ahead. The military operates on paperwork, and whether you're trying to get more supplies (submit necessary logistical requisitions) or get the assignment you want (application for personnel career-enhancement programs), you need to develop a good vocabulary.

Word Knowledge is what the military calls the vocabulary subtest on the ASVAB. Because a strong vocabulary is essential to success in the military, the Department of Defense has made this vocabulary test a part of the all-important AFQT score — the score that determines whether you're qualified to join the military service of your choice (see Chapter 1). The military considers clear communication so important that this skill is taught and graded at all levels of leadership training and is often required for promotion.

REMEMBER

Word knowledge isn't part of the AFQT score just because the military likes to use big words. It's included because words stand for ideas, and the more words you understand, the more ideas you can understand (and the better you can communicate with others). Society (including people in the military) often equates a large vocabulary with intelligence and success.

Getting Acquainted with the Test Format

The Word Knowledge portion of the ASVAB measures your vocabulary knowledge. It consists of 15 questions on the version most people take: the CAT-ASVAB. (There are 35 questions on the paper version, but most people don't take that one.) The questions come in three styles: synonyms, context, and antonyms. Your task is to choose the answer closest in meaning to the underlined word unless the test specifically tells you to choose the answer *most opposite* in meaning. Look at the following examples:

EXAMPLE

<u>Abatement</u> most nearly means

(A) encourage.

(B) relax.

(C) obstruct.

(D) terminate.

In this case, the correct answer is Choice (D) because *abatement* means putting an end to something or subsiding.

In the second type of question, you see an underlined word used in the context of a sentence. Again, your goal is to choose the answer closest in meaning to the underlined word as it's used in the sentence. For example:

EXAMPLE

His painting was <u>garish</u>.

(A) offensive

(B) tacky

(C) pretty

(D) expensive

REMEMBER

"Closest in meaning" doesn't mean "the exact same thing." You're looking for words most similar in meaning.

In case you're wondering, the answer is Choice (B).

Finally, you'll encounter a handful of questions about antonyms. You'll know you're facing an antonym question when you see the words *most opposite in meaning*. Consider the following question:

EXAMPLE

The word most opposite in meaning to <u>achieve</u> is

(A) win.

(B) junction.

(C) fail.

(D) championship.

The correct answer is Choice (C) because *achieve* means to successfully bring something about by effort, skill, or courage — and the opposite of that is to fail.

Bumping Up Your Test Score

Sometimes on the Word Knowledge subtest, you either know the answer at first glance, or you don't. Even with that restriction, however, you can pick up a few tricks to help you get the best score possible.

Keeping an eye on the clock

Like all the ASVAB subtests, the Word Knowledge subtest is timed. On the CAT-ASVAB, you get 8 minutes to answer 16 questions, meaning you get to spend about 30 seconds on each one.

If you're one of the few people taking the paper version, you have 11 minutes to answer the 35 questions, which translates into slightly less than 20 seconds to answer each question. For most people, that's plenty of time (as long as you're not thinking more about what you're missing on Facebook than you are about the test).

If you're taking the computerized version of the ASVAB, your remaining time appears on the computer screen. If you're taking the paper version of the test, a clock is clearly visible in the room, and the test proctor posts the start and stop time for the subtest on a blackboard or whiteboard.

Seeing homonyms in a sea of questions

A *homonym* is a word with multiple unrelated meanings (see Chapter 4). The word may be spelled the same for both or all meanings, or it may be spelled differently. If it's spelled the same, it may have a different pronunciation. Some homonyms spelled differently can have the same pronunciation.

The ASVAB doesn't contain any trick questions. In other words, the test doesn't present you with two legitimate answers and ask you to try to decide which one is the "best." However, homonyms can still trip you up if you don't pay attention. Look at the following example:

EXAMPLE

Isle most nearly means

(A) walkway.

(B) island.

(C) intention.

(D) description.

Isle and *aisle* are homonyms. *Isle* means island, and *aisle* means walkway (like in the grocery store). They're two words that sound the same, but they're spelled differently and mean different things. In this case, the correct answer is Choice (B).

Some homonyms are spelled the same but have different meanings. Just for the record, these are called *heteronyms* (one new word for your vocabulary: check!). You won't see multiple correct definitions on the Word Knowledge subtest when you're doing a direct definition problem, but you may see such multiple correct definitions when the word is used in the context of a sentence. For example:

EXAMPLE

Jack tied a <u>bow</u> around the gift.

(A) knot

(B) weapon

(C) ship front

(D) triangle

All the answer choices are proper definitions for the word *bow*. However, only one choice, Choice (A), makes sense for *bow* in the context of the sentence. It just wouldn't make sense for Jack to tie a weapon, the front of a ship, or a triangle around a gift.

Considering guessing

Sometimes on the Word Knowledge subtest, you just don't know the answer. In that case, don't leave it blank. (You can't leave answers blank on the computerized version of the test anyway.)

The paper version of the ASVAB doesn't penalize you for wrong answers. If you leave the answer blank, you have a 0 percent chance of getting it right. But if you make a wild guess, you have a 25 percent chance of stumbling upon the right answer.

WARNING

On the CAT-ASVAB, make sure your guesses are educated and that you don't click random answer buttons quickly just to get through. The test's creators designed the grading software to issue a pretty hefty penalty for multiple wrong answers toward the end of your subtests. They figure this scenario implies you were running out of time and didn't read the questions; to do well on the ASVAB and AFQT, you need to be prepared with adequate time for each question.

TIP

Keep in mind that although you may know the word in the question, you may not know one or more of the words in the multiple-choice answers. In that case, use the process of elimination to narrow down your choices. Eliminate the words you know *aren't* correct and guess which of the remaining words is most *likely* correct.

Before making a wild guess, take a few seconds to look at the word from a different perspective. You may find that you know the word after all — just in a different form. In English, one root word can be changed slightly to perform all sorts of roles; it might be able to act as a noun, a verb, an adjective, or an adverb with just a little modification. So if you know what the root word *attach* means, you can figure out what the word *attachment* means. If you know *adherent*, you can deduce what *adherence* means. (You can find much more information on this topic in Chapter 4.)

You can use root word clues to identify unfamiliar words on the ASVAB. Say you run across the word *memento* on the Word Knowledge test:

EXAMPLE

<u>Memento</u> most nearly means

(A) souvenir.

(B) beauty.

(C) speed.

(D) trouble.

If you don't have a clue what the word *memento* means, all is not lost. Take a closer look. What other word starting with the letters *mem-* do you know? How about the word *memory*? *Memory* is a noun that means something you remember, so the word *memento* is likely related to memories. Other words you might know are *memoir*, *memorable*, and even the word *memo*. So when you look over the possible choices, you can choose the one that has something to do with memory.

But wait. None of the answers actually says "memory." Now what? Just use the process of elimination. One of the answers has a lot to do with memory: Choice (A), *souvenir*.

Trying On Some Sample Questions

Now you're ready to pit your skills against the Word Knowledge subtest of the ASVAB. Try these sample questions to see how you do. They're similar to what you'll see on the ASVAB.

1. Bestial most nearly means
   - **(A)** playful.
   - **(B)** animal-like.
   - **(C)** tantalizing.
   - **(D)** pregnant.

2. The enemy was relentless with negotiations.
   - **(A)** overwhelmed
   - **(B)** happy
   - **(C)** strict
   - **(D)** peaceful

3. Malignant most nearly means
   - **(A)** tumor.
   - **(B)** angry.
   - **(C)** kind.
   - **(D)** evil.

4. Bernard wanted to ask a lawyer whether his friend's investment idea was licit.
   - **(A)** legal
   - **(B)** profitable
   - **(C)** illegal
   - **(D)** sensible

5. Achromatic most nearly means
   - **(A)** automatic.
   - **(B)** tasty.
   - **(C)** colorless.
   - **(D)** manual.

6. The legal team was impressed with her dynamic ideas.
   - **(A)** offensive
   - **(B)** fun
   - **(C)** powerful
   - **(D)** cowering

7. Wry most nearly means
   - **(A)** smile.
   - **(B)** distorted.
   - **(C)** angry.
   - **(D)** happy.

8. Melissa was justifiably proud of her recent abstinence.
   - **(A)** grades
   - **(B)** sobriety
   - **(C)** trustworthiness
   - **(D)** awards

9. Tolerate most nearly means
   - **(A)** accept.
   - **(B)** conserve.
   - **(C)** annoy.
   - **(D)** rush.

10. Lyle's landlord instructed him to vacate the apartment.
    - **(A)** paint
    - **(B)** leave
    - **(C)** clean
    - **(D)** sell

11. Jupiter's plucky attitude made him a great dog to hike unfamiliar territory with.
    - **(A)** courageous
    - **(B)** cowardly
    - **(C)** fearful
    - **(D)** obnoxious

12. The word most opposite in meaning to plausible is
    - **(A)** believable
    - **(B)** genuine
    - **(C)** unreasonable
    - **(D)** ridiculous

13. There was very little variation in the music they played.
    - **(A)** a stringed instrument
    - **(B)** significance
    - **(C)** singing
    - **(D)** difference

14. The group <u>zealously</u> defended the separation of church and state.

    (A) enthusiastically

    (B) angrily

    (C) sustainably

    (D) happily

15. <u>Inquisitive</u> most nearly means

    (A) fast.

    (B) nosy.

    (C) curious.

    (D) dismissive.

Answers and Explanations

Use this answer key to score the practice Word Knowledge questions.

1. **B.** *Bestial* is an adjective that means having animal characteristics. Noting the similarity between the words *bestial* and *beast* can lead you in the right direction with this question.

2. **C.** Used as an adjective, *relentless* means unyieldingly severe, strict, or harsh. The other words don't fit the context of the sentence.

3. **D.** *Malignant* is an adjective that means evil or harmful. You may have been tempted to select Choice (A) because you've heard of a malignant tumor, but *tumor* and *malignant* don't mean the same thing.

4. **A.** *Licit* is an adjective that means lawful. Although you may not have been familiar with the word *licit*, chances are good that you've come across the opposite-meaning word, *illicit*, and you probably know that it means illegal. So you can deduce that *licit* means the opposite of illegal, or legal.

5. **C.** *Achromatic* is an adjective that means having no color. If you knew that the word root *chrom* refers to color and that the prefix *a-* means without, you could figure out that *achromatic* means without color.

6. **C.** Used as an adjective, *dynamic* refers to a process or system that's characterized by constant progress, activity, or change. You can use clues in the sentence to rule out Choices (A) and (D) because if the legal team is impressed, she's probably not offensive or cowering. Although *dynamic* can mean fun, the word closest in meaning to what's in the sentence is *powerful*.

7. **B.** *Wry* is an adjective that means crooked or twisted.

8. **B.** *Abstinence* is a noun that means the willful avoidance of something — for example, a substance such as alcohol or drugs.

9. **A.** *Tolerate* is a verb meaning to allow or accept without hindrance.

10. **B.** *Vacate* is a verb that means to give up occupancy of a location. The word root, *vac*, is key here. A *vacation* involves leaving your normal place of residence. When people *evacuate* an area, they leave that area. A *vacuum* is created when matter leaves a given area.

11. **A.** *Plucky* is an adjective that means having or showing determined courage in the face of difficulties. Although it may be tough to find this word's meaning based on its construction, the context of the sentence provides a pretty good hint; you'd want a courageous dog with you on an unfamiliar hike. (A cowardly, fearful, or obnoxious one? Not so much.)

12. **C.** *Plausible* is a noun meaning reasonable, probable, or believable. The question asked what word is most opposite in meaning, and among your choices, Choice (C), unreasonable, is the way to go.

13. **D.** *Variation* is a noun that means a change or difference in condition, amount or level; in this sentence, it means the music mostly sounded the same. The prefix *vari-* may have tipped you off because it means *different* or *diverse*.

14. **A.** *Zealously* is an adverb — a word that modifies a verb — that means with great energy or enthusiasm toward a cause or objective. (*Zealously* modifies the verb *defended* in this sentence.)

15. **C.** *Inquisitive* is an adjective meaning curious or inquiring. If you chose Choice (B), you were on the right track, but the question asks you for the word closest in meaning. Though some inquisitive people are definitely nosy, the word only means curious.

Chapter **6**

Reading for Comprehension

The military services want their members to understand what they're reading. This skill is known as *reading comprehension*, but on the ASVAB, it's called *paragraph comprehension*, and it makes up part of your AFQT score.

The military runs on paperwork and verbal instructions. As a newly enlisted member, you'll have to read and understand your share of memos, policy letters, regulations, manuals, and forms. In some branches, your promotions are based — in part — on how well you can read, comprehend, and retain information from written material. And the higher rank you earn, the more paperwork you'll see.

Reading comprehension involves several skills that nearly anyone can develop with practice. To thoroughly understand what you read, you must develop the abilities to recognize the main idea, recall details, and make inferences. The information in this chapter helps you improve your reading comprehension skills, making it possible for you to nail the Paragraph Comprehension subtest of the ASVAB.

Taking Pointers about Points

When someone writes something, they're almost always trying to make a point. This message is called the *main point* or *principal idea* of the writing. The paragraph or passage may also contain information that supports or reinforces the main point; these little gems are called *subpoints*.

Here's an example: The main point of this chapter is to give you the scoop on the Paragraph Comprehension subtest, and each section covers a subpoint that helps you understand it even more. But on the test, you don't have to read whole chapters — just passages of up to a few paragraphs.

Picking out the main point

The main point is the most important part of a paragraph or passage. It's the primary theme that the writer wants you to understand. In many cases, the writer states the main point simply. In other cases, the writer may imply the main point rather than state it directly.

Quite often, the main point of a paragraph or passage is contained in the first sentence. You may recall from school that your English teacher referred to this sentence as the *topic sentence*. Sometimes a writer also rephrases or summarizes the main point in the passage's last sentence.

In the following passage, the main idea is stated in the first sentence:

> U.S. military forces will increasingly be called upon in the immediate future for peaceful military-to military contacts, humanitarian intervention, peace support, and other nontraditional roles. The end of the Cold War transformed U.S. national security. The United States entered the 21st century with unprecedented prosperity and opportunities threatened by complex dangers. Problems associated with fostering a stable global system require the U.S. military to play an essential role in building coalitions and shaping the international environment in ways that protect and promote U.S. interests.

The main point is stated clearly in the very first sentence: "U.S. military forces will increasingly be called upon in the immediate future for peaceful military-to-military contacts, humanitarian intervention, peace support, and other nontraditional roles." The sentences that follow are sub-points that help clarify and emphasize the paragraph's main point.

Sometimes the main point isn't in the first sentence. Look at the passage again, slightly reworded:

> The end of the Cold War transformed U.S. national security. The United States entered the 21st century with unprecedented prosperity and opportunities threatened by complex dangers. Problems associated with fostering a stable global system require the U.S. military to play an essential role in building coalitions and shaping the international environment in ways that protect and promote U.S. interests. A key assumption is that U.S. military forces will increasingly be called upon for peaceful military-to-military contacts, humanitarian intervention, peace support, and other nontraditional roles.

The paragraph's main point remains the same, but it isn't stated until the last sentence.

Sometimes the main point isn't clearly stated but is rather implied. Take a look at the following paragraph:

> The plane landed at 9 p.m. The children were disappointed that new security rules prevented them from meeting their father at the gate. They waited with their mother in the car outside the airport doors, amidst dozens of other people in vehicles, there for similar purposes. With each passing moment, their excitement grew. Finally, the automatic doors opened, and he walked out. "Dad! Hey, Dad!" the excited children yelled.

Though it's not directly stated, the main point of this paragraph is obviously that the children's father is coming home.

Take another look at the preceding passage. When trying to determine the main point of a paragraph, ask yourself the following:

>> **Who or what is this paragraph about?** A father returning to his family.

» **What aspect of this subject is the author talking about?** The moments before and the moment of the father's appearing at the airport doors.

» **What is the author trying to get across about this aspect of the subject?** The drama of the father's reunion with his family.

Simplifying subpoints

Most writers don't stick to just one point. If they did, most paragraphs could be reduced to just one sentence. But it doesn't work that way. Writers usually try to reinforce their main points by providing details. These subpoints may include facts, statistics, or descriptions that support the passage's main point. Subpoints help you see what the author is saying. Take, for instance, the following passage:

> For the purposes of drill, Air Force organizations are divided into elements, flights, squadrons, groups, and wings. The "rule of two" applies (that is, an element must consist of at least two people, a flight must consist of at least two elements, and so on). Usually, an element consists of between eight and ten people, and a flight has six or eight elements. Drill consists of certain movements by which the flight or squadron is moved in an orderly manner from one formation to another or from one place to another.

Notice how the writer uses the second, third, and fourth sentences to explain in detail how Air Force organizations are divided for the purposes of drill. These supporting details are subpoints.

TIP

Look for signal words in the passage — words like *again, also, as well as, furthermore, moreover,* and *significantly*. These signal words may call your attention to supporting facts.

Analyzing What You've Read

Understanding what you read involves more than just picking out main points and subpoints. To analyze a paragraph, you need to examine the passage carefully to identify causes, key factors, and possible results. Analyzing a passage requires you to draw conclusions from what you've read and understand relationships among the ideas in the text.

Say what? Figuring out what the passage means

By drawing conclusions about a passage's meaning, you reach new ideas that the author implies but doesn't come right out and state. You must analyze the information the author presents to make inferences from what you've read. What conclusions can you infer from the following paragraph?

> The local school district is facing a serious budgetary crisis. The state, suffering a revenue shortfall of more than $600 million, has cut funding to the district by $18.7 million. Already, 65 teachers have been laid off, and more layoffs are expected.

Can you conclude that the local school district is one that parents want to avoid? Possibly, but that's not the point the author is trying to make. Although the author doesn't come straight out and say so, you can draw the conclusion that if the state revenue shortfall could somehow be corrected — by increasing state sales tax or income tax, for example — the local school district's budgetary crisis could be resolved. The author never actually makes this point, but you can draw this conclusion from the facts presented by using reason and logic.

When analyzing a passage for the ASVAB, leave your baggage at the door. For example, if you read this passage in your local newspaper and didn't like your state's current governor, it would be easy to conclude that you and your neighbors need to elect a new governor. However, nothing in the passage suggests that the writer supports electing a new governor to solve the budget problem. Analyze *only* what the writer says and *only* in the context of taking the ASVAB.

Say it again, Sam: Paraphrasing

Paraphrasing means to rewrite a passage using your own words. This strategy is often useful when you're trying to understand a complex idea. Putting the passage in your own words can help you understand the main idea, which can in turn help you discover information that may not be stated directly. Paraphrasing can also be helpful in making inferences and drawing conclusions from the information provided. Look at the following short passage:

> On-the-job training (OJT) is often the most effective method of training because the employer tailors the training to meet the specific job requirements. OJT can be as casual as giving a few pointers to a new worker or as formal as a fully structured training program with timetables and specified subjects.

How would you paraphrase this passage? If you wrote something like the following, you'd be on the right track:

> Some OJT programs involve a formal lesson plan, while others simply tell a new employee what to do and how to do it. OJT works well because new employees can be taught what they need to do the specific job.

REMEMBER

Paraphrasing is just saying the same thing using different words. In basic training, your drill instructor may say, "You really need to work on your running time," or they may say, "Get the %$@* lead out of your pants and run faster!" Both mean the same thing.

Improving Your Reading Comprehension Skills

Some people read and comprehend better than others, but one thing is for certain: You're not born with the ability to read. It's something you learn. Like almost anything that is learned, you can use proven techniques to help you do it better:

>> Read more and watch TV less.

>> Practice skimming and scanning.

>> Learn to identify the main ideas and the all-important subpoints.

>> Work on the meanings of strange or difficult words.

>> Practice paraphrasing.

>> Reflect on what you've read.

Taking the time to read

Joseph Addison once noted that "Reading is to the mind what exercise is to the body." My dad has been painting walls to look like stone, precious metals, and all kinds of other materials — anything other than drywall — for more than 30 years. As a result, you wouldn't be able to tell the difference between one of his walls and the real deal. My brother's been wielding a tattoo gun for more than 20 years. He practiced on grapefruits and oranges (and a few brave volunteers). With more practice, he got better (thankfully!), and he gets better each time he creates a new tattoo.

The point is that you can improve any skill with practice. If you don't read well, the chances are good that you don't read much. People who read a lot are more likely to be better readers than people who don't read so much.

If you learn to read for fun, you'll automatically read more, and I guarantee that your reading skills will improve immeasurably after a relatively short time. So how do you learn to read for fun? Simple: Choose reading material in subject areas that interest you.

TIP

You don't have to pick up *A Tale of Two Cities* or *War and Peace*. You can start with a biography of a person you admire, manga, comic books, informational websites that cater to one of your hobbies or interests, or magazines you find at the library. Personally, I like *For Dummies* books. If you devote at least one hour a day to improving your reading comprehension, you'll see results fast — maybe within a month or so.

Skimming and scanning

Different situations call for different styles of reading. The technique you choose depends on your purpose for reading. For example, you may be reading for enjoyment, to find information, or to complete a task. If you're reading for enjoyment, you usually read and savor every word. However, in other situations — such as when you're just trying to find the main ideas or look up specific information — you may not want to read every single word.

Skimming

You can skim to quickly identify the main ideas of a text. For example, most people don't read a newspaper word for word. Instead, they skim through the text to see whether they want to read an article in more depth. Most people can skim three to four times faster than normal reading. Skimming is especially useful if you have lots of material to read in a limited amount of time.

TIP

Here are some points to keep in mind when you practice skimming:

>> If the article or passage has a title, read it. It's often the shortest possible summary of the content.

>> Read the first sentence or paragraph. This introductory text often consists of the main point(s).

>> If the text has subheadings, read each one, looking for relationships among them.

>> Look for clue words that answer who, what, where, how, why, and when.

>> Pay attention to qualifying adjectives, such as *best, worst, most,* and so on.

>> Look for typographical clues such as boldface, italics, underlining, or asterisks.

Scanning

Scanning involves moving your eyes quickly down the page seeking specific words and phrases. When you scan, you must be willing to skip over several lines of text without actually reading and understanding them.

Scanning is a useful technique when you're looking for keywords or specific ideas. For example, when you look up a word in the dictionary, you probably use the scanning technique. In most cases, you know what you're looking for, so you concentrate on finding a particular answer.

TIP

When scanning a document:

>> Keep in mind what you're scanning for. If you keep a picture in your mind, the information is more likely to jump out at you from among all the other printed words.

>> Anticipate what form the information is likely to appear in. Will it be numbers? Proper nouns?

>> Let your eyes run over several lines of print at a time.

>> When you find the information you're looking for, read the entire sentence.

TIP

Skimming and scanning are useful techniques for many of the Paragraph Comprehension problems. I talk more about this subtest in Chapter 7.

Looking for the main ideas and subpoints

Reading wouldn't have much purpose if you just let your eyes wander over the words without walking away with some sense of what the author is talking about. The author's ideas are included in the main point and subpoints of the writing. You need to practice extracting this information from your reading material. See the section "Taking Pointers about Points" earlier in this chapter.

Building your vocabulary

It's hard to understand what you're reading if you don't understand the individual words. Effective reading comprehension involves developing a solid vocabulary. Use the techniques in Chapter 4 to strengthen your vocabulary, and you'll simultaneously improve your reading comprehension skills. The two skills go hand in hand.

TIP

When practicing reading, try not to look up new words in a dictionary right away. Stopping to look up words often impairs your concentration and lessens your ability to comprehend what you've read.

Instead, start by trying to puzzle out the meaning of a new word by looking at the context in which the word is used in the sentence or phrase. For example, take the following passage:

> It had been three days since the shipwreck, and Tammy was unable to find food or much drinkable water. At that point, she would have done anything to get off that wretched island.

You can derive several important clues about the meaning of the word *wretched* based on its context in the passage. Obviously, Tammy isn't having a very good time, nor does she find the island to be a pleasant environment. Therefore, you can surmise that *wretched* has something to do with unpleasantness.

Paraphrasing

Putting the text in your own words can help you understand what the writer is talking about. I talk more extensively about this in the "Say it again, Sam: Paraphrasing" section earlier in this chapter.

You probably won't have time on the Paragraph Comprehension subtest to rewrite passages on your scratch paper. But by practicing the technique while you hone your reading comprehension skills, you'll develop the ability to paraphrase in your mind.

Remembering by reflecting

Reflecting simply means thinking about what you've read. If you take a few minutes to think about it, you're more likely to remember it. Did you enjoy the passage or article? Did you find it interesting? Do you agree or disagree with the author's views? Thinking about what you've read will help solidify the passage and its meaning in your mind, which makes it easier to answer questions about it later.

Speaking about Speed

Dozens of speed-reading courses, software, and online programs absolutely guarantee, without qualification, to turn you into a speed-reading wizard. However, if your goal is to score well on the Paragraph Comprehension subtest, I recommend you save your money.

The Paragraph Comprehension subtest isn't a speed-reading test. You'll get 27 minutes to answer 10 questions on the computerized version of the test; if you're one of the few people who takes it on paper, you'll have 13 minutes to answer 15 questions. If you get tryout questions on this subtest, you'll answer 25 questions and get 75 minutes to do it. (Tryout questions don't affect your score. See Chapter 1 to find out more about why they're on the test and what they're for.) In any case, this is plenty of time for most people. The best part is that usually you answer multiple questions about the same passage. That means by the time you get to the second or third question, you've already gained a good understanding of what the passage is about.

If you're still worried about your reading speed, just remember: The more you read, the better (and faster) you'll get at it. Read to comprehend by using the information in this chapter, and your speed will automatically get faster as you practice.

Diving for Facts: Paragraph Comprehension Practice

The Paragraph Comprehension subtest of the ASVAB is designed to keep you on your toes. You'll have to dig for the main idea, pull out facts, draw conclusions about what you've read, and find out what the author of the passage is implying. Each of these exercises is designed to help you do those things — and to gauge where you need a little more practice.

Finding the main idea

Read each of the following passages and underline (or circle — it's your book!) the clues that help you figure out the main idea; then put it into your own words in the space below the passage. Refer back to "Taking Pointers about Points" if you need a refresher. Check your answers by flipping to the "Answers and Explanations" section at the end of this chapter.

Passage 1

About 70 percent of people are eligible for a home office deduction on their taxes, but many are afraid to claim it because they think it'll get them audited. The truth is that the law allows you to claim a home office deduction if you use some space in your house exclusively for work (so guest bedrooms with a computer don't count). If you're eligible, you probably should claim it — but you should talk to a tax professional to be sure.

Main idea: _____

_____

Passage 2

The sliding boundary between the Pacific Plate and the North American Plate is called the San Andreas Fault. It effectively divides California into two parts, with San Diego and Los Angeles on the Pacific Plate; San Francisco and Sacramento are on the North American Plate. When the two plates build up enough pressure, one finally gives way and causes earthquakes. It's a common myth that the San Andreas Fault will eventually crack and send California into the ocean. One thing remains certain, though: The fault isn't going away, and neither are the earthquakes it causes.

Main idea: _____

_____

Passage 3

Currently serving or honorably discharged veterans may be eligible for the Forever G.I. Bill, which is an education benefit from the Veterans Administration. The Forever G.I. Bill pays for you to go to college or a trade school, and if you enroll full-time, you'll also get a monthly stipend to help pay for your housing. In some cases, a parent can transfer the benefit to their children or to a spouse.

Main idea: _____

_____

Passage 4

In 1990, the U.S. Supreme Court ruled that it's unconstitutional to ban people from burning the American flag, saying that preventing people from doing so would violate their First Amendment rights. As you know, the First Amendment to the U.S. Constitution guarantees us freedom of speech and a number of other freedoms, such as the freedom to exercise our religious beliefs, the freedom to peaceably assemble, and the freedom to petition the government when we disagree with elected officials. In the Supreme Court case *United States v. Eichman*, the Court upheld the right to burn the flag in this context. The U.S. Flag Code actually prescribes burning the flag when it becomes "so tattered that it no longer fits to serve as a symbol of the United States." Several organizations, including the Veterans of Foreign Wars, the American Legion, and the Boy and Girl Scouts of America, conduct dignified flag-burning ceremonies when necessary.

Main idea: _____

_____

Going on a fact-finding mission

Some of the Paragraph Comprehension questions on the ASVAB require you to hunt for specific facts in written passages. The questions you encounter may ask you to find out who, what, when, where, why, or how, and you'll most likely have to return to the passage to find the correct answers. Use the following exercises to test your fact-hunting skills; then flip to the "Answers and Explanations" section at the end of this chapter to see how accurate you were.

Passage 5

When it comes to voting rights (and the responsibilities that come with them), Americans are very clear about what they want. Four out of five Americans support early voting, and 63 percent support automatic voter registration. As many as 19 percent of all citizens are completely against requiring some form of voter identification at the polls. No matter what people prefer, though, that doesn't change the fact that just over half of all eligible voters turn out for general elections and even fewer show up for midterm elections.

How many Americans support early voting?

_____

How many Americans support automatic voter

registration? _____

_____

How many Americans are against requiring voter

identification at the polls? _____

_____

How many eligible voters vote in general elections?

_____

Passage 6

Nice is a beautiful city on the coast of France, less than an hour's drive from Cannes (the city famous for its film festival) and about 932 kilometers from Paris. The city is known for its natural beauty, and painters — including Marc Chagall, Henri Matisse, and Niki de Saint Phalle — have been trying to capture its essence for centuries. After a tumultuous history, the city itself was annexed by France in 1860, and it has remained part of the country ever since.

What artists have created famous paintings of Nice?

_____

_____

How far is Nice from Paris? _____

_____

When was Nice annexed by France? _____

_____

Passage 7

The National Museum of Natural History, run by the Smithsonian Institution, is located in the heart of Washington, D.C., between the White House and Capitol Hill. It offers free admission, although some of the attractions inside (most notably the butterfly exhibit and the IMAX theater) do charge a fee. The three-story museum has only two floors of exhibits; the ground floor contains shops and a few cafés offering drinks and prepackaged foods. On the first floor, you'll find the Ocean Hall, a modern mammal exhibit, and the Human Origins Exhibit. You can take stairs or an elevator to the second floor, where you'll find a remarkable dinosaur exhibit that includes a full T-Rex skeleton, the Hope Diamond, and the Live Insect Zoo.

Where is the National Museum of Natural History

located? _____

_____

_____

How many stories is the museum? _____

_____

Where would you go to learn about human

evolution? _____

Passage 8

The "terrible twos," according to most parents, are very real and very difficult. Dr. Vanessa LoBue says that this tough time actually begins when toddlers are about 18 months old, and it's because little ones aren't good at emotion regulation or self-control... and that those two factors combine to create the perfect storm. Dr. Jeremy Friedman, who wrote a book about dealing with toddlers, says that you can minimize tantrums and defuse meltdown situations by staying calm, being loving, and providing reassurance to your toddler.

Who said that the "terrible twos" start when kids are 18 months old? _____

_____

What is Dr. Jeremy Friedman's book about?

_____

According to the passage, why do toddlers go through such difficulty? _____

_____

Drawing conclusions on your own

In some cases, the ASVAB's Paragraph Comprehension questions want you to figure out what the passage is telling you when it doesn't actually say what you need to know. You'll have to draw conclusions based on what the passage does contain and choose the best answer from the four choices the test makers created for you. Use these passages to draw your own conclusions, and when you're done, head to the "Answers and Explanations" section to find out how you did.

Passage 9

Simón could smell the sweet scent of mantecada baking in the house when he dropped his bike near the porch stairs after school. He burst through the door, hoping they were done and ready to eat. Mom was standing in the kitchen, laughing at Paloma, whose tiny hands were covered in flour, and Dad was snapping pictures with his phone as the little girl toddled across the floor. Simón said, "Mom, may I have a piece of mantecada?" Mom smiled and said, "Yes, as soon as you've had your dinner."

What is mantecada? _____

_____

How old is Paloma likely to be? _____

_____

What time of day is it? _____

_____

Passage 10

The twins were both surprised when their mother took them to the mall on Sunday afternoon — the Sunday right before the big day — but the festive music, snowy seasonal décor, and throng of shoppers were distracting... and exciting. A long line of people trailed into the food court; young parents with strollers, grandparents peering over boxes and bags to smile at their grandkids, and everyone in between were slowly inching forward. The occasional flash of a camera brightened the space toward the front of the line, and both girls squealed happily when they figured out why they were there.

When does this story take place? _____

_____

Why are so many people waiting in line? _____

_____

Passage 11

The littlest one tumbled over the pile of his playful littermates. He made his way to Cheryl, his tail wagging as he panted. She bent down to scratch his pointed ears, and when he looked up into her eyes, she made her decision. "I'm going to call you Jack," she whispered.

What is Jack? _____

_____

What was Cheryl's decision? _____

_____

Heather watched the lizard dart up the tree, took a huge gulp of water, and wiped the sweat from her face with a towel. As her breathing slowed, she knew she could've been faster. She knew that she'd *have* to be faster if she wanted to stand a chance against the other competitors. The problem: she didn't really want to compete. Even if she did, she wasn't sure she had the skill to keep up. She pushed aside her negative thoughts, bent down to tie her shoe, and thought she could still see a handful of competitors near the bend in the road ahead. "Twenty-three miles down and three more to go," she thought, the dread ebbing away as she took off again at a comfortable pace.

Why is Heather sweating? _____

_____

What is Heather participating in? _____

_____

Answers and Explanations

Check your answers against these and see how close you were to finding the correct ones.

Passage 1: The main idea of this passage is that some people can claim a home office deduction on their taxes. It's mentioned in the first and second sentences, and it's alluded to (hinted at) in the final sentence.

Passage 2: The main idea of this passage is the San Andreas Fault and why it causes earthquakes.

Passage 3: The main idea of this passage is the Forever G.I. Bill — what it is and who can use it.

Passage 4: This passage is about burning the American flag. It mentions why it's legal to do so as freedom of speech and when the U.S. Flag Code prescribes (calls for) it.

Passage 5: Four out of five Americans support early voting; 63 percent of Americans support automatic voter registration; 19 percent of Americans oppose voter identification requirements; and just over half of all eligible voters vote in general elections.

Passage 6: Marc Chagall, Henri Matisse, and Niki de Saint Phalle have painted Nice; the city is 932 kilometers from Paris; and France annexed it in 1860.

Passage 7: The National Museum of Natural History is located in Washington, D.C., between the White House and Capitol Hill; the museum is three stories high; you'll find the exhibit about evolution on the first floor, in the Human Origins section.

Passage 8: Dr. Vanessa LoBue said that the "terrible twos" begin around 18 months; Dr. Jeremy Friedman's book is about dealing with toddlers; and 18-month-old kids aren't good at emotion regulation or self-control.

Passage 9: Mantecada is most likely a dessert; Paloma is most likely a toddler; and the story takes place in the afternoon.

Passage 10: The story takes place the Sunday before Christmas; the girls are excited because they're waiting to have their pictures taken with Santa Claus.

Passage 11: Jack is a dog; Cheryl decided she was going to keep him.

Passage 12: Heather is sweating because she has run 23 miles; she's competing in a marathon.

Chapter **7**

The Paragraph Comprehension Subtest

The Paragraph Comprehension subtest has the fewest questions of any of the ASVAB subtests. However, it's one of the most important subtests of the ASVAB. The military uses this test (along with the Word Knowledge subtest; see Chapters 4 and 5) to compute your verbal expression (VE) score, which in turn is an important part of your AFQT score. (If you want to see how these scores combine, turn to Chapter 1.)

This subtest is nothing more than a reading comprehension test, much like many of the reading tests you took in school. You're asked to read a short passage (a paragraph) and then answer one to four questions about information contained in that paragraph. Unfortunately, you probably won't find the reading to be very interesting. No passages from *Harry Potter* or about aliens shooting ray guns here. You're more likely to read about the corn crop harvest rates in Nebraska or the principles of time management. The key is to stay focused. After all, you have to answer only 10 or 15 questions, depending on your version of the test, and the paragraphs aren't that long.

REMEMBER

A large percentage of military jobs require a solid score on this subtest. If you're interested in which military jobs require you to score well on the Paragraph Comprehension subtest, I humbly recommend you head to your favorite book retailer and buy a copy of the best-selling *ASVAB For Dummies* (John Wiley & Sons, Inc.). You'll be glad you did.

Tackling the Test Format: Types of Questions

The Paragraph Comprehension subtest requires you to read a short paragraph and then answer one or more multiple-choice questions about what you've read. These questions can generally be broken down into one of four types, which I like to call the treasure hunt, getting the point, dictionary, and deep thinking.

The treasure hunt

Treasure hunt questions require you to find specific information within the paragraph. The good thing about this type of question is that by employing the scanning techniques in Chapter 6, you can often find the answer without having to read the entire paragraph. Try the following example:

EXAMPLE

A new study has found that 21 percent of people arrested in the United States for driving under the influence were arrested again for the same crime within five years. The study, commissioned by the U.S. Department of Justice, analyzed recidivism rates for DUI between 2002 and 2007. During this period, there were more than 930,000 arrests for DUI. Of these, 195,300 — or 21 percent — were arrested again for violating DUI laws a second time within the established time frame. The study found that 34 percent of the repeat offenses occurred within six months of the original arrest.

How many people were arrested for DUI more than once between 2002 and 2007?

(A) 930,000

(B) 195,300

(C) 210,000

(D) None of the above

By letting your eyes quickly scan the paragraph, you notice that all the large numbers are contained in the middle. If you stop and read the two sentences that include large numbers, you find the answer to the question: Choice (B).

Sometimes the answer isn't so obvious, and you have to dig a little deeper to find the treasure. Take the following question, for example:

EXAMPLE

George Armstrong Custer (December 5, 1839–June 25, 1876) was a U.S. Army officer and cavalry commander in the Civil War and the American Indian Wars. At the start of the Civil War, Custer was a cadet at the U.S. Military Academy at West Point, and his class's graduation was accelerated so that they could enter the war. Early in the Gettysburg Campaign, Custer's association with cavalry commander Major General Alfred Pleasonton earned him a promotion at the age of 23 from first lieutenant to brigadier general of volunteers. By the end of the Civil War (April 9, 1865), Custer had achieved the rank of major general of volunteers but was reduced to his permanent grade of captain in the regular army when the troops were sent home.

How old was George Custer at the end of the Civil War?

(A) 24

(B) 25

(C) 26

(D) 34

The answer is still right there in the paragraph, but you have to use a little judgment (and math) to find it. General Custer was born on December 5, 1839 (which you can find in the first sentence) and the Civil War ended on April 9, 1865 (which the last sentence tells you). Therefore, Custer was 25 years old, Choice (B), at the end of the war. (He didn't turn 26 until December of that year.)

Getting the point

This type of question asks you to discern the main topic, point, or idea of the paragraph (see Chapter 6 for more information). When you look for the main point, skimming the paragraph rather than reading it in its entirety is often helpful. Try this one on for size:

The farmers' market reopened the second weekend of May. Amid the asparagus and flowers, shoppers chatted about the return of temperatures in the seventies. Across the street, children (and their dogs) were playing Frisbee in the park. Finally, spring had come to town.

What is the main point of the passage?

(A) The farmers' market has reopened.

(B) Children like playing Frisbee.

(C) Spring had come to town.

(D) Shoppers were chatting.

In this paragraph, you may think that the farmers' market reopening is the main point, but the other information about the temperature and the kids playing Frisbee tells you that the main idea is something a bit broader than the market opening. The main idea is stated in the last sentence: "Finally, spring had come to town." Therefore, Choice (C) is the correct answer.

TIP

When skimming for the main point of a paragraph, start with the first sentence, and then read the last sentence. The main idea is often contained in one of these sentences.

Dictionary

Much like the Word Knowledge subtest (covered in Chapters 4 and 5), this type of question requires you to define a word as used in the context of the passage. The correct definition that the question is looking for can be the most common meaning of the word, or it can be a less well-known meaning of the word.

In either case, you have to read the passage, make sure you understand how the word is being used, and select the answer option that is closest in meaning to the word as it's used in the passage. Consider this example:

EXAMPLE

In the 18th century, it was common for sailors to be pressed into service in Britain. Young men found near seaports could be kidnapped, drugged, or otherwise hauled aboard a ship and made to work doing menial chores. They were not paid for their service, and they were given just enough food to keep them alive.

In this passage, <u>pressed</u> means

(A) hired.

(B) ironed.

(C) enticed.

(D) forced.

The correct answer is Choice (D). The descriptions of the conditions these sailors found themselves in should help you decide that they weren't hired or enticed; ironed is one meaning of the word *pressed*, but it isn't correct in this context.

Deep thinking

If the Paragraph Comprehension questions on the ASVAB simply asked you to scan a passage and find the main point or supporting details, it would be a pretty simple test. But the subtest goes beyond that. In order to properly answer some of the questions on the test, you have to analyze what you've read and draw conclusions.

REMEMBER

The *conclusion* — which may be called an *inference* or *implication* — must be reasonably based on what the passage says. You have to use good judgment when deciding what conclusions you can logically draw from what you've read. Be careful not to confuse passage content with your opinion.

Try this example:

EXAMPLE

One of the main reasons motorcyclists are killed in crashes is that the motorcycle itself provides virtually no protection in a crash. For example, approximately 80 percent of reported motorcycle crashes result in injury or death; a comparable figure for automobiles is about 20 percent.

Safe motorcycle riding means

(A) always wearing a helmet.

(B) using premium gas.

(C) selecting the most expensive motorcycle.

(D) always riding with a buddy.

The correct answer is Choice (A). The author didn't specifically state in the passage that wearing a helmet is important, but you can infer the correct answer because the author gives the reason for fatalities: Motorcycles themselves offer virtually no protection in a crash. Based on the information provided in the passage, you can logically conclude that even the small degree of protection offered by a helmet increases the safety of riding motorcycles. None of the other choices is as closely connected to the idea of safety.

Planning Your Attack

The best way to score well on the Paragraph Comprehension subtest is to improve your reading comprehension skills by following the advice I give Chapter 6. However, you can also do a few things on test day to make sure you score as high as possible:

>> **Watch the time.** As with all the ASVAB subtests, this test is timed. You have 27 minutes to read through and answer 10 questions on the CAT-ASVAB or 13 minutes for 15 questions on the paper version. If you get tryout questions on this subtest (head to Chapter 1 to find out more about those), you have 75 minutes to answer 27 questions. This period is plenty of time, so you shouldn't feel rushed. Don't relax *too* much, though; you don't have time for daydreaming, either.

>> **If you don't know the answer, you may take an educated guess by using the process of elimination.** On the paper version, you may guess freely at your discretion (hopefully, you won't have to after reading this book). However, on the computerized test, you risk receiving a penalty for too many wrong answers at the end of the subtest. (Those clever test graders have figured out that means you've run out of time and have become desperate to finish.) If you need to guess, make sure to eliminate as many choices as possible before choosing your answer.

>> **Question first, read later.** Your first instinct may be to read the entire paragraph before looking at the questions. However, many reading comprehension test experts recommend the opposite. If the question asks you to find specific information or discern the main idea of the paragraph, skimming or scanning (see Chapter 6) can save loads of time. Read the question first so you can best decide what reading technique to use.

>> **Take it one question at a time.** Some passages have more than one question associated with them, but you should look at only one question at a time. If you're taking the CAT-ASVAB, you don't have a choice — and you can't skip ahead and come back. You must answer a question to move on to the next.

>> **Understand each question.** What is the question asking you to do? Are you supposed to find the main point? Draw a conclusion? Find a word that is nearest in meaning? Make sure you know what the question is asking before you choose among the answer options. This tip may seem obvious, but when you're in a hurry, you can make mistakes by misunderstanding the questions.

>> **Read each answer option carefully.** Don't just select the first answer that seems right. *Remember:* On the Paragraph Comprehension subtest, one answer is often "most correct," while others are "almost right." You want to choose the "most correct" answer, not the "almost right" answer. And to do that, you have to read *all* the answers.

>> **Check your baggage at the door.** Answer each question based on the passage, not your own opinions or views on the topic.

>> **Don't choose ambiguous answer options.** They're incorrect 99.99 times out of 100. (Oh, heck, call it 100 times out of 100.) If an answer strikes you as not quite true but not totally false, that answer is incorrect. The people who wrote the questions put that choice there to throw you off. Don't give them the satisfaction of falling for their trap!

>> **Always be cautious about *never*.** For the most part, answer options that are absolutes are incorrect. *Never, always,* and related words are often a sign that you should select a different answer. Words like *generally* and *usually* are more likely to be part of the correct answer.

Surveying Sample Test Questions

Time for you to put all the great advice I provide in this chapter and Chapter 6 to good use. (You can see that I'm not usually accused of being too modest.) Quiz yourself on the following sample test questions to see whether your reading comprehension is up to speed. Read each short paragraph, which is followed by one or more questions regarding information contained in that passage. Make sure to read the paragraph carefully before selecting the choice that most correctly answers the question.

First, stick to one excuse. Thus, if a tradesman, with whom your social relations are slight, should chance to find you taking coppers from his till, you may possibly explain that you are interested in Numismatics and are a Collector of Coins; and he may possibly believe you. But if you tell him afterwards that you pitied him for being overloaded with unwieldy copper discs and were in the act of replacing them by a silver sixpence of your own, this further explanation, so far from increasing his confidence in your motives, will (strangely enough) actually decrease it. And if you are so unwise as to be struck by yet another brilliant idea and tell him that the pennies were all bad pennies, which you were concealing to save him from a police prosecution for coining, the tradesman may even be so wayward as to institute a police prosecution himself.

—G. K. Chesterton

1. The author is giving the reader advice about

    (A) collecting coins.

    (B) stealing.

    (C) dealing with tradesmen.

    (D) becoming a police officer.

Ethics are standards by which one should act based on values. Values are core beliefs such as duty, honor, and integrity that motivate attitudes and actions. Not all values are ethical values (integrity is — happiness is not). Ethical values relate to what is right and wrong and thus take precedence over nonethical values when making ethical decisions.

2. According to the paragraph, values can best be defined as

    (A) ethics.

    (B) stealing.

    (C) core beliefs.

    (D) right and wrong.

Questions 3 and 4 refer to the following passage.

Although the average consumer replaces the tires on his or her automobile every 50,000 miles, steel-belted radials can last for 60,000 miles. However, they must be properly maintained. The tires must be inflated to the correct air pressure at all times, and tires must be rotated and balanced according to a routine maintenance schedule. The tread should be checked for correct depth regularly.

3. How long can steel-belted radials last?

    (A) 25,000 miles

    (B) 50,000 miles

    (C) 60,000 miles

    (D) No one knows.

4. Proper tire maintenance, as described in the passage, does *not* include

    (A) keeping tires properly inflated.

    (B) balancing and rotating tires.

    (C) checking the tread.

    (D) checking the lug nuts.

Questions 5 and 6 refer to the following passage.

Some people argue that baking is an art, but Chef Debra Dearborn says that baking is a science. She says that if you follow a recipe carefully, assembling the ingredients accurately, cooking at the specified temperature for the specified period of time, your cookies will always turn out right. Chef Dearborn says the best baking is like the best experiment; anyone can duplicate it.

5. In this passage, the word *assembling* most nearly means

    (A) measuring.

    (B) putting together.

    (C) buying.

    (D) storing.

6. According to the passage, a person who can't make a decent batch of cookies

    (A) should get out of the kitchen.

    (B) is an artist.

    (C) isn't following the recipe carefully.

    (D) is Chef Dearborn.

Boiler technicians operate main and auxiliary boilers. They maintain and repair all parts, including pressure fittings, valves, pumps, and forced-air blowers. Technicians may have to lift or move heavy equipment. They may have to stoop and kneel and work in awkward positions.

7. According to this job description, a good candidate for this job would be

    (A) a person with management experience.

    (B) an individual with keen eyesight.

    (C) a person who isn't mechanically minded.

    (D) a person who is physically fit.

In June 2004, the city council passed a resolution requiring all residents to paint their address numbers on their homes using a bright color. This was done to assist firefighters, police, and paramedics in finding an address during an emergency. In August, 300 residences were randomly sampled, and it was found that 150 had complied with the new ordinance.

8. According to the passage, what percentage of the randomly sampled residences had complied with the new ordinance?

    (A) 10 percent

    (B) 20 percent

    (C) 50 percent

    (D) 60 percent

Questions 9 and 10 refer to the following passage.

The younger the child, the trickier using medicine is. Children under 2 years shouldn't be given any over-the-counter (OTC) drug without a doctor's approval. Your pediatrician can tell you how much of a common drug, like acetaminophen (Tylenol), is safe for babies. Prescription drugs also can work differently in children than adults. Some barbiturates, for example, which make adults feel sluggish, will make a child hyperactive. Amphetamines, which stimulate adults, can calm children. When giving any drug to a child, watch closely for side effects. If you're not happy with what's happening with your child, don't assume that everything's okay. Always be suspicious. It's better to make the extra calls to the doctor or nurse practitioner than to see a child have a bad reaction to a drug. And before parents dole out OTC drugs, they should consider whether they're truly necessary. Americans love to medicate — perhaps too much. A study published in the October 1994 issue of the *Journal of the American Medical Association* found that more than half of all mothers surveyed had given their 3-year-olds an OTC medication in the previous month. Not every cold needs medicine. Common viruses run their course in seven to ten days with or without medication. Although some OTC medications can make children more comfortable and help them eat and rest better, others may trigger allergic reactions or changes for the worse in sleeping, eating, and behavior. Antibiotics, available by prescription, don't work at all on cold viruses.

9. A common problem in America is

    (A) over-medication.

    (B) parents not heeding the advice of their doctors.

    (C) OTC drugs not requiring a prescription.

    (D) the cost of prescription medication.

10. When a parent is in doubt about giving a child medication, it's best to

    (A) speak with a pharmacist.

    (B) call a doctor or nurse practitioner.

    (C) read the label closely.

    (D) research the side effects.

Questions 11, 12, and 13 refer to the following passage.

Sadie and Jeff adopted Jupiter in the summer and brought him to live in their beautiful high-rise apartment. He's fluffy, brown, and incredibly energetic, and the three of them are inseparable. They spend time going to parks and restaurants, visiting family, and vacationing together. They even exercise together, running miles along Baltimore's streets so Sadie and Jeff can maintain passing scores on their Air Force Physical Assessments — the Air Force's physical test for body composition, muscular strength and endurance, and cardiovascular respiratory fitness. Like most pets, Jupiter has all kinds of nicknames from family and friends; some of the best are Joop-Dogg and Jupacabra. He's a confident pooch and barks when his people are too busy to play, but at the end of the day, Jupiter lets them join him on the sofa wherever they fit so the whole family can relax together.

11. Jupiter is a

    (A) dog.

    (B) cat.

    (C) hamster.

    (D) child.

12. The author's main point in this passage is that

    (A) Sadie and Jeff are in the Air Force.

    (B) Jupiter has his own personality.

    (C) dogs make great pets for servicemembers.

    (D) all dogs should have nicknames.

13. Where does this family probably live?

    (A) Washington, D.C.

    (B) Baltimore

    (C) Delaware

    (D) None of the above

Questions 14 and 15 refer to the following passage.

Around 80 million people live in the Democratic Republic of the Congo, and among them, there are more than 200 distinct ethnic groups. Most people in the Congo speak Lingala, Kikongo, Tshiluba, Swahili, or French; many people speak multiple languages. Kinshasa, the capital, was once called Léopoldville and is now one of the world's fastest growing megacities with a population of more than 17 million.

14. The capital of the Democratic Republic of the Congo is

   (A) Lingala.

   (B) Kikongo.

   (C) Kinshasa.

   (D) None of the above.

15. How many people live in the capital city?

   (A) 17 million

   (B) 80 million

   (C) 200 million

   (D) 120 million

Answers and Explanations

Use this answer key to score the practice Paragraph Comprehension questions.

1. **B.** Mr. Chesterton is expounding on how sticking to one excuse may help you if you're caught taking coins from the tradesman's till.

2. **C.** The second sentence defines the word *values*.

3. **C.** If you used the scanning technique explained in Chapter 6, you would've found this answer quickly.

4. **D.** This example is a negative question that requires extra care in answering. A negative question asks you for something that is not true or not included in the paragraph. If you're rushed or in a hurry, you can easily misread the question.

5. **B.** Although measuring is something you do when baking, it doesn't "most nearly" mean the same thing as assembling. *Putting together* does.

6. **C.** The passage states that if you follow a recipe carefully, your cookies will always turn out right.

7. **D.** Although the passage doesn't say, "This job requires a physically fit person," the duties listed imply that it does. A person with management experience or keen eyesight may make a good candidate, but the passage doesn't list these traits as requirements for the job. A person who isn't mechanically minded may not have the knowledge necessary to maintain and repair boilers and all their parts. This leaves Choice (D), and it's true that a person who is physically fit would be a good choice for the job.

8. **C.** The author didn't specifically say that 50 percent hadn't complied, but she included enough information in the passage that you can calculate it on your own.

9. **A.** The 11th and 12th sentences in the passage suggest that Americans probably medicate too much.

10. **B.** The passage states that making the extra calls to a doctor or nurse practitioner is better than giving the child a drug that causes a bad reaction. Although the other choices may be good advice, they aren't stated or implied in the paragraph.

11. **A.** Jupiter is a dog. Though plenty of pets are fluffy, brown, and energetic, there are a couple giveaways in the passage's language — the words *pooch* and *bark*, plus the fact that "Joop-Dogg" runs with Sadie and Jeff, should lead you to believe that the couple's four-legged pal belongs to a human family *and* the Canidae family (that's scientist lingo for dogs).

12. **B.** The passage is mostly about Jupiter's big personality, although there's some information about Sadie and Jeff being in the Air Force to distract you. In the section "Planning Your Attack" earlier in this chapter I tell you to leave your baggage at the door when you read passages. Even if you think Choices (C) and (D) are true, like I do, they're not really what the passage is about.

13. **B.** The passage mentions Sadie and Jeff's high-rise apartment, which is common in cities, and it comes right out and says that they run on the streets of Baltimore.

14. **C.** Kinshasa is the capital of the Democratic Republic of the Congo. Choices (A) and (B) are languages that many people in the country speak; the others are Tshiluba, Swahili, and French.

15. **A.** Somewhere in the neighborhood of 17 million people live in Kinshasa, which the passage's last sentence tells you.

3

Calculating Better Math Knowledge

Review the basics of fractions, decimals, algebra, and geometry to prepare for the Mathematics Knowledge subtest.

Figure out how to translate words into mathematical equations so you can solve word problems on the Arithmetic Reasoning subtest.

Test yourself with Mathematics Knowledge and Arithmetic Reasoning practice questions.

IN THIS CHAPTER

» Understanding math language and basic concepts

» Finagling fractions and decimals

» Brushing up on positive and negative numbers

» Getting into roots, exponents, and quadratics

» Digging into algebra and geometry

Chapter **8**

Knowing Your Math

I remember one of my high-school math teacher's favorite sayings: "You won't always have a calculator in your pocket." That was her way of reinforcing the need for my classmates and I to learn how to solve math problems on paper. (Joke's on you, Mrs. Smith. I have a calculator in my pocket, on my laptop, and on my tablet — and I can simply be near a device and say, "Hey Google! How much is 7,365 divided by 18.3?" to get an answer in seconds.)

But the military is with Mrs. Smith: It wants you to know how to solve math problems on paper. You know, in case you don't have a calculator in your pocket.

You have to prove your mathematical prowess by taking the ASVAB. Fully 50 percent of your AFQT score is based on your ability to solve math problems. And as I indicate in Chapter 1, your AFQT score determines whether you can join the military.

The good news is that although the military wants you well-grounded in math, it's not looking for rocket scientists. That's NASA's job. The two math subtests of the AFQT test your math ability only at the high school level, so you don't have to break out any advanced calculus or plot the orbit of subatomic particles.

While I was deciding what to cover in this chapter, I quickly realized that I can't give you an entire high school math education in one chapter. I couldn't do that in one whole book. Then I realized that I don't have to try to cram all the math you learned in 13 years of school into one chapter. If you're reading this book, you're obviously interested in joining the military. And to join the military, you must be either a high school graduate or have a high school equivalency certificate, or you must have at least some college credits. That means you've already learned this stuff. All I need to do is provide you a bit of a refresher to remind you of all those math rules you may have forgotten or stashed away in the back of your mind. And that's what you find here: a refresher course, designed to draw out all the math you should already know.

Look at it this way: You already know what you need to know in order to ace the AFQT. Your job is just to remind yourself of what you know. In this chapter, I help you do exactly that.

Making the Most of Math Terminology

Some people are intimidated by math in part because it has its own language. In Chapter 10, I explain how to use keywords in math word problems to translate English into mathematical equations. But that's not enough. You need to know basic math terminology to solve many of the problems you see on the two math subtests that make up the AFQT.

Although you don't need to know every math term, you should memorize the most common ones because you're likely to see them used in one way or another on the Mathematics Knowledge subtest or the Arithmetic Reasoning subtest. Here's some of what you need to know:

>> **Average:** The *average* usually refers to the *arithmetic mean* or just the *mean average.* To find the mean of a set of *n* numbers, add the numbers in the set and divide the sum by *n.* For example, the average (or arithmetic mean) of 3, 7, 10, and 12 is $\frac{3+7+10+12}{4}$, or 8.

>> **Coefficient:** The *coefficient* is a number multiplied by a variable or by a product of variables or by powers of variables in a term. For example, 123 is the coefficient in the term $123x^3y$.

>> **Evaluate:** *Evaluate* means to figure out or calculate. If you're asked to evaluate $5 + 3$, that means to simplify the expression to 8.

>> **Integer:** An *integer* is a whole number that can be expressed without a decimal or fraction component. Examples of integers include 1, 70, and –583.

>> **Pi:** In math equations and terms, pi is usually expressed by its Greek letter, π. *Pi* represents the ratio of the circumference of a circle to its diameter, and it's used in several formulas, especially formulas involving geometry. Pi's value is 3.141592653589793 . . . (on and on forever), but using the value 3.14 or $\frac{22}{7}$ is traditional in common math problems.

>> **Prime/composite numbers:** A *prime number* is a positive integer that can be divided evenly only by itself and 1. For example, 2, 3, 5, 7, 11, 13 are the first six primes. One afternoon, all the famous mathematicians got together over a beer and agreed among themselves that 1 isn't a prime number.

Positive numbers that have factors other than themselves and 1 as factors are called *composite numbers.* Again, by convention, 1 isn't considered a composite number.

>> **Product:** The *product* is the result of multiplication. The product of 2 and 9 is 18. Multiplication can be expressed by an x, ·, or parentheses.

>> **Quotient/remainder:** The *quotient* is the result of division. 40 divided by 5 has a quotient of 8.

But what if one number doesn't divide evenly into the other? The *remainder* is what's left over in that scenario. 43 divided by 5 has a quotient of 8 and a remainder of 3.

>> **Reciprocal:** A *reciprocal* is a fraction flipped upside down. The reciprocal of x is $\frac{1}{x}$. The reciprocal of $\frac{1}{x}$ is x, and $x \neq 0$.

>> **Sum:** The *sum* is the result of addition. The sum of 3 and 6 is 9.

You're not done with math vocabulary yet. You still need to know many more math words and terms. I explain them throughout the rest of the chapter.

The Heart of Math: Exploring Expressions and Equations

Math without expressions and equations is like a fire hydrant without a dog; they just go together. So what's the difference between a mathematical *expression* and an *equation*?

>> An *expression* is any mathematical calculation or formula combining numbers and/or variables. Expressions don't include equal signs (=). For example, $3 + 2$ is an expression, and so is $x(x+2) - 3$.

>> An *equation*, on the other hand, is a mathematical sentence built from expressions connected by an equal sign (=). For example, $3 + 2 = 5$ is an equation, and $x(x+2) - 3 = 30$ is also an equation.

This section gives you the lowdown on keeping equations balanced and simplifying expressions.

Keeping equations balanced

One of the coolest things about equations is that you can do almost anything you want to them as long as you remember to do the exact same thing to both sides of the equation. This rule is called keeping the equation *balanced*. For example, if you have the equation $4 + 1 = 3 + 2$, you can add 3 to both sides of the equation, and it still balances out: $4 + 1 + 3 = 3 + 2 + 3$. You can divide both sides by 3, and it still balances: $(4 + 1) \div 3 = (3 + 2) \div 3$.

TIP

Equation balancing becomes especially handy in algebra (see the later section "Alphabet Soup: Tackling Algebra Review").

Obeying the order of operations

In math, you must solve equations by following steps in a proper order. If you don't, you won't get the right answer. Many of the most frequent math errors occur when people don't follow the *order of operations* when solving mathematical problems.

REMEMBER

Keep in mind the following order of operations:

1. **Start with any calculations in parentheses or brackets.**

   When you have *nested* parentheses or brackets (parentheses or brackets inside other parentheses or brackets), do the inner ones first and work your way outward.

   Groupings where parentheses are implied, such as numerators or denominators (like $\frac{1}{2+3}$) or the numbers under a radical (like $\sqrt{1+2}$), are performed first, just as they would be if there were official parentheses around them.

2. **Do any terms with exponents and roots.**

3. **Complete any multiplication and division, in order from left to right.**

4. **Do any addition and subtraction, in order from left to right.**

TIP

An easy way to remember this order is to think of the phrase "**P**lease **E**xcuse **M**y **D**ear **A**unt **S**ally" (**P**arentheses, **E**xponents, **M**ultiply and **D**ivide, **A**dd and **S**ubtract). The order of operations isn't absolute, though, because you can simplify *different parts* of an expression in the same step — as long as you're simplifying and not combining terms that don't belong together. (The more you can simplify an equation, the better. You'll save precious time on the ASVAB and reduce the possibility of copying errors, too.)

Take the following expression out for a ride.

EXAMPLE

Solve: $3 \times (5 + 2) + 5^2 \div 2$.

Do the calculations in the parentheses first: $3 \times 7 + 5^2 \div 2$

Next, simplify the exponents: $3 \times 7 + 25 \div 2$

Do multiplication and division from left to right: $21 + 12.5$

Finally, perform addition and subtraction from left to right: 33.5

Mental math: Mixing it up with the commutative, associative, and distributive properties

Although the order of operations tells you to do steps in a certain order (see the preceding section), some mathematical properties let you choose a different path. Using the commutative, associative, and distributive properties can make numbers smaller and easier to work with — sometimes easy enough that you can do calculations in your head instead of relying on your scratch paper. Anything that saves you time and brain power on the ASVAB is great because you're working on a limited time budget . . . and you can't use a calculator.

The commutative and associative properties: Moving numbers in your head

The commutative and associative properties let you break the rules about adding or multiplying from left to right. The *commutative property of addition* says you can rearrange the numbers you're adding without changing the result:

$$28 + 27 + 2 = 28 + 2 + 27$$
$$= 30 + 27$$
$$= 57$$

Similarly, the *associative property of addition* lets you decide how to group the numbers you're adding:

$$19 + 46 + 4 = 19 + (46 + 4)$$
$$= 19 + (50)$$
$$= 69$$

Together, these properties let you add a string of numbers in whatever order you like. For example, you can make calculations easier by pairing up numbers whose ones digits add up to 10 before adding other numbers in the list.

Because subtracting is essentially the same thing as adding a negative number, you can extend these addition properties to subtraction problems, too — just be careful to keep track of the negative signs (see the later section "Playing with Positive and Negative Numbers" for details). The following example shows how smart groupings can let you add and subtract figures faster. Notice which calculations are easier to do in your head.

Left to Right	Reordered and Regrouped
$27 - 98 - 27 + 8$	$27 - 98 - 27 + 8$
$= -71 - 27 + 8$	$= (27 - 27) + (-98 + 8)$
$= -98 + 8$	$= 0 + (-90)$
$= -90$	$= -90$

Similarly, the *commutative and associative properties of multiplication* let you multiply numbers in any order you like. Check out how switching the numbers around can make mental math easier:

Left to Right	Reordered and Regrouped
$5 \times 13 \times 2$	$(5 \times 2) \times 13$
$= 65 \times 2$	$= 10 \times 13$
$= 130$	$= 130$

You can even use these multiplication properties with division, as long as you remember that division is the same thing as multiplying by a fraction (see the later section "Multiplying fractions"):

Left to Right	Reordered and Regrouped
$35 \times 23 \div 7$	$35 \times 23 \times \dfrac{1}{7}$
$= 805 \div 7$	$= \dfrac{35}{7} \times 23$
$= 115$	$= 5 \times 23$
	$= 115$

The distributive property: Breaking up large numbers

Have you ever envied those people who can perform calculations on large numbers in their heads? What if I told you that you can be one of those people? That's right. All you have to do is practice the distributive property of math.

The *distributive property*, often referred to as the *distributive law of math*, lets you separate or break larger numbers into parts for simpler arithmetic. It basically says that $a(b+c)$ is the same as $(a \times b) + (a \times c)$.

Suppose you want to mentally multiply 4 by 53; 4×53 is the same as $(4 \times 50) + (4 \times 3)$. Four times 50 is easy; it's 200. Four times 3 is also easy. It's 12. Two hundred plus 12 is 212.

Try another one with a bit of a twist.

EXAMPLE

Mentally perform the calculation 12×19.

12×19 is equivalent to $12(20 - 1) = (12 \times 20) - (12 \times 1)$.

You can quickly mentally calculate that 12 times 20 is 240 and that 12 times 1 is 12. Subtract 12 from 240, and you have 228.

Figure 8-1 illustrates how this process works.

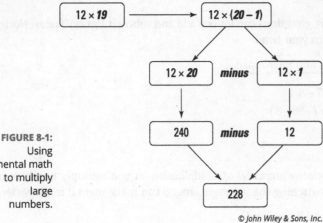

FIGURE 8-1:
Using mental math to multiply large numbers.

© John Wiley & Sons, Inc.

If 12×20 is still too large for mental calculation, you can break it down as $(12 \times 10) + (12 \times 10)$, or $120 + 120$.

You can also use the distributive property for division, although that takes a bit more practice: $340 \div 4$ is the same as $(340 \div 2) \div 2$. You can quickly calculate that 340 divided by 2 is 170, and 170 divided by 2 is 85.

Or you can express $340 \div 4$ as $(100 \div 4) + (100 \div 4) + (100 \div 4) + (40 \div 4)$. You can mentally calculate 100 divided by 4 as 25. Forty divided by 4 is also easy — it's 10. So $25 + 25 + 25 + 10 = 85$. Keep practicing, and you'll be known as the neighborhood lightning calculator.

Having Fun with Factors

A *factor* is simply a number that is multiplied to get a product. *Factoring* a number means taking the number apart. It's kind of like multiplying in reverse. For example, the factors of 12 are 1, 2, 3, 4, 6, and 12 because all these numbers can be divided evenly into 12.

Here are some other factors:

>> **2:** 1, 2

>> **3:** 1, 3

>> **4:** 1, 2, 4

>> **5:** 1, 5

>> **6:** 1, 2, 3, 6

>> **16:** 1, 2, 4, 8, 16

>> **20:** 1, 2, 4, 5, 10, 20

>> **45:** 1, 3, 5, 9, 15, 45

Understanding types of factors

A factor can be either a prime number or a composite number (except 1 and 0 are neither prime nor composite). As I mention in the section "Making the Most of Math Terminology" earlier in this chapter, prime numbers have only themselves and 1 as factors, while composite numbers can be divided evenly by other numbers.

The prime numbers up to 100 are 2, 3, 5, 7, 11, 13, 17, 19, 23, 29, 31, 37, 41, 43, 47, 53, 59, 61, 67, 71, 73, 79, 83, 89, and 97.

Finding prime factors

Any composite number can be written as a product of prime factors. Mathematicians call this process *prime factorization.* To find the prime factors of a number, you divide the number by the smallest possible prime number and work up the list of prime numbers until the result is itself a prime number.

Say you want to find the prime factors of 240. Because 240 is even, start by dividing it by the smallest prime number, which is 2: $240 \div 2 = 120$. The number 120 is also even, so it can be divided by 2: $120 \div 2 = 60$. Then $60 \div 2 = 30$ and $30 \div 2 = 15$. Now, 15 isn't even, so check to see whether you can divide it by 3 (the next highest prime number); $15 \div 3 = 5$, which itself is a prime number, so 240 is now fully factored.

$$240 \div 2 = 120$$
$$120 \div 2 = 60$$
$$60 \div 2 = 30$$
$$30 \div 2 = 15$$
$$15 \div 3 = 5$$

Now, simply list what you divided by to write the prime factors of 240. The prime factors of 240 are $2 \times 2 \times 2 \times 2 \times 3 \times 5$.

Looking at Least Common Multiples

A *common multiple* is a number that is a multiple of two or more numbers. For example, 20, 30, and 40 are common multiples of the numbers 5 and 10. The *least common multiple* (LCM) of two or more numbers is the smallest number (not zero) that's a multiple of both or all the numbers. The LCM is useful in solving many math problems — especially those involving fractions (check out the following section for info on working with fractions).

One way to find the LCM is to list the multiples of each number, one at a time, until you find the smallest multiple that's common to all the numbers.

Find the LCM of 45 and 50.

>> **Multiples of 45:** 45, 90, 135, 180, 225, 270, 315, 360, 405, 450

>> **Multiples of 50:** 50, 100, 150, 200, 250, 300, 350, 400, 450

The LCM of 45 and 50 is 450.

That's rather cumbersome, isn't it? Wouldn't it be great if you had an easier way? You do, and I'm here to let you in on the secret: An easier way to find the LCM is first to list the prime factors of each number (as explained in the preceding section):

>> The prime factors for 45 are $3 \times 3 \times 5$.

>> The prime factors for 50 are $2 \times 5 \times 5$.

Then multiply each factor the greatest number of times it occurs in either number. If the same factor occurs more than once in both numbers, you multiply the factor the greatest number of times it occurs. For example, 5 occurs as a prime factor of both 45 (where it occurs once) and 50 (where it occurs twice); the two occurrences in the factorization of 50 beat the single occurrence in the factorization of 45. The number 3 occurs two times, 5 occurs two times, and 2 occurs once, so you have $3 \times 3 \times 5 \times 5 \times 2 = 450$.

REMEMBER

Checking your answer to see whether the original numbers divide evenly into the LCM you calculate is always a great idea. You can in fact divide 45 and 50 evenly into 450, so you're good to go in this example.

Now that you're getting the hang of it, try another one:

EXAMPLE

What is the least common multiple of 5, 27, and 30?

List the prime factors of each number:

» **Prime factors of 5:** 5

» **Prime factors of 27:** $3 \times 3 \times 3$

» **Prime factors of 30:** $2 \times 3 \times 5$

The number 3 occurs a maximum of three times, 5 occurs a maximum of one time, and 2 occurs a maximum of one time: $3 \times 3 \times 3 \times 5 \times 2 = 270$. Check your answer by seeing whether 5, 27, and 30 can all divide evenly into 270.

Conquering the Fear of Fractions

I don't know why, but most people I've talked to don't like to do math with fractions. Maybe it's because teachers always used pies as examples, and that just makes people hungry. The pies were all imaginary, too, so you didn't even get a piece after all the figuring was done. I'm going to break convention and use squares of cardboard instead. Sure, they're harder to cut than pies, but they don't smell as enticing.

A *fraction* is nothing more than part of a whole. Take a look at Figure 8-2.

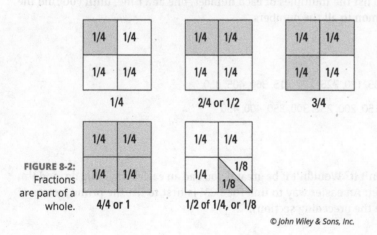

FIGURE 8-2: Fractions are part of a whole.

© John Wiley & Sons, Inc.

Each shaded area represents part of a whole, or a fraction of the whole. It doesn't have to be fourths. If I had divided the cardboard into two equal pieces, each shaded area would represent one-half. If the cardboard were cut into three equal pieces, each piece would be one-third of the whole.

Fractions aren't difficult to work into your mathematical skills as long as you remember a few rules and techniques.

Defining parts and types of fractions

The top number of a fraction is called the *numerator*. The bottom number is known as the *denominator*. For example, in the fraction $\frac{7}{16}$, 7 is the numerator and 16 is the denominator.

TIP

You may also see numerators and denominators separated by a / sign rather than one on top of the other; $1/4$ is the same as $\frac{1}{4}$.

If the numerator is smaller than the denominator, the fraction is less than a whole (smaller than 1). This kind of fraction is called a *proper fraction*. The fraction $\frac{3}{16}$ is a proper fraction, as is $\frac{1}{3}$.

If the numerator is larger than the denominator, the fraction is larger than a whole (larger than 1), and the fraction is called an *improper fraction*. The fraction $\frac{17}{16}$ is an improper fraction.

REMEMBER

Converting improper fractions to mixed numbers is customary in math, especially after all mathematical operations are complete. A *mixed number* is a whole number plus a fraction. The easiest way to convert an improper fraction to a mixed number is to divide the numerator by the denominator. You convert $\frac{17}{16}$ to a mixed number by dividing 17 by 16: $17 \div 16 = 1$, with a remainder of 1, so the improper fraction converts to $1\frac{1}{16}$.

Simplifying fractions

Simplifying (or *reducing*) fractions means to make the fraction as simple as possible. You're usually required to simplify fractions on the ASVAB math subtests before you can select the correct answer. For example, if you worked out a problem and the answer was $\frac{4}{8}$, the correct answer choice on the math subtest would probably be $\frac{1}{2}$, which is the simplest equivalent to $\frac{4}{8}$.

Many methods of simplifying fractions are available. In this section, I give you the two that I think are the easiest; you can decide which is best for you.

Method 1: Dividing by the lowest prime numbers

Try dividing the numerator and denominator by the lowest prime numbers until you can't go any further. (The earlier section "Understanding types of factors" has details on this process.)

EXAMPLE

Simplify $\frac{24}{108}$.

Both the numerator and denominator are even numbers, so they can be divided by the lowest prime number, which is 2. Then $24 \div 2 = 12$, and $108 \div 2 = 54$. The result is $\frac{12}{54}$.

The numerator and denominator are both still even numbers, so divide by 2 again: $12 \div 2 = 6$, and $54 \div 2 = 27$. The result is $\frac{6}{27}$.

This time the denominator is an odd number, so you know it isn't divisible by 2. Try the next highest prime number, which is 3: $6 \div 3 = 2$, and $27 \div 3 = 9$. The result is $\frac{2}{9}$.

Because no common prime numbers divide evenly into both 2 and 9, the fraction is fully simplified.

Method 2: Listing prime factors

This method of simplification is my favorite. Simply list the prime factors of both the numerator and the denominator as explained in the earlier section "Finding prime factors" and then see whether any cancel out (are the same).

EXAMPLE

Simplify $\frac{24}{108}$.

The prime factors of 24 are $2 \times 2 \times 2 \times 3$.

The prime factors of 108 are $2 \times 2 \times 3 \times 3 \times 3$.

You can now write the fraction as $\frac{2 \times 2 \times 2 \times 3}{2 \times 2 \times 3 \times 3 \times 3}$.

Two of the 2s and one of the 3s cancel out, so you can remove them from both the numerator and the denominator. What's left is $\frac{2}{3 \times 3}$, or $\frac{2}{9}$.

Multiplying fractions

Multiplying fractions is very easy. All you have to do is multiply the numerators by each other, multiply the denominators by each other, and then simplify the result, as shown in the following equation:

$$\frac{4}{5} \times \frac{3}{7} \times \frac{9}{15} = \frac{4 \times 3 \times 9}{5 \times 7 \times 15} = \frac{108}{525}$$

The fraction $\frac{108}{525}$ can be simplified to $\frac{36}{175}$ (see the earlier section "Simplifying fractions").

If you can cross-cancel before you multiply, multiplying fractions is even easier. Here's the same problem. The 3 in the numerator and the 15 in the denominator have a common factor: They're both divisible by 3. If you divide both by 3 before multiplying, you don't have to reduce the fraction at the end:

$$\frac{4}{5} \times \frac{\overset{1}{\cancel{3}}}{7} \times \frac{9}{\underset{5}{\cancel{15}}} = \frac{36}{175}$$

TIP

Before multiplying mixed numbers, change them to improper fractions by multiplying the denominator by the integer and adding it to the numerator. For example, $2\frac{5}{8}$ is a mixed number. To convert it to an improper fraction, multiply 8 by 2 and add 5 to the result:

$$2 \times 8 = 16$$
$$16 + 5 = 21$$

The end result is $\frac{21}{8}$.

Dividing fractions

Dividing fractions is almost the same as multiplying, with one important difference: You have to convert the second fraction (the *divisor*) to the reciprocal and then multiply. As I explain in the earlier "Making the Most of Math Terminology" section, the reciprocal is simply a fraction flipped over.

EXAMPLE

Solve: $\frac{3}{5} \div \frac{2}{5}$.

Take the reciprocal of the second fraction and multiply it by the other fraction:

$$\frac{3}{5} \div \frac{2}{5} = \frac{3}{5} \times \frac{5}{2} = \frac{3 \times 5}{2 \times 5} = \frac{15}{10}$$

The fraction $\frac{15}{10}$ is an improper fraction, which you can convert to $1\frac{5}{10}$ (see the earlier section "Defining parts and types of fractions"). Then you can simplify $1\frac{5}{10}$ to $1\frac{1}{2}$ (see the earlier section "Simplifying fractions").

Adding and subtracting fractions

Adding and subtracting fractions can be as simple as multiplying and dividing them, or it can be more difficult. As the following sections show, it all depends on whether the fractions have the same denominator.

Adding and subtracting fractions with like denominators

To add or subtract two fractions with the same denominator, add (or subtract) the numerators and place that sum (or difference) over the common denominator:

$$\frac{2}{9} + \frac{3}{9} = \frac{2+3}{9} = \frac{5}{9}$$
$$\frac{3}{9} - \frac{2}{9} = \frac{3-2}{9} = \frac{1}{9}$$

Adding and subtracting fractions with different denominators

You can't add or subtract fractions with different denominators. You have to convert the fractions so they all have the same denominator, and then you perform addition or subtraction as I explain in the preceding section.

Converting fractions so they share the same denominator involves finding a *common denominator*. A common denominator is nothing more than a common multiple of all the denominators, as I describe in the earlier section "Looking at Least Common Multiples."

EXAMPLE

Find a common denominator for the fractions $\frac{3}{5}$ and $\frac{1}{8}$.

The multiples of 5 are 5, 10, 15, 20, 25, 30, 35, and 40.

The multiples of 8 are 8, 16, 24, 32, and 40.

A common denominator for the fractions $\frac{3}{5}$ and $\frac{1}{8}$ is 40.

The next step in the addition/subtraction process is to convert the fractions so they share the common denominator. To do this, divide the original denominator into the new common denominator and then multiply the result by the original numerator.

Start with $\frac{3}{5}$. Divide the original denominator (5) into the new common denominator (40): $40 \div 5 = 8$. Next, multiply the result (8) by the original numerator (3): $8 \times 3 = 24$. The equivalent fraction is $\frac{24}{40}$.

Perform the same operation with the second fraction, $\frac{1}{8}$. Divide the original denominator (8) into the new common denominator (40): $40 \div 8 = 5$. Next, multiply this (5) by the original numerator (1): $5 \times 1 = 5$. The equivalent fraction is $\frac{5}{40}$.

Now that the fractions have the same denominator, you can add or subtract them as shown in the preceding section:

$$\frac{3}{5} + \frac{1}{8} = \frac{24}{40} + \frac{5}{40} = \frac{29}{40}$$

Performing multiple operations

Sometimes you have to work through more than one operation on a set of fractions. Give this one a try:

EXAMPLE

$$\frac{\frac{1}{8} + \frac{3}{4}}{\frac{3}{5} - \frac{2}{10}} \times \frac{4}{5}$$

On the surface, this problem looks complicated. But if you remember the *order of operations* (see the earlier section "Obeying the order of operations") and take the problem one step at a time, it's really easy.

Under the order of operations, you do the work in the implied sets of parentheses (the top and bottom of the big fraction) first:

$$\frac{1}{8} + \frac{3}{4} = \frac{1}{8} + \frac{6}{8} = \frac{7}{8}$$

and

$$\frac{3}{5} - \frac{2}{10} = \frac{6}{10} - \frac{2}{10} = \frac{4}{10} = \frac{2}{5}$$

If you write the big fraction bar as a division sign, the problem now reads $\left(\frac{7}{8} \div \frac{2}{5}\right) \times \frac{4}{5}$.

Continue by performing the next operation in the parentheses:

$$\frac{7}{8} \div \frac{2}{5} = \frac{7}{8} \times \frac{5}{2} = \frac{35}{16}$$

The problem is now much simpler: $\frac{35}{16} \times \frac{4}{5}$.

$$\frac{35}{16} \times \frac{4}{5} = \frac{35 \times 4}{16 \times 5} = \frac{140}{80} = \frac{70}{40} = \frac{35}{20} = 1\frac{15}{20} = 1\frac{3}{4}$$

Converting fractions to decimals

Some math problems require you to perform operations on both decimal numbers (see the later section "Dealing with Decimals") and fractions. To properly perform such calculations, you must either convert the fraction to a decimal number or convert the decimal to a fraction.

Converting a fraction to a decimal number is easy. You simply divide the numerator by the denominator. For example $\frac{3}{4}$ is

$$\begin{array}{r} 0.75 \\ 4\overline{)3.00} \\ -2\,8 \\ \hline 20 \\ -20 \\ \hline 0 \end{array}$$

EXAMPLE

Try the following:

Solve: $\frac{1}{2} + 0.34$.

Convert the fraction to a decimal by dividing the numerator by the denominator:

$$\begin{array}{r} 0.5 \\ 2\overline{)1.0} \\ -1\,0 \\ \hline 0 \end{array}$$

Now you can easily perform the operation: $0.5 + 0.34 = 0.84$.

Comparing fractions

The two math subtests of the ASVAB often ask you to compare fractions to determine which one is the largest or smallest. If the fractions all have the same denominator, it's easy. The fraction with the largest numerator is the largest, and the one with the smallest numerator is the smallest.

But how do you compare fractions that have different denominators? I'll leave it up to you to determine which of the following proven methods you like the best.

Method 1: Finding a common denominator

The first method is to convert the fractions so they all have a common denominator (see the earlier section "Adding and subtracting fractions with different denominators"). After conversion, the fraction with the largest numerator is the largest fraction, and the one with the smallest numerator is the smallest. This method is what you probably learned in school.

EXAMPLE

Which of the following fractions is the largest: $\frac{5}{12}$, $\frac{3}{4}$, $\frac{9}{15}$, or $\frac{13}{16}$?

First, find a common multiple for the denominators:

>> **The multiples of 12:** 12, 24, 36, 48, 60, 72, 84, 96, 108, 120, 132, 144, 156, 168, 180, 192, 204, 216, 228, 240.

>> **The multiples of 4:** 4, 8, 12, 16, 20, 24, 28, 32, 36, 40, 44, 48, 52, 56, 60, 64, 68, 72, 76, 80, 84, 88, 92, 100, 104, 108, 112, 116, 122, . . . , 240.

>> **The multiples of 15:** 15, 30, 45, 60, 75, 90, 105, 120, 135, 150, 165, 180, 195, 210, 225, 240.

>> **The multiples of 16:** 16, 32, 48, 64, 80, 96, 112, 128, 144, 160, 176, 192, 208, 224, 240.

The lowest common denominator for all four fractions is 240.

Next, convert all the fractions so they have a denominator of 240 by dividing the new common denominator by the original denominator of the fraction and then multiplying the result by the original numerator:

>> $\frac{5}{12} = \frac{100}{240}$

>> $\frac{3}{4} = \frac{180}{240}$

$$\gg \quad \frac{9}{15} = \frac{144}{240}$$

$$\gg \quad \frac{13}{16} = \frac{195}{240}$$

The largest fraction is the one with the largest numerator: $\frac{195}{240}$, or $\frac{13}{16}$.

Method 2: The cross-product method

You may find Method 1 to be a bit time-consuming. If so, I think you'll enjoy this method. I certainly wish my teachers had heard of it when I was in high school. Maybe they explained it and I was sleeping that day.

The second method is called the *cross-product method*. To use it, you compare the cross-products of two fractions. The first cross-product is the product of the first numerator and the second denominator. The second cross-product is the product of the second numerator and the first denominator. If the cross-products are equal, the fractions are equivalent. If the first cross-product is larger, the first fraction is larger. If the second cross-product is larger, the second fraction is larger.

EXAMPLE

Which of the following fractions is the largest: $\frac{5}{12}$, $\frac{3}{4}$, $\frac{9}{15}$, or $\frac{13}{16}$?

Compare the first two fractions, $\frac{5}{12}$ and $\frac{3}{4}$: $5 \times 4 = 20$ and $12 \times 3 = 36$. The second fraction is larger.

Compare the larger fraction, $\frac{3}{4}$, with the third fraction, $\frac{9}{15}$: $3 \times 15 = 45$ and $4 \times 9 = 36$, so $\frac{3}{4}$ is still the largest fraction.

Now compare $\frac{3}{4}$ to the final fraction, $\frac{13}{16}$: $3 \times 16 = 48$ and $4 \times 13 = 52$.

The final fraction, $\frac{13}{16}$, is the largest.

Getting rational about ratios

Ratios represent how one quantity is related to another quantity. A ratio may be written as *A:B* or $\frac{A}{B}$ or using the phrase "*A* to *B*."

A ratio of 1:3 says that the second quantity is three times as large as the first. A ratio of 2:3 means that the second quantity is three times as large as one-half of the first quantity. A ratio of 5:4 means the second quantity is four times as large as one-fifth of the first quantity.

A ratio is actually a fraction. For example, the fraction $\frac{3}{4}$ is also a ratio of 3 to 4. Solve problems including ratios the same way you solve problems that include fractions.

Dealing with Decimals

Decimals are a method of writing fractional numbers without using a numerator and denominator. You can write the fraction $\frac{7}{10}$ as the decimal 0.7; you pronounce it "seven-tenths" or "zero point seven." The period or decimal point indicates that the number is a decimal.

Other decimals exist, such as hundredths or thousandths. They're all based on the number ten:

» **0.7:** Seven-tenths $\left(\dfrac{7}{10}\right)$

» **0.07:** Seven-hundredths $\left(\dfrac{7}{100}\right)$

» **0.007:** Seven-thousandths $\left(\dfrac{7}{1,000}\right)$

» **0.0007:** Seven-ten-thousandths $\left(\dfrac{7}{10,000}\right)$

» **0.00007:** Seven-hundred-thousandths $\left(\dfrac{7}{100,000}\right)$.

If a decimal is less than 1, it's traditional in mathematics to place a zero before the decimal point. Write "0.7," not ".7."

A decimal may be greater than 1. The decimal 3.7 would be pronounced as "three and seven-tenths" $\left(3\dfrac{7}{10}\right)$.

Converting decimals to fractions

To convert a decimal to a fraction, write all the digits following the decimal point in the numerator. If you see zeros before any nonzero digits, you can ignore them.

The denominator is always a one followed by zeros. The number of zeros in the denominator is determined by the total number of digits to the right of the decimal point (including the leading zeros):

» **One digit:** Denominator = 10. Example: $0.7 = \dfrac{7}{10}$

» **Two digits:** Denominator = 100. Example: $0.25 = \dfrac{25}{100}$

» **Three digits:** Denominator = 1,000. Example: $0.351 = \dfrac{351}{1,000}$

» **Four digits:** Denominator = 10,000. Example: $0.0041 = \dfrac{41}{10,000}$

If necessary, reduce the fraction (see the earlier section "Simplifying fractions").

Of course, you can also convert fractions to decimals (see the "Converting fractions to decimals" section earlier in this chapter).

Adding and subtracting decimals

You add and subtract decimals just as you do regular numbers (integers), except that before you perform your operation, you arrange the numbers in a column with the decimal points lined up one over the other.

EXAMPLE

Add the numbers 3.147, 148.392, and 0.074.

Put the numbers in an addition column with the decimal points lined up and perform the addition:

$$\begin{array}{r} 3.147 \\ 148.392 \\ +\ \ 0.074 \\ \hline 151.613 \end{array}$$

Multiplying decimals

Multiplying decimals requires three steps:

1. **Convert the decimals to whole numbers by moving the decimal points to the right, remembering to count how many spaces you move each decimal point.**

2. **Multiply the whole numbers just as you'd perform any other multiplication.**

3. **Place the decimal point in the product by moving the decimal point to the left the same number of total spaces you moved the decimal points to the right at the beginning.**

EXAMPLE

Multiply: $3.724 \times 0.0004 \times 9.42$.

First, convert the decimals to whole numbers by moving the decimal points to the right (remember to count).

  3.724 becomes 3,724 (decimal moved three spaces).

  0.0004 becomes 4 (decimal moved four spaces).

  9.42 becomes 942 (decimal moved two spaces).

Next, perform the multiplication on the whole numbers:

  $3,724 \times 4 \times 942 = 14,032,032$

Finally, put the decimal point in the correct position by moving it to the left the same number of places you moved the points to the right. You moved the decimal points a total of nine spaces to the right at the beginning, so now place the decimal point nine spaces to the left:

  14,032,032 becomes 0.014032032

REMEMBER

If you run out of numbers before you're finished counting spaces to the left, add zeros (as shown in the example) until you've finished counting.

Dividing decimals

Dividing decimals can be a challenge. You have to use both subtraction and multiplication. You also need to be pretty good at rounding (see the later "Rounding" section) and estimating numbers.

REMEMBER

You're not allowed to use a calculator on the ASVAB math subtests.

You can divide decimals in two ways: long division and conversion.

Method 1: Long division

To do long division with decimals, follow these steps:

1. **If the divisor isn't a whole number, move the decimal point in the divisor all the way to the right (to make it a whole number), and move the decimal point in the dividend the same number of places to the right.**

2. **Position the decimal point in the result directly above the decimal point in the dividend.**

3. **Divide as usual.**

   If the divisor doesn't go into the dividend evenly, add zeros to the right of the last digit in the dividend and keep dividing until it comes out evenly or a repeating pattern shows up.

Try the following division problem:

$$7.42 \div 0.7$$

Write the problem on your scratch paper in long-division form:

$$0.7\overline{)7.42}$$

Now move the decimal point one place to the right, which makes the divisor a whole number. Also move the decimal point in the dividend one place to the right:

$$7\overline{)74.2}$$

Position the decimal point in the result directly above the decimal point in the dividend:

$$7\overline{)74.\overset{.}{2}}$$

Divide as usual. Seven goes into 70 ten times with 4 left over; then drop the 2 down:

$$
\begin{array}{r}
10. \\
7\overline{)74.2} \\
70 \\
\hline
042
\end{array}
$$

Seven goes into 42 six times:

$$
\begin{array}{r}
10.6 \\
7\overline{)74.2} \\
70 \\
\hline
042 \\
42 \\
\hline
0
\end{array}
$$

When you're finished dividing decimals, you're finished. You don't have to move the decimal point around like you do after you've multiplied decimals.

Method 2: Conversion

The other way to divide decimals is to convert the decimals to fractions and then divide the fractions (see the earlier sections "Converting decimals to fractions" and "Dividing fractions," respectively).

Try the problem from the preceding section, using the conversion method.

$$7.42 \div 0.7$$

First, convert the decimals to fractions:

$$7.42 = 7\frac{42}{100} = \frac{742}{100}$$

$$0.7 = \frac{7}{10}$$

$$7.42 \div 0.7 = \frac{742}{100} \div \frac{7}{10}$$

Take the reciprocal of the divisor (flip the second fraction upside down) and then multiply:

$$\frac{742}{100} \times \frac{10}{7} = \frac{742 \times 10}{100 \times 7} = \frac{7,420}{700}$$

The fraction $\frac{7,420}{700}$ can be simplified (see "Simplifying fractions") to $10\frac{3}{5}$. Convert $\frac{3}{5}$ to a decimal (see "Converting fractions to decimals"), and the answer is 10.6.

Rounding

Rounding a number means limiting a number to a few (or no) decimal places. For example, if you have a $1.97 in change in your pocket, you may say, "I have about $2." The rounding process simplifies mathematical operations.

To round a number, you first determine what place you're rounding to. For example, the math subtests that make up the AFQT may ask you to round to the nearest tenth. Then look at the number immediately to the right of that place. If the number is 5 or greater, round the digit to the left up; for any number under 5, round the digit to the left down. Thus, you'd round 1.55 up to 1.6 and 1.34 down to 1.3.

TIP

You can also round other numbers, such as whole numbers. For example, 1,427 becomes 1,400 when you round to the nearest 100. However, most of the rounding operations you encounter on the Mathematics Knowledge subtest involve rounding decimals to the nearest tenth or nearest hundredth.

Perusing percents

Percent literally means "part of 100." That means, for example, that 25 percent (25%) is equal to $\frac{25}{100}$, which is equal to 0.25.

If a problem asks you to find 25 percent of 250, it's asking you to multiply 250 by 0.25.

TIP

To convert a percent to a decimal number, remove the percent sign and move the decimal point two places to the left: 15 percent is 0.15, and 15.32 percent is 0.1532. Conversely, to change a decimal number to percent, add the percent sign and move the decimal point two places to the right: 4.321 is equal to 432.1 percent.

Playing with Positive and Negative Numbers

Numbers can be positive or negative. A *positive* number is any number greater than zero. So 4; 3.2; 793; $\frac{3}{4}$; $\frac{1}{2}$; and 430,932,843,784 are all positive numbers.

Numbers smaller than zero are *negative* numbers. Every positive number has a negative number equivalent. You express negative numbers by putting a negative (minus) sign (–) in front of the number: –7, –18, $-\frac{3}{4}$, and –743.42 are all negative numbers.

In the math subtests of the ASVAB, you'll often be asked to perform mathematical operations on positive and negative numbers. Just remember the following rules:

>> **Adding two positive numbers always results in a positive number:** $3 + 3 = 6$

>> **Adding two negative numbers always results in a negative number:** $-3 + -3 = -6$

>> **Adding a negative number is the same as subtracting a positive number:**
$-3 + (-3) = 3 - 3 = 0$

>> **Subtracting a negative number is the same as adding a positive number:**
$3-(-3)=3+3=6$

>> **Multiplying or dividing two positive numbers always results in a positive number:**
$3 \div 3 = 1$

>> **Multiplying or dividing two negative numbers always results in a positive number:**
$-3 \times -3 = 9$

>> **Multiplying or dividing a negative number by a positive number always results in a negative number:** $-3 \times 3 = -9$

TIP

When you multiply a series of positive and negative numbers, count the number of negative numbers. If the number is even, the result will be positive. If the number is odd, the result will be negative.

REMEMBER

Everyone knows that 10 is larger than 5 and that 20 is larger than 15. With negative numbers, however, it works just the opposite: −10 is smaller than −5, and −20 is smaller than −15.

As you'll recall from your math in school, any number multiplied by zero is zero.

Rooting for Roots and Powers

Many of the problems you see on the ASVAB math subtests require you to perform calculations involving roots, such as square roots and cube roots, and numbers raised to exponents. If that sounds confusing, don't worry; it's really not. Read on.

Advice about exponents

Exponents are an easy way to show that a number is to be multiplied by itself a certain number of times. For example, 5^2 is the same as 5×5, and 4^3 is the same as $4 \times 4 \times 4$. The number or variable that is to be multiplied by itself is called the *base*, and the number or variable showing how many times it's to be multiplied by itself is called the *exponent*.

Here are important rules when working with exponents:

>> **Any base raised to the power of 1 equals itself.** For example, $6^1 = 6$.

>> **Any base raised to the zero power (except 0) equals 1.** For example, $3^0 = 1$.

In case you were wondering, according to most calculus textbooks, 0^0 is an "indeterminate form." What mathematicians mean by "indeterminate form" is that in some cases it has one value, and in other cases it has another. This stuff is advanced calculus, however, and you don't have to worry about it on the ASVAB math subtests.

TECHNICAL STUFF

>> **To multiply terms with the same base, you add the exponents.** For example, $7^2 \times 7^3 = 7^5$.

>> **To divide terms with the same base, you subtract the exponents.** For example, $4^5 \div 4^3 = 4^2$.

>> **If a base has a negative exponent, it's equal to its reciprocal with a positive exponent.** For example, $3^{-4} = \frac{1}{3^4}$.

>> **When a product has an exponent, each factor is raised to that power.** For example, $(5 \times 3)^3 = 5^3 \times 3^3$.

Roots

A root is the opposite of a power or an exponent. There are infinite kinds of roots. You have the *square root*, which means "undoing" a base to the second power; the cube root, which means "undoing" a base raised to the third power; a fourth root, for numbers raised to the fourth power; and so on. However, on the ASVAB math subtests, the only questions you're likely to see will involve square roots and possibly a couple of cube roots.

Square roots

A math operation requiring you to find a square root is designated by the *radical symbol* $(\sqrt{\ })$. The number underneath the radical line is called the *radicand*. For example, in the operation $\sqrt{36}$, the number 36 is the radicand.

A square root is a number that, when multiplied by itself, produces the radicand. Take the square root of 36 $(\sqrt{36})$, for example. If you multiply 6 by itself (6×6), you come up with 36, so 6 is the square root of 36.

However, as I mention in the earlier section "Playing with Positive and Negative Numbers," when you multiply two negative numbers together, you get a positive number. For example, -6×-6 also equals 36, so -6 is also the square root of 36.

That brings me to an important rule: When you take a square root, the results include two square roots — one positive and one negative.

TECHNICAL STUFF

Computing the square roots of negative numbers, such as $\sqrt{-36}$, is also possible, but it involves concepts such as imaginary numbers, which are more advanced than what you're asked to do on the ASVAB.

There are two types of square roots:

>> **Perfect squares:** Only some numbers, called *perfect squares,* have exact square roots.

>> **Irrational numbers:** All the rest of the numbers have square roots that include decimals that go on forever and have no pattern that repeats (non-repeating, non-terminating decimals), so they're called *irrational numbers.*

PERFECT SQUARES

Finding a square root can be difficult without a calculator, but because you can't use a calculator during the test, you're going to have to use your mind and some guessing methods. To find the square root of a number without a calculator, make an educated guess and then verify your results.

The radical symbol indicates that you're to find the principal square root of the number under the radical. The principal square root is a positive number. But if you're solving an equation such as $x^2 = 36$, then you give both the positive and negative roots: 6 and -6.

To use the educated-guess method, you have to know the square roots of a few perfect squares. One good way to do so is to study the squares of the numbers 1 through 12:

>> 1 and -1 are both square roots of 1.

>> 2 and -2 are both square roots of 4.

- » 3 and –3 are both square roots of 9.

- » 4 and –4 are both square roots of 16.

- » 5 and –5 are both square roots of 25.

- » 6 and –6 are both square roots of 36.

- » 7 and –7 are both square roots of 49.

- » 8 and –8 are both square roots of 64.

- » 9 and –9 are both square roots of 81.

- » 10 and –10 are both square roots of 100.

- » 11 and –11 are both square roots of 121.

- » 12 and –12 are both square roots of 144.

IRRATIONAL NUMBERS

When the ASVAB asks you to figure square roots of numbers that don't have perfect squares, the task gets a bit more difficult. If you have to find the square root of a number that isn't a perfect square, the ASVAB usually asks you to find the square root to the nearest tenth.

Suppose you run across this problem:

$\sqrt{54} =$

Think about what you know:

- » The square root of 49 is 7, and 54 is slightly greater than 49. You also know that the square root of 64 is 8, and 54 is slightly less than 64. (If you didn't know that, check out the preceding section.)

- » If the number 54 is somewhere between 49 and 64, the square root of 54 is somewhere between 7 and 8.

- » Because 54 is closer to 49 than to 64, the square root will be closer to 7 than to 8, so you can try 7.3 as the square root of 54:

  1. **Multiply 7.3 by itself.**

     $7.3 \times 7.3 = 53.29$, which is very close to 54.

  2. **Try multiplying 7.4 by itself to see whether it's any closer to 54.**

     $7.4 \times 7.4 = 54.76$, which isn't as close to 54 as 53.29.

  3. **7.3 is the square root of 54 to the nearest tenth.**

Cube roots

A *cube root* is a number that when multiplied by itself three times equals the number under the radical. For example, the cube root of 27 is 3 because $3 \times 3 \times 3 = 27$. A cube root is expressed by the radical sign with a 3 written on the left of the radical. For example, the cube root of 27 would be expressed as $\sqrt[3]{27}$.

You may see one or two cube-root problems on the math subtests of the ASVAB but probably not more than that. Plus, the problems you encounter will probably be perfect cubes and won't involve irrational numbers.

Each number has only one cube root (unlike square roots). If the radicand is positive, the cube root will be a positive number.

Also, unlike with square roots, finding the cube root of a negative number without involving advanced mathematics is possible. If the radicand is negative, the cube root will also be negative. For example, $\sqrt[3]{-27} = -3$.

Just like square roots, you should memorize a few common cube roots:

>> 1 is the cube root of 1, and –1 is the cube root of –1.

>> 2 is the cube root of 8, and –2 is the cube root of –8.

>> 3 is the cube root of 27, and –3 is the cube root of –27.

>> 4 is the cube root of 64, and –4 is the cube root of –64.

>> 5 is the cube root of 125, and –5 is the cube root of –125.

>> 6 is the cube root of 216, and –6 is the cube root of –216.

>> 7 is the cube root of 343, and –7 is the cube root of –343.

>> 8 is the cube root of 512, and –8 is the cube root of –512.

>> 9 is the cube root of 729, and –9 is the cube root of –729.

>> 10 is the cube root of 1,000, and –10 is the cube root of –1,000.

Scientific notation

Scientific notation is a compact format for writing very large or very small numbers. Although it's most often used in scientific fields, you may find a question or two on the Mathematics Knowledge subtest of the ASVAB asking you to convert a number to scientific notation, or vice versa.

Scientific notation separates a number into two parts: a *characteristic*, which is always greater than or equal to 1 and less than 10, and a *power of ten*. Thus, 1.25×10^4 means 1.25 times 10 to the fourth power, or 12,500; 5.79×10^{-8} means 5.79 times 10 to the negative eighth power. (Remember that a negative exponent is equal to its reciprocal with a positive exponent, so 10^{-8} means $\frac{1}{100,000,000}$). In this case, the scientific notation comes out to 0.0000000579.

Alphabet Soup: Tackling Algebra Review

Algebra problems are equations, which means that the quantities on both sides of the equal sign are equal — they're the same: $2 = 2$, $1 + 1 = 2$, and $3 - 1 = 2$. In all these cases, the quantities are the same on both sides of the equal sign. So, if $x = 2$, then x is 2 because the equal sign says so.

Visiting variables

Most algebraic equations involve using one or more variables. A *variable* is a symbol that represents a number. Usually, algebra problems use letters such as n, t, or x for variables. In most algebra problems, your goal is to find the value of the variable. For example, in the equation $x + 4 = 60$, you'd try to find the value of x by using the rules of algebra.

Following the rules of algebra

Algebra has several rules or properties that — when combined — allow you to simplify equations. Some (but not all) equations can be simplified to a complete solution:

>> **You may combine like terms.** This rule means adding or subtracting terms with variables of the same kind. The expression $4x + 4x$ simplifies to $8x$. $2y + y$ is equal to $3y$. The expression $13 - 7 + 3$ simplifies to 9.

>> **You may use the distributive property to remove parentheses around unlike terms (see "The distributive property: Breaking up large numbers" earlier in this chapter).**

>> **You may add or subtract any value as long as you do it to both sides of the equation.**

>> **You may multiply or divide by any number (except 0) as long as you do it to both sides of the equation.**

Combining like terms

One of the most common ways to simplify an expression is to combine like terms. Numeric terms may be combined, and any terms with the same variable part may be combined.

Take, for instance, the expression $5x + 3 + 3x - 6y + 4 + 7y$.

TIP

In algebra, when two or more variables are multiplied, it's traditional to place the variables next to each other and omit the multiplication sign ($\times$): $a \times b = ab$. The same rule applies to variables multiplied by numbers: $4 \times y = 4y$.

$5x$ and $3x$ are like terms. So are $-6y$ and $7y$. 3 and 4 are also like terms because they're numbers without variables. By combining the like terms, you get

$5x + 3x = 8x$

$-6y + 7y = 1y$ (or just y)

$3 + 4 = 7$

By combining the like terms, the expression $5x + 3 + 3x - 6y + 4 + 7y$ simplifies to $8x + y + 7$.

Using the distributive property

I know what you're thinking: Combining like terms is pretty cool, but what if you have unlike terms contained within parentheses? Doesn't the order of operations require you to deal with terms in parentheses first? Indeed, it does, and that's where the distributive property comes in.

As I explain in the section "Mental math: Mixing it up with the commutative, associative, and distributive properties" earlier in this chapter, $a(b + c) = ab + ac$. For example, $6(4 + 3)$ is mathematically the same as $(6 \times 4) + (6 \times 3)$.

Applying the same principle to algebra, the distributive property can be very useful in getting rid of those pesky parentheses:

$4(x + y) = 4x + 4y$

Using addition and subtraction

You can use addition and subtraction to get all the terms with variables on one side of an equation and all the numeric terms on the other. That's an important step in finding the value of the variable.

The equation $3x = 21$ has only the variable term on one side and only a number on the other. The equation $3x + 4 = 25$ doesn't.

REMEMBER

You can add and subtract any number as long as you do it to both sides of the equation. In this case, you want to get rid of the number 4 on the left side of the equation. How do you make the 4 disappear? Simply subtract 4 from it:

$$3x + 4 - 4 = 25 - 4$$

The equation simplifies to $3x = 21$.

Using multiplication and division

The rules of algebra also allow you to multiply and divide both sides of an equation by any number except zero. Say you have an equation that reads $3x = 21$, or 3 times x equals 21. You want to find the value of x, not three times x.

What happens if you divide a number by itself? The result is 1. Therefore, to change $3x$ to $1x$ (or x), divide both sides of the equation by 3:

$$3x = 21$$
$$\frac{3x}{3} = \frac{21}{3}$$
$$1x = 7$$
$$x = 7$$

But what if the equation were $\frac{2}{3}b = 21$? What would you do then?

I'll give you a hint: If you multiply any fraction by its reciprocal, the result is 1. Remember, a reciprocal is a fraction flipped upside down.

$$\frac{2}{3}b = 21$$
$$\frac{3}{2} \cdot \frac{2}{3}b = 21 \cdot \frac{3}{2}$$

Remember to multiply both sides of the equation by $\frac{3}{2}$.

$$1b = \frac{21}{1} \cdot \frac{3}{2}$$
$$b = \frac{21 \cdot 3}{1 \cdot 2}$$
$$b = \frac{63}{2}$$
$$b = 31\frac{1}{2}$$

All Is Not Equal: Examining Inequalities

In the earlier section, "The Heart of Math: Exploring Expressions and Equations," I say that all equations include equal signs (=), and I stand by that statement. However, some math problems look very much like equations, but they use signs other than the equal sign.

These problems are called *inequalities*. An equation states that each side of the equation separated by the equal sign is equal to the other. An inequality, on the other hand, says that the two sides separated by an inequality sign are *not* equal to each other.

Just as with equations, the solution to an inequality is all the values that make the inequality true. For the most part, you solve inequalities the same as you'd solve a normal equation. You need to keep some facts of inequality life in mind, however. Short and sweet, here they are:

>> **Negative numbers** are less than zero and less than positive numbers.

>> **Zero** is less than positive numbers but greater than negative numbers.

>> **Positive numbers** are greater than negative numbers and greater than zero.

Although there's only one equal sign (=), several signs are associated with inequalities:

>> ≠ means *does not equal* in the way that 3 does not equal 4, or $3 \neq 4$.

>> > means *greater than* in the way that 4 is greater than 3, or $4 > 3$.

>> < means *less than* in the way the 3 is less than 4, or $3 < 4$.

>> ≤ means *less than or equal to* in the way that x may be less than or equal to 4, or $x \leq 4$.

>> ≥ means *greater than or equal to* in the way that x may be greater than or equal to 3, or $x \geq 3$.

You solve inequalities by using the same principles of algebra used to solve equations, with the exception of multiplying or dividing each side by a negative number (check out the earlier "Following the rules of algebra" section). Take the following example:

Solve: $3x + 4 < 25$.

EXAMPLE

The inequality says that 3x plus 4 is less than 25. You solve it in the same way as you would the equation $3x + 4 = 25$:

$$3x + 4 < 25$$
$$3x + 4 - 4 < 25 - 4$$
$$3x < 21$$
$$\frac{3x}{3} < \frac{21}{3}$$
$$x < 7$$

Although you solve inequalities the same way you solve equations, keep two important rules in mind when working with inequalities:

REMEMBER

>> In algebra, if $a = b$, then $b = a$. In other words, you can swap the data on each side of the equal sign, and the equation means the same thing. So $2x + 4 = 18$ and $18 = 2x + 4$ are the same thing. This interchangeability doesn't work with inequalities. In other words, $2x + 4 > 18$ isn't the same as $18 > 2x + 4$. When you swap the data in an inequality, you have to change the inequality sign to balance the inequality (keep the inequity true). So $2x + 4 > 18$ is the same as $18 < 2x + 4$.

>> When you multiply or divide both sides of the inequality by a negative number, the inequality sign is reversed. That means if you multiply both sides of the inequality $3 < 4$ by –4, your answer is $-12 > -16$.

Solving Quadratics

A *quadratic equation* is an algebraic equation in which the unknown is raised to an exponent of 2 (and no higher), as in x^2. Quadratic equations can be very simple or very complex (or several degrees of difficulty in between). Here are some examples:

» $x^2 = 36$

» $x^2 + 4 = 72$

» $x^2 + 3x - 33 = 0$

REMEMBER

The exponent in a quadratic is never higher than 2 (because it would then no longer be the *square* of an unknown but a cube or something else). An equation that includes the variable x^3 or x^4 is *not* a quadratic.

You can solve quadratics in three primary ways: the square-root method, factoring, or the quadratic formula. Which method you choose depends on the difficulty of the equation.

Method 1: The square-root method

Simple quadratic equations (those that consist of just one squared term and a number) can be solved by using the *square-root rule*:

If $x^2 = k$, then $x = \pm\sqrt{k}$, as long as k isn't a negative number.

Remember to include the $\pm$ sign, which indicates that the answer is a positive or negative number. Take the following simple quadratic equation:

EXAMPLE

Solve: $3x^2 + 4 = 31$.

1. **First, isolate the variable by subtracting 4 from each side.**

   The result is $3x^2 = 27$.

2. **Next, get rid of the 3 by dividing both sides of the equation by 3.**

   The result is $x^2 = 9$.

3. **You can now solve by using the square-root rule.**

   $x^2 = 9$
   $x = \pm\sqrt{9}$
   $x = 3$ and $x = -3$

Method 2: The factoring method

Most quadratic equations you encounter on the ASVAB math subtests can be solved by putting the equation into the quadratic form and then factoring.

The *quadratic form* is $ax^2 + bx + c = 0$, where a, b, and c are just numbers. All quadratic equations can be expressed in this form. Want to see some examples?

» **$2x^2 - 4x = 32$:** This equation can be expressed in the quadratic form as $2x^2 + (-4x) + (-32) = 0$. In this case, $a = 2$, $b = -4$, and $c = -32$.

» $x^2 = 36$: You can express this equation as $1x^2 + 0x + (-36) = 0$. So $a = 1$, $b = 0$, and $c = -36$.

» $3x^2 + 6x + 4 = -33$: Expressed in quadratic form, this equation reads $3x^2 + 6x + 37 = 0$. So $a = 3$, $b = 6$, and $c = 37$.

Ready to factor? How about trying the following equation?

EXAMPLE

Solve: $x^2 + 5x + 6 = 0$.

Because I like you, I've already expressed the equation in quadratic form (the expression on the left is equal to zero), saving you a little time.

TIP

You can use the factoring method for most quadratic equations where $a = 1$ and c is a positive number.

The first step in factoring a quadratic equation is to draw two sets of parentheses on your scratch paper, and then place an x at the front of each, leaving some extra space after it. As with the original quadratic, the equation should equal zero:

$$(x \quad)(x \quad) = 0$$

The next step is to find two numbers that equal c when multiplied together and equal b when added together. In the example equation, $b = 5$ and $c = 6$, so you need to hunt for two numbers that multiply to 6 and add up to 5. For example, $2 \times 3 = 6$ and $2 + 3 = 5$. In this case, the two numbers you're seeking are positive 2 and positive 3.

Finally, put these two numbers into your set of parentheses:

$$(x + 2)(x + 3) = 0$$

Any number multiplied by zero equals zero, which means that $x + 2 = 0$ and/or $x + 3 = 0$. The solution to this quadratic equation is $x = -2$ and/or $x = -3$.

REMEMBER

When choosing your factors, remember that they can be either positive or negative numbers. You can use clues from the signs of b and c to help you find the numbers (factors) you need:

» If c is positive, then the factors you're looking for are either both positive or both negative:

   • If b is positive, then the factors are positive.

   • If b is negative, then the factors are negative.

   • b is the sum of the two factors that give you c.

» If c is negative, then the factors you're looking for are of alternating signs; that is, one is negative and one is positive:

   • If b is positive, then the larger factor is positive.

   • If b is negative, then the larger factor is negative.

   • b is the difference between the two factors that gives you c.

Try another one, just for giggles:

EXAMPLE

Solve: $x^2 - 7x + 6 = 0$.

Start by writing your parentheses:

$$(x\quad)(x\quad)=0$$

In this equation, $b=-7$ and $c=+6$. Because b is negative and c is positive, both factors will be negative.

You're looking for two negative numbers that multiply to 6 and add to -7. Those numbers are -1 and -6. Plugging the numbers into your parentheses, you get $(x-1)(x-6)=0$. That means $x=1$ and/or $x=6$.

Method 3: The quadratic formula

The square-root method can be used for simple quadratics, and the factoring method can easily be used for many other quadratics, as long as $a=1$. (See the two preceding sections.) But what if a doesn't equal 1, or you can't easily find two numbers that multiply to c and add up to b?

You can use the quadratic formula to solve any quadratic equation. So why not just use the quadratic formula and forget about the square-root and factoring methods? Because the quadratic formula is kind of complex:

$$x=\frac{-b\pm\sqrt{b^2-4ac}}{2a}$$

The quadratic formula uses the a, b, and c from $ax^2+bx+c=0$, just like the factoring method.

Armed with this knowledge, you can apply your skills to a complex quadratic equation:

EXAMPLE

Solve: $2x^2-4x-3=0$.

In this equation, $a=2$, $b=-4$, and $c=-3$. Plug the known values into the quadratic formula and simplify:

$$x=\frac{-b\pm\sqrt{b^2-4ac}}{2a}$$

$$x=\frac{-(-4)\pm\sqrt{(-4)^2-4(2)(-3)}}{2(2)}$$

$$x=\frac{4\pm\sqrt{16+24}}{4}$$

$$x=\frac{4\pm\sqrt{40}}{4}$$

$$x=\frac{4\pm6.3}{4}$$

$$x=\frac{4+6.3}{4}\text{ and }x=\frac{4-6.3}{4}$$

$$x=2.58\text{ and }x=-0.58$$

Rounded to the nearest tenth, $x=2.6$ and $x=-0.6$.

Knowing All the Angles: Geometry Review

According to my handy pocket dictionary, *geometry* is "the branch of mathematics that deals with the deduction of the properties, measurement, and relationships of points, lines, angles, and figures in space from their defining conditions by means of certain assumed properties of space." Sounds interesting!

Really, geometry is simply the branch of mathematics that's concerned with shapes, lines, and angles. From the perspective of the ASVAB math subtests, you should be able to identify basic geometric shapes and know certain properties about them so you can determine their angles and measurements. You see a lot of geometry-related questions on both the Mathematics Knowledge and the Arithmetic Reasoning subtests of the ASVAB.

Knowing all the angles

Angles are formed when two lines intersect at a point. Many geometric shapes are formed by intersecting lines, which form angles. Angles can be measured in degrees, which are often represented by the ° symbol. The greater the number of degrees, the wider the angle is:

>> A straight line is exactly 180°.

>> A *right angle* is exactly 90°.

>> An *acute angle* is more than 0° and less than 90°.

>> An *obtuse angle* is more than 90° but less than 180°.

>> *Complementary angles* are two angles that equal 90° when added together.

>> *Supplementary angles* are two angles that equal 180° when added together.

Take a look at the different types of angles in Figure 8-3.

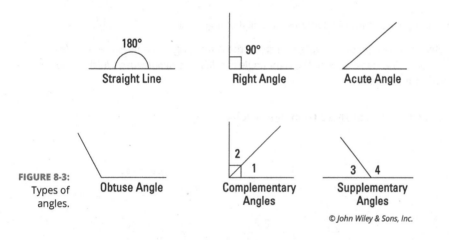

FIGURE 8-3:
Types of
angles.

© John Wiley & Sons, Inc.

Common geometric shapes

I'm not going to explain all the possible geometric shapes for two reasons: Doing so would take this entire book, and you don't need to know them all to solve the math problems you find on the ASVAB. However, you should recognize the most common shapes associated with geometry.

Getting square with quadrilaterals

A *quadrilateral* is a geometric shape with four sides. All quadrilaterals contain interior angles totaling 360°. Here are the five most common types of quadrilaterals:

>> **Squares** have four sides of equal length, and all the angles are right angles.

>> **Rectangles** have all right angles.

>> **Rhombuses** have four sides of equal length, but the angles don't have to be right angles.

>> **Trapezoids** have at least two sides that are parallel.

>> **Parallelograms** have opposite sides that are parallel, and their opposite sides and angles are equal.

Figure 8-4 gives you an idea of what these five quadrilaterals look like.

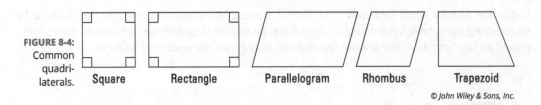

FIGURE 8-4: Common quadrilaterals.

Square   Rectangle   Parallelogram   Rhombus   Trapezoid

Trying out triangles

A *triangle* consists of three straight lines whose three interior angles always add up to 180°. The sides of a triangle are called *legs*. Triangles can be classified according to the relationship among their angles, the relationship among their sides, or some combination of these relationships. You should know the three most common types of triangles:

>> **Isosceles triangle:** Has two equal sides, and the angles opposite the equal sides are also equal.

>> **Equilateral triangle:** Has three equal sides, and all the angles measure 60°.

>> **Right triangle:** Has one right angle (90°); therefore, the remaining two angles are *complementary* (add up to 90°). The side opposite the right angle is called the *hypotenuse*, which is the longest side of a right triangle.

Check out Figure 8-5 to see what these triangles look like.

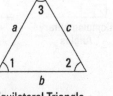
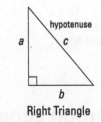

FIGURE 8-5: The three most common types of triangles.

Isosceles Triangle
If sides *a* and *c* are equal, then angles 1 and 2 are equal.

Equilateral Triangle
Sides *a*, *b*, *c* are equal. Angles 1, 2, 3 are equal.

Right Triangle
$a^2 + b^2 = c^2$

Settling on circles

A *circle* is formed when the points of a closed line are all located equal distances from a point called the *center* of the circle. A circle always has 360°. The closed line of a circle is called its *circumference*. The *radius* of a circle is the measurement from the center of the circle to any point on the circumference of the circle. The *diameter* of the circle is measured as a line passing through the center of the circle, from a point on one side of the circle to a point on the other side of the circle. The diameter of a circle is always twice as long as the radius. Figure 8-6 shows these relationships.

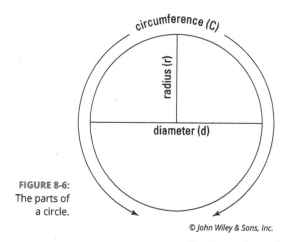

FIGURE 8-6:
The parts of
a circle.

© John Wiley & Sons, Inc.

Tackling famous geometry formulas

The math subtests of the ASVAB often ask you to use basic geometry formulas to calculate geometric measurements. You should commit these simple formulas to memory.

Quadrilateral formulas you should know

You may be asked to calculate the perimeter (distance around), the area, or the diagonal of a square or rectangle. Use the following formulas:

» **Perimeter of a square:** $P = 4s$, where s = one side of the square

» **Area of a square:** $A = s^2$

» **Diagonal of a square:** $d = s\sqrt{2}$

» **Perimeter of a rectangle:** $P = 2l + 2w$, where l = the length and w = the width of the rectangle; you can also write this formula as $P = 2(l + w)$

» **Area of a rectangle:** $A = lw$

» **Diagonal of a rectangle:** $d = \sqrt{l^2 + w^2}$

Good-to-know triangle formulas

Some math problems on the ASVAB may ask you to calculate the perimeter or area of a triangle. The following formulas are used for these two purposes:

» **Perimeter of a triangle:** $P = s_1 + s_2 + s_3$, where s = the length of each side of the triangle

» **Area of a triangle:** $A = \frac{1}{2}bh$, where b = the length of the triangle's base (bottom) and h = the height of the triangle

TIP

A special formula called the *Pythagorean theorem* says that if you know the length of any two sides of a right triangle, you can find the length of the third side. It works only on right triangles, however. The formula is $a^2 + b^2 = c^2$, where c equals the length of the triangle's hypotenuse and a and b equal the lengths of the remaining two sides.

Circle formulas

Circles are a bit more complex than squares, rectangles, and triangles and often involve invoking the value of π. In the "Making the Most of Math Terminology" section earlier in this chapter, I tell you that π is approximately equal to 3.14.

- » **Radius of a circle:** $r = \frac{1}{2}d$, where d = the diameter of the circle
- » **Diameter of a circle:** $d = 2r$
- » **Circumference of a circle:** $C = 2\pi r$
- » **Area of a circle:** $A = \pi r^2$

Handy formulas for three-dimensional shapes

Sometimes the math subtests require you to calculate measurements for solid (three-dimensional) shapes. These types of questions generally come in two flavors: calculating volume or calculating surface area.

Volume is the space a shape takes up. You can think of volume as how much a shape would hold if you poured water into it. *Surface area* is the area of the outside of the shape — for example, the amount of area you'd have to cover if you were to paint the outside of the solid shape.

- » **Volume of a cube:** $V = s^3$, where s = the length of one side of the cube
- » **Volume of a box (also called a rectangular prism):** $V = lwh$, where l = the length, w = the width, and h = the height of the box
- » **Volume of a cylinder:** $V = \pi r^2 h$, where r = the radius of the cylinder and h = the height of the cylinder
- » **Surface area of a cube:** $SA = 6s^2$
- » **Surface area of a box (rectangular prism):** $SA = 2lw + 2wh + 2lh$

You Got a Problem? Math Knowledge Exercises

The best way to get better at math is to practice, and I couldn't let you leave this chapter without giving you a few run-throughs on the material you just read. These exercises are designed to help you flex your math muscles. You'll practice terminology (I promise not to quiz you on the word *brachistochrone*), run around with Dear Aunt Sally, and convert fractions. You'll also keep equations balanced and identify which formulas you should use to solve problems on the ASVAB.

Math terminology practice

Remember when your mother said, "It's not *what* you say; it's *how* you say it"? She wasn't talking about math. In mathematics, it's exactly what you say that matters. Use Activity 1 to determine which mathematical operations (addition, subtraction, multiplication, or division) go with the signal words in the left column, and then check the "Answers and Explanations" section at the end of this chapter to make sure you're right.

Math Terminology

Signal Word	Operation (addition, subtraction, multiplication, or division)
1. Increase	
2. Deduct	
3. Product	
4. Quotient	
5. Sum	
6. Of	
7. Difference	
8. Total	
9. Less	
10. Combine	

Order of operations practice

Math is a lot like the military: There are right ways and wrong ways to do everything. In mathematics, it's all about the order of operations. Remember that Aunt Sally — although we always have to apologize for her (Please Excuse My Dear Aunt Sally) — can show you how to solve any math problem in the right order (refer back to "Obeying the order of operations," earlier in this chapter). In Activity 2, look at the problem and determine which operations you'll do first, then which you'll do second. You don't need to perform the calculations. When you're done, see whether you're right in the "Answers and Explanations" section at the end of this chapter. When you're only simplifying things, it's often okay to switch the first and second operations you perform.

ACTIVITY 2 **Order of Operations**

Problem	First	Second
Example: $5+6+(17\cdot2)$	$(17\cdot2)$	Add 5, 6, and the product of 17 and 2
1. $(4-3)(3+19)$		
2. $12^2-(13+22)$		
3. $\frac{18}{3}+27$		
4. $14+x(18^2)$		
5. $7^3\div4$		
6. $6\div3+12$		
7. $\frac{3}{4}+38.6+24.2$		
8. $\frac{0.3^{17}}{2}$		
9. $(4^3+17)+y$		
10. $4+4+8-\left(\frac{18^2}{2}\right)$		

Converting fractions and decimals

When you run into an ASVAB question that contains fractions and decimals, you'll most likely need to convert one or the other to solve the problem (see "Dealing with Decimals" earlier in this chapter). Use Activity 3 to practice switching between fractions and decimals, and then check the "Answers and Explanations" section at the end of this chapter to see how well you did.

ACTIVITY 3 **Fractions and Decimals**

Problem	Your Conversion
1. 0.17	
2. $\frac{2}{5}$	
3. $1\frac{3}{10}$	
4. 4.75	
5. 18.925	
6. $\frac{21}{8}$	
7. $7\frac{21}{5}$	
8. 9.217	
9. −37.2	
10. $8\frac{81}{8}$	

Solving equations and inequalities

When you take the ASVAB, you'll do plenty of mental math — but you'll also use some of the unlimited supply of scratch paper the test proctor gives you to write equations. Simple errors in an equation can throw off your entire game, though, so use Activity 4 to practice solving each equation or inequality. When you're finished, check your work in the "Answers and Explanations" section at the end of this chapter. (If you need to brush up on balancing equations, see the "Following the rules of algebra" section earlier in this chapter.)

ACTIVITY 4 **Solving Equations and Inequalities**

Problem	Your Work
1. $3x + 7 = 25$	
2. $20x - 3 < 57$	
3. $x - 3 = 17$	
4. $4x + 5 = 1 + 5x$	
5. $9y - 7 = 7y - 11$	

Identifying formulas

Many of the algebra and geometry questions on the ASVAB require you to plumb the depths of your memory for a specific mathematical formula. If you can't remember it, you're going to have a tough time coming up with the right answer. Use Activity 5 to match each type of problem with the appropriate formula to solve it. (*Note:* Not all of these formulas appear in this chapter.) Make sure you connected the right pairs by checking your answers in the "Answers and Explanations" section at the end of this chapter.

ACTIVITY 5 Identifying Formulas

Answer	Formula Type	Formula
1.	1. Quadratic equation	A. $A = lw$
2.	2. Pythagorean theorem	B. $d = rt$
3.	3. Area of a triangle	C. $A = \pi r^2$
4.	4. Area of a rectangle	D. $ax^2 + bx + c = 0$
5.	5. Circumference of a circle	E. $C = 2\pi r$
6.	6. Slope-intercept form	F. $A = \frac{1}{2}bh$
7.	7. Distance traveled	G. $a^2 + b^2 = c^2$
8.	8. Simple interest	H. $V = lwh$
9.	9. Area of a circle	I. $I = prt$
10.	10. Volume of a rectangular prism	J. $y = mx + b$

Answers and Explanations

Check your answers for each of the exercises here, and take some time to review the explanations if you're not sure where you went wrong.

Activity 1: Math Terminology

1. Increase: addition

2. Deduct: subtraction

3. Product: multiplication

4. Quotient: division

5. Sum: addition

6. Of: multiplication

7. Difference: subtraction

8. Total: addition

9. Less: subtraction

10. Combine: addition

Activity 2: Order of Operations

Problem	First	Second
1. $(4-3)(3+19)$	$(4-3)$	multiply 1 by $(3+19)$
2. $12^2 - (13+22)$	$13+22$	subtract 35 from 12^2
3. $\frac{18}{3} + 27$	$18 \div 3$	add 6 and 27
4. $14 + x(18^2)$	18^2	multiply 18^2 by x then add 14
5. $7^3 \div 4$	7^3	divide by 4
6. $6 \div 3 + 12$	$6 \div 3$	add 2 and 12
7. $\frac{3}{4} + 38.6 + 24.2$	$3 \div 4$	add the remaining numbers
8. $\frac{0.3^{17}}{2}$	0.3^{17}	divide by 2
9. $(4^3 + 17) + y$	4^3	add 64 and 17 then add y
10. $4 + 4 + 8 - \left(\frac{18^2}{2}\right)$	18^2	divide by 2 then total the remaining numbers

Activity 3: Fractions and Decimals

Problem	Your Conversion
1. 0.17	$\frac{17}{100}$
2. $\frac{2}{5}$	0.4
3. $1\frac{3}{10}$	1.3
4. 4.75	$4\frac{3}{4}$
5. 18.925	$18\frac{37}{40}$
6. $\frac{21}{8}$	2.625
7. $7\frac{21}{5}$	11.2
8. 9.217	$9\frac{217}{1,000}$
9. −37.2	$-37\frac{1}{5}$
10. $8\frac{81}{8}$	18.125

Activity 4: Solving Equations and Inequalities

1. $3x + 7 = 25$
$3x + 7 - 7 = 25 - 7$
$3x = 18$
$\dfrac{3x}{3} = \dfrac{18}{3}$
$x = 6$

2. $20x - 3 < 57$
$20x - 3 + 3 < 57 + 3$
$20x < 60$
$\dfrac{20x}{20} < \dfrac{60}{20}$
$x < 3$

3. $x - 3 = 17$
$x - 3 + 3 = 17 + 3$
$x = 20$

4. $4x + 5 = 1 + 5x$
$4x + 5 = 5x + 1$
$4x + 5 - 5x = 5x + 1 - 5x$
$-x + 5 = 1$
$-x + 5 - 5 = 1 - 5$
$-x = -4$
$x = 4$

5. $9y - 7 = 7y - 11$
$9y - 7 - 7y = 7y - 11 - 7y$
$2y - 7 = -11$
$2y - 7 + 7 = -11 + 7$
$2y = -4$
$\dfrac{2y}{2} = \dfrac{-4}{2}$
$y = -2$

Activity 5: Identifying Formulas

1. D. The quadratic equation is $ax^2 + bx + c = 0$.

2. G. The Pythagorean theorem is $a^2 + b^2 = c^2$.

3. F. The formula to find the area of a triangle is $A = \frac{1}{2}bh$, where A represents area, b represents the length of the base, and h represents the triangle's height.

4. A. The formula to find the area of a rectangle is $A = lw$, where A represents area, l represents the rectangle's length, and w represents the rectangle's width.

5. **E.** The formula to find the circumference (the distance around) a circle is $C = 2\pi r$, where C represents circumference and r represents the circle's radius (the distance from the center of the circle to its outer edge).

6. **J.** The formula for slope-intercept form of a line is $y = mx + b$, where m is the slope and b is the y-intercept. In this formula, x and y represent coordinate points.

7. **B.** The formula to find distance traveled is $d = rt$, where d represents distance, r represents rate (speed), and t represents time.

8. **I.** The formula to figure out simple interest is $I = prt$, where I represents interest, p represents principal, r represents the rate of interest per year expressed as a decimal, and t represents the time periods involved.

9. **C.** The formula to find the area of a circle is $A = \pi r^2$, where A represents area and r represents the circle's radius (the distance, in a straight line, from the circle's center to its outer edge).

10. **H.** The formula to find the volume of a rectangular prism is $V = lwh$, where V represents volume, l represents length, w represents width, and h represents height.

Chapter **9**

The Mathematics Knowledge Subtest

The Mathematics Knowledge subtest is one of two math subtests on the ASVAB that help the military determine your AFQT score. This chapter and Chapter 8 prepare you for the types of questions and knowledge you need in order to feel confident and score competitively on the Mathematics Knowledge portion of the ASVAB. Chapters 10 and 11 review your ability to correctly answer word problems for the Arithmetic Reasoning subtests.

Most of the time, the Mathematics Knowledge subtest contains only one or two questions testing each specific mathematical concept. For example, one question may ask you to multiply fractions, the next question may ask you to solve a mathematical inequality, and the question after that may ask you to find the value of an exponent. (If you've suddenly become nervous after reading the preceding sentence, don't worry. I cover all this stuff in Chapter 8.)

All this variety forces you to constantly shift your mental gears to quickly deal with different concepts. You can look at this situation from two perspectives: These mental gymnastics can be difficult and frustrating, especially if you know everything about solving for x but nothing about deriving a square root. But variety can also be the spice of life. If you don't know how to solve a specific type of problem, this oversight may cause you to get only one question wrong (or maybe two — but think positively). On the flip side, having trouble in a specific area helps you zero in on what you need to focus your study on so you can improve your weaker areas.

Taking Stock of the Test Structure

On the CAT-ASVAB, the Mathematics Knowledge subtest consists of 15 questions covering the entire array of high-school math, and you have 23 minutes to complete the subtest. (If you're taking the paper version of the ASVAB, you have to answer 25 questions in 24 minutes.) You don't necessarily have to rush through each calculation, but the pace you need to set (about a minute per question) doesn't exactly give you time to daydream about what you're having for dinner. You have to concentrate to solve each problem quickly and accurately.

The people who made up the test's rules have dictated you can't use a calculator for any of the math questions on the ASVAB. When you enter the testing room, you get a pencil and a sheet of scratch paper. (I guess their thinking is that if you're in the middle of a combat zone and find a sudden need to solve for x, you won't have your phone in your pocket to look up the answer.) The good news is that all the questions on the math subtests of the ASVAB are designed so you can solve them without electronic calculation.

The Mathematics Knowledge subtest features three types of questions:

>> **Direct math:** This type of question presents you with a mathematical equation and asks you to solve it.

>> **Math law:** This type of question asks you about a mathematical law, rule, term, or concept.

>> **Combined:** This type of question asks you to use a mathematical law, rule, term, or concept to solve a problem.

Direct math questions

The direct math question is the most common type of question on the Mathematics Knowledge subtest. In a direct math question, you're presented with an equation and asked to solve it. You see a lot of these.

EXAMPLE

Solve for x: $2x + 4(2x + 7) = 3(2x + 4)$.

(A) 0.75

(B) −4

(C) 1.25

(D) −1.25

The correct answer is Choice (B), −4. This is an algebraic equation that you can solve using the rules of algebra (see Chapter 8):

$$2x + 4(2x + 7) = 3(2x + 4)$$
$$2x + 8x + 28 = 6x + 12$$
$$10x + 28 = 6x + 12$$
$$10x + 28 - 6x = 6x + 12 - 6x$$
$$4x + 28 = 12$$
$$4x = -16$$
$$x = -4$$

Math law questions

Sometimes the Mathematics Knowledge subtest asks you a question that doesn't involve solving a mathematical problem. Instead, you're expected to answer a question concerning a mathematical concept, math term, rule, or law. You're not likely to see more than two or three of these kinds of questions on the test, however.

EXAMPLE

In the expression $432xy + 124xy$, the "432" is called the

(A) multiplier.

(B) coefficient.

(C) matrix.

(D) prime.

The correct answer is Choice (B), coefficient. A *coefficient* is the number multiplied by a variable or by a product of variables or by powers of variables in a term. (You can find more useful math terms in Chapter 8.)

Combined questions

You may see several combined questions on the Mathematics Knowledge subtest. These questions require you to use a particular math term, rule, or concept to solve a mathematical problem.

EXAMPLE

What is the quotient of 4 and 4?

(A) 8

(B) 16

(C) 0

(D) 1

The right answer is Choice (D), 1. To solve this problem, you need to know that a *quotient* is the result of a division operation. When you've figured that out, you have to perform the operation:

$$4 \div 4 = 1$$

Planning Your Test Attack

For most people, scoring well on the Mathematics Knowledge subtest requires more than just showing up on time and borrowing a No. 2 pencil and piece of scratch paper. Maybe everything on the test will go perfectly, and you'll breeze through without a problem. On the other hand, maybe you'll get stuck on a question or run into other roadblocks. When this happens, having a plan of attack is helpful.

Keeping an eye on the all-important clock

Like all subtests of the ASVAB, the Mathematics Knowledge subtest is timed. If you're taking the computerized version of the ASVAB, you get 16 questions in 20 minutes, and your remaining time will be shown in the corner of your computer screen.

If you're taking the paper version of the test, you have just 24 minutes to try to correctly answer 25 questions. That's 57.6 seconds per question. (Do you like the way I used math to figure that out?) The room will have a clock in it, and the start time and stop time will be posted somewhere in the room, easily visible to you and the other test takers.

TIP

Keep an eye on the clock. You want to try to finish the test before time runs out. Try to average about 45 or 50 seconds per question. If you get stuck on a question, refer to the section "Playing the guessing game" later in this chapter.

Doubling your chances by double-checking

If you have time, double-check your answers. Those crafty test makers often provide wrong answer choices that work if you made a common error, so don't assume that your answer is the right one just because it matches one of the possible answer choices. Look at the following example:

Solve: $\frac{1}{4} \div \frac{1}{2} =$

(A) $\frac{1}{8}$

(B) 2

(C) 17

(D) $\frac{1}{2}$

To correctly solve this problem, you multiply the first fraction by the *reciprocal* (flipped over) value of the second fraction:

$$\frac{1}{4} \div \frac{1}{2} = \frac{1}{4} \times \frac{2}{1} = \frac{2}{4} = \frac{1}{2}$$

The correct answer is Choice (D), $\frac{1}{2}$. If you multiplied the fractions instead of dividing, you would've gotten Choice (A). If you took the reciprocal of the first fraction rather than the second, you would've gotten Choice (B). If you took a wild guess, you might've gotten Choice (C).

Although double-checking your answers is always a good idea, remember to watch the time. You don't want to run out of time with only half the questions answered because you've spent too much time double-checking all your answers.

Using the answer choices to your advantage

If you're stuck on a particular problem, sometimes plugging the possible answer choices into the equation can help you find the right answer.

Solve: $\frac{1}{2}x - 45 = 5$.

(A) 25

(B) 50

(C) 100

(D) 75

The right answer is Choice (C), 100. Suppose you experience a complete brain freeze and can't remember how to handle a variable multiplied by a fraction. You don't have to jump straight to random guessing at this point. You can replace x in the equation with the known possible answer choices and see whether any of them work.

First, recognize that you can simplify the equation to $\frac{1}{2}x = 50$ by adding 45 to both sides. Now start substituting the answer choices for *x*:

>> *x* = 25: $\frac{1}{2} \times 25 = 50 \rightarrow 12.5 = 50$. That doesn't work.

>> *x* = 50: $\frac{1}{2} \times 50 = 50 \rightarrow 25 = 50$. That certainly doesn't work.

>> *x* = 100: $\frac{1}{2} \times 100 = 50 \rightarrow 50 = 50$. You can stop here because Choice (C) is the correct answer.

Don't forget that plugging in all the answers is time-consuming, so save this procedure until you've answered all the problems you can answer. If you're taking the computer version, you can't skip a question, so budget your time wisely; if you don't have much time, just make a guess and move on. You may be able to solve the next question easily.

Playing the guessing game

If time is running short on the CAT-ASVAB, try to read and legitimately answer the questions instead of filling in random guesses for the remaining items. The CAT-ASVAB applies a relatively large penalty when you provide several incorrect answers toward the end of the subtest.

If you're taking the paper version of the ASVAB, you can always skip the tough questions and come back to them after you've finished the easier ones. If you're taking the computerized version of the ASVAB, the software doesn't let you skip questions.

Guessing incorrectly on any of the paper ASVAB subtests doesn't count against you. It's okay to fill in an answer — any answer — on your answer sheet because if you don't, your chances of getting that answer right are zero. But if you take a shot at it, your chances increase to 25 percent, or one in four.

If you're taking the paper version of the test and elect to skip questions until later, make sure you mark the next answer in the correct space on the answer sheet. Otherwise, you may wind up wearing out the eraser on your pencil when you discover your error at the end of the test. Or, even worse, you may not notice the error and wind up getting several answers wrong because you mismarked your answer sheet.

The process of elimination

Guessing doesn't always mean "pick an answer, any answer." You can increase your chances of picking the right answer by eliminating answers that can't be right.

Solve: $\frac{1}{8} \times \frac{4}{5} =$

(A) $1\frac{1}{8}$

(B) $1\frac{1}{4}$

(C) $\frac{1}{10}$

(D) $\frac{1}{5}$

Any fraction that is less than 1 that is multiplied by another fraction that is less than 1 is going to result in an answer that is less than 1. That means Choices (A) and (B) can't be correct. Your odds of guessing the right answer have just improved from one in four to one in two, or a 50/50 chance. (By the way, the correct answer is Choice (C).)

Solving what you can and guessing the rest

Sometimes you may know how to solve part of a problem but not all of it. If you don't know how to do all the operations, don't give up. You can still narrow your choices by doing what you can. Suppose this question confronts you:

EXAMPLE

What is the value of $(-0.4)^3$?

(A) −0.0027

(B) −0.000064

(C) 0.000064

(D) 0.0009

What if you don't remember how to multiply decimals? All is not lost! If you remember how to use exponents, you'll remember that you have to multiply $-0.04 \times -0.04 \times -0.04$. If you simplify the problem and just multiply $-4 \times -4 \times -4$ without worrying about those pesky zeros, you know that your answer will be negative and will end in the digits 64. With this pearl of wisdom in mind, you can see that Choices (A), (C), and (D) are all wrong. You logically guessed your way to the correct answer, Choice (B)!

Applying Your Knowledge to Practice Questions

How about putting all the knowledge you've gained about the Mathematics Knowledge subtest to the test? Here are ten questions that are very similar to those you're likely to see when you take the actual test.

1. Which of the following fractions is the smallest?

   (A) $\frac{3}{4}$

   (B) $\frac{14}{17}$

   (C) $\frac{4}{7}$

   (D) $\frac{5}{8}$

2. What is the product of $\sqrt{36}$ and $\sqrt{49}$?

   (A) 1,764

   (B) 42

   (C) 13

   (D) 6

3. Solve: $2x - 3 = x + 7$

   (A) 10

   (B) 6

   (C) 21

   (D) −10

4. A circle has a radius of 15 feet. What is most nearly its circumference?

   (A) 30 feet

   (B) 225 feet

   (C) 94 feet

   (D) 150 feet

5. At 3 p.m., the angle between the hands of the clock is

(A) 90 degrees.

(B) 180 degrees.

(C) 120 degrees.

(D) 360 degrees.

6. If $3 + y \geq 13$, what is the value of y?

(A) Greater than or equal to 10

(B) Less than or equal to 10

(C) 10

(D) 6

7. $y^3 \times y^2 \times y^{-3} =$

(A) y^2

(B) y^{-13}

(C) y^8

(D) x^{23}

8. 14 yards + 14 feet =

(A) 16 yards

(B) 15 yards

(C) 28 feet

(D) 56 feet

9. What is 35 percent of 85?

(A) 33.2

(B) 65.32

(C) 21.3

(D) 29.75

10. What is most nearly the average of 37, 22, 72, and 44?

(A) 43.8

(B) 55.2

(C) 175

(D) 77.1

11. 224 inches equals

(A) 18 feet, 8 inches

(B) 18 feet, 6 inches

(C) 18 feet, 4 inches

(D) 18 feet, 2 inches

12. The area of a square is 36 ft². How long is each side?

(A) 3 feet

(B) 4 feet

(C) 6 feet

(D) 9 feet

13. The formula to find the area of a circle is

(A) $c = 2\pi r$

(B) $A = \pi r^2$

(C) $A = \frac{1}{2} \times (\text{base}_1 + \text{base}_2) \times \text{height}$

(D) $P = 2lw$

14. Find the equation of a line with a slope of −5 and a y-intercept of 3.

(A) $y = (3)x - 5$

(B) $y = 5x + 3$

(C) $y = -5x + 3$

(D) $y = 3x + 15$

15. $4^4 \times 3^4 =$

(A) 2,800

(B) 20,736

(C) 28,886

(D) 12,880

Answers and Explanations

Use this answer key to score the practice Mathematics Knowledge questions.

1. **C.** One method of comparing fractions is called the *cross-product method* (see Chapter 8).

    The cross-products of the first fraction and the second fraction are $3 \times 17 = 51$ and $14 \times 4 = 56$. The first fraction is smaller.

    The cross-products of the first fraction and the third fraction are $3 \times 7 = 21$ and $4 \times 4 = 16$. The third fraction is smaller.

    The cross-products of the third fraction and the fourth fraction are $4 \times 8 = 32$ and $5 \times 7 = 35$. The third fraction, Choice (C), is still smaller, so it's the smallest of all the fractions.

2. **B.** The square root of 36 is 6, and the square root of 49 is 7. The product of those two numbers is $6 \times 7 = 42$.

3. **A.** Rearrange the equation and solve as follows:

    $$2x - 3 = x + 7$$
    $$2x - x = 7 + 3$$
    $$x = 10$$

4. **C.** The circumference of a circle is $\pi \times$ diameter, the diameter equals two times the radius, and π is approximately 3.14. Therefore, $30 \times 3.14 \approx 94$.

    The $\approx$ sign means *approximately equals*. It's used here because the answer, 94, is a rounded number.

    TIP

5. **A.** At 3 p.m., one hand is on the 12, and the other is on the 3. This setup creates a *right angle* — a 90-degree angle.

6. **A.** Solve the inequality the same way you'd solve an algebraic equation:

    $$3 + y \geq 13$$
    $$y \geq 13 - 3$$
    $$y \geq 10$$

7. **A.** When you multiply powers with the same base, add the exponents:
    $$y^3 \times y^2 \times y^{-3} = y^{3+2+(-3)} = y^2.$$

8. **D.** Convert the yards to feet by multiplying by 3: $14 \times 3 = 42$ feet. Add this to 14 feet: $42 + 14 = 56$ feet.

9. **D.** Multiply 85 by the decimal equivalent of 35 percent, or 0.35: $0.35 \times 85 = 29.75$.

10. **A.** Add the numbers and then divide by the number of terms: $37 + 22 + 72 + 44 = 175$, and $175 \div 4 = 43.75$. Round this number up to 43.8.

11. **A.** There are 12 inches in a foot, and you can fit 18 of those into 224 inches (with 8 inches left to spare). Look at it this way: 12 inches $\times 18$ inches $= 216$ inches. Then, 224 inches − 216 inches = 8 inches.

12. C. The formula for the area of a square is $A = a^2$, where A represents area and a represents the length of each side (because all the sides on a square are the same length). If you know what number squared equals 36 — that is, if you know the square root of 36 — you know that the sides of a square measuring 36 ft.² must each be 6 feet long. $6 \times 6 = 36$, so the answer is Choice (C).

13. B. When you want to find the area of a circle, you need the formula $A = \pi r^2$. The other formulas listed as choices are also real formulas, but not for the area of a circle. In case you were wondering, $c = 2\pi r$ gives you the circumference of a circle; $A = \frac{1}{2} \times (\text{base}_1 + \text{base}_2) \times \text{height}$ gives you the area of a trapezoid, and $P = 2lw$ helps you figure out the perimeter of a circle.

14. C. The formula for slope-intercept form is $y = mx + b$, where m represents the slope of the line and b represents the y-intercept. Both x and y represent the points. Replace the variables with what you know:

$$y = mx + b$$
$$y = (-5)x + (3)$$
$$y = -5x + 3$$

15. B. This one's just a matter of math. 4^4 really means $4 \times 4 \times 4 \times 4$, which equals 256. Along the same lines, 3^4 is the same as $3 \times 3 \times 3 \times 3$, and that's 81. Then, multiply 256 by 81 to get 20,736 — that's your answer.

Chapter **10**

Working with Word Problems

Two types of mathematics tests are part of the AFQT. The first type is the Mathematics Knowledge subtest that I discuss in Chapters 8 and 9. The second type is the Arithmetic Reasoning subtest, which is the topic of this chapter and Chapter 11.

In the Mathematics Knowledge subtest, you have it pretty easy. You see a mathematical equation, and you do your best to solve it. The Arithmetic Reasoning subtest is more involved. You have to set up your own equations to solve the problem, which means a little more work on your scratch paper. The crafty folks who create ASVAB questions are asking you to whip up an equation and solve it... which sounds suspiciously like they want to see how much you know so they can find you the right job!

Lots of people have difficulty translating a word problem into a mathematical equation. If you're starting to sweat at the mere thought of math word problems, you're not alone. Just take a deep breath, relax, and don't worry. I'm here to guide you through the process.

Making Sense of Word Problems

The purpose of math word problems is to test your ability to use general mathematics to solve everyday, real-world problems. That's what all the textbooks say. However, in my "real world," I've never once wondered how old Anna is if she's three years older than Chuck, and in five years, her age and Chuck's age would equal 54. I'd just ask Anna how old she is.

In all fairness, arithmetic reasoning can actually be quite helpful in sharpening your ability to figure out dimensions of spaces, construction information, travel time, and the probability of being late if you decide to go shopping at the Post Exchange before your important meeting with your first sergeant. You may even want to understand how much interest you've acquired in your bank account, how much cash you have left over after lunch, and how much that beer pong set really costs after you take 20 percent off.

When you realize that math word problems are designed to measure your ability to use basic math to solve *fictional* problems, they can be kind of fun — sort of like solving a puzzle.

Setting Up the Problem

Word problems are nothing more than a series of expressions that fit into an equation. An equation is a combination of math expressions. (If that sounds like Greek to you, check out Chapter 8.) The expressions in math word problems are generally stated in English. Your job is to dig out the relevant facts and state them in mathematical terms. You do so by

>> Getting organized

>> Understanding the problem

>> Identifying the information you need

>> Translating the problem into one or more solvable mathematic equations

I cover all these tasks in greater detail in the following sections.

Getting organized

Getting organized isn't really a step as much as it is a method. You need to be organized throughout the problem-solving process. Being organized helps you think clearly and ensures you don't get lost while trying to define and solve the problem.

TIP

When using your scratch paper, draw and label your pictures and graphs clearly. And be sure to mark your calculations with the question number. If you go back to your notes and can't remember what you were thinking about when you drew that picture, you'll be frustrated and will waste valuable time — and you don't have any time to waste on the Arithmetic Reasoning subtest. (For more on pictures, see the nearby sidebar.)

Understanding the problem

Make sure you read the entire problem, but be careful: Don't try too hard to understand the problem on the first read-through. I know that doesn't seem to make any sense, but bear with me.

Math word problems can be broken down into two parts:

WARNING

>> **The problem statement:** The problem statement isn't really an object to be understood. It's simply a source of information you can use, as needed, to solve the equation.

 The information included in the problem statement is often confusing or disorganized. Sometimes *distracters* (information that has nothing to do with solving the problem) are mixed in, leading to confusion and making the problem difficult to solve. (See the "Dealing with distracters" sidebar for more information.)

>> **The problem question:** The problem question is the meat of the matter. Exactly what is the questioner asking you to find? This part of the problem is the one you really need to understand.

A PICTURE CAN BE WORTH A THOUSAND EQUATIONS

When you walk in to take the ASVAB, the test proctor is going to give you a piece of blank scratch paper. If you want more, they'll gladly give you more; they'll even give you more if you run out during the exam. And while the scratch sheet is handy for figuring out equations, it's also useful for drawing diagrams and pictures to help you clarify problems in your mind.

Sometimes, drawing a simple diagram can save you loads of time when you're trying to get a quick grasp on how to solve a math word problem. Here's one of my favorite examples:

A ladybug walks 5 inches directly south. She then turns and walks 10 inches directly east. If she then sprouts her wings and flies directly back to her starting point, how far will she have to fly?

This problem becomes instantly clear with a quick diagram on your scratch paper, like the sketch shown here.

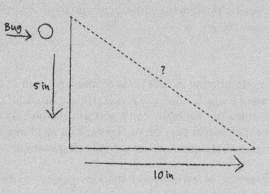

The crudely drawn diagram on your scratch paper makes it instantly clear that you need to find the length of the hypotenuse of a right triangle. If you read Chapter 8, you know that you can use the Pythagorean theorem $\left(a^2 + b^2 = c^2\right)$ to figure out this problem. Without that sketch, you may not realize how simple this problem really is.

Identifying the information you need

After you've separated the question from the statement (see the preceding section), list the facts in a clear, concise list. Identify exactly what the question is asking of you. Figure out what you need but don't have, and name things. Pick variables (a, b, x, and so on) to stand for the unknowns, clearly labeling these variables with what they stand for.

REMEMBER

Be as clear as possible when you identify the information you need. You don't want to spend five minutes on a word problem solving for x, only to reach the end and forget what x is supposed to stand for.

DEALING WITH DISTRACTERS

If math word problems were all straightforward questions, such as "What is 10 multiplied by 10?" you could skip this chapter. However, the people on the Department of Defense's payroll who write the questions stay awake at night to think up ways to complicate things. The use of distracters is one such way.

A *distracter* is any piece of information included in the problem statement that has absolutely nothing to do with solving the problem. Consider the following example:

> In November, the National Weather Service recorded 1 inch of snow and 3 inches of rain in Grand Forks, North Dakota. In December, these numbers were reversed, with 3 inches of snow and only 1 inch of rain. How much snow did Grand Forks receive in total?

You don't need to know how much rain fell in Grand Forks to solve this problem. The amount of rain has absolutely nothing to do with the problem question. It's a distracter; its purpose is to distract you from focusing on the real question. The problem mentions rain, so it has to figure into the problem in some way, doesn't it? Wrong! Be sure to read the question carefully and ignore any information that's just there to trip you up.

TIP

Pay particular attention to include units of measure, such as feet, miles, inches, pounds, dollars, and so on. One of the fastest ways to mess up on a math word problem is by forgetting the apples-and-oranges rule. You generally can't perform mathematical operations on different units of measurement. Ten apples plus ten oranges equals 20 pieces of fruit; it does *not* equal 20 apples, nor does it equal 20 oranges. Look at the following example:

> A carpenter buys 44 feet of wood. If she adds the wood to the 720 inches of wood she already owns, how many feet of wood will she have?

If you add 44 to 720, you're going to get the wrong answer. Before you can add the numbers, you have to either convert 44 feet of wood to inches ($44 \cdot 12 = 528$ inches) or convert 720 inches to feet ($720 \div 12 = 60$ feet).

TIP

Make sure when you select your answer, it has the correct unit of measurement. Those tricky test writers often give several options with different units to make sure you're paying attention and can correctly identify what unit to use.

Translating the problem

Now you're at the tough part. The hardest thing about doing word problems is taking the English words and translating them into mathematics. Luckily, math word problems often contain certain *keywords* that can help.

WARNING

Although the following keywords *often* indicate a mathematical operation in a word problem, that's not always the case. You have to use a little common sense. "A man was walking down the street" doesn't mean a division operation. "Matt and Paul were working *together*" doesn't necessarily mean you're going to perform addition regarding Matt and Paul.

Addition keywords

Several words and phrases used in math word problems indicate an addition operation:

- » Increased by
- » More than
- » Combined
- » Together
- » Total of
- » Sum
- » Added to

"The drill sergeant can do 100 pushups more than Private Jones can" is equivalent to Private Jones + 100 = drill sergeant. "Together, they can do 300 pushups" can be mathematically stated as drill sergeant + Private Jones = 300.

Try the following example, just to see if you're getting the hang of things:

EXAMPLE

The drill sergeant can do 100 pushups more than Private Jones. Together, they can do 300 pushups. How many pushups can Private Jones do?

The question is asking you how many pushups Private Jones can do. You're not really interested in how many the drill sergeant can do, and the problem statement tells you that they can do 300 pushups together. You also know that the drill sergeant can do 100 more than Private Jones.

List the important information:

- » Let j = the number of pushups that Private Jones can do. This figure is what you really want to find out, so you need to define it first.

- » Let d = the number of pushups that the drill sergeant can do. You don't really want to know this information, but it's a necessary fact in order to solve the problem.

- » You know another definition of d. The problem statement tells you that the drill sergeant can do 100 more pushups than Private Jones, which means that $d = j + 100$, which is the same (mathematically) as saying $j = d - 100$.

- » You know that together they can do 300 pushups, which tells you that $d + j = 300$.

All you need to do now is to solve that final equation in terms of j. First, subtract d from both sides to express the equation in terms of j: $d + j = 300$ is the same as $j = 300 - d$. (I cover algebraic properties in Chapter 8.)

You already have a definition for d from above ($d = j + 100$). Substitute this value for d in the equation you're now working to solve:

$$j = 300 - d$$
$$j = 300 - (j + 100)$$
$$j = 300 - j - 100$$
$$2j = 200$$
$$j = 100$$

Private Jones can do 100 pushups.

TIP

As an alternative, you can also substitute "$j + 100$" for d in the equation $d + j = 100$. The answer will be the same.

Even if you can do this particular problem in your head (300 total − 100 more = 200, divide by two to get 100), try to avoid doing so. You want to get in the practice of setting up and solving equations for each question. Often, you'll stumble on a word problem that can be solved only by using an equation, and you want to be an expert at the proper procedures.

REMEMBER

Because math can be a tricky thing (I've been known to believe $2 + 2 = 3$ before my morning coffee), it's always a good idea to check your answer to make sure it makes sense. Plug your answer into the original problem and see whether it works out: The drill sergeant can do 100 pushups more than Private Jones: $100 + 100 = 200$. The drill sergeant can do 200 pushups. Together, they can do 300 pushups: $100 + 200 = 300$. Makes sense.

Subtraction keywords

If you see any of the following words and phrases in a math word problem, it generally indicates a subtraction operation:

>> Decreased by

>> Minus

>> Less

>> Difference between/of

>> Less than

>> Fewer than

"Becky's pay decreased by $10" can be stated mathematically as Becky − 10. This phrasing is also the same as "Becky's pay minus $10," or "Becky's pay, less $10."

"The difference between Bob's pay and Becky's pay" can be expressed as Bob − Becky.

WARNING

The *less than* and *fewer than* terms work backward in English from what they are in the math. Although "Becky's pay minus $10" is Becky − 10, "Becky's pay less than x" is *not* Becky − x; it's x − Becky.

Multiplication keywords

The following words and phrases usually mean a multiplication operation when included in a math word problem:

>> Of

>> Times

>> Multiplied by

>> Product of

>> Increased/decreased by a factor of

"15 percent of x" is mathematically expressed as $x \cdot 0.15$. "x times y" and "x multiplied by y" mean $x \cdot y$. "The product of x and y" is the same as $x \cdot y$.

Increased by a factor of and *decreased by a factor of* can involve addition and subtraction in combination with multiplication. "*x* increased by a factor of 10 percent" is expressed as $x + (x \cdot 0.10)$.

Division keywords

If you see the following words/phrases in a math word problem, "division operation" should pop into your mind:

» A
» Per
» Average
» Ratio of
» Quotient of

The first two terms in this list mean "divided by" — for example, "I bought 2 gallons of milk at the grocery store and paid \$3, so milk was \$1.50 a gallon," or "Milk was \$1.50 per gallon."

To find the average of a group of numbers, you add the numbers and then divide by the number of terms. "The average of *a*, *b*, and *c*" is $(a + b + c) \div 3$.

Mathematically, *ratios* are expressed as fractions. A ratio of five to three is written as $\frac{5}{3}$, which is the same as saying $5 \div 3$. Chapter 8 has more detail about how to work with ratios.

The "quotient of *x* and *y*" is the same as $x \div y$.

Practicing keywords

Learning how to recognize keywords is essential in translating English into mathematical expressions. Try a few examples, just to see if you're getting the hang of it:

» **Translate "the sum of 13 and *y*" into a math expression.** This phrase translates to $13 + y$. The keyword *sum* indicates an addition operation.

» **How do you write "the quotient of *a* and 6" as an expression?** The keyword *quotient* means division, so this example translates to $a \div 6$.

» **How do you write "7 less than *y*" as a mathematical expression?** It's $y - 7$. If you answered $7 - y$, you forgot that "less than" is backward in math from how it's used in English.

» **Translate "the ratio of *x* plus 6 to 8" into an expression.** "*x* plus 6" is an addition operation, while the keyword *ratio* indicates division. This problem translates to $\frac{x + 6}{8}$.

Are you ready to try a couple of longer ones? I knew you were!

» **The length of a rectangle is 45 inches more than its width. Let the width = *w*; express the length in mathematical terms.** *More than* is a keyword that means addition. Because the width = *w*, you write the length mathematically as $w + 45$.

» **Paul is three years older than Marsha, who is four times the age of Brian. Express Marsha's age as an algebraic expression.** You can express Paul's age, Marsha's age, and Brian's age with any variables you choose, but using the first letters of their names just makes sense. That way, you have less chance of forgetting what variable stands for what. "Four *times*" indicates multiplication. Marsha's age can be written as $4 \cdot b$, or $4b$. Paul's age can be expressed as $m + 3$, so Marsha's age can also be written as $p - 3$.

Confused? Check out Chapter 8 for the properties of algebraic equations.

Trying Out Typical Word Problems

When you can recognize common keywords and translate them into mathematical expressions as I describe earlier in the chapter, you're ready to take on a few math word problems.

Because math word problems generally represent fictional real-life situations, the test writers can theoretically come up with an infinite number of possible problems. However, math word problem test writers must have limited imaginations because certain types of questions seem to pop up more often than others. This observation is true whether you're taking the SAT or the Arithmetic Reasoning subtest of the ASVAB.

Age problems

Age problems involve figuring out how old someone is, was, or will be. You generally solve them by comparing someone's age to the ages of other people.

Sometimes you can solve an age problem by using a one-variable solution, and sometimes it takes several variables. In the following sections, I show you how to solve the same problem by using either a one-variable solution or a two-variable solution.

One-variable solution

EXAMPLE

Sid is twice as old as Mary. In three years, the sum of their ages will be 66. How old are they now?

Let Mary's age = x. Because Sid is twice as old as Mary, his age can be represented as $2x$.

In three years, Mary's age will be $x + 3$, and Sid's age will be $2x + 3$. The sum of their ages will be 66.

You now have an equation you can work with:

$$(x+3)+(2x+3)=66$$
$$3x+6=66$$
$$3x=60$$
$$x=\frac{60}{3}$$
$$x=20$$

REMEMBER

What did x stand for again? Was it Mary's age or Sid's age? Be sure to clearly label variables on your scratch paper so you don't get frustrated and tear your hair out in front of everyone else. That causes talk.

The x represents Mary's age, so Mary is 20 years old. Because Sid is twice Mary's age, Sid is 40 $(2 \cdot 20 = 40)$.

REMEMBER

If you have time, check your answer to see that it makes sense: Sid (age 40) is twice as old as Mary (age 20). In three years, the sum of their ages will be $(40 + 3) + (20 + 3) = 43 + 23 = 66$. It fits! Isn't math fun?

Two-variable solution

EXAMPLE

Sid is twice as old as Mary. In three years, the sum of their ages will be 66. How old are they now?

Let m = Mary's age and s = Sid's age. You know that Sid is twice as old as Mary, so $s = 2m$. That gives you your first equation.

You also know that in three years, the sum of their ages will be 66. Stated mathematically:

$$(m+3)+(s+3)=66$$

You can simplify this equation:

$$m+s+6=66$$
$$m+s=60$$

You now have two equations with two variables that you can use to solve the problem:

$$s=2m$$
$$m+s=60$$

Replace s in the second equation with the definition of s in the first equation:

$$m+2m=60$$
$$3m=60$$
$$m=\frac{60}{3}$$
$$m=20$$

Mary is 20 years old. That's the same answer you get when you use the one-variable solution in the preceding section.

Geometric problems

These problems require you to compute the volume, perimeter, area, circumference, diameter, and so on of various geometric shapes.

You're painting a fence that is 20 feet long and 6 feet high. How much square footage of fence are you covering with paint?

EXAMPLE

The area formula for a rectangle is $A = lw$, where l is length and w is width, so the answer to this simple problem is $A = 6 \cdot 20 = 120$ square feet.

Generally, the Arithmetic Reasoning test makers don't let you off so easy, though. The problem is more likely to be written something like the following.

You're painting a fence that is 20 feet long and 6 feet high. Paint costs $20 per gallon, and 1 gallon of paint covers 60 square feet of fence. How much do you need to spend on paint to complete the project?

EXAMPLE

The problem now requires a couple of extra steps to answer. First, you have to compute the area of the fence. You already did that: 120 square feet.

Now you have to determine how many gallons of paint you need to buy to cover 120 square feet. Because 1 gallon of paint covers 60 square feet, you need $120 \div 60 = 2$ gallons of paint.

Finally, you need to figure how much 2 gallons of paint cost. Paint is $20 per gallon, and you need 2 gallons, so $20 \cdot 2 = 40.

You get quite a few geometric problems on the Arithmetic Reasoning subtest. To make sure you're ready for them, memorize the basic geometric formulas in Table 10-1.

TIP

TABLE 10-1   Basic Geometric Formulas

Shape	Function	Formula
Square	Area	$A = s^2$
	Perimeter	$P = 4s$
	Diagonal	$d = s\sqrt{2}$
Rectangle	Area	$A = lw$
	Perimeter	$P = 2l + 2w$
	Diagonal	$d = \sqrt{l^2 + w^2}$
Triangle	Perimeter	$P = s_1 + s_2 + s_3$
	Area	$A = \frac{1}{2}bh$
Right Triangle	Pythagorean theorem	$a^2 + b^2 = c^2$
Circle	Radius	$r = \frac{d}{2}$
	Diameter	$d = 2r$
	Circumference	$C = 2\pi r$
	Area	$A = \pi r^2$
Cube	Volume	$V = s^3$
	Surface Area	$SA = 6s^2$
Rectangular Box	Volume	$V = lwh$
	Surface Area	$SA = 2lw + 2wh + 2lh$
Cylinder	Volume	$V = \pi r^2 h$

TIP

Because many of these formulas relate to each other, remembering (or recreating) them might be easier if you connect them. Remember:

>> Drawing a diagonal through a square or rectangle creates two right triangles, which means the diagonal formulas are just the Pythagorean theorem solved for the hypotenuse.

>> The volume formulas are the area of a base shape (a rectangle or circle) times the height.

>> Surface area formulas for boxes and cubes are based on the area of a rectangle — it's just that you're working with six rectangles instead of one.

You can find more information about using all these formulas in Chapter 8.

Coin problems

I think mathematicians must have big piggy banks. Many math word problems ask you to figure out how many coins of various types a person has.

EXAMPLE

Jeremy has 12 more nickels than quarters. How many coins does he have if the total value of his coins is $2.70?

Let q = quarters. Because Jeremy has 12 more nickels than quarters, you can represent the number of nickels as $q + 12$. Jeremy has $2.70 worth of coins, which is equal to 270¢. A quarter is 25¢, and a nickel is 5¢. Jeremy's total coins together must equal 270¢. Therefore,

$$(25¢ \cdot \text{number of quarters}) + (5¢ \cdot \text{number of nickels}) = 270¢$$

Or, writing it another way:

$$25q + 5(q + 12) = 270$$
$$25q + 5q + 60 = 270$$
$$30q = 210$$
$$q = \frac{210}{30}$$
$$q = 7$$

Jeremy has 7 quarters. Because he has 12 more nickels than quarters, he has $7 + 12 = 19$ nickels, for a total of $19 + 7 = 26$ coins.

Does this answer make sense? Always remember to check your answer. Jeremy has 12 more nickels (19 nickels) than quarters (7 quarters). How much money does he have? 19 nickels = 95¢ and 7 quarters = 175¢, so 95¢ + 175¢ = 270¢ = $2.70. It looks good to me.

Travel problems

I wish I could travel as much as word problem test writers seem to. They come up with a lot of travel problems. They especially seem to like trains and planes.

Travel problems involve using the distance formula, $d = rt$, where d is the distance, r is the rate, and t is the time. Generally, the problems come in three basic types: traveling away from each other, traveling in the same direction, and traveling at 90-degree angles.

Traveling away from each other

When two planes (or trains, cars, people, or even bugs) travel in opposite directions, they increase the distance between them in direct proportion. To solve these types of problems, you compute the distance traveled from the starting point for each plane (or train, car, person, or bug).

EXAMPLE

Train A travels north at 60 mph. Train B travels south at 70 mph. If both trains leave the station at the same time, how far apart will they be at the end of two hours?

To solve this problem, you compute the distance traveled by train A and then the distance traveled by train B and add the results together.

The distance formula is $d = rt$. The rate of travel for train A is 60 mph, and it travels for two hours:

$$d = 60 \times 2$$
$$d = 120$$

Train A travels 120 miles during the two-hour period.

WARNING

When using the distance formula, you have to pay attention to the units of measurement. Remember the apples-and-oranges rule (see "Identifying the information you need" earlier in this chapter). If rate (r) is expressed in kilometers per hour, your result (d) will be kilometers. If rate (r) is expressed as miles per second, you must either convert it to mph or convert time (t) to seconds.

Math word problems require you to make basic assumptions. In the train problem in the section "Traveling away from each other," you're to assume that both trains travel at a constant rate of speed. You're supposed to ignore the fact that they may slow down for a curve, or that they'll probably need a little time to get up to cruising speed.

If a question gives you the average daily output of a factory and asks you what the output will be in a year, you're supposed to assume that the year is 365 days long.

If you're asked how high the kite is flying 300 feet away from you, you must assume that the ground is perfectly level.

If . . . well, you get the point.

The rate of travel for train B is 70 mph, and it also travels for two hours:

$$d = 70 \times 2$$
$$d = 140$$

Train B travels 140 miles during the two-hour period.

Train A is 120 miles from the station and train B is 140 miles from the station, in the opposite direction. The two trains are $120 + 140 = 260$ miles apart.

Traveling in the same direction

If two trains are traveling in the same direction but at different rates of speed, one train travels farther in the same time than the other travels. The distance between the two trains is the difference between the distance traveled by train A and the distance traveled by train B.

EXAMPLE

Train A travels north at 60 mph. Train B also travels north, on a parallel track, at 70 mph. If both trains leave the station at the same time, how far apart will they be at the end of two hours?

Train A traveled 120 miles, and train B traveled 140 miles. (If you're wondering why I didn't show my work here, check out the calculations in the preceding section.) Because they're traveling in the same direction, you subtract to find the distance between them: $140 - 120 = 20$. The two trains are 20 miles apart.

Traveling at 90-degree angles

Some travel problems involve two people or things moving at 90-degree angles and then stopping; the problem then asks you what the distance is (as the crow flies) between the two people or things, which means you need to use the distance formula and a little basic geometry.

EXAMPLE

Train A travels north at 60 mph. Train B travels east at 70 mph. Both trains travel for two hours. Then a bee flies from Train A and lands on Train B. Assuming the bee flew in a straight line, how far did the bee travel between the two trains?

Train A travels 120 miles, and Train B travels a distance of 140 miles. (Head to the earlier section "Traveling away from each other" for the math that gets you those distances.)

Because the trains are traveling at 90-degree angles (one north and one east), the lines of travel form two sides of a right triangle. Figure 10-1 should make this setup easy to visualize.

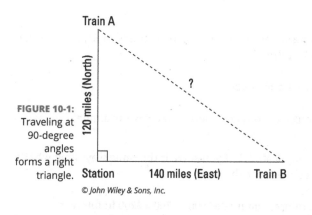

FIGURE 10-1: Traveling at 90-degree angles forms a right triangle.

The Pythagorean theorem says that if you know the length of two sides of a right triangle, you can find the length of the third side by using the formula $a^2 + b^2 = c^2$, where c is the longest side:

$$120^2 + 140^2 = c^2$$
$$14,400 + 19,600 = c^2$$
$$c = \sqrt{34,000}$$
$$c = 184.39$$

The bee flies 184.39 miles. I'm not going to lie: I spent too much time online trying to figure out how far bees can fly. Though a bee technically *could* fly this distance, it would take just under 10 hours if it — wait for it — made a beeline for the second train. (Western honey bees can travel at speeds of up to 20 mph, in case you were wondering.) By then, the trains would probably be on their way somewhere else, so the bee would be better off calling it a day and heading home.

Finding the square root of a very large number can be a little overwhelming, especially because you don't have a calculator available during the ASVAB. When you reach this point of the equation, just squaring the possible answers to see which one works is often easier.

TIP

Investment/loan problems

These problems are primarily focused on simple interest rates for investments and loans, using the formula $I = prt$, where I is the interest, p is the principal, r is the rate of interest, and t is the time.

The investment/loan problems you see on the Arithmetic Reasoning subtest are pretty simple. They're nowhere near as difficult as similar situations in real life, where interest is compounded.

To solve these problems, replace what's known in the interest formula and then solve for anything else.

John invests $1,500 for three years at an annual interest rate of 7 percent. How much will John have at the end of the three-year period?

EXAMPLE

Plug the known information into the interest formula, $I = prt$:

$$I = \$1,500 \times 0.07 \times 3$$
$$I = \$315$$

Percent means "part of 100." To convert percentage into a decimal, divide the percentage by 100.

REMEMBER

That means 7 percent equals $\frac{7}{100}$ and 0.07. To convert a decimal into percentage, multiply by 100. You get $0.07 = 0.07 \cdot 100 = 7$ percent. (Flip to Chapter 9 for more information about working with percentages and decimals.)

John will make $315 in interest. Adding this amount to his original investment of $1,500 tells you that John will have a total of $1,500 + $315 = $1,815.

That was pretty easy, so let me throw another one at you.

EXAMPLE

You invest $700, and after five years you receive a total of $900. What was the annual interest rate?

On the surface, this one looks a bit more complicated, but you solve it the same way: Plug what's known into the interest formula, $I = prt$, and solve for the rest.

You invested $700 and received $900. Therefore, you made $900 – $700 = $200 in interest.

$$\$200 = \$700 \times r \times 5$$
$$\$200 = \$3,500r$$
$$r = \frac{\$200}{\$3,500}$$
$$r = 0.057$$

Expressed as a percentage, this amount is $0.057 \cdot 100 = 5.7$ percent.

Mixture problems

Mixture problems often involve mixing different items at different costs and determining the final cost of the mixture. They can also involve mixing various solutions and determining percentages of the solution mixture. This concept sounds difficult, but it's really pretty easy when you know how. Are you ready to try a couple of problems?

EXAMPLE

How many quarts of a 70-percent alcohol solution must be added to 50 quarts of a 40-percent alcohol solution to produce a 50-percent alcohol solution?

Let x = the number of quarts of 70-percent solution needed. The amount of alcohol contained in x quarts of the 70-percent solution is represented by $0.7x$. (I explain how to convert a percentage into a decimal in the preceding section.)

You have 50 quarts of the 40-percent solution, so the amount of alcohol contained in those 50 quarts is represented by $50 \cdot 0.4 = 20$ quarts.

The total number of quarts of solution can be represented as $50 + x$ (the number of quarts of 40-percent solution plus the unknown number of quarts of 70-percent solution). Half (50 percent) of that solution will be alcohol, so $0.5(50 + x)$.

Maybe Table 10-2 can make this scenario a bit clearer:

TABLE 10-2 Alcohol Mixtures

	Quarts of Solution	Percent Alcohol (as Decimal)	Total Quarts of Alcohol
70% solution	x	0.7	$0.7x$
40% solution	50	0.4	$0.4(50) = 20$
50% solution	$50 + x$	0.5	$0.5(50 + x)$

The fourth column of the table gives you your equation: $0.7x + 20 = 0.5(50 + x)$. First, distribute the 0.5 to the terms in parentheses. Then work the equation as follows:

$$0.7x + 20 = 25 + 0.5x$$
$$0.7x = 5 + 0.5x$$
$$0.7x - 0.5x = 5$$
$$0.2x = 5$$
$$x = \frac{5}{0.2}$$
$$x = 25$$

The final mixture will require 25 quarts of 70-percent solution.

EXAMPLE

A grocery store wants to offer a mixture of green and red grapes to sell for $4.20 per pound. If green grapes cost $3 per pound and red grapes retail for $6 per pound, how many pounds of red grapes should the grocer add to 12 pounds of green grapes to produce the desired mixture?

Let x = the pounds of red grapes. The total amount of grapes will be the pounds of green grapes (12) plus the unknown pounds of red grapes (x), or $12 + x$. The total cost of green grapes at $3 per pound is $12 \cdot \$3 = \$36$.

Red grapes sell for $6 per pound, so their total cost is represented as $6x$.

The total cost of the mixture is to be $4.20 per pound, so you can represent it as $4.2(12 + x)$.

Table 10-2 worked so well for the last problem that I want to use one again. Check out Table 10-3.

TABLE 10-3 Grape Mixtures

Type	Cost per Pound	Pounds	Total Cost
Green	$3	12	$3·12 = $36
Red	$6	x	$6x
Mixture	$4.20	$12 + x$	$4.20(12 + x)$

Again, the last column gives you your equation: $36 + 6x = 4.2(12 + x)$. First, distribute the 4.2 to the terms in parentheses. Then work the equation as follows:

$$36 + 6x = 50.4 + 4.2x$$
$$6x - 4.2x = 50.4 - 36$$
$$1.8x = 14.4$$
$$x = \frac{14.4}{1.8}$$
$$x = 8$$

The mixture will require 8 pounds of red grapes.

Percent problems

Percent problems involve working with percentages, such as discount savings, pay raises, and so on. You often see them on the Arithmetic Reasoning subtest. They're relatively simple to solve.

EXAMPLE

Leroy makes $8.95 per hour. He's such a good worker that his boss gives him a 25-percent raise. How much per hour does Leroy make now?

To find the dollar amount of the raise, multiply Leroy's previous salary by the decimal equivalent of 25 percent: $8.95 \cdot 0.25 = 2.237$. Round this number up to $2.24, just to make Leroy smile. (You can read about rounding decimals in Chapter 9.) Now add the raise to Leroy's original salary: $8.95 + $2.24 = $11.19.

EXAMPLE

Katie is very excited. For only $45, she bought a set of towels that usually sells for $60. What was the percentage of her discount?

Divide the new price by the original price: $45 \div 60 = 0.75$. The new price is 75 percent of the original price, which means Katie's discount was 25 percent.

Work problems

These problems involve two or more people or things working together. You're expected to figure out how long they'll take to complete a task together.

EXAMPLE

Patrick can build a wall in five hours. Dennis can build the same wall in seven hours. How long will they take to build the wall together?

TIP

You can use a general formula to solve such work problems. It's $\frac{a \times b}{a+b}$, where a is the time the first person or thing takes to do the job and b is the time it takes the second person or thing to do the job.

Patrick needs five hours to build the wall, and Dennis seven hours. Plugging the data into the work formula gets you the following:

$$\frac{5 \times 7}{5 + 7} = \frac{35}{12} = 2\frac{11}{12}$$

It will take them $2\frac{11}{12}$ hours to build the wall together.

Wasn't that fun? I bet you're eager to try another one.

EXAMPLE

One hose can fill an aboveground pool in three hours. Another hose will fill it in six hours. How long will filling the pool take using both hoses?

Just plug the numbers into your handy-dandy work equation:

$$\frac{3 \times 6}{3 + 6} = \frac{18}{9} = 2$$

It will take two hours to fill the pool when using both hoses.

Number problems

Number problems are pretty straightforward. The questions ask you to manipulate numbers with basic addition, subtraction, multiplication, or division. Most people find these types of word problems to be pretty easy.

Do you want to try a few, just to get your feet wet? Sure you do.

EXAMPLE

Jesse is a bartender at a local pub. On Friday, he made $27.40 in tips; on Saturday, he made $34.70 in tips; and on Sunday, he made $7 less than he made on Friday. How much did Jesse earn in tips during the three days?

See what I mean? Pretty straightforward. Jesse made $\$27.40 + \$34.70 + (\$27.40 - \$7) = \$82.50$ in tips.

EXAMPLE

Shea ran 1.5 miles in 9:57. The next day, she ran it in 10:02. On the third day, she ran it in 10:07. What is her average time for the 1.5-mile run?

First, convert all the times into seconds, just to make the math a little easier:

$$9:57 = (9 \cdot 60) + 57 = 597 \text{ seconds}$$
$$10:02 = (10 \cdot 60) + 2 = 602 \text{ seconds}$$
$$10:07 = (10 \cdot 60) + 7 = 607 \text{ seconds}$$

Add the seconds together: $597 + 602 + 607 = 1{,}806$ seconds. Now, divide by the number of times Shea ran the 1.5-mile run (three times) to discover that her average speed is $1{,}806 \div 3 = 602$ seconds. Finally, convert the seconds to minutes by dividing by 60: $602 \div 60 = 10$ minutes, with 2 seconds left over. Shea's average time for the 1.5-mile run is 10:02.

EXAMPLE

The sum of two consecutive odd positive numbers is 112. What are the numbers?

As I note in the "Addition keywords" section earlier in this chapter, *sum* means addition. Let $n =$ the first number. That means that $n + 2 =$ the second number (because they're consecutive *odd* numbers). Here's your equation:

$$n + (n + 2) = 112$$

Solve for *n*:

$$2n + 2 = 112$$
$$2n = 110$$
$$n = \frac{110}{2}$$
$$n = 55$$

The first number is 55. The second number is $55 + 2 = 57$.

Practical Mathematicals: Arithmetic Reasoning Exercises

Just like your physical fitness level will inch up the more you conduct PT (that's short for *physical training*) with your fellow servicemembers, you'll get better at solving word problems with more practice. Use these exercises to gauge your performance and figure out where you need to break more of a mental sweat. The answers to each practice exercise are at the end of this chapter, so head there when you're finished with each activity to check your work.

Fact-finding to figure out which formulas to use

In Chapter 6, I mention that some of the ASVAB's Paragraph Comprehension questions require you to go into a passage and pull out facts. Just add math, and you have Arithmetic Reasoning questions. You'll have to figure out what problem the question is asking you to solve and then determine which formula you need to solve it. (There's more on specific formulas in Chapter 8.) Read the sentences in Activity 1 and, in the column next to the problem, write which formula(s) you'll need to solve a problem with that type of sentence in it. When you're done, check out the "Answers and Explanations" section at the end of this chapter to see how many you got right.

ACTIVITY 1 Fact-Finding

Problem	Required Formula
1. Two people are traveling in opposite directions.	
2. Find the area of a rectangle with dimensions of x by y.	
3. The diameter of a circle is x. Find its area.	
4. Someone invested x for y years and receives z percent in interest.	
5. Two people worked together to do something.	
6. Find the area of a triangle with sides measuring x and y.	
7. Find the circumference of a circle with a radius of x.	
8. Find the length of a side of a right triangle.	
9. Find the volume of a swimming pool with sides of x and y and a depth of z.	
10. Find the perimeter of a yard that is x feet long and y feet wide.	

Real-world formula problems

In Activity 1, you determined which formulas to use for specific types of problems. In Activity 2, you do something similar — but this time, you match the appropriate formula to the word problem provided. (Save your actual problem-solving for Chapter 12, where you'll take your first ASVAB practice test.) When you're finished, check the "Answers and Explanations" section at the end of this chapter.

ACTIVITY 2 Applying Formulas to Problems

Answer	Question	Formula
1.	A circular swimming pool measures 15 feet across. What is its circumference?	A. $I = prt$
2.	Mary and Shelley are filling the swimming pool for Frank. It takes Shelley 5 hours to fill the pool alone, and it takes Mary 8 hours. How long will it take them together?	B. $t = \dfrac{d}{r}$
3.	Two dogs, Tonka and Cujo, are running north and east, respectively. Cujo runs 15 miles, while Tonka runs 13 miles. When they're done, another dog, Achilles, runs in a straight line from Cujo to Tonka. How far did Achilles travel between the two dogs?	C. $V = s^3$
4.	Abigail and Matthew invest \$2,500 for four years at an annual interest rate of 3.5 percent. How much will they have at the end of four years?	D. $\dfrac{a \times b}{a + b}$
5.	A gift box measures 12 inches across on each side, and it's 14 inches deep. What is the gift box's volume?	E. $A = \dfrac{1}{2}bh$
6.	You're painting a wall that's 11 feet high and 13 feet long. How many square feet will you paint?	F. $P = 2l + 2w$
7.	A man traveled 86 miles at a speed of 7 miles per hour. How long did it take him?	G. $C = 2\pi r$
8.	A woman is ordering prefabricated fencing for her yard, which is 45 feet long and 38 feet wide. How many feet of fencing should she order?	H. $A = lw$
9.	Three people put their money together and bought a square safe. One side of the safe is 13 inches long, and it's an inch thick all around. How much room is left inside the safe?	I. $V = lwh$
10.	You want to pass a triangle-shaped note in math class, but you know your eagle-eyed teacher can see notes that have an area of more than 4 square inches. Is a triangle-shaped piece of paper with a 3.5-inch base and a height of 2.5 inches small enough to pass in class?	J. $a^2 + b^2 = c^2$

Putting together tables to make calculations easier

In many cases, sketching a table to help you solve a problem can be a huge help — especially when you're pressed for time (check out "Mixture problems" earlier in this chapter for a little more guidance). Creating a table can give you the equation you need to solve the problem, so use Activity 3 to practice drawing your own table and coming up with an equation that solves the problem. When you're done (or if you're not sure what to do next), flip to the "Answers and Explanations" section at the end of this chapter.

ACTIVITY 3 Creating Tables

Question	Your Table	Your Equation
1. A scientist needs to add a 70-percent alcohol solution to 30 gallons of a 20-percent alcohol solution to create a 50-percent alcohol solution. How many quarts of the 70-percent alcohol solution is necessary?		
2. A candy shop is selling a combination of caramels and chocolate-covered pretzels for $5 per pound. Caramels cost $4 per pound, and chocolate-covered pretzels cost $6 per pound. How many pounds of pretzels should the shopkeeper add to 10 pounds of caramel to produce the right mixture?		
3. A pilot in the D.C. National Guard flew 600 nautical miles. For the first part of the 7-hour trip, he flew at 150 knots. For the last part of the trip, he flew at 130 knots. How long did he fly the helicopter at each speed?		
4. How many pounds of carrots that cost $0.80 per pound must be mixed with 8 pounds of celery, which costs $1.25 per pound, to create a mixture that costs $1 per pound?		
5. A river flows at about 2 miles per hour. A motorboat can travel 15 miles down the river (with the current) in the same amount of time it takes to travel 10 miles up the river (against the current). How fast is the boat in still water?		

Answers and Explanations

After you've completed the exercises, check your answers here. If you don't quite grasp the concepts you need for the Arithmetic Reasoning subtest, go back to the appropriate sections earlier in this chapter to brush up on them.

Activity 1: Fact-Finding

1. Travel problems require you to use the distance formula, which is $d = rt$, where d represents distance, r represents rate (speed), and t represents time. You can also use variations of the formula to find speed and time; just isolate the variable you need. (For example, you can find speed if you know distance and time by using the formula $r = \dfrac{d}{t}$, and you can find time when you know distance and speed by using the formula $t = \dfrac{d}{r}$.)

2. The formula for the area of a rectangle is $A = lw$, where A represents area, l represents length, and w represents width.

3. The formula for the area of a circle is $A = \pi r^2$, where A represents area and r represents radius. (Remember, a circle's radius is half its diameter, and pi is about equal to 3.14.)

4. You can figure out this type of simple-interest problem using the formula $I = prt$, where I represents interest, p represents principal, r represents the interest rate, and t represents time. (You can figure out principal with the formula $p = \dfrac{I}{rt}$, the interest rate with the formula $r = \dfrac{I}{pt}$, and the amount of time for the investment with the formula $t = \dfrac{I}{pr}$.)

5. Work problems are best solved with the formula $\dfrac{a \times b}{a + b}$, where a represents one person's work and b represents the other person's work.

6. The formula to find the area of a triangle is $A = \dfrac{1}{2}bh$, where A represents area, b represents the length of the base, and h represents the triangle's height.

7. If you know a circle's radius or diameter (radius is half of the diameter), you can find a circle's circumference (the distance all the way around the outside) using the formula $C = 2\pi r$, where C represents circumference and r represents the circle's radius.

8. You have to find the length of a side of a right triangle in problems that ask you to determine the distance between two objects traveling at a 90-degree angle, which means you need the Pythagorean theorem. It's $a^2 + b^2 = c^2$. In the Pythagorean theorem, a and b represent the lengths of the triangle's legs (the two sides that form a right angle), and c represents its hypotenuse.

9. The formula to find the volume of a box (or rectangular prism) is $V = lwh$, where V represents volume, l represents length, and h represents height. You can also find the volume of a cube, in which all the sides are equal, by using the formula $V = s^3$, where V still represents volume and s represents the length of one side.

10. The formula to find the perimeter of a rectangle is $P = 2l + 2w$, where P represents perimeter, l represents length, and w represents width. If you're dealing with a square, the formula is just $P = 4s$, where P represents perimeter and s represents the length of one of its sides.

Activity 2: Applying Formulas to Problems

1. **G.** The problem asks you to find the circumference of a circle, and the formula for that is $C = 2\pi r$, where C represents circumference and r represents the circle's radius. Remember, the radius of a circle is half its diameter.

2. **D.** The formula to solve a work problem that asks you how long it will take two people together to accomplish a task is $\frac{a \times b}{a + b}$.

3. **J.** Because this problem deals with a right triangle (the two dogs are running north and east, which forms a right angle, and the third dog travels from one dog to the other), you can use the Pythagorean theorem, which is $a^2 + b^2 = c^2$, to solve it. First, you have to figure out how far each dog got while running for 30 minutes. When you've done that, you can use the Pythagorean theorem to get an answer (and tell the dogs' owners to start using leashes). In this formula, a and b represent Tonka's and Cujo's distances.

4. **A.** Investment and loan problems can typically be solved with the interest formula, which is $I = prt$. I stands for interest, p represents the principal, r represents the interest rate, and t represents the amount of time you're evaluating.

5. **I.** You need to find the volume of a rectangular prism (or box), and the formula for that is $V = lwh$, where V represents volume, l represents length, w represents width, and h represents height.

6. **H.** When a problem asks you, "How many square feet...," it's looking for an area. The formula for the area of a rectangle is $A = lw$, where A represents area, l represents length, and w represents width.

7. **B.** Modify the distance formula so you can figure out how long it took the man to travel 86 miles at 7 miles per hour; you use $t = \frac{d}{r}$, where t represents time, d represents distance, and r represents rate (or speed).

8. **F.** The problem asks you to find the perimeter of a rectangle, and the formula for that is $P = 2l + 2w$, where P represents perimeter, l represents length, and w represents width.

9. **C.** In this problem, you need to use the formula for the volume of a cube, which is $V = s^3$, where V represents volume and s represents the length of a side.

10. **E.** If you want to sneak the note past the teacher, you need to figure out the area of a triangle. The formula for that is $A = \frac{1}{2}bh$, where A represents area, b represents the length of the base, and h represents the triangle's height. (For the record, the triangle-shaped note in the problem would've gotten you detention.)

Activity 3: Creating Tables

1. Your table should look like this:

	Gallons of Solution	Percent of Alcohol	Total Gallons of Alcohol Solution
70% solution	x	0.7	$0.7x$
20% solution	30	0.3	$0.3(50) = 15$
50% solution	$50 + x$	0.5	$0.5(50 + x)$

2. The table tells you that your equation will be $0.7x + 15 = 0.5(50 + x)$.

3. Your table should look like this:

Candy Type	Cost per Pound	Pounds	Total Cost
Caramels	$4	10	$4 \times 10 = 40$
Pretzels	$6	x	$6x$
Mixture	$5	$10 + x$	$5(10 + x)$

4. Your table tells you your equation should be $40 + 6x = 5(10 + x)$.

5. Your table should look like this:

	Distance	Rate	Time
First part of trip	d	150	t
Last part of trip	$600 - d$	130	$7 - t$
Total	600		7

6. The table tells you that, using the distance formula ($d = rt$) — where d represents distance, r represents rate (speed), and t represents time — your equation will look like this: $600 - d = 130(7 - t)$.

7. Your table should look like this:

	Total Cost	Price per Pound	Amount in Pounds
Carrots	$0.8x$	$0.80	x
Celery	10	$1.25	8
Mixture	$x + 8$	$1.00	$x + 8$

8. Based on what's in the table, your equation should be $0.8x + 10 = x + 8$.

9. Your table should look like this:

	Distance	Rate	Time
Downriver	15	$x + 2$	$\dfrac{15}{x+2}$
Upriver	10	$x - 2$	$\dfrac{9}{x-2}$

10. The table shows you that your equation to find the boat's speed should be $\dfrac{15}{x+2} = \dfrac{9}{x-2}$.

Chapter **11**

The Arithmetic Reasoning Subtest

The ASVAB has two math subtests — Mathematics Knowledge and Arithmetic Reasoning — and both are used for computing your AFQT score. Of the two, the Arithmetic Reasoning subtest may be considered the more difficult for most people (probably because you first have to decide what the problem is before you can solve it).

Among other things, math word problems measure your reasoning skills. That's why the military services put so much emphasis on this particular subtest. They want recruits who can figure things out — recruits who can solve problems.

REMEMBER

If you're starting to get nervous, don't. You've been doing arithmetic word problems since the third grade. Sure, they're a little more difficult now than when Mrs. Grundy was telling you that you had three apples and gave one to Tammy, but the fact is, this material isn't new for you. You've done it before. The military is just asking you to do it again, that's all.

I'm here to help you get ready. In this chapter, I tell you what you can expect on the Arithmetic Reasoning subtest, give you a few methods that may help improve your score and get you through those rough spots, and then — just for fun — toss a few practice questions at you. For help on the Mathematics Knowledge subtest, check out Chapters 8 and 9.

Looking at the Test Structure

The Arithmetic Reasoning subtest is the second subtest on the ASVAB, right after the General Science subtest. Therefore, it's the first subtest you encounter on the ASVAB that affects your AFQT score.

The Arithmetic Reasoning subtest asks you to read a word problem, determine what the question is asking, solve the problem with mathematics, and select the correct answer. (Then you have to repeat the process numerous times.) Most of the problems look like this:

EXAMPLE

Janae walks 5 miles to work each morning and 5 miles home each evening. How many miles does Janae walk in a day?

(A) 6 miles

(B) 8 miles

(C) 7 miles

(D) 10 miles

I hope you picked Choice (D), 10 miles! That was an easy question just to get you warmed up. Unfortunately, the questions the military writes are a bit tougher.

You have 55 minutes to answer 15 questions for the CAT-ASVAB (computerized version); if you happen to take the paper test, you must answer 30 questions in 36 minutes (makes sense, doesn't it?).

You see a mixture of hard questions, medium questions, and easy questions on this subtest. The hard ones are worth more points than the medium ones, which are worth more points than the easy ones. If you're taking the CAT-ASVAB (see Chapter 1), the computer automatically selects the question difficulty based on how you answered the preceding question. If you're really good at math word problems, you may only see hard questions!

The test administrator supplies you with scratch paper so you can work out some of the problems on paper, if necessary. The people who make up the rules don't allow recruits (or anyone else) to use calculators on the ASVAB. All you're allowed is your brain, your trusty No. 2 pencil, and scratch paper.

Developing a Test Strategy

The U.S. military doesn't win wars without a strategy, and you should have a set strategy for conquering the Arithmetic Reasoning subtest. A strategy is more than "I'll try to solve all the problems quickly and correctly." That works fine if everything goes right and you know how to solve the questions instantly when you see them, but the test probably won't go that way. Your strategy needs to include plans to keep things going smoothly, as well as ideas of what to do if things start going wrong.

Keeping track of the time

This chapter is supposed to be about the Arithmetic Reasoning subtest, so I think it's time for a practice question. Ready?

EXAMPLE

You have to take a math test consisting of 30 multiple-choice questions. You have 36 minutes to complete the test. How much time do you have for each question?

(A) 1 minute, 12 seconds

(B) 90 seconds

(C) 1 minute

(D) 1 minute, 20 seconds

First, convert the minutes to seconds so you don't have to deal with fractions or decimals: $36 \times 60 = 2,160$ seconds. Now, divide the total number of seconds by the number of test questions: $2,160 \div 30 = 72$ seconds. You have 72 seconds, or Choice (A), 1 minute and 12 seconds, to complete each question.

You can take a different approach by simplifying the problem before you start to solve it, too. Look at it this way: You know you have more than a minute for each question, because there are more minutes than there are questions (if you had less than a minute, there would be more questions than there are minutes). If 30 questions take at least 30 minutes, you can divide the remaining 6 minutes you have (remember, you get 36 minutes to complete the test) among the 30 questions:

$$\frac{360 \text{ seconds}}{30 \text{ questions}} = \frac{36 \text{ seconds}}{3 \text{ questions}} = 12 \text{ seconds per question}$$

Add the 12 seconds per question to the 1 minute you knew you had when you started. You still have 1 minute, 12 seconds to answer each question.

You can also leave the time in minutes until the end of the problem by creating a ratio and reducing it:

$$\frac{36 \text{ minutes}}{30 \text{ questions}} = \frac{6 \text{ minutes}}{5 \text{ questions}} = 1.2 \text{ minutes per question}$$

Now convert the 0.2 minutes to seconds:

$$0.2 \text{ minutes} = (0.2)(60 \text{ seconds}) = 12 \text{ seconds}$$

No matter which way you solve it, you still get a minute and 12 seconds to solve each problem.

That's not much time, considering that you have to read the question, determine what it's asking, translate the problem into mathematical equations, solve those equations, and then answer the question — and, if you have time, check your answer. But that's how Arithmetic Reasoning goes, at least on the paper test.

If you're taking the computerized version of the ASVAB, the time remaining for the subtest ticks down right there on your computer screen. If you're taking the paper version of the ASVAB, you'll see a large clock clearly visible somewhere on the wall. The test proctor also posts the start time and end time of the subtest where you can easily see it.

TIP

Don't spend too much time on any one question. If a question is stumping you, admit defeat, choose an answer (see the "Logical guessing" section later in this chapter), and move on. You don't want to find yourself in a position where you only have 15 minutes left and you're on question 3.

Choosing an answer and checking it twice

Checking your answer to ensure it makes sense in relation to the question is always a good idea if you have time. You don't always have time on the Arithmetic Reasoning subtest, but if you find yourself running ahead of the clock, take a few seconds to check your answer by running through the calculations again, trying a different method to solve the problem, or simply making sure the answer seems reasonable.

TIP

Don't assume that the answer you got is correct just because it's one of the answer choices. Those crafty test makers often use common mistakes as possible answer choices.

If you're taking the paper version of the ASVAB, you should also leave enough time at the end of the subtest to check and make sure you've marked your answer sheet correctly. Make sure the answer blocks are completely filled in, and make sure you didn't make the rookie mistake of answering the wrong question with the right answer.

Using the answer choices: There's more than one way to solve an equation

If you're stumped and just can't seem to write equations to solve a problem, you can often answer the question by seeing which of the answer choices works. Look at the following example:

EXAMPLE

The product of two consecutive negative even integers is 24. Find the lower number.

(A) −2

(B) −4

(C) −6

(D) −7

Say you set up an algebra problem; you decide that if you let the lower integer be n, then $n(n+2) = 24$. Correctly solving this problem involves factoring a quadratic equation (see the end of this section if that sentence scares you). Perhaps quadratic equations aren't your cup of tea, and you get stuck at $n^2 + 2n - 24 = 0$. (If so, Chapter 8 may be of some help.) But before giving up and making a wild guess, try seeing which of the answer choices works:

> ➤ **−2:** No negative even integer is larger than −2, so Choice (A) doesn't work.

> ➤ **−4:** $-4 \times -2 = 8$, so Choice (B) doesn't work.

> ➤ **−6:** $-6 \times -4 = 24$. Choice (C) works!

WARNING

Don't test all the answer choices unless you're absolutely stuck. It can use up a lot of time. In essence, you're computing the problem (up to) three times; if you're confident in your first three efforts, you may as well just pick the last answer.

There are other ways to settle on the right answer, too. Maybe you automatically thought of factors of 24, noted that 4 and 6 are consecutive even numbers, and turned them into negative numbers. Or maybe you recognized that 24 is very near the square number 25, which equals 5×5, so you knew that consecutive even factors of 24 would probably be 4 and 6, the even numbers just above and below 5. No matter which way you look at it, knowing there are usually a handful of ways to solve a problem can help you get over hurdles meant to trip you up on the ASVAB.

Thought I forgot about the original problem? Here's the "proper" (algebraic) way to solve it. Let the first integer equal n. Then the next consecutive even integer is $n+2$.

$$n(n+2) = 24$$
$$n^2 + 2n = 24$$
$$n^2 + 2n - 24 = 0$$
$$(n+6)(n-4) = 0$$
$$n = -6 \text{ and } n = 4$$

The answer can't be 4, because the problem asks for a negative number. The first number (the smallest, n) is −6, which means the second number ($n+2$) is −4.

Logical guessing

Sometimes nothing else works, and you just have to guess. If you're taking the paper version of the ASVAB, you can always skip the hard questions and go back to them when you finish the other questions. If you choose to do so, remember to leave enough time to go back and answer, even if your method is "eeny-meeny-miny-mo." There is no penalty for wrong answers on the paper version of the ASVAB. If you get the question wrong, you get zero points. If you leave the answer blank, you also get zero points. If you make a wild guess, you have at least a one in four chance of getting the answer right and getting points. Be careful, however, of guessing on a series of questions at the end of the test if you're taking the computer version. If you give a lot of wrong answers toward the end of the CAT-ASVAB, the computer dings you in the score department because it's programmed to believe you mismanaged your time.

You can't skip questions on the CAT-ASVAB. The computer doesn't present you with the next question until you answer the current one. Unfortunately, you don't have the option of going back and giving the question another try when you finish the rest of the subtest. You have to decide whether to use more of your precious time to figure it out or guess and move on.

Guessing doesn't have to be wild, however. Sometimes you can improve your chances by eliminating obviously wrong answers. Consider the brain stumper from the preceding section:

EXAMPLE

The product of two consecutive negative even integers is 24. Find the lower number.

(A) −2

(B) −4

(C) −6

(D) −7

Choice (A) is obviously incorrect because no number larger than −2 can be both negative and even. You can quickly see that Choice (D) is wrong because it's an odd number, and the question is asking for a negative even number. Now, if you have to guess, you've just changed the odds from a one in four chance to a 50/50 chance.

Taking Arithmetic Reasoning out for a Spin

I promised you a chance to practice, and here it is. In this section, I give you ten fairly simple math word problems, similar to what you see on the Arithmetic Reasoning subtest.

Don't worry about time here; use these questions to get used to the general test structure and to practice some of the concepts from this chapter and Chapter 10. When you're ready, you can move on to the full-blown AFQT practice tests that start in Chapter 12.

1. If apples are on sale at 15 for $3, what is the cost of each apple?

    (A) 50¢

    (B) 25¢

    (C) 20¢

    (D) 30¢

2. A noncommissioned officer challenged her platoon of 11 enlisted women to beat her record of performing a 26-mile training run in four hours. If all the enlisted women match her record, how many miles will they have run?

    (A) 71.5 miles

    (B) 6.5 miles

    (C) 286 miles

    (D) 312 miles

3. Carter gets their hair cut and colored at an expensive salon in town. They are expected to leave a 15 percent tip for services. If a haircut is $45 and a color treatment is $150, how much of a tip should Carter leave?

   (A) $22.50
   (B) $29.25
   (C) $20.00
   (D) $195.00

4. A bag of sand holds 1 cubic foot of sand. How many bags of sand are needed to fill a square sandbox measuring 5 feet long and 1 foot high?

   (A) 5 bags
   (B) 10 bags
   (C) 15 bags
   (D) 25 bags

5. The day Samantha arrived at Space Force boot camp on the lunar surface, the temperature reached a high of 90 degrees in the shade and a low of −20 degrees at night. What is the average between the high and low temperatures for the day?

   (A) 35 degrees
   (B) 45 degrees
   (C) 70 degrees
   (D) 62 degrees

6. Beth has received an offer to sell her 320-acre farm for $3,000 per acre. She agrees to give the buyer $96,000 worth of land. What fraction of Beth's land is the buyer getting?

   (A) $\frac{1}{4}$
   (B) $\frac{1}{10}$
   (C) $\frac{1}{5}$
   (D) $\frac{2}{3}$

7. A map is drawn so that 1 inch equals 3 miles. On the map, the distance from Kansas City to Denver is 192.5 inches. How far is the round trip from Kansas City to Denver in miles?

   (A) 192.5 miles
   (B) 577.5 miles
   (C) 385 miles
   (D) 1,155 miles

8. Jakson and Julian can sell their store for $150,000. They plan to divide the proceeds according to the ratio of the money they each invested in the business. Jakson put in the most money, at a 3:2 ratio to Julian. How much money should Julian get from the sale?

   (A) $50,000
   (B) $30,000
   (C) $60,000
   (D) $90,000

9. In the military, $\frac{1}{4}$ of an enlisted person's time is spent sleeping and eating, $\frac{1}{12}$ is spent standing at attention, $\frac{1}{6}$ is spent staying fit, and $\frac{2}{5}$ is spent working. The rest of the time is spent at the enlisted person's own discretion. How many hours per day does this discretionary time amount to?

   (A) 6 hours
   (B) 1.6 hours
   (C) 2.4 hours
   (D) 3.2 hours

10. Train A is headed east at 55 mph. Train B is also heading east on an adjacent track at 70 mph. At the end of four hours, how much farther will train B have traveled than train A?

    (A) 40 miles
    (B) 50 miles
    (C) 60 miles
    (D) 70 miles

11. Lifeguards at a community pool may work no more than 6-hour shifts from Monday through Friday and 8-hour shifts on Saturday and Sunday. Last week, Bianca, Crisean, Genesis, Charles, and India each worked six fewer hours than Sailor worked. Sailor worked the maximum allowable number of hours on Monday, Tuesday, Friday, Saturday, and Sunday. How much money did Crisean earn last week if he makes $25 per hour?

    (A) $650
    (B) $700
    (C) $750
    (D) It's impossible to tell.

12. A group of college professors divided their students into groups of three. Each group wrote a report containing 9 pictures. If the students used 585 pictures altogether, how many students were there in all?

(A) 21

(B) 65

(C) 130

(D) 195

13. Katarina and Bonnie drove 2,000 miles from West Bloomfield, Michigan, to Las Vegas, Nevada. If they drove 6 hours per day at an average of 60 miles per hour, about how many days did it take them to reach Las Vegas?

(A) 5.5

(B) 6

(C) 7

(D) 7.5

14. Maria and Robert have 40 chickens and rabbits. If there are 100 legs in the barnyard, how many chickens are there?

(A) 25

(B) 30

(C) 32

(D) 35

15. Dante wanted to give his mom a plant for her birthday. She has an empty rectangular pot that measures 8 inches long, 6 inches wide, and 6 inches tall. How many cubic inches of soil does Dante need to buy at the home improvement store to fill the pot to the top?

(A) 480

(B) 240

(C) 270

(D) 288

Answers and Explanations

Use this answer key to score the practice Arithmetic Reasoning questions.

1. **C.** Divide $3 by 15.

2. **C.** Multiply 26×11. The other information in the question is irrelevant; it's there to throw you off.

3. **B.** Add $45 and $150 and multiply the answer by 15 percent, or 0.15. A shortcut: Find 15 percent of the original $150, which is $22.50. The only choice possible is Choice (B) because it's the only one that's a little higher than $22.50. You can estimate to solve this problem, too, because $150 + $45 is about $200, and 15 percent of $200 is $30; Choice (B) is the closest answer.

4. **D.** The volume formula for a square or rectangular box is $V = lwh$, so $V = 5 \times 5 \times 1 = 25$ cubic feet. Each bag holds 1 cubic foot of sand.

5. **A.** Add the two temperatures given and then divide by the number of terms, 2:
$(90 + -20) \div 2 = 70 \div 2 = 35$.

6. **B.** $96,000 divided by $3,000 (the price per acre) equals 32 acres, and 32 acres divided by 320 acres (the total size of the farm) equals 10 percent, or $\frac{1}{10}$ of the land. *Tip:* You may find the division easier if you write this problem out as a fraction and reduce it, like this:

$$\frac{96,000}{3,000} = \frac{96,\cancel{000}}{3,\cancel{000}} = \frac{96}{3} = 32$$

7. **D.** Multiply 192.5×3 to get the distance in miles, and then double the answer to account for both legs of the trip.

8. **C.** According to the ratio, Jakson should get $\frac{3}{5}$ of the money, and Julian should get $\frac{2}{5}$ of the money. You calculate these fractions by adding both sides of the ratio together $(3 + 2 = 5)$ to determine the denominator. Each side of the ratio then becomes a numerator, so Jakson's investment is $\frac{3}{5}$ of the total investment, and Julian's is $\frac{2}{5}$ of the total investment. (You can check these fractions by adding $\frac{3}{5}$ and $\frac{2}{5}$ to get $\frac{5}{5}$ or 1, which is all the money.) Divide $150,000 by 5, and then multiply the answer by 2 to determine Julian's share of the money.

9. **C.** Calculate this answer by first assigning a common denominator of 60 to all the fractions and adjusting the numerators accordingly: $\frac{15}{60}, \frac{5}{60}, \frac{10}{60}, \frac{24}{60}$. Add the fractions to find out how much time is allotted to all these tasks. The total is $\frac{54}{60}$, which leaves $\frac{6}{60}$ or $\frac{1}{10}$ of the day to the enlisted person's discretion. $\frac{1}{10}$ of 24 hours is 2.4 hours.

10. **C.** The distance formula is $d = rt$. Plug in the known values:

   - Train A: $d = 55 \times 4 = 220$ miles
   - Train B: $d = 70 \times 4 = 280$ miles

Train B traveled $280 - 220 = 60$ miles farther than train A.

You can also find the difference in speed, and then multiply by 4:

$70 - 55 = 15$ and $15 \times 4 = 60$.

11. **B.** Crisean made $700. Don't let the wordy nature of this math problem distract you — it doesn't matter how many hours Bianca, Genesis, Charles, or India worked; only Sailor's and Crisean's hours matter. The problem tells you that Sailor worked 34 hours last week (she worked the maximum allowable shifts on Monday, Tuesday, Friday, Saturday and Sunday, so three six-hour shifts and two eight-hour shifts). Crisean worked six fewer hours than Sailor did, so he clocked in at 28 hours. Multiply 28 by $25 to get $700, which is what Crisean earned (before taxes, of course).

12. **D.** There were 195 students. First, divide the total number of pictures by 9; that tells you how many groups there were. $585 \div 9 = 65$, so there were 65 groups. There were three students per group, so multiply 65 by 3 to get 195.

13. **A.** Katarina and Bonnie drove six hours per day at about 60 miles per hour, so they traveled a total of 360 miles every day. The trip is 2,000 miles, so divide 2,000 by 360; that's approximately 5.5, so that's how long it took the pair to get across the country.

14. **B.** These types of problems — sometimes called *heads and legs problems* — are easiest to solve if you know how to build an equation. In this case, you need to know how many two-legged chickens and four-legged rabbits there are. There are 100 legs and 40 heads in this problem. Let r represent rabbits and c represent chickens. To figure out the number of legs, let $4r$ represent the rabbits and $2c$ represent the chickens (rabbits have four each, while chickens have two).

$$100 = 4r + 2c$$
$$40 = r + c$$

Shuffle the heads around first to find the value of r: $r = 40 - c$. Then, replace the variable r in the first equation with $40 - c$.

$$100 = 4(40 - c) + 2c$$
$$100 = 160 - 4c + 2c$$
$$100 = -2c + 160$$
$$100 - 160 = -2c$$
$$-60 = -2c$$
$$\frac{-60}{-2} = \frac{-2c}{2}$$
$$c = 30$$

That tells you there are 30 chickens in the barnyard. The rest of the animals — all 10 of them — must be rabbits. (Check your work by counting legs — 30 chickens have 60 legs, and 10 rabbits have 40 legs — $60 + 40 = 100$.)

15. **D.** This question asks you to find the volume of a rectangular prism; that's the pot's shape. To do that, you need the formula $V = lwh$, where V represents volume, l represents length, w represents width, and h represents height. Plug in what you know:

$$V = (8)(6)(6)$$
$$V = 288$$

Dante needs 288 cubic inches of dirt to fill the pot to the brim.

AFQT Practice Exams

4

Take four practice AFQT exams that simulate the paper version of the Arithmetic Reasoning, Word Knowledge, Paragraph Comprehension, and Mathematics Knowledge subtests.

Score your tests and check your answers to see which topics you've mastered and which topics you need to spend more time on.

Chapter **12**
Practice Exam 1

The Armed Forces Qualification Test (AFQT) consists of four of the 10 subtests given on the Armed Services Vocational Aptitude Battery (ASVAB). The four subtests used to determine your AFQT score are Arithmetic Reasoning, Word Knowledge, Paragraph Comprehension, and Mathematics Knowledge.

Your AFQT score is very important. Although all the ASVAB subtests are used to determine which military jobs you may qualify for, the AFQT score determines whether you're even qualified to join the military. All the military service branches have established minimum AFQT scores, according to their needs (see Chapter 1 for more information).

The AFQT is not a stand-alone test (it's part of the ASVAB), but in this chapter, I present the subtests applicable to the AFQT in the same order in which you'll encounter them when you take the actual ASVAB.

After you complete the entire practice test, check your answers against the answer key in Chapter 13.

REMEMBER

The test is scored by comparing your raw score to the scores of other people, which produces a scaled score. So just because you missed a total of 20 questions doesn't mean that your score is 80. (That would be too simple.) Turn to Chapter 1 to find out how the AFQT score is derived from these four subtests.

Your goal in taking this practice test is to determine which areas you may still need to study. If you miss only one question on the Word Knowledge subtest, but you miss 15 questions on Arithmetic Reasoning, you probably want to devote some extra study time to developing your math skills before you take the ASVAB.

Answer Sheet for Practice Exam 1

Part 1: Arithmetic Reasoning

1. Ⓐ Ⓑ Ⓒ Ⓓ
2. Ⓐ Ⓑ Ⓒ Ⓓ
3. Ⓐ Ⓑ Ⓒ Ⓓ
4. Ⓐ Ⓑ Ⓒ Ⓓ
5. Ⓐ Ⓑ Ⓒ Ⓓ
6. Ⓐ Ⓑ Ⓒ Ⓓ

7. Ⓐ Ⓑ Ⓒ Ⓓ
8. Ⓐ Ⓑ Ⓒ Ⓓ
9. Ⓐ Ⓑ Ⓒ Ⓓ
10. Ⓐ Ⓑ Ⓒ Ⓓ
11. Ⓐ Ⓑ Ⓒ Ⓓ
12. Ⓐ Ⓑ Ⓒ Ⓓ

13. Ⓐ Ⓑ Ⓒ Ⓓ
14. Ⓐ Ⓑ Ⓒ Ⓓ
15. Ⓐ Ⓑ Ⓒ Ⓓ
16. Ⓐ Ⓑ Ⓒ Ⓓ
17. Ⓐ Ⓑ Ⓒ Ⓓ
18. Ⓐ Ⓑ Ⓒ Ⓓ

19. Ⓐ Ⓑ Ⓒ Ⓓ
20. Ⓐ Ⓑ Ⓒ Ⓓ
21. Ⓐ Ⓑ Ⓒ Ⓓ
22. Ⓐ Ⓑ Ⓒ Ⓓ
23. Ⓐ Ⓑ Ⓒ Ⓓ
24. Ⓐ Ⓑ Ⓒ Ⓓ

25. Ⓐ Ⓑ Ⓒ Ⓓ
26. Ⓐ Ⓑ Ⓒ Ⓓ
27. Ⓐ Ⓑ Ⓒ Ⓓ
28. Ⓐ Ⓑ Ⓒ Ⓓ
29. Ⓐ Ⓑ Ⓒ Ⓓ
30. Ⓐ Ⓑ Ⓒ Ⓓ

Part 2: Word Knowledge

1. Ⓐ Ⓑ Ⓒ Ⓓ
2. Ⓐ Ⓑ Ⓒ Ⓓ
3. Ⓐ Ⓑ Ⓒ Ⓓ
4. Ⓐ Ⓑ Ⓒ Ⓓ
5. Ⓐ Ⓑ Ⓒ Ⓓ
6. Ⓐ Ⓑ Ⓒ Ⓓ
7. Ⓐ Ⓑ Ⓒ Ⓓ

8. Ⓐ Ⓑ Ⓒ Ⓓ
9. Ⓐ Ⓑ Ⓒ Ⓓ
10. Ⓐ Ⓑ Ⓒ Ⓓ
11. Ⓐ Ⓑ Ⓒ Ⓓ
12. Ⓐ Ⓑ Ⓒ Ⓓ
13. Ⓐ Ⓑ Ⓒ Ⓓ
14. Ⓐ Ⓑ Ⓒ Ⓓ

15. Ⓐ Ⓑ Ⓒ Ⓓ
16. Ⓐ Ⓑ Ⓒ Ⓓ
17. Ⓐ Ⓑ Ⓒ Ⓓ
18. Ⓐ Ⓑ Ⓒ Ⓓ
19. Ⓐ Ⓑ Ⓒ Ⓓ
20. Ⓐ Ⓑ Ⓒ Ⓓ
21. Ⓐ Ⓑ Ⓒ Ⓓ

22. Ⓐ Ⓑ Ⓒ Ⓓ
23. Ⓐ Ⓑ Ⓒ Ⓓ
24. Ⓐ Ⓑ Ⓒ Ⓓ
25. Ⓐ Ⓑ Ⓒ Ⓓ
26. Ⓐ Ⓑ Ⓒ Ⓓ
27. Ⓐ Ⓑ Ⓒ Ⓓ
28. Ⓐ Ⓑ Ⓒ Ⓓ

29. Ⓐ Ⓑ Ⓒ Ⓓ
30. Ⓐ Ⓑ Ⓒ Ⓓ
31. Ⓐ Ⓑ Ⓒ Ⓓ
32. Ⓐ Ⓑ Ⓒ Ⓓ
33. Ⓐ Ⓑ Ⓒ Ⓓ
34. Ⓐ Ⓑ Ⓒ Ⓓ
35. Ⓐ Ⓑ Ⓒ Ⓓ

Part 3: Paragraph Comprehension

1. Ⓐ Ⓑ Ⓒ Ⓓ   4. Ⓐ Ⓑ Ⓒ Ⓓ   7. Ⓐ Ⓑ Ⓒ Ⓓ   10. Ⓐ Ⓑ Ⓒ Ⓓ   13. Ⓐ Ⓑ Ⓒ Ⓓ
2. Ⓐ Ⓑ Ⓒ Ⓓ   5. Ⓐ Ⓑ Ⓒ Ⓓ   8. Ⓐ Ⓑ Ⓒ Ⓓ   11. Ⓐ Ⓑ Ⓒ Ⓓ   14. Ⓐ Ⓑ Ⓒ Ⓓ
3. Ⓐ Ⓑ Ⓒ Ⓓ   6. Ⓐ Ⓑ Ⓒ Ⓓ   9. Ⓐ Ⓑ Ⓒ Ⓓ   12. Ⓐ Ⓑ Ⓒ Ⓓ   15. Ⓐ Ⓑ Ⓒ Ⓓ

Part 4: Mathematics Knowledge

1. Ⓐ Ⓑ Ⓒ Ⓓ   6. Ⓐ Ⓑ Ⓒ Ⓓ   11. Ⓐ Ⓑ Ⓒ Ⓓ   16. Ⓐ Ⓑ Ⓒ Ⓓ   21. Ⓐ Ⓑ Ⓒ Ⓓ
2. Ⓐ Ⓑ Ⓒ Ⓓ   7. Ⓐ Ⓑ Ⓒ Ⓓ   12. Ⓐ Ⓑ Ⓒ Ⓓ   17. Ⓐ Ⓑ Ⓒ Ⓓ   22. Ⓐ Ⓑ Ⓒ Ⓓ
3. Ⓐ Ⓑ Ⓒ Ⓓ   8. Ⓐ Ⓑ Ⓒ Ⓓ   13. Ⓐ Ⓑ Ⓒ Ⓓ   18. Ⓐ Ⓑ Ⓒ Ⓓ   23. Ⓐ Ⓑ Ⓒ Ⓓ
4. Ⓐ Ⓑ Ⓒ Ⓓ   9. Ⓐ Ⓑ Ⓒ Ⓓ   14. Ⓐ Ⓑ Ⓒ Ⓓ   19. Ⓐ Ⓑ Ⓒ Ⓓ   24. Ⓐ Ⓑ Ⓒ Ⓓ
5. Ⓐ Ⓑ Ⓒ Ⓓ   10. Ⓐ Ⓑ Ⓒ Ⓓ   15. Ⓐ Ⓑ Ⓒ Ⓓ   20. Ⓐ Ⓑ Ⓒ Ⓓ   25. Ⓐ Ⓑ Ⓒ Ⓓ

Part 1: Arithmetic Reasoning

TIME: 36 minutes for 30 questions

DIRECTIONS: Arithmetic Reasoning is the second subtest of the ASVAB. These questions are designed to test your ability to use mathematics to solve various problems that may be found in real life — in other words, math word problems.

Each question is followed by four possible answers. Decide which answer is correct, and then mark the corresponding space on your answer sheet. Use your scratch paper for any figuring you want to do. You may *not* use a calculator.

1. Amy and Dan bought each of their four kids an ice cream cone and one iced coffee for themselves to share. Each ice cream cone cost $1.25, and their total bill was $7.50. How much did the iced coffee cost?

   (A) $2.75
   (B) $2.50
   (C) $1.25
   (D) $1.75

2. Sergeant Major Stanley is drawing a map in the sand for his troops. He draws the Tuz Mayor's Compound as a square measuring 18 inches on one side. What is the area of the square?

   (A) 36 square inches
   (B) 72 square inches
   (C) 324 square inches
   (D) 583 square inches

3. Currently, Danielle is twice as old as Abigail. In three years, the sum of their ages will be 30. What is Danielle's current age?

   (A) 16
   (B) 14
   (C) 10
   (D) 8

4. Tamika bought a set of rims for her truck for $500. She spent some money on window tint and twice as much on a new radio. Her total bill for all of these modifications was $950. How much did she spend on the radio?

   (A) $300
   (B) $325
   (C) $150
   (D) $450

5. Half a number plus 17 is 57. What is the number?

   (A) 20
   (B) 90
   (C) 80
   (D) 40

6. A recipe to make 10 pancakes requires 3 cups of flour and 2 tablespoons of baking powder. If you only need to make six pancakes, how many cups of flour do you need?

   (A) $1\frac{8}{5}$ cups
   (B) $1\frac{1}{8}$ cups
   (C) $1\frac{4}{5}$ cups
   (D) $1\frac{1}{4}$ cups

7. Antwon and Jason are painting a room. It takes Tim 10 hours to paint a room of that size alone, but Jason can get it done in 8 hours. Approximately how long will it take them to paint the room together?

   (A) 4.2 hours
   (B) 4.4 hours
   (C) 9 hours
   (D) 9.4 hours

8. Ebony is building a rectangular garden in her backyard. To fit in everything she wants to grow, she needs a garden with an area of 156 square feet. If her garden is 12 feet long, how wide should it be?

   (A) 10 feet
   (B) 15.6 feet
   (C) 13 feet
   (D) 12 feet

9. Two consecutive odd numbers have a sum of 92. What are the numbers?

   (A) 41 and 51

   (B) 44 and 48

   (C) 43 and 45

   (D) 45 and 47

10. Davy gets $17 per month in allowance. He saved two months' worth of allowance and then spent $\frac{3}{5}$ of it on apps for his phone. He spent $\frac{1}{8}$ of the remaining money on a bumper sticker. Of the money left after purchasing the sticker, Davy spent $\frac{1}{2}$ of it on candy. How much did Davy spend on the candy?

    (A) $5.95

    (B) $2.85

    (C) $1.70

    (D) $13.60

11. Three baristas, Pilar, Maria, and Tatiana, made $187 in tips on Saturday. Pilar made $12 more than Maria, and Maria made twice as much as Tatiana. How much did Tatiana make in tips?

    (A) $70

    (B) $35

    (C) $25

    (D) $65.50

12. Mr. Brown confiscated a triangle-shaped note from a student during his fourth-period math class. The note's base was 8 centimeters and its height was 12 centimeters. What was the note's area?

    (A) 48 square inches

    (B) 96 square inches

    (C) 52 square inches

    (D) 32 square inches

13. A car travels at a speed of 7^2 miles per hour. If the car travels at that speed for 2^4 hours, how many miles has the car gone?

    (A) 112 miles

    (B) 392 miles

    (C) 594 miles

    (D) 784 miles

14. Two runners are racing on a 2-mile course. The start gun fires at 1:15 p.m. The first runner speeds along at an average pace of 10.3 miles per hour, while the second runner travels at a pace of 10 miles per hour. How long does it take for the second runner to reach the finish line?

    (A) 12 minutes

    (B) 13.3 minutes

    (C) 14 minutes

    (D) 14.8 minutes

15. A man in a boat travels downstream for three hours. The current averages 4 miles per hour. The man then turns around and travels the same distance upstream, against the current. It takes him four hours to return to his starting point. The boat's speed is constant the entire trip. How far did the man travel round-trip?

    (A) 96 miles

    (B) 112 miles

    (C) 192 miles

    (D) 216 miles

16. Sadie spent $447 shopping for school clothes. Sweatshirts cost $27.50 each, and jeans cost $33.25 per pair. Sadie purchased 15 items of clothing, so how many pairs of jeans did she buy?

    (A) 5

    (B) 6

    (C) 8

    (D) 9

17. Luka's microscope has an objective lens that can magnify something 11^8 times. Its eyepiece can further magnify something 11^2 times. What is Luka's microscope's maximum magnification?

    (A) 11^6

    (B) 11^{10}

    (C) 121^{16}

    (D) 11^{16}

18. Miguel spends $27 on chocolate that costs $4.50 per pound. How many pounds of chocolate did he buy?

    (A) 4.5 pounds

    (B) 5 pounds

    (C) 6 pounds

    (D) 6.8 pounds

19. A kite has one diagonal length of 18.5 cm and another diagonal length of twice that. What is the kite's area?

    (A) 111 cm²

    (B) 256.75 cm²

    (C) 342.25 cm²

    (D) 684.5 cm²

20. If the height-to-width ratio of an American flag is 1:1.5, how wide is the flag if it is 60 inches high?

    (A) 40 inches

    (B) 60 inches

    (C) 90 inches

    (D) 120 inches

21. The price of a car has increased by 5 percent. It was originally listed for $23,550. What is the current price of the car?

    (A) $23,950

    (B) $24,323.50

    (C) $24,727.50

    (D) $31,975

22. If you walk around the outside edge of a field that measures 300 feet by 160 feet and end where you started, how many feet did you walk?

    (A) 460 feet

    (B) 800 feet

    (C) 920 feet

    (D) 1,100 feet

23. Carter used all of his quarters at the car wash, but he still has 23 coins in his pocket. Some of them are nickels, and some are dimes, but the total in his pocket is $1.50. How many of the coins are dimes?

    (A) 7

    (B) 8

    (C) 9

    (D) 10

24. Henry is building a toy UFO for his daughter. He cuts a circle from a piece of tin with a diameter of 12.5 inches. What is the approximate area of the shape Henry cut?

    (A) 78.5 square inches

    (B) 115.3 square inches

    (C) 122.7 square inches

    (D) 490.7 square inches

25. Vicki is packing a suitcase for her vacation. She knows she'll be picking up a music box as a gift for her friend. The hand-carved music box measures 8 inches wide, 8 inches high, and 8 inches long. Vicki's suitcase measures 19 inches wide, 30 inches high, and 10 inches long. How much space will Vicki have left for her clothes if she plans to pack the music box when she comes home?

    (A) 5,188 cubic inches

    (B) 3,894 cubic inches

    (C) 5,700 cubic inches

    (D) 6,212 cubic inches

26. How many legs do six horses, four dogs, and two kangaroos have?

    (A) 36

    (B) 38

    (C) 41

    (D) 44

GO ON TO NEXT PAGE

27. Chloe is graphing her weight loss, which falls on a line perpendicular to $2y = 4x + 3$. What is the slope of the line representing Chloe's weight loss?

(A) $-\dfrac{2}{3}$

(B) $-\dfrac{1}{2}$

(C) $\dfrac{1}{2}$

(D) 2

28. Suri has two-thirds of a gallon of almond milk and $\dfrac{7}{12}$ gallon of fruit juice. She has a total of $2\dfrac{1}{8}$ gallons of beverages in her refrigerator. How many gallons of beverages are neither almond milk nor fruit juice?

(A) $1\dfrac{1}{4}$

(B) $2\dfrac{7}{8}$

(C) $1\dfrac{3}{8}$

(D) $\dfrac{7}{8}$

29. Kai took four tests in his criminal justice class. He scored 91, 79, 88, and 84. His final exam is worth two test grades, so what grade does Kai need to get on his final exam to get an A (90 percent or better) in the class?

(A) 95

(B) 96

(C) 99

(D) 100

30. Alberto wants to paint one wall in his living room blue. The wall is 7.5 feet high and 15 feet wide. One quart of paint covers exactly 100 square feet. How much paint does Alberto need to cover the entire wall in two coats of paint?

(A) 1.125 quarts

(B) 1.25 quarts

(C) 2 quarts

(D) 2.25 quarts

Part 2: Word Knowledge

TIME: 11 minutes for 35 questions

DIRECTIONS: The Word Knowledge subtest is the third subtest of the ASVAB. The questions are designed to measure your vocabulary knowledge. You'll see three types of questions on this subtest. The first type simply asks you to choose a word or words that most nearly mean the same as the underlined word in the question. The second type includes an underlined word used in a sentence, and you are to choose the word or words that most nearly mean the same as the underlined word, as used in the context of the sentence. The third type of question asks you to choose the word that has the opposite or nearly opposite meaning as the underlined word. Each question is followed by four possible answers. Decide which answer is correct, and then mark the corresponding space on your answer sheet.

1. The teacher's instructions were ambiguous, and I didn't understand what she wanted.

   (A) clear

   (B) debatable

   (C) concise

   (D) disgusting

2. It's a transient heatwave; the temperatures will return to normal on Monday.

   (A) short-lived

   (B) mobile

   (C) unbearable

   (D) permanent

3. The word most opposite in meaning to sedentary is

   (A) hungry.

   (B) dirt.

   (C) lazy.

   (D) active.

4. The soldiers worked in close proximity with civilians while they were deployed.

   (A) confidence

   (B) nearness

   (C) relations

   (D) obsequiousness

5. Petulant most nearly means

   (A) bad-tempered.

   (B) agreeable.

   (C) floral.

   (D) friendly.

6. Incredulous most nearly means

   (A) skeptical.

   (B) believable.

   (C) brilliant.

   (D) remarkable.

7. Gratuitous most nearly means

   (A) provocative.

   (B) costly.

   (C) ridiculous.

   (D) unwarranted.

8. We plan to boycott the companies that advertise on that website.

   (A) purchase

   (B) visit

   (C) reject

   (D) patronize

9. Don't believe the fallacy that money can buy you happiness.

   (A) truth

   (B) misconception

   (C) saying

   (D) argument

10. Foreign diplomats in the U.S. are typically immune from legal action.

    (A) exempt

    (B) prone

    (C) susceptible

    (D) reluctant

11. Mosaic most nearly means
    (A) wander.
    (B) collage.
    (C) transfusion.
    (D) batter.

12. The most elite soldiers are in the Special Forces.
    (A) snobbish
    (B) overweight
    (C) best
    (D) moderate

13. Mutate most nearly means
    (A) chop.
    (B) maim.
    (C) ignore.
    (D) change.

14. Excerpt most nearly means
    (A) snippet.
    (B) excuse.
    (C) exempt.
    (D) disallow.

15. Nobody could believe that the outrageous candidate made it so far.
    (A) brilliant
    (B) shocking
    (C) charming
    (D) moderate

16. Invariably most nearly means
    (A) always.
    (B) occasionally.
    (C) algebraically.
    (D) theoretically.

17. Encumber most nearly means
    (A) vegetate.
    (B) relax.
    (C) hamper.
    (D) exacerbate.

18. Flair most nearly means
    (A) burn.
    (B) flippancy.
    (C) restriction.
    (D) talent.

19. The stray dog seemed to accept his lot in life with equanimity.
    (A) hopefulness
    (B) composure
    (C) agitation
    (D) confusion

20. Grope most nearly means
    (A) fumble.
    (B) fruit.
    (C) complain.
    (D) fall.

21. Sleek is most opposite in meaning to
    (A) polished.
    (B) shiny.
    (C) clumsy.
    (D) dull.

22. The man's callous comments about his ex-wife made the judge cringe.
    (A) original
    (B) sympathetic
    (C) heartless
    (D) cautious

23. Impervious most nearly means
    (A) waterproof.
    (B) dense.
    (C) repelled.
    (D) proof.

24. Revenue most nearly means
    (A) income.
    (B) taxation.
    (C) musical.
    (D) publicity.

25. Pulverize most nearly means
   (A) transfix.
   (B) grind.
   (C) disseminate.
   (D) transcend.

26. The stranded pilots were in dire need of a communication device.
   (A) inescapable
   (B) frustrated
   (C) urgent
   (D) terrifying

27. Chastise most nearly means
   (A) careful.
   (B) engaged.
   (C) argue.
   (D) scold.

28. The word most opposite in meaning to conspicuous is
   (A) imperceptible.
   (B) garish.
   (C) noticeable.
   (D) quiet.

29. We moved so the kids would have a greater opportunity to get a good education.
   (A) favorability
   (B) chance
   (C) luck
   (D) likelihood

30. Vengeance most nearly means
   (A) forgiveness.
   (B) ignorance.
   (C) punishment.
   (D) vindictiveness.

31. Deplorable most nearly means
   (A) disgraceful.
   (B) honorable.
   (C) gross.
   (D) fanatical.

32. The word most opposite in meaning to recede is
   (A) abate.
   (B) develop.
   (C) dwindle.
   (D) advance.

33. The Wind Talkers could decipher their own secret codes.
   (A) define
   (B) unscramble
   (C) create
   (D) confuse

34. If you keep rereading what you've already read, you'll only protract the process.
   (A) shorten
   (B) write out
   (C) convolute
   (D) lengthen

35. She provided an articulate account of her experience.
   (A) understandable
   (B) long-winded
   (C) expressionless
   (D) disjointed

Part 3: Paragraph Comprehension

TIME: 13 minutes for 15 questions

DIRECTIONS: Paragraph Comprehension is the fourth subtest on the ASVAB. The questions are designed to measure your ability to understand what you read. This section includes one or more paragraphs of reading material, followed by incomplete statements or questions. Read the paragraph and select the choice that best completes the statement or answers the question. Then mark the corresponding space on your answer sheet.

Questions 1 and 2 refer to the following passage, which is from Amphibians and Reptiles of the Rainforests of Southern El Petén, Guatemala *by William E. Duellman.*

In this tropical area having a high amount of rainfall most of the species of amphibians and reptiles have extensive ranges in the wet forests on the Atlantic lowlands of southern México and northern Central America; some species that more frequently are found in sub-humid forests also occur. Ecologically the fauna is divided into five major habitats—aquatic, aquatic margin, fossorial, terrestrial, and arboreal. Forty-two per cent of the 78 species are wholly or partly arboreal. The fauna is most closely related to that in Alta Verapaz, Guatemala, but includes many species that occur in the Tikal-Uaxactún area in northeastern Guatemala.

1. What is *not* a major habitat the author describes?

    (A) aquatic

    (B) terrestrial

    (C) aquatic margin

    (D) territorial

2. According to this passage, what percentage of species of amphibians and reptiles are completely or partly arboreal?

    (A) 78

    (B) 42

    (C) 32.76

    (D) The passage doesn't say.

Questions 3 through 5 refer to the following passage, which is from Prisoners in Devil's Bog *by Hugh Lloyd.*

He had never before visited one of these commercial palaces and he gazed about him in speechless awe. He found the revolving door so delightful that it seemed like some freakish entertainment in an amusement park, and he indulged himself with the giddy sensation of going around and around in it until a uniformed elevator starter brusquely ordered him out.

Instead, he went in.

Observing the rather ornate cigar and candy booth, he invested in a gooey chocolate bar which he ate while studying the alphabetical list of offices. He was deeply impressed with this imposing directory and experienced a thrill of triumph when at last his searching eyes discovered the name, INTERNATIONAL DETECTIVE AGENCY—7-721-728.

3. Based on the passage, you can assume the man is in

    (A) a palace.

    (B) an amusement park.

    (C) an office building.

    (D) an elevator.

4. What is the man in the passage looking for in the office building?

    (A) an elevator

    (B) a chocolate bar

    (C) a building directory

    (D) a detective agency

5. What does the man buy?

    (A) tickets

    (B) a cigar

    (C) candy

    (D) nothing

Question 6 refers to the following passage, which is from The Cliff Ruins of Canyon de Chelly, Arizona *by Cosmos Mindeleff.*

To the traveler on foot, or even on horseback, Canyon de Chelly is easily accessible from almost any direction. Good trails run northward to the San Juan and northeastward over the Tunicha mountains to the upper part of that river; Fort Defiance is but half a day's journey to the southeast; Tusayan and Zuñi are but three days distant to the traveler on foot; the Navaho often ride the distance in a day or a day and a half. The canyon is accessible to wagons, however, only at its mouth.

6. According to the passage, how long does it take to hike to Tusayan from Canyon de Chelly?

    (A) 1.5 days

    (B) 3 days

    (C) 0.5 days

    (D) The passage doesn't say.

Questions 7 and 8 refer to the following passage.

General Braxton Bragg, born in 1817 in Warrenton, North Carolina, was a high-profile commander for the Confederacy during the Civil War. Educated at West Point, Bragg led a group of volunteers to capture a federal arsenal in Baton Rouge, Louisiana. Despite the recognition he earned for training his troops, Bragg was almost universally disliked by his peers. One artillery officer, E.P. Alexander, called him "simply muddle-headed." General Nathan Bedford Forrest once called Bragg a scoundrel and a coward (and threatened to slap him). Although most of the actual battles Bragg fought ended in defeat (former general and U.S. Vice President John C. Breckinridge challenged Bragg to a duel after one such lost battle), the U.S. Army installation in Fayetteville, North Carolina — Fort Bragg — was named for the late general, who's been called "the Confederacy's worst general" by a number of historians. Today, the installation has a new name: Fort Liberty.

7. According to the passage, why was General Braxton Bragg "the Confederacy's worst general"?

    (A) He lost most of the battles he fought.

    (B) Few of his peers liked him.

    (C) Bragg trained troops.

    (D) Both A and B are correct.

8. Where was the military installation named after General Braxton Bragg?

    (A) Warrenton, North Carolina

    (B) West Point

    (C) Fayetteville, North Carolina

    (D) Baton Rouge, Louisiana

Question 9 refers to the following passage, which is from Susan B. Anthony: Rebel, Crusader, Humanitarian *by Alma Lutz.*

The attic of the tavern had been finished off for a ballroom with bottles laid under the floor to give a nice tone to the music of the fiddles, and now the young people of the village wanted to hold their dancing school there. Susan's father, true to his Quaker training, felt obliged to refuse, but when they came the second time to tell him that the only other place available was a disreputable tavern where liquor was sold, he relented a little, and talked the matter over with his wife and daughters. Lucy Anthony, recalling her love of dancing, urged him to let the young people come. Finally he consented on the condition that Guelma, Hannah, and Susan would not dance.

9. According to the passage, what made Susan's father reconsider holding dance classes in his ballroom?

    (A) It had good acoustics.

    (B) Dancing went against his Quaker training.

    (C) The only other place available was a disreputable tavern.

    (D) He decided that his daughters couldn't dance.

GO ON TO NEXT PAGE

Questions 10 and 11 refer to the following passage, which is from Knights of Art: Stories of the Italian Painters *by Amy Steedman.*

Life was rough and hard in that country home, but the peasant baby grew into a strong, hardy boy, learning early what cold and hunger meant. The hills which surrounded the village were grey and bare, save where the silver of the olive-trees shone in the sunlight, or the tender green of the shooting corn made the valley beautiful in early spring. In summer there was little shade from the blazing sun as it rode high in the blue sky, and the grass which grew among the grey rocks was often burnt and brown. But, nevertheless, it was here that the sheep of the village would be turned out to find what food they could, tended and watched by one of the village boys.

10. According to the passage, what made the valley beautiful?

    (A) blue skies and bright sun

    (B) cornfields that bloomed in early spring

    (C) grass that grew among the rocks

    (D) large herds of sheep

11. What does the author of this passage mean by "learning early what cold and hunger meant"?

    (A) Winters are uncomfortable in the village.

    (B) The village was too hot in the summer, and there was very little food from about June to August.

    (C) The boy's family was poor.

    (D) The boy was forced to tend sheep during winter.

Question 12 refers to the following passage, which is from Knights of Art: Stories of the Italian Painters *by Amy Steedman.*

The tramontana, that keen wind which blows from over the snow mountains, was sweeping down the narrow streets, searching out every nook and corner with its icy breath. Men flung their cloaks closer round them, and pulled their hats down over their eyes, so that only the tips of their noses were left uncovered for the wind to freeze. Women held their scaldinoes, little pots of hot charcoal, closer under their shawls, and even the dogs had a sad, half-frozen look. One and all longed for the warm winds of spring and the summer heat they loved.

12. According to the passage, why did women carry scaldinoes?

    (A) to keep warm

    (B) to remember the spring and summer

    (C) to bring to the men

    (D) The passage doesn't say.

Question 13 refers to the following passage, which is from White Fang *by Jack London.*

The porcupine rolled itself into a ball, radiating long, sharp needles in all directions that defied attack. In his youth One Eye had once sniffed too near a similar, apparently inert ball of quills, and had the tail flick out suddenly in his face. One quill he had carried away in his muzzle, where it had remained for weeks, a rankling flame, until it finally worked out. So he lay down, in a comfortable crouching position, his nose fully a foot away, and out of the line of the tail. Thus he waited, keeping perfectly quiet. There was no telling. Something might happen. The porcupine might unroll.

13. What does "a rankling flame" describe in the context of this passage?

    (A) a blister

    (B) fire

    (C) pain

    (D) the porcupine's tail

Questions 14 and 15 refer to the following passage, which is from Project Trinity, 1945–1946 *by Carl Maag and Steve Rohrer.*

In order to prevent eye damage, Dr. Bainbridge ordered the distribution of welder's filter glass. Because it was not known exactly how the flash might affect eyesight, it was suggested that direct viewing of the fireball not be attempted even with this protection. The recommended procedure was to face away from ground zero and watch the hills or sky until the fireball illuminated the area. Then, after the initial flash had passed, one could turn around and view the fireball through the filter glass. Despite these well-publicized instructions, two participants did not take precautions. They were temporarily blinded by the intense flash but experienced no permanent vision impairment.

14. Based on the context of the passage, you can assume that the flash is caused by

(A) a house fire.

(B) solar flares.

(C) beacons.

(D) a nuclear explosion.

15. According to the passage, where were people supposed to look during the initial flash?

(A) into welder's glasses

(B) at the hills or sky

(C) at the flash

(D) ground zero

Part 4: Mathematics Knowledge

TIME: 24 minutes for 25 questions

DIRECTIONS: Mathematics Knowledge is the fifth subtest on the ASVAB. The questions are designed to test your ability to solve general mathematical problems. Each question is followed by four possible answers. Decide which answer is correct, and then mark the corresponding space on your answer sheet. Use your scratch paper for any figuring you want to do. You may *not* use a calculator.

1. Which of the following fractions has the least value?

   (A) $\frac{2}{9}$

   (B) $\frac{1}{2}$

   (C) $\frac{5}{6}$

   (D) $\frac{2}{3}$

2. Solve for x: $3x + 8x = 44$

   (A) 4

   (B) 5

   (C) 8.8

   (D) 11

3. Which formula can you use to find the volume of a rectangular prism?

   (A) $V = \frac{1}{2}bh$

   (B) $V = \pi r^2 h$

   (C) $V = lwh$

   (D) $V = 6s^2$

4. What is the approximate circumference of a circle with a radius of 6 centimeters?

   (A) 37.88 cm

   (B) 37.68 cm

   (C) 18.84 cm

   (D) 6.28 cm

5. What is the area of a square measuring 9 feet on one side?

   (A) 36 cubic feet

   (B) 18 square feet

   (C) 81 cubic feet

   (D) 81 square feet

6. Find the perimeter of this figure:

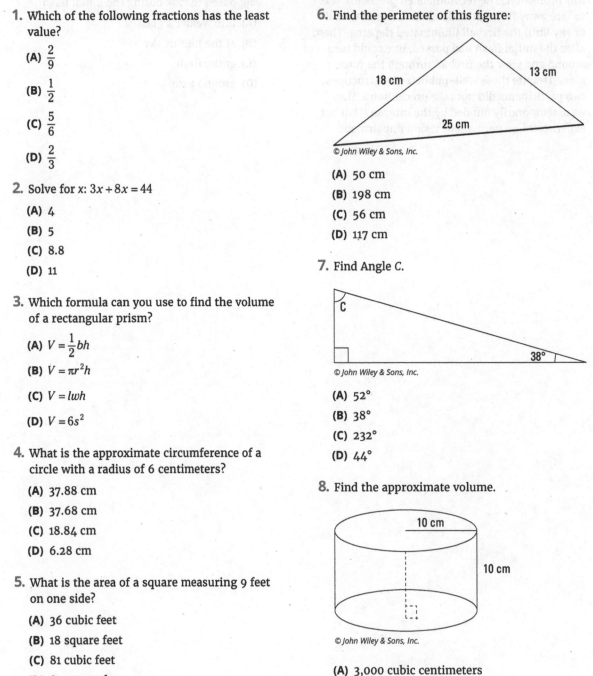

© John Wiley & Sons, Inc.

   (A) 50 cm

   (B) 198 cm

   (C) 56 cm

   (D) 117 cm

7. Find Angle C.

© John Wiley & Sons, Inc.

   (A) 52°

   (B) 38°

   (C) 232°

   (D) 44°

8. Find the approximate volume.

© John Wiley & Sons, Inc.

   (A) 3,000 cubic centimeters

   (B) 314 cubic centimeters

   (C) 3,140 cubic centimeters

   (D) 1,000 cubic centimeters

9. What is the value of b when $a = 4$?

$2a + b = 15$

(A) 5.5

(B) 7

(C) 8

(D) 11

10. Solve for x: $14(x + 9) = 252$

(A) 4

(B) 9

(C) 16

(D) 27

11. Find the approximate area of the circle.

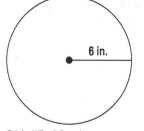

© John Wiley & Sons, Inc.

(A) 110 square inches

(B) 113.04 square inches

(C) 114.03 square inches

(D) 18.84 square inches

12. Find y:

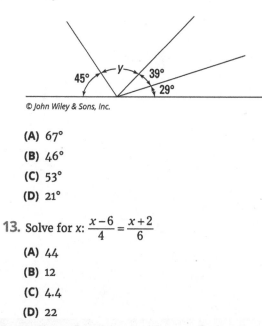

© John Wiley & Sons, Inc.

(A) 67°

(B) 46°

(C) 53°

(D) 21°

13. Solve for x: $\dfrac{x - 6}{4} = \dfrac{x + 2}{6}$

(A) 44

(B) 12

(C) 4.4

(D) 22

14. Solve for y: $7 + y + 4y \geq 51 + y$

(A) $y \geq 44$

(B) $y \geq 25$

(C) $y \geq 11$

(D) $y \geq 8$

15. Solve for x: $\dfrac{7}{8} \div x = \dfrac{7}{96}$

(A) 12

(B) 13

(C) 13.5

(D) 7

16. Solve for x: $18x = 655.5 - x$

(A) 12.5

(B) 17

(C) 34.5

(D) 38.78

17. Find the area of the figure.

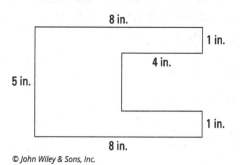

© John Wiley & Sons, Inc.

(A) 30 square inches

(B) 28 square inches

(C) 26 square inches

(D) 25.5 square inches

18. Solve for x: $4x = 32\dfrac{5}{8}$

(A) $8\dfrac{5}{32}$

(B) $8\dfrac{6}{32}$

(C) $8\dfrac{17}{32}$

(D) $9\dfrac{1}{2}$

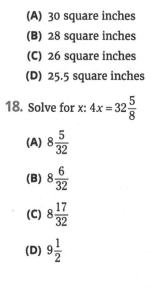

GO ON TO NEXT PAGE

19. Simplify: $\sqrt{12a^3b^2}$

(A) $2\sqrt{3}ab$

(B) $2\sqrt{3}a^{\frac{2}{3}}b$

(C) $2b\sqrt{3a^3}$

(D) $2\sqrt{3a^{\frac{3}{2}}b}$

20. Solve for a: $14a = -60 + 2a$

(A) -3.75

(B) 8

(C) 5

(D) -5

21. Express 7,700,000 in scientific notation.

(A) 7.7×10^6

(B) 7.7×10^7

(C) 7.7×10^{-6}

(D) 7.7×6^{10}

22. Find the equation for a line that passes through the points (6, 7) and (2, 1).

(A) $y = \frac{3}{2}(7) - 2$

(B) $7 = \frac{3}{2}x - 2$

(C) $y = \frac{3}{2}x - 4$

(D) $y = \frac{3}{2}x - 2$

23. Identify the appropriate formula to find one unknown length of a side in a right triangle when you know the lengths of the other two sides.

(A) $a = \frac{1}{2}bh$

(B) $a^2 + b^2 = c^2$

(C) $c^2 = ab^2$

(D) $a^3 + b^4 = c^5$

24. Find 35 percent of 200.

(A) 75

(B) 46

(C) 70

(D) 21

25. Solve for a if $b = -5.75$:

$$\frac{3a}{2} + b = 3.25$$

(A) -1.7

(B) 2.5

(C) 7

(D) 6

Chapter **13**

Practice Exam 1: Answers and Explanations

Did you do well on the first practice exam? I sure hope so! Use this answer key to score the practice exam in Chapter 12 and check out the answer explanations. If you didn't do well, don't worry — there are three more practice tests in this book to help you hone your English and math skills.

REMEMBER

The AFQT isn't scored based on number correct, number wrong, or even percent of questions correct. Instead, the score is derived by comparing your raw score with the raw score of others who have taken the test before you. In determining the raw score, harder questions are worth more points than easier questions. (For more on scoring, turn to Chapter 1.)

Don't waste time trying to equate your score on this practice test with your potential score on the actual AFQT. It can't be done. Instead, use the results of this practice test to determine which areas you should devote more study time to.

Part 1: **Arithmetic Reasoning**

Mathematical word problems can be tough. You have to develop a skill for determining which factors are relevant to the problem and then be able to convert those factors into a mathematical formula to arrive at a correct solution. Yikes! No wonder so many math books are on the market! A few good ones that may help are *Basic Math & Pre-Algebra For Dummies* by Mark Zegarelli; *Math Word Problems For Dummies, Algebra I For Dummies,* and *Algebra II For Dummies,* all by Mary Jane Sterling; *Geometry For Dummies* by Mark Ryan; and *SAT II Math For Dummies* by Scott Hatch, JD, and Lisa Zimmer Hatch, MA — all published by John Wiley & Sons, Inc.

Reviewing Chapters 8 and 10 and the additional practice questions in Chapter 11 may also help. Finally, Chapters 20 and 21 may help you improve your scores.

1. **B. $2.50**

   You can create an equation to solve this problem, where c represents coffee.

   $$c + 4(1.25) = 7.5$$
   $$c + 5 = 7.5$$
   $$c + 5 - 5 = 7.5 - 5$$
   $$c = 2.5$$

2. **C. 324 square inches**

   The formula to find the area of a square is $A = s^2$, where s represents the length of a side. Replace s with 18 to solve:

   $$s^2 = 18^2 = 18 \times 18 = 324$$

   The area of the square is 324 square inches.

3. **A. 16**

   It's often helpful to plan your attack on these types of problems by creating your own variables. Let a represent Abigail's age; because Danielle is twice as old, her age is $2a$.

   In three years, Abigail will be $a + 3$ years old, and Danielle will be $2a + 3$ years old. The sum of their ages will be 30.

   Your equation should represent adding their future ages and setting the sum equal to 30.

   $$(a + 3) + (2a + 3) = 30$$
   $$3a + 6 = 30$$
   $$3a + 6 - 6 = 30 - 6$$
   $$3a = 24$$
   $$\frac{3a}{3} = \frac{24}{3}$$
   $$a = 8$$

   Abigail is 8 years old, and the problem tells you that Danielle is twice as old. Multiply Abigail's age by two to find Danielle is now 16.

4. **A. $300**

   First, subtract how much Tamika spent on rims from her total:

   $$\$950 - \$500 = \$450$$

   Between window tint and the new radio, Tamika spent $450. Let x represent how much she spent on window tint and $2x$ represent how much she spent on the radio; then solve for x:

   $$x + 2x = 450$$
   $$3x = 450$$
   $$\frac{3x}{3} = \frac{450}{3}$$
   $$x = 150$$

   Remember that x represents how much Tamika spent on window tint. She spent $150 on window tint and twice as much on the radio. Therefore, she spent $300 on the radio.

5. C. 80

Let x represent the number you need to find. Your equation looks like this:

$$\frac{1}{2}x + 17 = 57$$

$$\frac{1}{2}x + 17 - 17 = 57 - 17$$

$$\frac{1}{2}x = 40$$

$$\frac{1}{2}x(2) = 40(2)$$

$$x = 80$$

The original number is 80.

6. C. $1\frac{4}{5}$ cups

This ratio problem requires you to set a proportion. You don't have to worry about the baking powder, though; this question asks you how much flour you need.

If you can make 10 pancakes with 3 cups of flour, your ratio looks like this:

$$\frac{\text{flour}}{\text{pancakes}} = \frac{3}{10}$$

To find out how much flour you need to make just six pancakes, create an expression that looks like this, letting x represent how much flour you need:

$$\frac{\text{flour}}{\text{pancakes}} = \frac{x}{6}$$

The two ratios are equivalent, so create an equation and cross-multiply to solve for x:

$$\frac{3}{10} = \frac{x}{6}$$

$$10x = 18$$

$$\frac{10x}{10} = \frac{18}{10}$$

$$x = \frac{18}{10}$$

$$x = 1\frac{8}{10} = 1\frac{4}{5}$$

7. B. 4.4 hours

Both men are painting the room together, so it's a shared-work problem. Start by considering what portion of the room each man paints per hour. In one hour, Antwon paints $\frac{1}{10}$ of the room, because it takes 10 hours for him to paint an entire room. Create an equation to find the total portion of the room painted per hour when they work together.

$$\frac{1}{10} + \frac{1}{8} = x$$

Find a common denominator and solve for x:

$$\frac{1}{10} + \frac{1}{8} = x$$

$$\frac{1}{10}\left(\frac{4}{4}\right) + \frac{1}{8}\left(\frac{5}{5}\right) = x$$

$$\frac{4}{40} + \frac{5}{40} = x$$

$$x = \frac{9}{40}$$

In one hour, the two men paint $\frac{9}{40}$ of the room. Let t stand for the total time they take to paint the room together.

$$\frac{9}{40} = \frac{1}{t}$$

$$9t = 40$$

$$t = \frac{40}{9} \approx 4.4$$

Together, the two men can paint the room in about 4.4 hours. You can also solve this problem using the shared-work formula from Chapter 10.

8. **C. 13 feet**

The area of a rectangle is its length times its width, or $A = lw$. The area and the length are given in the problem, so create an equation to solve for the unknown width. Let w represent the garden's width:

$$156 = 12w$$

$$\frac{156}{12} = \frac{12w}{12}$$

$$w = 13$$

Ebony's garden must be 13 feet wide.

9. **D. 45 and 47**

The question asks you to find two consecutive odd numbers, so Choices (A) and (B) can't be correct. Check the other choices. Choice (C) is $43 + 45 = 88$, and Choice (D) is $45 + 47 = 92$, so Choice (D) is correct.

If you don't read all the answer choices, you'll have to do more math. To solve the problem algebraically, let n represent the first number and $n + 2$ represent the second number. Note that n and $n + 2$ are the variables used to represent any pair of consecutive odd *or* even numbers.

Your equation looks like this:

$$n + (n + 2) = 92$$

$$2n + 2 = 92$$

$$2n + 2 - 2 = 92 - 2$$

$$2n = 90$$

$$\frac{2n}{2} = \frac{90}{2}$$

$$n = 45$$

The first number is 45. Because the next consecutive odd number is 47, Choice (D) is correct. You can double-check your math by adding both numbers together; you get 92.

10. **A. $5.95**

This problem requires you to go through several steps. First, double Davy's monthly allowance because he saved it for two months: $17 \times 2 = 34.

The problem tells you Davy spent $\frac{3}{5}$ of his allowance on apps, which means he had $\frac{2}{5}$ left. Figure out how much that is by multiplying:

$$\$34\left(\frac{2}{5}\right) = \$34(0.4) = \$13.60$$

He spent $\frac{1}{8}$ of the remainder, so he has $\frac{7}{8}$ of $13.60 left. Multiply again to see how much money that is:

$$\$13.60\left(\frac{7}{8}\right) = \$13.60(0.875) = \$11.90$$

Davy has half of that left:

$$\$11.90 \div 2 = \$5.95$$

Another way to solve this problem is to multiply all the fractions listed before you multiply by the dollar amount:

$$\frac{2}{5} \cdot \frac{7}{8} \cdot \frac{1}{2} = \frac{\cancel{2}}{5} \cdot \frac{7}{8} \cdot \frac{1}{\cancel{2}} = \frac{7}{40} = 0.175$$
$$0.175(\$34) = \$5.95$$

11. **B. $35**

The key to this type of problem is to define each variable in the same terms. If you choose to represent each barista with a different variable, you have a single equation with three variables, which is unsolvable.

Start with Tatiana, the person who made the least. Let x represent how much Tatiana made, and because Maria made twice that much, let $2x$ represent Maria's earnings. Let $2x + 12$ represent Pilar's earnings.

The sum of their earnings is $187. Write an equation to represent the sum and solve for x:

$$x + 2x + (2x + 12) = 187$$
$$5x + 12 = 187$$
$$5x + 12 - 12 = 187 - 12$$
$$5x = 175$$
$$\frac{5x}{5} = \frac{175}{5}$$
$$x = 35$$

Tatiana made $35. (And, if you're interested, Maria made $70, while Pilar racked up $82 in tips. Add them all together and you get their total, $187.)

12. A. 48 square inches

The formula to find the area of a triangle is $A = \frac{1}{2}bh$, where A represents area, b represents the length of the base, and h represents the triangle's height. Replace the variables with the values given in the problem and solve:

$$A = \frac{1}{2}(8)(12)$$
$$= \frac{1}{2}(96)$$
$$= 48$$

The area of the triangle is 48 square inches.

13. D. 784 miles

Start by simplifying each exponential term. First, $7^2 = 7 \times 7 = 49$ miles per hour. The car traveled for 2^4 hours, and $2^4 = 2 \times 2 \times 2 \times 2 = 16$. Now multiply the rate by the time to determine that the car traveled 49 mph $\times 16$ hours $= 784$ miles.

14. A. 12 minutes

There's plenty of unnecessary information for you to ignore in this problem. First, it doesn't matter what time the start gun fires. Second, it doesn't matter how fast the first runner moves. The problem only asks how long it takes the second runner to reach the finish line, which is 2 miles from the starting point.

You can use a modified form of the distance formula ($d = rt$, where d represents distance, r represents rate, and t represents time) to find out how long it takes the second runner to complete the race:

$$t = \frac{d}{r}$$
$$= \frac{2}{10}$$
$$= \frac{1}{5}$$

Because you're working in miles per hour, the runner reaches the end in one-fifth of an hour, or 12 minutes ($60 \div 5 = 12$).

15. C. 192

Let x represent the boat's speed, and use the distance formula ($d = rt$, where d represents distance, r represents rate, and t represents time) to create a table. The rate of travel is the boat's speed plus or minus the speed of the current, and the distance is the rate times the time.

	Rate	Time	Distance
Downstream	$x+4$	3	$3(x+4)$
Upstream	$x-4$	4	$4(x-4)$

The problem tells you that the distances are equal, so put set the distances equal to each other and solve for x:

$$3(x+4) = 4(x-4)$$
$$3x + 12 = 4x - 16$$
$$3x + 12 - 12 = 4x - 16 - 12$$
$$3x = 4x - 28$$
$$3x - 4x = -28 + 4x - 4x$$
$$-x = -28$$
$$x = 28$$

The boat's speed is 28 miles per hour. Now use the distance formula with the man's upstream trip (or the downstream trip, which works just as well) to figure out how far the man traveled:

$$d = rt$$
$$= 3(x+4)$$
$$= 3(28+4)$$
$$= 3(32)$$
$$= 96$$

The man traveled 96 miles in one direction, and because the trip back was also 96 miles, he traveled 192 miles round-trip.

16. **B. 6**

Although it doesn't look like it on the surface, this is a mixture word problem. Let s represent the number of sweatshirts Sadie bought and create a table to help build the correct equation:

	Number	Price per Item	Total
Sweatshirts	s	$27.50	27.5s
Jeans	$15-s$	$33.25	33.25(15−s)
Total	15		$447

Create an equation by looking at the "Total" column; then solve for s:

$$27.5s + 33.25(15-s) = 447$$
$$27.5s + 498.75 - 33.25s = 447$$
$$-5.75s + 498.75 = 447$$
$$-5.75s + 498.75 - 498.75 = 447 - 498.75$$
$$-5.75s = -51.75$$
$$\frac{-5.75s}{-5.75} = \frac{-51.75}{-5.75}$$
$$s = 9$$

That means Sadie bought nine sweatshirts. Because she bought fifteen items of clothing, the remaining six were jeans.

17. B. 11^{10}

Because the magnification of the eyepiece compounds the magnification of the lens, you multiply the two terms. These two exponential terms have the same base (11), so when multiplying, simply add the exponents. Your work looks like this:

$$11^8 \times 11^2 = 11^{8+2} = 11^{10}$$

18. C. 6 pounds

Let x represent the number of pounds of chocolate that Miguel bought. The total cost is the number of pounds times the price per pound, so your equation looks like this:

$$4.5x = 27$$
$$\frac{4.5x}{4.5} = \frac{27}{4.5}$$
$$x = 6$$

Miguel bought 6 pounds of chocolate.

19. C. 342.25 cm²

The problem tells you that one diagonal is 18.5 centimeters long and the other is twice that, or 37 centimeters.

The formula to find the area of a kite is $A = \frac{(d_1 \times d_2)}{2}$, where d_1 represents the length of the first diagonal and d_2 represents the length of the second diagonal. Replace the variables and solve:

$$A = \frac{(18.5 \times 37)}{2}$$
$$= \frac{684.5}{2}$$
$$= 342.25 \text{ cm}^2$$

If you don't remember the formula to find the area of a kite, you're definitely not alone — but you can still solve this problem. A kite is a pair of identical triangles stuck together. The base of the triangle is one diagonal, and the height of the triangle is half the other diagonal. Use the formula to find the area of a triangle, and double it:

$$A = 2\left(\frac{1}{2}bh\right) = bh$$

Using this formula, your work looks like this:

$$A = 18.5 \cdot 18.5$$
$$A = 342.25$$

20. C. 90 inches

According to the question, the American flag's height-to-width ratio is 1:1.5. For every one unit the flag is high, it must be 1.5 units wide.

Multiply 60 by 1.5 to find out how wide the flag must be at that height:

$$60 \times 1.5 = 90$$

The flag must be 90 inches wide.

21. **C. $24,727.50**

There are at least two ways to solve this problem.

You can multiply the original amount by 1.05 (that's 100% + 5%) to find the new price. Turn the percentage into a decimal:

$$23,550 \times 1.05 = 24,727.50$$

Alternatively, you can figure out 5% of the original price and then add it to the original price:

$$x = 23,550 + (23,550 \times 0.05)$$
$$x = 23,550 + 1,177.5$$
$$x = 24,727.5$$

Remember that you have limited time when you take the ASVAB. The shortest route to the answer is your best bet (unless you forget the shortest route)!

22. **C. 920 feet**

This problem is asking you to find the perimeter of a rectangle. To find perimeter, you add the lengths of all the sides together. In this case, you're adding two sides that measure 300 feet each and two sides that measure 160 feet each.

$$300 + 300 + 160 + 160 = 920$$

You've walked 920 feet.

Alternatively, you can add double the length and double the width: $2(300) + 2(160) = 920$.

Or you can add the length and width, then double the sum: $2(300 + 160) = 920$.

These are all versions of the perimeter formula, and the method you're most comfortable with is the one you should use on the ASVAB.

23. **A. 7**

Remember that with money problems involving change, your calculations will most likely be easier if you multiply by 100. This is not a necessary step if you find it's quicker to solve using decimals!

Let d represent the number of dimes in Carter's pocket. You know he has 23 coins, so the number of nickels in his pocket is $23 - d$ (because all the coins that aren't dimes must be nickels).

Each dime is worth $0.10, and each nickel is worth $0.05. The sum of the values of the coins equals $1.50, so create an equation and solve for d:

$$0.1d + 0.05(23 - d) = 1.5$$
$$(0.1d \times 100) + (0.05 \times 100)(23 - d) = (1.5 \times 100)$$
$$10d + 5(23 - d) = 150$$
$$5d + 115 = 150$$
$$5d + 115 - 115 = 150 - 115$$
$$5d = 35$$
$$\frac{5d}{5} = \frac{35}{5}$$
$$d = 7$$

Carter has 7 dimes in his pocket.

24. C. 122.7 square inches

The formula to find the area of a circle is $A = \pi r^2$, where A represents area and r represents the circle's radius. A circle's radius is half its diameter, so divide 12.5 by 2 to find the circle's radius is 6.25 inches.

Replace the variable r in the formula with 6.25 and solve, using 3.14 for π:

$$A = 3.14\left(6.25^2\right)$$
$$= 3.14(39.0625)$$
$$= 122.65625 \text{ in.}^2$$

Because all the answer choices contain one digit after the decimal point, you'll have to round your answer. 122.65625 rounds up to 122.7.

25. A. 5,188 cubic inches

This problem requires you to solve two volume formulas: One for a cube and one for a rectangular box (or prism, if you want to get fancy about it). When you figure out the volume of each, you'll subtract the cube from the rectangle to figure out how much room Vicki has left.

The formula to find the volume of a cube is $V = s^3$, where V represents volume and s represents the length of one side of the cube. The problem says one side of the music box is 8 inches, so find that volume first:

$$V = 8^3$$
$$= 512 \text{ in.}^3$$

The music box takes up 512 cubic inches.

Finding the volume of Vicki's suitcase requires you to use the formula $V = lwh$, where V represents volume, l represents length, w represents width, and h represents height. Replace the variables with what you know from the problem:

$$V = 10 \times 19 \times 30$$
$$= 5,700 \text{ in.}^3$$

Subtract the space the music box will occupy to find out how much room Vicki will have left: $5,700 - 512 = 5,188 \text{ in.}^3$

26. D. 44

Horses and dogs each have four legs, and kangaroos have two. Let a represent the number of horses and dogs together, because they each have an equal number of legs. Let b represent the number of kangaroos. Let c represent the total number of all the animals' legs. Your equation should look like this:

$$4a + 2b = c$$

Replace the variables with the values you know (there are ten horses and dogs, and two kangaroos):

$$c = 4(10) + 2(2)$$
$$c = 40 + 4$$
$$c = 44$$

Together, these animals have 44 legs.

If you're like many people, though, you didn't create an algebraic formula; you just multiplied and added. That's fine, too — you don't need to create extra work for yourself when you only have a limited time to come up with all the answers.

(And if you were guessing instead of doing the math, you could immediately rule out Choice (C), because there's no way *any* number of animals who have even numbers of legs could total 41.)

27. B. $-\dfrac{1}{2}$

Solve the equation for y to put the equation in slope-intercept form, $y = mx + b$, where m represents the slope of the line and b represents where the line intercepts the y-axis:

$$2y = 4x + 3$$
$$\frac{2y}{2} = \frac{4x + 3}{2}$$
$$y = 2x + \frac{3}{2}$$

The coefficient in front of the x tells you that the slope of this line is 2.

To find the slope of any line that's perpendicular to this one, you need its negative reciprocal. (*Remember:* All pairs of perpendicular lines have negative reciprocal slopes, and all parallel lines have the same slope!) The negative reciprocal of 2 is $-\dfrac{1}{2}$.

28. D. $\dfrac{7}{8}$

First, figure out how many gallons of fruit juice and almond milk Suri has in total by adding $\dfrac{2}{3}$ and $\dfrac{7}{12}$. Start by finding the lowest common denominator; then add:

$$\frac{2}{3} + \frac{7}{12} = \frac{8}{12} + \frac{7}{12} = \frac{15}{12}$$

Convert your answer to a mixed number and reduce:

$$\frac{15}{12} = 1\frac{3}{12} = 1\frac{1}{4}$$

Suri has $1\dfrac{1}{4}$ gallons of almond milk and fruit juice combined. Subtract that from the total number of gallons she has in the fridge by finding a common denominator. In this case, $1\dfrac{1}{4}$ needs to become $1\dfrac{2}{8}$:

$$2\frac{1}{8} - 1\frac{2}{8} = \frac{7}{8}$$

29. C. 99

Let x represent what Kai needs to score on his final exam. Remember, there are six tests that count toward his final grade (he's already taken four, and the final exam is worth two). Your equation should look like this:

$$\frac{91 + 79 + 88 + 84 + x + x}{6} = 90$$

Simplify the equation. Then solve for x:

$$\frac{342 + 2x}{6} = 90$$

$$\frac{342 + 2x}{\cancel{6}} \times \frac{\cancel{6}}{1} = 90 \times 6$$

$$342 + 2x = 540$$

$$2x + 342 - 342 = 540 - 342$$

$$2x = 198$$

$$\frac{2x}{2} = \frac{198}{2}$$

$$x = 99$$

Kai needs to score 99 on his final exam to get an A in the class.

30. D. 2.25 quarts

First figure out the area of Alberto's living room wall by using the formula for the area of a rectangle, which is $A = lw$, where A represents area, l represents length, and w represents width:

$$A = 7.5 \times 15$$
$$= 112.5 \text{ ft}^2$$

The area of the wall is 112.5 square feet.

Because Alberto wants to use two coats of paint, he'll need enough paint for twice that, which is 225 square feet.

Each quart of paint covers exactly 100 square feet, so divide the total area by the area covered per quart. Alberto will need 2.25 quarts of paint for this job.

Part 2: Word Knowledge

I hope you did well on this subtest. (I was crossing my fingers the whole time!) If not, you may want to take another gander at Chapter 4 and the practice questions in Chapter 5.

If you need additional study references to improve your vocabulary ability, you may want to consider *Vocabulary For Dummies* by Laurie E. Rozakis, PhD, and *SAT Vocabulary For Dummies* by Suzee Vlk (both published by John Wiley & Sons, Inc.).

1. B. debatable

Ambiguous is an adjective that means open to multiple interpretations or having a double meaning.

2. A. short-lived

Transient is an adjective that means lasting for only a short time. It's also used as a noun to refer to a person who's staying or working in a place for a short time.

3. D. active.

Sedentary is an adjective that refers to spending too much time being inactive. It also applies to work that's characterized by a lack of physical activity or to a seated position.

"Carolyn's sedentary lifestyle contributed to her weight gain."

4. **B. nearness**

Proximity is a noun that means nearness in space, time, or relationship.

5. **A. bad-tempered.**

Petulant is an adjective that describes people or their mannerisms as childishly sulky or bad-tempered.

"He acted like a petulant child when he stormed out of the office like that."

6. **A. skeptical.**

Incredulous is an adjective that means unwilling (or unable) to believe something.

"The journalist was incredulous that the politician lied right to her face."

7. **D. unwarranted.**

Gratuitous is an adjective that means uncalled for or unwarranted. It can also refer to something that's done for free or given freely.

"The movie was filled with gratuitous violence."

8. **C. reject**

Boycott is a verb that means to withdraw from commercial or social relations with an organization. It's also a noun that refers to a ban against relations with certain groups or against cooperation with a certain policy.

9. **B. misconception**

Fallacy is a noun that means a mistaken belief, especially one that's based on an unsound argument.

10. **A. exempt**

Immune is an adjective that describes someone or something as protected or exempt from an obligation or the effects of something.

11. **B. collage.**

Mosaic is a noun that means a picture or pattern produced by arranging multiple small, colored pieces together.

"That beautiful mosaic has been in the entryway since 1910."

12. **C. best**

Elite is a noun that refers to a select part of a group that's superior to the rest.

13. **D. change.**

Mutate is a verb that means to change or cause to change.

"Cancer cells are more likely to mutate than other cells are."

14. **A. snippet.**

Excerpt is a noun that means a short extract from a piece of writing or music, a film, or a broadcast.

"Because the excerpt was so terrible, we decided not to buy the book."

15. **B. shocking**

Outrageous is an adjective that describes someone or something that's shockingly bad or excessive. It can also mean extremely bold, unusual, and startling.

16. **A. always.**

Invariably is an adverb that describes something that happens on every occasion, in every case.

"He was invariably optimistic, even when things weren't going his way."

17. **C. hamper.**

Encumber is a verb that means to restrict or burden someone or something to make free action or movement difficult.

"Those boots will only encumber you when you try walking up that sand dune."

18. **D. talent.**

Flair is a noun that means a special or instinctive talent, ability, or aptitude for doing something well. It can also mean stylishness or originality.

19. **B. composure**

Equanimity is a noun that means mental calmness, composure, and self-possession, especially in a difficult situation.

20. **A. fumble.**

Grope is a verb that means to feel or search blindly or uncertainly.

"The child woke from his nightmare and groped for the light switch."

21. **D. dull.**

Sleek is an adjective that means smooth and glossy.

"She had sleek, blond hair that gleamed in the sun."

22. **C. heartless**

Callous is an adjective that means showing or having an insensitive, cruel disregard for other people. Don't get it mixed up with *callus*, which is what you get on your pencil-gripping fingers when you take too many ASVAB practice tests in a row.

23. **A. waterproof.**

Impervious is an adjective that means not allowing fluid to pass through. It also means unable to be affected by.

"The outer shell of the sleeping bag is impervious, so you can sleep just about anywhere."

24. **A. income.**

Revenue is a noun that means income, especially as it pertains to a company or organization.

"This year's revenue exceeded our goal by $1,500."

25. B. grind.

Pulverize is a verb that means to reduce to fine particles.

"The seeds are pulverized into flour during the final step of the process."

26. C. urgent

Dire is an adjective that means extremely serious or urgent; it also describes a warning or threat that comes before a disaster.

27. D. scold.

Chastise is a verb that means to rebuke or reprimand severely.

"The teacher will definitely chastise you for forgetting your homework for the fifth time this week."

28. A. imperceptible.

Conspicuous is an adjective that means standing out so as to be clearly visible. It also means attracting attention.

"The skunk's conspicuous white stripe set off my internal alarm bells, and I ran."

29. B. chance

Opportunity is a noun that refers to a set of circumstances that makes it possible to do something.

30. C. punishment.

Vengeance is a noun that means punishment inflicted or retribution given for an injury or wrong.

"William the Conqueror's desire for vengeance led him to invade King Harold's domain."

31. A. disgraceful.

Deplorable is an adjective that means deserving strong condemnation.

"The prisoners lived in deplorable conditions while they were incarcerated at Alcatraz."

32. D. advance.

Recede is a verb that means to move back from a previous position.

"If we stay long enough, we can watch the tide recede."

33. B. unscramble

Decipher is a verb that means to convert a text written in code (or a coded signal) into normal language.

34. D. lengthen

Protract is a verb that means to prolong.

35. A. understandable

Articulate is an adjective that means having or showing the ability to speak coherently and fluently; it can refer to a person or to his or her words. It's also used as a verb that means to express an idea or feeling coherently and fluently.

Part 3: Paragraph Comprehension

So, how did you do? If you didn't do very well on this subtest, you may want to engage in some more reading practice. Improving your vocabulary can also help improve your reading comprehension skills; See Chapters 4 and 5 for some tips. You may also want to try a few of the practice questions in Chapter 7.

1. D. territorial

The author describes five major habitats: aquatic, aquatic margin, fossorial, terrestrial, and arboreal. Choice (D), territorial, is the only one of the answer choices not on that list.

2. B. 42

The passage says, "Forty-two per cent of the 78 species are wholly or partly arboreal." You don't have to do any math because the question asks you for the percentage of reptiles and amphibians that are arboreal.

3. C. an office building.

The passage calls the space a "commercial palace" and describes the revolving door, and it mentions an "alphabetical list of offices."

4. D. a detective agency

The passage describes the man's "thrill of triumph" when he finds "INTERNATIONAL DETECTIVE AGENCY" on the directory. Although he does see an elevator, buy a chocolate bar, and find the directory, it's the detective agency he wanted to find.

5. C. candy

The passage says, "he invested in a gooey chocolate bar," which means he bought candy.

6. B. 3 days

The passage says, "Tusayan and Zuñi are but three days distant to the traveler on foot."

7. D. Both A and B are correct.

The passage says that General Bragg lost most of the battles he fought ("most of the actual battles Bragg fought ended in defeat") and that he was "almost universally disliked by his peers." The passage also describes what other officers called him, from "muddle-headed" to a scoundrel and a coward.

Although Bragg did train troops, that didn't have anything to do with why he was considered "the Confederacy's worst general."

8. C. Fayetteville, North Carolina

Although each of the locations listed in the answer choices is mentioned in the passage, only one is noted as the location of an installation named after the general. The passage says, "The U.S. Army installation in Fayetteville, North Carolina — Fort Bragg — is named for the late general."

Choice (A), Warrenton, North Carolina, is where General Bragg was born. Choice (B), West Point, is where he learned to operate as an officer in the military, and Choice (D), Baton Rouge, Louisiana, is where Bragg led a group of volunteers to capture a federal arsenal.

9. **C. The only other place available was a disreputable tavern.**

The passage says Susan's father "relented a little" when the young people of the village asked about using his ballroom a second time because "the only other place available was a disreputable tavern where liquor was sold."

10. **B. cornfields that bloomed in early spring**

The passage says, "The tender green of the shooting corn made the valley beautiful in early spring."

Although the author mentions the blue skies and bright sun from Choice (A) and the grass that grows between the rocks from Choice (C), she means neither as a compliment. She mentions the sheep, too, but says nothing about them contributing to the valley's beauty.

11. **C. The boy's family was poor.**

The passage says, "Life was rough and hard in that country home, but the peasant baby grew into a strong, hardy boy." Because the boy was a peasant, and because life was "rough and hard," you can assume that the author means the boy's family was poor.

12. **A. to keep warm**

The passage says that scaldinoes are "little pots of hot charcoal" that women carried under their shawls. The author describes cold, wintry weather and mentions that men "flung their cloaks closer round them," while "even the dogs had a sad, half-frozen look." Therefore, you can assume that the women carried scaldinoes to keep warm.

13. **C. pain**

The passage says the quill remained in One Eye's muzzle for weeks until it worked its way out — and that One Eye is very careful to stay far enough away from the porcupine's tail so it can't hurt him. Choice (C) is the correct answer because the phrase "a rankling flame" describes the pain the quill caused One Eye.

14. **D. a nuclear explosion.**

The passage doesn't directly say that the flash is from a nuclear explosion, but there are several clues, such as calling the area "ground zero" and saying that "direct viewing of the fireball" should not be attempted, even with welder's glass.

15. **B. at the hills or sky**

The passage says, "The recommended procedure was to face away from ground zero and watch the hills or sky until the fireball illuminated the area."

Part 4: Mathematics Knowledge

This subtest would have been much easier if the ASVAB folks allowed you to use a calculator, wouldn't it? Fortunately, the problems on this subtest are designed so they can be solved using only scratch paper, a good ol' No. 2 pencil, and a little brain sweat.

If you're still having difficulty, give Chapter 9 a gander. *Basic Math & Pre-Algebra For Dummies* by Mark Zegarelli; *Algebra I For Dummies* and *Algebra II For Dummies*, both by Mary Jane Sterling; *Geometry For Dummies* by Mark Ryan; and *SAT II Math For Dummies* by Scott Hatch, JD, and Lisa Zimmer Hatch, MA (all published by John Wiley & Sons, Inc.) can also help you improve your math knowledge score. You can find additional practice questions in Chapter 10.

1. A. $\frac{2}{9}$

TIP

When a question on the ASVAB asks you to find the fraction with the least (or greatest) value, eliminate obviously wrong answers first. When the numerator is more or less than half its denominator, you have a clearer picture of which answers don't make sense. In this case, finding the lowest common denominator isn't necessary, because Choice (A) is the only one that's less than $\frac{1}{2}$.

If eliminating answers leaves you with two or more choices, find the lowest common denominator so you can see how the fractions compare. In this case, the lowest common denominator of all the choices is 18 (each of the denominators given in the problem is a factor of 18).

Order each fraction based on its new numerator:

$$\frac{2}{9} = \frac{4}{18}$$

$$\frac{1}{2} = \frac{9}{18}$$

$$\frac{5}{6} = \frac{15}{18}$$

$$\frac{2}{3} = \frac{12}{18}$$

Now you can see that because $\frac{2}{9} = \frac{4}{18}$, that's the fraction with the least value.

2. A. 4

Combine like terms. Then isolate the variable x to solve:

$$3x + 8x = 44$$
$$11x = 44$$
$$\frac{11x}{11} = \frac{44}{11}$$
$$x = 4$$

3. C. $V = lwh$

The formula to find the volume of a rectangular prism, or box, is $V = lwh$, where V represents volume, l represents the length of a side, w represents width, and h represents height.

In case you were wondering, Choice (A) is based on the formula to find the area of a triangle, Choice (B) is the formula you need if you're finding the volume of a cylinder, and Choice (D) is based on the formula to find the surface area of a cube.

4. B. 37.68 cm

Using the approximation 3.14 for π, substitute the given information into the formula for the circumference of a circle:

$$C = 12\pi = 12(3.14) = 37.68$$

TIP

Here's a tip that can speed up your problem-solving on the ASVAB: Because the approximation for pi has multiple digits and decimal places, leave calculations in terms of pi until you've solved everything you can in the equation.

5. D. 81 square feet

The formula to find the area of a square is $A = s^2$, where A represents area and s represents the length of a side. All the sides have equal length in a square, so replace the variable s with 9:

$$A = s^2$$
$$= 9^2$$
$$= 9 \times 9$$
$$= 81 \text{ ft}^2$$

Remember, when you're finding the area of something, you're using square measurements — area is two-dimensional, like the flat surface of the ground or a wall. Cubic measurements are three-dimensional, and they relate to volume, like filling up a box or a swimming pool.

6. C. 56 cm

To find the perimeter of any shape, simply add the lengths of all the sides together. The perimeter of this triangle is $13 + 25 + 18 = 56$ centimeters.

7. A. 52°

All the angles in a triangle must add up to 180°. Because this triangle is labeled as a right triangle by the box in the corner, you know that angle is 90°. The question tells you another angle is 38°, so you can figure out the measure of Angle C by adding 90 and 38, then subtracting the total from 180:

$$90 + 38 = 128$$
$$180 - 128 = 52$$

Angle C measures 52°.

8. C. 3,140 cubic centimeters

The formula to find the volume of a cylinder is $V = \pi r^2 h$, where V represents volume, r represents the cylinder's radius, and h represents its height.

Replace the variables with the values shown in diagram and use 3.14 to approximate π:

$$V = 3.14\left(10^2\right)(10)$$
$$= 3.14(100)(10)$$
$$= 314(10)$$
$$= 3,140 \text{ cm}^3$$

The volume of this right cylinder is 3,140 cubic centimeters.

In many problems, it's easier to leave pi intact so you don't have to work with decimals right away. You could solve this problem this way, too:

$$1,000\pi = 1,000(3.14) = 3,140$$

(Try to remember that you should leave the pi for dessert. I don't want to do it either, but sometimes it's for the best!)

9. B. 7

Replace the variable *a* with 4, and then solve for *b*:

$$2(4)+b=15$$
$$8+b=15$$
$$b+8-8=15-8$$
$$b=7$$

10. B. 9

Simplify the equation by distributing the 14. Then solve for *x*:

$$14(x+9)=252$$
$$14x+126=252$$
$$14x+126-126=252-126$$
$$14x=126$$
$$\frac{14x}{14}=\frac{126}{14}$$
$$x=9$$

11. B. 113.04 square inches

The formula to find the area of a circle is $A=\pi r^2$, so replace the variable *r* with the circle's radius (6 inches) and use 3.14 to approximate pi:

$$A=\pi\left(6^2\right)$$
$$=3.14(36)$$
$$=113.04 \text{ in.}^2$$

The area of this circle is 113.04 square inches.

12. A. 67°

All the angles on a line must add up to 180°, and the problem gives you three of the four angles measures.

Add all three angles, and then subtract the sum from 180 to find *y*:

$$45+39+29=113$$
$$180-113=67$$

The value of *y* is 67°.

13. D. 22

This problem requires you to cross-multiply to clear the fractions:

$$\frac{x-6}{4}=\frac{x+2}{6}$$
$$6(x-6)=4(x+2)$$

Then you can isolate x to solve:

$$6x - 36 = 4x + 8$$
$$6x - 36 - 4x = 4x + 8 - 4x$$
$$2x - 36 = 8$$
$$2x - 36 + 36 = 8 + 36$$
$$2x = 44$$
$$\frac{2x}{2} = \frac{44}{2}$$
$$x = 22$$

14. **c.** $y \geq 11$

Although the $\geq$ can make this inequality look confusing, you'll solve it just like a regular equation. Start by combining like terms (the y, in this case) and then isolate the variable y to solve:

$$7 + y + 4y \geq 51 + y$$
$$7 + 5y \geq 51 + y$$
$$7 + 5y - 7 \geq 51 + y - 7$$
$$5y \geq 44 + y$$
$$5y - y \geq 44 + y - y$$
$$4y \geq 44$$
$$\frac{4y}{4} \geq \frac{44}{4}$$
$$y \geq 11$$

Remember: When solving inequalities, if you divide both sides by a negative number, you must also flip the inequality symbol. If the problem had involved dividing by -4 in the last step (instead of 4), the final answer would have been $y \leq -11$.

15. **A.** 12

Start by multiplying both sides by x to make the problem look more familiar:

$$\frac{7}{8} \div x = \frac{7}{96}$$
$$\frac{7}{8} \div x \cdot \frac{x}{1} = \frac{7}{96} \cdot \frac{x}{1}$$
$$\frac{7}{8} = \frac{7}{96} x$$

Isolate x by multiplying both sides by the reciprocal of $\frac{7}{96}$ (because the 7s cancel out):

$$\frac{7}{8} = \frac{7}{96} x$$
$$\frac{7}{8} \cdot \frac{96}{7} = x$$
$$\frac{\cancel{7}}{8} \cdot \frac{96}{\cancel{7}} = x$$
$$12 = x$$

16. **C. 34.5**

Sometimes it's easier to multiply both sides of the problem by 10 right out of the gate to avoid working with decimals. Add x to both sides first so you can skip using the distributive property, and then isolate x to solve:

$$18x = 655.5 - x$$
$$18x + x = 655.5$$
$$19x = 655.5$$
$$19x(10) = (655.5)(10)$$
$$190x = 6,555$$
$$\frac{190x}{190} = \frac{6,555}{190}$$
$$x = \frac{69}{2}$$
$$x = 34.5$$

17. **B. 28 square inches**

You can see that there's a 4-inch-x-3-inch rectangle cut out of a larger rectangle, so the simplest way to solve this problem is to imagine you're looking at a whole rectangle and find its area first. Then subtract the area of the smaller rectangle to get the final answer.

If you look at the larger rectangle in whole, its length is 5 inches and its width is 8 inches. The formula to find the area of a rectangle is $A = lw$, where l represents length and w represents width. The area of the larger rectangle is $8 \times 5 = 40$ square inches.

The smaller rectangle measures 4 inches wide by 3 inches long. Its area is $4 \times 3 = 12$ square inches.

Subtract the area of the smaller rectangle from the area of the larger rectangle to get your answer: $40 - 12 = 28$ square inches.

18. **A. $8\frac{5}{32}$**

A problem like this is easier to tackle if you turn $\frac{5}{8}$ into the decimal 0.625 before you start. Once that's done, you can multiply both sides by 1,000 to ditch the decimals and solve:

$$4x = 32\frac{5}{8}$$
$$4x = 32.625$$
$$4x \cdot 1,000 = 32.625(1,000)$$
$$4,000x = 32,625$$
$$\frac{4,000x}{4,000} = \frac{32,625}{4,000}$$
$$x = \frac{261}{32}$$
$$x = 8\frac{5}{32}$$

Because all the answer choices are in fraction form, you didn't have to convert your answer to a decimal.

Here's an even faster approach: Isolate x by dividing both sides by 4, treating the whole number (32) and the fraction separately:

$$4x = 32\frac{5}{8}$$

Whole number part: $32 \div 4 = 8$

Fractional part: $\frac{5}{8} \div 4 = \frac{5}{8} \cdot \frac{1}{4} = \frac{5}{32}$

Add the two parts of the problem back together. The answer is still $8\frac{5}{32}$.

19. **C.** $2b\sqrt{3a^3}$

To solve this problem, you'll have to separate the variables from the real numbers:

$$\sqrt{12a^3b^2} = \sqrt{12}\sqrt{b^2}\sqrt{a^3}$$

Then break 12 into its primes (2^2 and 3); your work looks like this:

$$2\sqrt{3}\sqrt{b^2}\sqrt{a^3}$$

Break down the variable b, because the square of a squared number is itself, and apply the radical rule $\sqrt[n]{a^m} = a^{\frac{m}{n}}$ to what's left: $2b\sqrt{3a^3}$

20. **D.** −5

Collect all terms with an a on one side. Then divide both sides by 12 to solve.

$$14a = -60 + 2a$$
$$14a - 2a = -60 + 2a - 2a$$
$$12a = -60$$
$$\frac{12a}{12} = \frac{-60}{12}$$
$$a = -5$$

21. **A.** 7.7×10^6

Scientific notation requires you to write a number in two parts: A real number between 1 and 10, multiplied by 10 raised to a power. The power shows you how many places to move the decimal point to get back to the original number.

In scientific notation, only one digit goes before the decimal point. For 7,700,000, the decimal point goes after the first 7 but before the second. There are then six digits after the decimal point, which tells you what power you need to use. The answer is 7.7×10^6.

22. **D.** $y = \frac{3}{2}x - 2$

Remember the point-slope form of a line is $y = mx + b$, where m represents the slope and b represents the point where the line intersects the y-axis. The first thing you need to find is the slope. Use the formula $m = \frac{y_2 - y_1}{x_2 - x_1}$, and plug in the given x and y values given by the coordinates.

$$m = \frac{1-7}{2-6} = \frac{-6}{-4} = \frac{3}{2}$$

Now you have the first piece of the puzzle, so plug it into the equation:

$$y = mx + b$$
$$y = \frac{3}{2}x + b$$

Substitute the given values for x and y from the coordinates of one of the points into the equation and then solve for b. Here are the calculations if you choose the first point:

$$7 = \frac{3}{2}(6) + b$$

$$\frac{3}{2}(6) + b = 7$$

$$9 + b = 7$$

$$9 + b - 9 = 7 - 9$$

$$b = -2$$

Now that you know $b = -2$, you know the complete equation is $y = \frac{3}{2}x - 2$.

You could've used the second set of points to find the equation, too. Either way, the answer is the same.

23. **B.** $a^2 + b^2 = c^2$

Using the Pythagorean theorem, you can find an unknown side's length in a right triangle if you know the lengths of the other two sides.

In this formula, a and b stand for the lengths of the legs, and c stands for the length of the hypotenuse.

24. **C. 70**

Before you work on percentage problems, convert the percentage to a decimal. 35 percent translates into 0.35.

The word *of* in the problem tells you to multiply the two quantities. 35% *of* 200 = 35% times 200:

$$0.35 \times 200 = 70$$

Tip: If you're doing mental math, you could reason that 35 is 35 percent of 100. If you double that to find 35 percent of 200, you'll come up with 70 again. This works because multiplication is commutative. Mathematically, $35 \cdot \frac{1}{100} \cdot 200 = 200 \cdot \frac{1}{100} \cdot 35$, and because 200% is 2, you can double 35 to get the answer on this (or a similar) problem.

25. **D. 6**

The problem tells you that $b = -5.75$, so replace the variable b in the equation with the given value; then simplify:

$$\frac{3a}{2} + b = 3.25$$

$$\frac{3a}{2} + (-5.75) = 3.25$$

$$\frac{3a}{2} - 5.75 + 5.75 = 3.25 + 5.75$$

$$\frac{3a}{2} = 9$$

$$\frac{3a}{2} \times \frac{2}{1} = 9 \times \frac{2}{1}$$

$$3a = 18$$

$$a = 6$$

Answer Key

Part 1: Arithmetic Reasoning

1.	B	9.	D	17.	B	25.	A
2.	C	10.	A	18.	C	26.	D
3.	A	11.	B	19.	C	27.	B
4.	A	12.	A	20.	C	28.	D
5.	C	13.	D	21.	C	29.	C
6.	C	14.	A	22.	C	30.	D
7.	B	15.	C	23.	A		
8.	C	16.	B	24.	C		

Part 2: Word Knowledge

1.	B	10.	A	19.	B	28.	A
2.	A	11.	B	20.	A	29.	B
3.	D	12.	C	21.	D	30.	C
4.	B	13.	D	22.	C	31.	A
5.	A	14.	A	23.	A	32.	D
6.	A	15.	B	24.	A	33.	B
7.	D	16.	A	25.	B	34.	D
8.	C	17.	C	26.	C	35.	A
9.	B	18.	D	27.	D		

Part 3: Paragraph Comprehension

1.	D	5.	C	9.	C	13.	C
2.	B	6.	B	10.	B	14.	D
3.	C	7.	D	11.	C	15.	B
4.	D	8.	C	12.	A		

Part 4: Mathematics Knowledge

1.	A	8.	C	15.	A	22.	D
2.	A	9.	B	16.	C	23.	B
3.	C	10.	B	17.	B	24.	C
4.	B	11.	B	18.	A	25.	D
5.	D	12.	A	19.	C		
6.	C	13.	D	20.	D		
7.	A	14.	C	21.	A		

Chapter 14

Practice Exam 2

The Armed Services Vocational Aptitude Battery (ASVAB) includes four subtests that make up the Armed Forces Qualification Test (AFQT) score: Arithmetic Reasoning, Word Knowledge, Paragraph Comprehension, and Mathematics Knowledge.

The military branches use the AFQT score as an initial qualifier to determine whether the military considers you to be "trainable." Each service has established its own minimum score. You can find much more information about how the AFQT is scored, and how the services use those scores, in Chapter 1.

REMEMBER

You can't take the AFQT by itself. You have to take the entire ASVAB exam, which includes 10 total subtests (on the computerized version of the ASVAB, the Auto and Shop Information subtests are presented separately, but on the paper-and-pencil version of the test, they're combined — most people take the computerized version.) All the subtests of the ASVAB are used to determine military job qualifications, while the four subtests that make up the AFQT score are used to determine military qualification.

After you complete the entire sample test, check your answers against the answers and explanations in Chapter 15. On the actual AFQT, hard questions are worth more points than easy questions, so you can't score your test by a simple number correct or number wrong. (Chapter 1 explains how the AFQT is scored.)

Consider using this test as a progress check after your first week or two of study. Adjust your study plan accordingly.

Answer Sheet for Practice Exam 2

Part 1: Arithmetic Reasoning

1. Ⓐ Ⓑ Ⓒ Ⓓ
2. Ⓐ Ⓑ Ⓒ Ⓓ
3. Ⓐ Ⓑ Ⓒ Ⓓ
4. Ⓐ Ⓑ Ⓒ Ⓓ
5. Ⓐ Ⓑ Ⓒ Ⓓ
6. Ⓐ Ⓑ Ⓒ Ⓓ

7. Ⓐ Ⓑ Ⓒ Ⓓ
8. Ⓐ Ⓑ Ⓒ Ⓓ
9. Ⓐ Ⓑ Ⓒ Ⓓ
10. Ⓐ Ⓑ Ⓒ Ⓓ
11. Ⓐ Ⓑ Ⓒ Ⓓ
12. Ⓐ Ⓑ Ⓒ Ⓓ

13. Ⓐ Ⓑ Ⓒ Ⓓ
14. Ⓐ Ⓑ Ⓒ Ⓓ
15. Ⓐ Ⓑ Ⓒ Ⓓ
16. Ⓐ Ⓑ Ⓒ Ⓓ
17. Ⓐ Ⓑ Ⓒ Ⓓ
18. Ⓐ Ⓑ Ⓒ Ⓓ

19. Ⓐ Ⓑ Ⓒ Ⓓ
20. Ⓐ Ⓑ Ⓒ Ⓓ
21. Ⓐ Ⓑ Ⓒ Ⓓ
22. Ⓐ Ⓑ Ⓒ Ⓓ
23. Ⓐ Ⓑ Ⓒ Ⓓ
24. Ⓐ Ⓑ Ⓒ Ⓓ

25. Ⓐ Ⓑ Ⓒ Ⓓ
26. Ⓐ Ⓑ Ⓒ Ⓓ
27. Ⓐ Ⓑ Ⓒ Ⓓ
28. Ⓐ Ⓑ Ⓒ Ⓓ
29. Ⓐ Ⓑ Ⓒ Ⓓ
30. Ⓐ Ⓑ Ⓒ Ⓓ

Part 2: Word Knowledge

1. Ⓐ Ⓑ Ⓒ Ⓓ
2. Ⓐ Ⓑ Ⓒ Ⓓ
3. Ⓐ Ⓑ Ⓒ Ⓓ
4. Ⓐ Ⓑ Ⓒ Ⓓ
5. Ⓐ Ⓑ Ⓒ Ⓓ
6. Ⓐ Ⓑ Ⓒ Ⓓ
7. Ⓐ Ⓑ Ⓒ Ⓓ

8. Ⓐ Ⓑ Ⓒ Ⓓ
9. Ⓐ Ⓑ Ⓒ Ⓓ
10. Ⓐ Ⓑ Ⓒ Ⓓ
11. Ⓐ Ⓑ Ⓒ Ⓓ
12. Ⓐ Ⓑ Ⓒ Ⓓ
13. Ⓐ Ⓑ Ⓒ Ⓓ
14. Ⓐ Ⓑ Ⓒ Ⓓ

15. Ⓐ Ⓑ Ⓒ Ⓓ
16. Ⓐ Ⓑ Ⓒ Ⓓ
17. Ⓐ Ⓑ Ⓒ Ⓓ
18. Ⓐ Ⓑ Ⓒ Ⓓ
19. Ⓐ Ⓑ Ⓒ Ⓓ
20. Ⓐ Ⓑ Ⓒ Ⓓ
21. Ⓐ Ⓑ Ⓒ Ⓓ

22. Ⓐ Ⓑ Ⓒ Ⓓ
23. Ⓐ Ⓑ Ⓒ Ⓓ
24. Ⓐ Ⓑ Ⓒ Ⓓ
25. Ⓐ Ⓑ Ⓒ Ⓓ
26. Ⓐ Ⓑ Ⓒ Ⓓ
27. Ⓐ Ⓑ Ⓒ Ⓓ
28. Ⓐ Ⓑ Ⓒ Ⓓ

29. Ⓐ Ⓑ Ⓒ Ⓓ
30. Ⓐ Ⓑ Ⓒ Ⓓ
31. Ⓐ Ⓑ Ⓒ Ⓓ
32. Ⓐ Ⓑ Ⓒ Ⓓ
33. Ⓐ Ⓑ Ⓒ Ⓓ
34. Ⓐ Ⓑ Ⓒ Ⓓ
35. Ⓐ Ⓑ Ⓒ Ⓓ

Part 3: Paragraph Comprehension

1. Ⓐ Ⓑ Ⓒ Ⓓ   4. Ⓐ Ⓑ Ⓒ Ⓓ   7. Ⓐ Ⓑ Ⓒ Ⓓ   10. Ⓐ Ⓑ Ⓒ Ⓓ   13. Ⓐ Ⓑ Ⓒ Ⓓ
2. Ⓐ Ⓑ Ⓒ Ⓓ   5. Ⓐ Ⓑ Ⓒ Ⓓ   8. Ⓐ Ⓑ Ⓒ Ⓓ   11. Ⓐ Ⓑ Ⓒ Ⓓ   14. Ⓐ Ⓑ Ⓒ Ⓓ
3. Ⓐ Ⓑ Ⓒ Ⓓ   6. Ⓐ Ⓑ Ⓒ Ⓓ   9. Ⓐ Ⓑ Ⓒ Ⓓ   12. Ⓐ Ⓑ Ⓒ Ⓓ   15. Ⓐ Ⓑ Ⓒ Ⓓ

Part 4: Mathematics Knowledge

1. Ⓐ Ⓑ Ⓒ Ⓓ   6. Ⓐ Ⓑ Ⓒ Ⓓ   11. Ⓐ Ⓑ Ⓒ Ⓓ   16. Ⓐ Ⓑ Ⓒ Ⓓ   21. Ⓐ Ⓑ Ⓒ Ⓓ
2. Ⓐ Ⓑ Ⓒ Ⓓ   7. Ⓐ Ⓑ Ⓒ Ⓓ   12. Ⓐ Ⓑ Ⓒ Ⓓ   17. Ⓐ Ⓑ Ⓒ Ⓓ   22. Ⓐ Ⓑ Ⓒ Ⓓ
3. Ⓐ Ⓑ Ⓒ Ⓓ   8. Ⓐ Ⓑ Ⓒ Ⓓ   13. Ⓐ Ⓑ Ⓒ Ⓓ   18. Ⓐ Ⓑ Ⓒ Ⓓ   23. Ⓐ Ⓑ Ⓒ Ⓓ
4. Ⓐ Ⓑ Ⓒ Ⓓ   9. Ⓐ Ⓑ Ⓒ Ⓓ   14. Ⓐ Ⓑ Ⓒ Ⓓ   19. Ⓐ Ⓑ Ⓒ Ⓓ   24. Ⓐ Ⓑ Ⓒ Ⓓ
5. Ⓐ Ⓑ Ⓒ Ⓓ   10. Ⓐ Ⓑ Ⓒ Ⓓ   15. Ⓐ Ⓑ Ⓒ Ⓓ   20. Ⓐ Ⓑ Ⓒ Ⓓ   25. Ⓐ Ⓑ Ⓒ Ⓓ

Part 1: Arithmetic Reasoning

TIME: 36 minutes for 30 questions

DIRECTIONS: Arithmetic Reasoning is the second subtest of the ASVAB; it comes after General Science, which isn't part of the AFQT. These questions are designed to test your ability to use mathematics to solve various problems that may be found in real life — in other words, math word problems.

Each question is followed by four possible answers. Decide which answer is correct, and then mark the corresponding space on your answer sheet. Use your scratch paper for any figuring you want to do. You may *not* use a calculator.

1. Marta is building a rectangular fence in her backyard and has 200 feet of fencing she can use. If the yard is to be 15 feet wide and she uses all the fencing, how long will the yard be?

   (A) 27 ft

   (B) 72 ft

   (C) 85 ft

   (D) 87 ft

2. Henry is 48 inches tall. His older brother is 25 percent taller. How tall is Henry's brother?

   (A) 60 in.

   (B) 64 in.

   (C) 63 in.

   (D) 73 in.

3. Janet, Alice, and Gabriel are collecting cans for recycling. Altogether, they collected 473 cans. Janet collected 124 cans, and Alice collected 205 cans. How many cans did Gabriel collect?

   (A) 329

   (B) 142

   (C) 144

   (D) 167

4. The floor of Mr. Gilbert's office is in the shape of a rectangle with an area of 168 square feet. The length of the floor is 12 feet. What is the width?

   (A) 12 ft

   (B) 14 ft

   (C) 9 ft

   (D) 16 ft

5. There are 10 decimeters in a meter and 10 meters in a decameter. How many decimeters are there in 3 decameters?

   (A) 3,000

   (B) 0.03

   (C) 300

   (D) 30

6. At 9:00 a.m., the outside temperature was −14° Fahrenheit. By noon, the temperature increased by 21° Fahrenheit. What was the outside temperature at noon?

   (A) 7°

   (B) 6°

   (C) −7°

   (D) −35°

7. An airplane flew a distance of 180 miles in an hour and a half. What was the speed of the plane?

   (A) 120 mph

   (B) 110 mph

   (C) 180 mph

   (D) 270 mph

8. The ratio of cars to trucks is 3:4. There are 15 cars. How many trucks are there?

   (A) 24

   (B) 10

   (C) 12

   (D) 20

9. A grocery store sells raisins for $3.50 per pound and almonds for $4 per pound. Keith bought just enough raisins and almonds to make a 2-pound mixture that is 40-percent raisins. How much did he pay for the raisins?

(A) $2.85

(B) $3.50

(C) $3.20

(D) $2.80

10. Patricia's age is one-third Ms. Chang's age. The sum of their ages is 56 years. What is Ms. Chang's age?

(A) 38

(B) 44

(C) 42

(D) 14

11. Ed worked 10 hours and earned $125. John also worked 10 hours, but his hourly rate is $0.50 less than Ed's hourly rate. How much did John earn for 10 hours of work?

(A) $118.50

(B) $60.00

(C) $119.50

(D) $120.00

12. A game board is in the shape of a square with a perimeter of 60 inches. What is the length of one side of the game board?

(A) 1 ft

(B) 1.25 ft

(C) 1.5 ft

(D) 1.75 ft

13. A recipe calls for $2\frac{3}{4}$ cups of milk, but you have only $1\frac{1}{2}$ cups of milk available. How much more milk do you need for the recipe?

(A) $1\frac{3}{5}$ cups

(B) $1\frac{1}{4}$ cups

(C) $1\frac{1}{5}$ cups

(D) $\frac{3}{4}$ cup

14. Maria invests $2,500 into a savings account. After 1 year, she has earned $100 in interest. What is the annual interest rate for the account?

(A) 4.5 percent

(B) 0.4 percent

(C) 4 percent

(D) 2.5 percent

15. What is the area of the region in this figure?

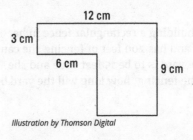

Illustration by Thomson Digital

(A) 72 cm²

(B) 36 cm²

(C) 90 cm²

(D) 30 cm²

16. Martha is teaching her first cooking class. 60 percent of the class — or 21 students — burned their quiche. How many total students are in the class?

(A) 27

(B) 31

(C) 35

(D) 39

17. Keisha walked a distance of 4.5 miles at a rate of 3 miles per hour. She started her walk at 3:40 p.m. What time did she finish her walk?

(A) 4:10 p.m.

(B) 3:55 p.m.

(C) 4:20 p.m.

(D) 5:10 p.m.

18. You earn $9.75 an hour and need to earn at least $150. Which inequality shows the number of hours, h, you must work?

(A) $9.75 < 150h$

(B) $9.75h \geq 150$

(C) $9.75h \leq 150$

(D) $\frac{19.75}{h} \geq 150$

19. Carlos has a model of his father's new truck. The model truck is 32 centimeters long. If the scale of the model is 2 centimeters = 0.25 meters, what is the approximate length of his father's truck?

(A) 4 m

(B) 8 m

(C) 10 m

(D) 12 m

20. Aaliyah is selling 3 paintings. She places them in a row so the cost increases by $15 from left to right. The painting on the far left costs $29. What is the cost of the painting on the far right?

(A) $59

(B) $15

(C) $44

(D) $75

21. Taraji is in a hurry to get to her friend's house Thanksgiving dinner in Wyoming. If she is traveling a constant 50 miles per hour, how many hours will it take her to make the 600-mile trip?

(A) 30 hours

(B) 12 hours

(C) 60 hours

(D) 15 hours

22. On the expressway, where the speed limit is 60 miles per hour, the formula for calculating a speeding fine, F, is $F = 10(x - 60) + 80$, where x is the speed of the car in miles per hour. If Steve was fined $230 for speeding down the highway, how fast was he driving?

(A) 70 mph

(B) 75 mph

(C) 85 mph

(D) 80 mph

23. Siraj recorded the odometer reading of 65,034 before filling his car with gas. The next time he filled his car with gas, the odometer reading was 65,322. He needed 12 gallons of gas to fill his tank. What is the best estimate of the car's gas mileage in miles per gallon (mpg)?

(A) 12 mpg

(B) 24 mpg

(C) 18 mpg

(D) 32 mpg

24. A can of beans is in the shape of a cylinder. The can has a diameter of 8 centimeters and a height of 10 centimeters. What is the volume of the can?

(A) 160π cm^3

(B) 640π cm^3

(C) 80π cm^3

(D) $1,600\pi$ cm^3

25. Matt must pay a $15 co-pay for each of his visits to a chiropractor. Then the insurance company pays 60 percent of the remaining cost of the visit. He made 10 visits to the chiropractor, each costing $305. How much did Matt pay for his chiropractor visits in total?

(A) $2,900

(B) $1,310

(C) $1,160

(D) $1,180

26. Marco can replace a truck tire in 20 minutes. His brother takes 10 minutes longer to do the same job. How long will replacing a truck tire take them if they work together?

(A) 18 minutes

(B) 16 minutes

(C) 12 minutes

(D) 25 minutes

27. Each squeeze of a spray bottle's trigger emits 0.024 ounces of water. Ten squeezes of the trigger emit 2 percent of the total amount of water the bottle holds. How many ounces of water can the bottle hold?

(A) 16 oz

(B) 20 oz

(C) 24 oz

(D) 12 oz

28. A shoe box has a length of 30 centimeters, a width of 15 centimeters, and a height of 10 centimeters. What is the surface area of the shoe box?

(A) 3,600 cm²

(B) 4,500 cm²

(C) 1,800 cm²

(D) 900 cm²

29. Two runners start in the same place and run in opposite directions. The first runner averages 5 miles per hour, and the second runner averages 6 miles per hour. After how many hours will they be 11 miles apart?

(A) 1 hour

(B) 2 hours

(C) 1.5 hours

(D) 1.1 hours

30. The coach bought pepperoni pizzas for the entire soccer team, including himself. Each pizza cost $12. When they were all finished eating, $2\frac{3}{4}$ pizzas were left over. Each of the 15 players on the team ate a quarter of a pizza, and the coach ate half of a pizza. How much did the coach pay for the pizzas before tax?

(A) $72

(B) $180

(C) $84

(D) $88

Part 2: Word Knowledge

TIME: 11 minutes for 35 questions

DIRECTIONS: The Word Knowledge subtest is the third subtest of the ASVAB; it follows Arithmetic Reasoning. The questions are designed to measure your vocabulary knowledge. You'll see three types of questions on this subtest. The first type simply asks you to choose a word or words that most nearly mean the same as the underlined word in the question. The second type includes an underlined word used in a sentence, and you are to choose the word or words that most nearly mean the same as the underlined word, as used in the context of the sentence. The third type of question asks you to choose the word that has the opposite or nearly opposite meaning as the underlined word. Each question is followed by four possible answers. Decide which answer is correct, and then mark the corresponding space on your answer sheet.

1. The word most opposite in meaning to savor is
   (A) deny.
   (B) enjoy.
   (C) detest.
   (D) keep.

2. Lackluster most nearly means
   (A) exuberant.
   (B) benign.
   (C) mediocre.
   (D) sharp.

3. The word most opposite in meaning to participate is
   (A) abstain.
   (B) join.
   (C) contribute.
   (D) shove.

4. The word most opposite in meaning to organize is
   (A) arrange.
   (B) mess up.
   (C) juggle.
   (D) disturb.

5. Unkempt most nearly means
   (A) clean.
   (B) orderly.
   (C) disastrous.
   (D) messy.

6. I knew the preliminary interview was merely to get my foot in the door.
   (A) falling
   (B) first
   (C) closing
   (D) binding

7. The clash between Keola and his boss was inevitable because of their different values.
   (A) unlikely
   (B) unavoidable
   (C) unrelenting
   (D) unusual

8. Toby took the sunset as a good omen for his new life in Florida.
   (A) fact
   (B) letter
   (C) decree
   (D) sign

9. The frigid wind on the chairlift was enough to give someone frostbite.
   (A) stale
   (B) warm
   (C) cold
   (D) boring

10. No one voted for Michael because he was such a <u>tyrant</u> last semester.

    (A) leader

    (B) oppressor

    (C) guide

    (D) teacher

11. <u>Counterfeit</u> most nearly means

    (A) authentic.

    (B) soiled.

    (C) phony.

    (D) credible.

12. The word most opposite in meaning to <u>burden</u> is

    (A) relieve.

    (B) bother.

    (C) trouble.

    (D) support.

13. The word most opposite in meaning to <u>animate</u> is

    (A) deflect.

    (B) stir.

    (C) enliven.

    (D) subdue.

14. <u>Plausible</u> most nearly means

    (A) impossible.

    (B) factual.

    (C) reasonable.

    (D) perishable.

15. <u>Pliable</u> most nearly means

    (A) dormant.

    (B) flexible.

    (C) stiff.

    (D) spontaneous.

16. <u>Resignation</u> most nearly means

    (A) approval.

    (B) acceptance.

    (C) denial.

    (D) disbelief.

17. <u>Obliterate</u> most nearly means

    (A) pamper.

    (B) wound.

    (C) destroy.

    (D) control.

18. <u>Heed</u> most nearly means

    (A) betray.

    (B) abide.

    (C) ignore.

    (D) escape.

19. Amelie felt <u>immense</u> pride as he accepted the gold medal.

    (A) massive

    (B) contained

    (C) minute

    (D) similar

20. Mei made a choice to <u>pursue</u> her dream of dancing despite her parents' disapproval.

    (A) follow

    (B) ignore

    (C) mediate

    (D) bring forth

21. I was impressed by how <u>tactful</u> my father was regarding my recent breakup.

    (A) cruel

    (B) oblivious

    (C) sensitive

    (D) doting

22. I loved watching my jock brother <u>endure</u> my sister's ballet recitals.

    (A) tolerate

    (B) approve

    (C) deny

    (D) abstain

23. Charli's <u>longevity</u> during the marathon training was better than she expected.

    (A) brevity

    (B) distance

    (C) number

    (D) endurance

24. The girl had to <u>console</u> her friend, who couldn't stop crying.

   (A) compartment

   (B) comfort

   (C) hide

   (D) push away

25. When the coach claps his hands, we're supposed to <u>disperse</u> to our positions in the field.

   (A) run

   (B) gather

   (C) scatter

   (D) formulate

26. <u>Enshrouded</u> most nearly means

   (A) illuminated.

   (B) enclosed.

   (C) revealed.

   (D) covered.

27. <u>Repudiate</u> most nearly means

   (A) disown.

   (B) waver.

   (C) reclaim.

   (D) adjust.

28. <u>Oblique</u> most nearly means

   (A) forward.

   (B) cordial.

   (C) indirect.

   (D) candid.

29. <u>Acquiesce</u> most nearly means

   (A) agree with.

   (B) argue with.

   (C) hide from.

   (D) move into.

30. <u>Tenuous</u> most nearly means

   (A) stable.

   (B) flimsy.

   (C) firm.

   (D) buoyant.

31. The children were <u>unbridled</u> during playtime, looking more like wild animals than 5-year-olds.

   (A) organized

   (B) relieving

   (C) rampant

   (D) joyous

32. I won't <u>ostracize</u> the new girl just because the other kids are jealous.

   (A) ridicule

   (B) befriend

   (C) exclude

   (D) restrict

33. <u>Replete</u> most nearly means

   (A) full.

   (B) barren.

   (C) meager.

   (D) coarse.

34. <u>Enigma</u> most nearly means

   (A) accessible.

   (B) mystery.

   (C) transparent.

   (D) profound.

35. Carlton stepped in to <u>assuage</u> the patron's fury after a waiter spilled soup on the man.

   (A) pacify

   (B) replace

   (C) order

   (D) determine

Part 3: Paragraph Comprehension

TIME: 13 minutes for 15 questions

DIRECTIONS: Paragraph Comprehension is the fourth subtest on the ASVAB; it comes after Word Knowledge. The questions are designed to measure your ability to understand what you read. In this part of the test, you see one or more paragraphs of reading material, followed by incomplete statements or questions. Read the paragraph and select the choice that best completes the statement or answers the question. Then mark the corresponding space on your answer sheet.

Questions 1 and 2 refer to the following passage.

Dog training isn't for the faint of heart. You have to be tough and let the dog know who's boss, or it'll never listen to anything you say. If your dog is a puppy, you may have to put it in a crate when you leave the house, which will cause the puppy to whine and become anxious. All these actions can be difficult when you're looking into the face of an adorable dog, so you have to be firm in your resolve even when you feel bad.

1. What is the main point of the passage?
   - (A) Crate training is the best way to train a dog.
   - (B) Dogs are easy to train.
   - (C) All dogs require training.
   - (D) Trainers should avoid becoming emotional.

2. In this passage, resolve means
   - (A) determination.
   - (B) indecision.
   - (C) prowess.
   - (D) fear.

The sudden death of Dale Earnhardt was a shock to not only the NASCAR community but also the world. His aggressiveness on the track and success behind the wheel made him a well-known figure and a household name. He started his career in 1975, racing as part of the Winston Cup Series in Charlotte, North Carolina. Before his fatal crash in 2001 during the Daytona 500, he won more than 76 races, including one Daytona 500 race in 1998. He shares the record for the most NASCAR Premier Series Championships with Richard Petty and Jimmie Johnson at seven apiece.

3. How many Daytona 500 races did Dale Earnhardt win?
   - (A) 7
   - (B) 76
   - (C) 1
   - (D) None of the above

Bipolar disorder is a mental issue that involves acute swings in mood, ranging from a heightened state of mania and an extreme state of depression. More than 4 percent of the population lives with bipolar disorder, which can be a debilitating factor in day-to-day functioning. The cause is still a topic of research for scientists, although they suspect that genetics and environment are responsible, at least in part, for the onset of the illness.

4. As used in this passage, acute most nearly means
   - (A) pointed.
   - (B) severe.
   - (C) sensitive.
   - (D) mild.

Questions 5 and 6 refer to the following passage.

For a sport to get into the Olympic Games, the International Olympic Committee must first recognize the activity as an official sport, and the sport must have a governing agency that isn't politically affiliated. In 2014, 12 sports were added to the Winter Olympics in Sochi, Russia, but many more have come and gone over the years. For instance, rugby was added and dropped from the games three times between 1900 and 1928. However, the sport was added again to the 2016 Summer Olympics in Rio de Janeiro, Brazil, due to a gap in the roster created by the elimination of softball and baseball from the 2012 Summer Games in London, England.

5. How many times has rugby been added to the roster of Olympic sports?

    (A) 3

    (B) 12

    (C) 4

    (D) 1

6. According to the passage, what country hosted the 2016 Summer Olympics?

    (A) Holland

    (B) England

    (C) Russia

    (D) Brazil

Making bread and cooking are different beasts. You can easily substitute ingredients and improvise the recipe as you go in cooking, but you must use exact ingredients and measurements for breadmaking. For example, if you want to use whole-grain flour instead of bread flour, you have to change the ratio of wet ingredients to get the same texture. Cooking is much more flexible than breadmaking.

7. What is the author trying to convey in this paragraph?

    (A) Making bread is easier than cooking.

    (B) Anyone can measure ingredients.

    (C) Breadmaking is more exact than cooking.

    (D) Whole grains are better for cooking.

Questions 8 and 9 refer to the following passage.

The history of the bald eagle in the United States is an interesting tale; the national bird came very close to extinction in the mid-20th century. An act of Congress in 1940 barred the trapping and killing of the eagles in the United States, but their numbers continued to decline. It was discovered that the pesticide DDT caused a calcium breakdown in bald eagles, resulting in sterilization or fragile eggshells and therefore low reproduction rates. With the ban of DDT use in 1972, the slow regrowth of the species began. In 1995, the eagles were removed from the endangered species list; in 1998, they were removed from the threatened species list. The bald eagles now live in abundance in North America.

8. In the passage, <u>barred</u> means

    (A) promoted.

    (B) outlawed.

    (C) approved.

    (D) disowned.

9. In what year did the action that eventually led to the growth of the bald eagle population begin?

    (A) 1972

    (B) 1998

    (C) 1995

    (D) 1940

Jill has danced her best many times in front of audiences, but this performance is the most important one of her life. Her audition for the famed Joffrey Ballet company is the end of a long journey of schooling and competitions, all of which were in preparation for this moment. She has spent the last 15 years improving her skills, and she is confident in her ability to achieve her goal. Dancing with the Joffrey Ballet would be a dream come true for Jill.

10. What is the main point of this passage about Jill?

    (A) Jill is a skilled ballet dancer.

    (B) Ballet is Jill's preferred form of exercise.

    (C) Joining the Joffrey Ballet is Jill's life's goal.

    (D) Jill is overly determined.

A good quilt was once simply fluffy, decorative, and cozy, creating the image of a grandmother lovingly sewing patches of material together by hand. Today, however, the art of quilting is more lucrative than just a hobby. National and international quilting contests are regular annual events with hundreds of entrants. The quilts depict a variety of scenes, from landscapes to skylines, and the prizes for best in show can reach up to $10,000. Quilting has become a serious activity for many, and the results are impressive.

11. According to the passage, quilt makers

(A) have plenty of time on their hands.

(B) have opportunities to make a lot of money.

(C) are in short supply.

(D) make quilts only with squares.

For sale: Inflatable lifeboat for use in calm, shallow water. Has some puncture holes on the surface. Water typically fills the bottom, and air must be pumped periodically to avoid sinking. This boat isn't good for water deeper than four feet or for people who don't swim. Asking market price of $200.

12. According to this advertisement, the lifeboat would be safe to use in

(A) a lake.

(B) the ocean.

(C) a river.

(D) None of the above

Questions 13 and 14 refer to the following passage.

A new study indicates that childhood obesity begins in the early years of life. Researchers followed more than 7,500 obese students between kindergarten (age 5) and eighth grade. The findings indicated that two-thirds of the children who were obese in kindergarten remained obese in eighth grade. The study also showed that children who were obese in eighth grade were likely to remain that way into adulthood. The researchers measured the children seven times for height and weight over the period of the study, and determinations of "obese" or "overweight" were made using body mass index levels.

13. Based on the information in the passage, which step might reduce adolescent obesity?

(A) promoting extracurricular activities

(B) removing a child from school

(C) forming a support group for obese children

(D) preventing a child from becoming overweight before the age of 5

14. According to the passage, approximately how many children who participated in the study fell out of the obese range?

(A) one-third

(B) 7,500

(C) two-thirds

(D) 25 percent

Crispin Glover is a cult actor famous for his dark and brooding characters. Finding success first in the thriller *The River's Edge*, he became the most famous studious character in the world with his portrayal of outcast bookworm George McFly in the box-office hit *Back to the Future*. He is often referred to as a shape shifter for his ability to fully become his characters. His role as the slick samurai in the movie adaptation of the TV series *Charlie's Angels* was no exception.

15. In this passage, <u>adaptation</u> can best be defined as

(A) version.

(B) copy.

(C) continuation.

(D) screenplay.

DO NOT TURN THE PAGE UNTIL TOLD TO DO SO **STOP** DO NOT RETURN TO A PREVIOUS TEST

Part 4: Mathematics Knowledge

TIME: 24 minutes for 25 questions

DIRECTIONS: Mathematics Knowledge is the fifth subtest on the ASVAB; it follows Paragraph Comprehension. The questions are designed to test your ability to solve general mathematical problems. Each question is followed by four possible answers. Decide which answer is correct, and then mark the corresponding space on your answer sheet. Use your scratch paper for any figuring you want to do. You may *not* use a calculator.

1. Which number is prime?
   - (A) 1
   - (B) 2
   - (C) 10
   - (D) 51

2. Which decimal is equal to eleven thousandths?
   - (A) 1.1
   - (B) 0.11
   - (C) 0.011
   - (D) 0.101

3. $1.091 + 0.19 =$
   - (A) 1.100
   - (B) 1.182
   - (C) 1.281
   - (D) 1.11

4. An equilateral triangle has a perimeter of 54 feet. What is the length of one side of the triangle?
   - (A) 18 ft
   - (B) 16 ft
   - (C) 27 ft
   - (D) 162 ft

5. What is 40 percent of 220?
   - (A) 8.8
   - (B) 55
   - (C) 44
   - (D) 88

6. What is $\frac{26}{8}$ expressed as a decimal?
   - (A) 4.25
   - (B) 3.5
   - (C) 2.75
   - (D) 3.25

7. Which of the following is equal to $p^3 \times p^{-1}$?
   - (A) p^2
   - (B) $2p^2$
   - (C) p^{-3}
   - (D) p

8. $\frac{8}{25} - \frac{3}{25} =$
   - (A) $\frac{5}{50}$
   - (B) $\frac{1}{5}$
   - (C) $\frac{1}{4}$
   - (D) $\frac{5}{0}$

9. For which value of y is the inequality $y + 2 < -6$ true?
   - (A) -9
   - (B) -8
   - (C) 7
   - (D) 9

10. Simplify: $3(x - 5) + 4x$
    - (A) $7x - 5$
    - (B) $7x - 15$
    - (C) $7x + 35$
    - (D) $12x - 15$

11. The longest side of a right triangle has a length of 17 feet, and the shortest side has a length of 8 feet. What is the length of the remaining side?

(A) 10 ft

(B) 12 ft

(C) 15 ft

(D) 16 ft

12. What is the result when the quotient of 40 and 20 is decreased by the sum of 1 and 5?

(A) −5.5

(B) 2

(C) 14

(D) −4

13. $15 - 3 \times 2^2 =$

(A) −21

(B) 576

(C) 3

(D) 48

14. What is the least common multiple of 12 and 20?

(A) 2

(B) 60

(C) 120

(D) 240

15. What is the product of $\frac{3}{4}$ and $\frac{8}{7}$?

(A) $\frac{6}{7}$

(B) $\frac{11}{28}$

(C) 1

(D) $\frac{24}{11}$

16. $3(-4)(1)(-2) =$

(A) −24

(B) 12

(C) 18

(D) 24

17. $\sqrt[3]{64} =$

(A) 8 and −8

(B) 4 and −4

(C) 8 only

(D) 4 only

18. $\frac{2}{5} + \frac{1}{3} =$

(A) $\frac{5}{50}$

(B) $\frac{1}{5}$

(C) $\frac{11}{15}$

(D) $\frac{3}{8}$

19. The length of one side of the square is 20 meters. Find the area of the region that is inside the square but outside the circle.

20 m

Illustration by Thomson Digital

(A) 314 m²

(B) 86 m²

(C) 856 m²

(D) 234 m²

20. The sum of three consecutive odd integers is 63. What is the middle number?

(A) 21

(B) 23

(C) 25

(D) 27

21. Solve the equation $x^2 + 4 = 20$ for x.

(A) 16 only

(B) 8 and −8

(C) 4 only

(D) 4 and −4

22. The measure of the supplement of an angle is equal to twice the measure of the angle. What is the measure of the angle?

(A) 60°

(B) 30°

(C) 120°

(D) 90°

23. Solve for x: $\dfrac{9}{x} = \dfrac{81}{10}$

(A) 90

(B) $1\dfrac{1}{9}$

(C) $\dfrac{1}{9}$

(D) $2\dfrac{1}{9}$

24. Simplify: $\dfrac{x^2 - 16}{x - 4}$

(A) $\dfrac{1}{x - 4}$

(B) $\dfrac{x - 16}{x + 4}$

(C) $x + 4$

(D) $x - 4$

25. The measures of the angles of a given quadrilateral are 55, 90, 111, and $2n$. What is the value of n?

(A) 45°

(B) 90°

(C) 110°

(D) 52°

DO NOT TURN THE PAGE UNTIL TOLD TO DO SO   STOP   DO NOT RETURN TO A PREVIOUS TEST

Chapter **15**

Practice Exam 2: Answers and Explanations

T he answers and explanations in the following sections help you determine how well you performed on the practice test in Chapter 14 — and give you some hints about where you may have dropped a decimal point or two. Don't worry; it happens to the best of us.

Don't focus too much on scores. On the actual AFQT, harder questions are worth more points than easier questions. The AFQT is one of those rare tests on which you can miss some questions and still max out your test score. As always, use the results to decide where you want to concentrate your study time. Do you need more work on math or reading and verbal skills? This chapter helps you find out.

If you want to skip the explanations for now and see which questions you got right or wrong, go to the Answer Key at the end of the chapter.

Part 1: **Arithmetic Reasoning**

The Arithmetic Reasoning subtest is not only one of the important subtests that make up the AFQT, but it's also used as a qualification factor for many of the military jobs you can choose from. You may want to glance at *ASVAB For Dummies* by Rod Powers and Angie Papple Johnston (published by John Wiley & Sons, Inc.) to see which military jobs require you to do well on this subtest.

If you missed more than five or six questions on this practice test, it's time to dig out that old high-school math textbook and wrap your brain around some math problems. Chapters 9 and 11 can also help you out. Some other great books that may help you score better on this subtest include *Math Word Problems For Dummies*, *Algebra I For Dummies*, and *Algebra II For Dummies*, all by

Mary Jane Sterling; *Basic Math & Pre-Algebra For Dummies* by Mark Zegarelli; *Geometry For Dummies* by Mark Ryan; and *SAT II Math For Dummies* by Scott Hatch, JD, and Lisa Zimmer Hatch, MA — all published by John Wiley & Sons, Inc.

1. **C. 85 ft**

   Marta has 200 feet of fencing and wants to fence in a rectangular yard. If the yard is to be 15 feet wide, then use the formula for perimeter to find the length:

   $$P = 2(l + w)$$
   $$200 = 2(l + 15)$$
   $$\frac{200}{2} = \frac{2(l + 15)}{2}$$
   $$100 - 15 = l + 15 - 15$$
   $$85 = l$$

   You can check your work by plugging the numbers for length and width back into the equation to make sure the answer comes out to 200 or less (the total amount of fencing Marta has).

2. **A. 60 in.**

   First, find 25 percent of 48: $0.25(48) = 12$ inches. (Instead of multiplying 48 by 0.25, you can also recognize that 25 percent is equal to $\frac{1}{4}$ of something and simply divide 48 by 4 to arrive at the same answer.) Henry's brother's height is $48 + 12 = 60$ inches.

3. **C. 144**

   Together, Janet and Alice collected 329 cans: $124 + 205 = 329$. Because the group collected 473 cans, subtract Janet and Alice's total to find how many cans Gabriel collected: $473 - 329 = 144$ cans.

4. **B. 14 ft**

   The area formula for a rectangle is $A = lw$, where A = area, l = length, and w = width. Substitute the known values into this formula and then isolate w by dividing both sides by 12:

   $$168 = 12w$$
   $$\frac{168}{12} = \frac{12w}{12}$$
   $$14 = w$$

5. **C. 300**

   A decameter equals 10 meters, so 3 decameters equals 30 meters. Because there are 10 decimeters in a meter, you multiply that number by the total number of meters: $10(30) = 300$ decimeters in a decameter.

6. **A. 7°F**

   Because the temperature increased, add to find the outside temperature at noon:

   $$-14 + 21 = 21 + (-14) = 21 - 14 = 7° \text{ Fahrenheit}$$

7. A. 120 mph

The distance formula is $d = rt$, where d is the distance, r is the rate, and t is the time. In this problem, you can save time by using fractions instead of decimals (that's not always the case, though). Turn 1.5 (the time the plane flew) into an improper fraction:

$$1\frac{1}{2} = \frac{3}{2}$$

Replace the variables with the values you know and cancel out everything you can:

$$\frac{180}{3/2} = 180 \cdot \frac{2}{3} = \frac{\overset{60}{\cancel{180}}}{1} \cdot \frac{2}{\underset{1}{\cancel{3}}} = 120$$

If you're not good with fractions, it's okay to stick with the decimal. Substitute the known values into this formula and then isolate r by dividing both sides by 1.5:

$$180 = r(1.5)$$
$$\frac{180}{1.5} = \frac{1.5r}{1.5}$$
$$120 = r$$

8. D. 20

Let x = the number of trucks, and express the two ratios of cars to trucks as a proportion. So $\frac{3}{4} = \frac{15}{x}$ because you know there are 15 cars. Cross-multiply to solve for x.

$$\frac{3}{4} = \frac{15}{x}$$
$$3x = 4(15)$$
$$3x = 60$$
$$\frac{3x}{3} = \frac{60}{3}$$
$$x = 20$$

9. D. $2.80

Forty percent of 2 pounds is $0.4(2) = 0.8$ pounds. The amount he paid for the raisins is $0.8(\$3.50) = \$2.80$.

10. C. 42

If x is Patricia's age, then Ms. Chang's age is $3x$. Set up the equation and solve for x:

$$x + 3x = 56$$
$$4x = 56$$
$$\frac{4x}{4} = \frac{56}{4}$$
$$x = 14$$

Patricia's age is 14, so Ms. Chang's age is $3(14) = 42$. To double-check, add the two ages together to make sure they equal 56 as the problem indicates: $14 + 42 = 56$.

11. D. $120.00

Ed's hourly rate is $125 \div 10 = \$12.50$ per hour. John's hourly rate is $\$12.50 - \$0.50 = \$12$ per hour. For 10 hours of work, John earns $10(\$12) = \$120$.

You can skip working out Ed's hourly rate if you multiply the $0.50 difference in the men's hourly wages by 10 hours of work ($0.50 × 10 = $5) and subtract that from Ed's total earnings: $125 − $5 = $120.

TIP

If you find a shortcut that works for you — and that you'll remember on test day — use it. But if you're a little shaky on the details, stick with what you know so you don't make mistakes that drop your AFQT score.

12. B. 1.25 ft

The length of one side of the square game board is $\frac{60}{4} = 15$ inches. There are 12 inches in 1 foot, so 15 inches is 1 foot and 3 inches, or $1\frac{3}{12} = 1\frac{1}{4} = 1.25$ feet.

13. B. $1\frac{1}{4}$ cups

Write each mixed number as an improper fraction. To do so, multiply the denominator by the whole number and then add the result to the numerator:

$$2\frac{3}{4} = \frac{4 \times 2 + 3}{4} = \frac{8 + 3}{4} = \frac{11}{4}$$

$$1\frac{1}{2} = \frac{2 \times 1 + 1}{2} = \frac{2 + 1}{2} = \frac{3}{2}$$

Write the fractions using a common denominator, and then subtract to find the amount of milk you need. The common denominator is 4 because 4 is the least common multiple (LCM) of 4 and 2:

$$\frac{11}{4} - \frac{3}{2} = \frac{11}{4} - \frac{6}{4}$$
$$= \frac{11 - 6}{4}$$
$$= \frac{5}{4}$$
$$= 1\frac{1}{4}$$

Another approach is to add to the first amount $\left(1\frac{1}{2}\right)$ until you reach the second amount $\left(2\frac{3}{4}\right)$. If you add $\frac{1}{2}$ cup, you'll hit an even 2 cups; another $\frac{3}{4}$ cup will bring you to $2\frac{3}{4}$ cups. Add the fractions $\left(\frac{1}{2} + \frac{3}{4}\right)$ to see how much milk you added altogether:

$$\frac{1}{2} + \frac{3}{4} = \frac{2}{4} + \frac{3}{4} = \frac{5}{4} = 1\frac{1}{4}$$

14. C. 4 percent

Use the interest formula $I = prt$, where I is the interest, p is the principal, r is the interest rate (as a decimal), and t is the time in years. Substitute known values into the formula and solve for r.

$$100 = 2,500(r)(1)$$
$$100 = 2,500r$$
$$\frac{100}{2,500} = \frac{2,500r}{2,500}$$
$$r = \frac{1}{25}$$
$$r = 0.04$$

Write 0.04 as a percent by moving the decimal point two places to the right: 0.04 = 4 percent.

15. **A. 72 cm²**

Divide the region into two rectangles and find the length of the missing sides.

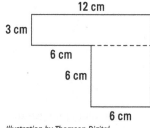

Illustration by Thomson Digital

The formula for the area of a rectangle is $A = lw$. Find the area of the upper rectangle and add it to the area of the lower rectangle.

Upper rectangle: $A = 3(12) = 36 \text{ cm}^2$

Lower rectangle: $A = 6(6) = 36 \text{ cm}^2$

The area of the total region is $36 + 36 = 72 \text{ cm}^2$.

16. **C. 35**

If 60 percent of Martha's cooking class is equal to 21 people, you must find the total number of students by using x for the total number of people in the class.

Write the equation like this:

$$0.60 = 21$$

Divide both sides by 0.60:

$$\frac{0.60x}{0.60} = \frac{21}{0.60}$$
$$x = 35$$

There are 35 total students in the class.

You can also set up a proportion if you know that $60\% = \frac{3}{5}$:

$$\frac{3}{5} = \frac{21}{x}$$

Increase the terms of the first fraction to get to the second; you get 21 by multiplying 3 by 7, and multiplying 5 by 7 gives you 35, so $x = 35$.

17. **D. 5:10 p.m.**

The distance formula is $d = rt$, where d is the distance, r is the rate, and t is the time. Substitute the known values and solve for t to find out how long Keisha walked:

$$4.5 = 3t$$
$$\frac{4.5}{3} = \frac{3t}{3}$$
$$1.5 = t$$

One hour and 30 minutes after 3:40 p.m. is 5:10 p.m. Add one hour to 3:40 p.m. to arrive at 4:40 p.m., and then add another 20 minutes to get to 5:00 p.m. Add the remaining 10 minutes to reach 5:10 p.m.

18. **B. $9.75h \geq 150$**

The amount you earn is the product of your hourly rate and the number of hours worked, which you can express as $9.75h$. Your earnings must be greater than or equal to $150, which is represented by the symbol $\geq$.

amount earned $\geq \$150$

$\$9.75h \geq \$150$

19. **A. 4 m**

Let x = the length of Carlos's father's truck. The ratio of the model length to the length of the actual truck should equal the ratio of 2 centimeters to 0.25 m. Set the two ratios equal to each other to make an equation. Cross-multiply to solve for x.

$$\frac{32}{x} = \frac{2}{0.25}$$
$$2x = 32(0.25)$$
$$\frac{2x}{2} = \frac{8}{2}$$
$$x = 4$$

In the equation above, an easy way to multiply 32 by 0.25 is to divide 32 by 4 (because $0.25 = \frac{1}{4}$).

20. **A. $59**

Use a sequence of numbers to represent the cost of the paintings in order from left to right. The first number on the left is 29. Add 15 to find the cost of the next painting: 29, 44, 59. The painting on the far right costs $59.

If it's easier, round 29 up to 30, add 15 three times, and subtract $1 at the end:

$\$15 + \$15 + \$15 = \$60$

$\$60 - \$1 = \$59$

21. **B. 12 hours**

Find how many hours it will take Taraji to travel by using the distance formula ($d = rt$), where $d = 600$ and $r = 50$:

$$600 = 50t$$
$$\frac{600}{50} = \frac{50t}{50}$$
$$t = 12$$

It will take Taraji 12 hours to get to her grandmother's house.

22. **B. 75 mph**

Substitute $F = 230$ into the formula and solve for x:

$$10(x-60)+80 = 230$$
$$10x-600+80 = 230$$
$$10x-520 = 230$$
$$10x-520+520 = 230+520$$
$$10x = 750$$
$$\frac{10x}{10} = \frac{750}{10}$$
$$x = 75$$

23. **B. 24 mpg**

Subtract to find the number of miles traveled: $65,322 - 65,034 = 288$ miles. The car's gas mileage is the distance traveled divided by the number of gallons of gas used: $\frac{288}{12} = 24$.

24. **A. 160π cm^3**

The formula for the volume of a cylinder is $V = \pi r^2 h$, where r is the radius and h is the height. The radius of the can is equal to half the diameter: $r = \frac{d}{2} = \frac{8}{2} = 4$. Substitute known values into the formula to find the volume: $V = \pi(4^2)(10) = \pi(16)(10) = 160\pi$.

25. **B. $1,310**

Subtract the co-pay for one visit from the cost of one visit: $305 - 15 = 290$. The insurance company pays 60 percent of the cost after the co-pay, so Matt pays 40 percent of the cost. Find 40 percent of $290: $0.4(290) = 116$. Add Matt's portion after the co-pay to the co-pay: $15 + 116 = 131$ total for each visit. Multiply Matt's total cost for one visit to the chiropractor by 10: $10(131) = 1,310$.

26. **C. 12 minutes**

You can figure out how long it will take Marco and his brother to change a tire together by determining how much work each person does in a set amount of time. Use one hour (60 minutes) to keep it simple: Marco can repair one tire in 20 minutes, so he can finish three tires in an hour. His brother can repair two tires in one hour.

In one hour together, they repair

$$\frac{3 \text{ tires}}{1 \text{ hour}} + \frac{2 \text{ tires}}{1 \text{ hour}} = \frac{5 \text{ tires}}{1 \text{ hour}}$$

The number of tires is expressed in the numerator, and the unit of time is expressed in the denominator. Because they can repair five tires in one hour together, divide the 60 minutes of an hour by 5 to get the time it takes them to repair just one:

$$60 \div 5 = 12$$

27. D. 12 oz

First, find out how many ounces of water ten squeezes of the trigger emit: $10(0.024) = 0.24$ ounces. That means 0.24 ounces of water is 2 percent of the total amount of water that the bottle can hold.

Let $x =$ the total number of ounces of water that the bottle will hold. You know that 2 percent of x is equal to 0.24, so write an equation and then solve for x.

$$x = \frac{0.24}{0.02}$$
$$x = \frac{24}{2}$$
$$x = 12$$

28. C. 1,800 cm²

A shoe box is a rectangular box. The formula for the surface area of a rectangular box is $SA = 2lw + 2wh + 2lh$, where $l =$ length, $w =$ width, and $h =$ height. Substitute the known values into the formula and simplify.

$$SA = 2(30)(15) + 2(15)(10) + 2(30)(10)$$
$$= 60(15) + 30(10) + 60(10)$$
$$= 900 + 300 + 600$$
$$= 1,800$$

29. A. 1 hour

You could create an algebraic equation and a chart to solve this problem, but the question is really asking you how far apart the runners will be in one hour. The first runner can run 5 miles per hour, and the second runs 6 miles per hour — and they're running in opposite directions. That means in one hour, they're $5 + 6 = 11$ miles apart.

For more complex problems, algebra comes in handy. You could solve this problem by letting x represent the amount of time the runners take to run 11 miles in opposite directions and then making a chart to help solve the problem.

	Rate	×	Time	=	Distance
Runner 1	5		x		$5x$
Runner 2	6		x		$7x$

Illustration by Thomson Digital

You need to figure out how far each runner ran; you can use a variation of the distance formula, $d = rt$, where $d =$ distance, $r =$ rate, and $t =$ time. The table shows you that Runner 1 will run a distance of $5x$ and Runner 2 will run a distance of $6x$. Because they are running in opposite directions and you want to know when they are 11 miles apart, you add the two distances together and set the sum equal to 11. The equation looks like this:

$$5x + 6x = 11$$
$$11x = 11$$
$$x = 1$$

It will take the runners 1 hour to get 11 miles apart.

30. **C. $84**

   Use the amount of pizza eaten to determine how many pizzas the coach bought. Excluding the coach, the team ate $15\left(\frac{1}{4}\right)=\frac{15}{4}$ pizzas. Add the amount of pizza the coach ate and the amount of pizza left over: $\frac{15}{4}+\frac{1}{2}+2\frac{3}{4}$. Convert the remaining pizza $\left(2\frac{3}{4}\right)$ to an improper fraction: $2\frac{3}{4}=\frac{11}{4}$.

   Come up with a common denominator and add to find the total number of pizzas:

   $$\frac{15}{4}+\frac{2}{4}+\frac{11}{4}=\frac{15+2+11}{4}$$
   $$=\frac{28}{4}$$
   $$=7$$

   For 7 pizzas, the total cost before tax is $7(\$12)=\$84$.

   If it's easier, you can add the fractional and whole parts of the pizza separately. If you add the players' pizza as a fraction, the coach's pizza, and the fractional part of the leftover pizza, then add the sum to the whole pizzas, your calculation looks like this:

   $$\frac{15}{4}+\frac{1}{2}+\frac{3}{4}=\frac{15}{4}+\frac{2}{4}+\frac{3}{4}=\frac{20}{4}=5\,\text{pizzas}$$
   $$5\,\text{pizzas}+2\,\text{pizzas}=7\,\text{pizzas}$$

Part 2: Word Knowledge

The Word Knowledge subtest is nothing more than a vocabulary test. However, it can be hard for some people. The good news is that vocabulary isn't an innate talent. It's something that everyone can improve. If you find you need to improve your vocabulary, see Chapters 4 and 5. A couple of other great study references are *Vocabulary For Dummies* by Laurie E. Rozakis and *SAT Vocabulary For Dummies* by Suzee Vlk (both published by John Wiley & Sons, Inc.). Additionally, see Chapter 6 for more practice questions.

1. **C. detest.**

   Savor is a verb that means to appreciate something.

   "Simón wanted to savor every bite of the meringue."

2. **C. mediocre.**

   Lackluster is an adjective that means lacking life or energy.

   "The actor gave a lackluster performance during his audition, so he didn't get the part."

3. **A. abstain.**

   Participate is a verb that means to take part in.

   "Marie didn't want to participate in marriage counseling after her husband had an affair."

4. **B. mess up.**

   Organize is a verb that means to coordinate or make orderly.

   "Cheryl took one look at the messy room and began to organize everything into neat stacks."

5. **D. messy.**

   Unkempt is an adjective describing something disorderly.

   "Tina's bedroom was so unkempt that Cheryl had to come in and organize it."

6. **B. first**

   Preliminary is an adjective describing something introductory.

7. **B. unavoidable**

   Inevitable is an adjective that means bound to happen.

8. **D. sign**

   Omen is a noun describing something prophetic.

9. **C. cold**

   As used in this sentence, *frigid* is an adjective meaning extremely cold.

10. **B. oppressor**

    Tyrant is a noun describing someone who rules over others unjustly.

11. **C. phony.**

    As used in this sentence, *counterfeit* is an adjective meaning fake or forged.

    "When the criminal tried to pay for his dinner with a counterfeit $100 bill, the server called her manager."

12. **A. relieve.**

    Used as a verb, *burden* means to provide a load or a difficult task to someone. It's also a noun that refers to something that's carried, or a duty or responsibility.

    "Robert thought that his complaints about work would burden his wife."

13. **D. subdue.**

    Used as a verb, *animate* means to rouse or make lively.

    "Playing loud, happy music animated the kids in gymnastics class."

14. **C. reasonable.**

    Plausible is an adjective that means something looks to be true or believable, though it may or may not actually be so.

    "The defendant's self-defense claim wasn't plausible, so the prosecutor encouraged the jury to find the man guilty."

15. **B. flexible.**

    Pliable is an adjective that means easily bent or changeable.

    "Good leather is pliable, so it won't crack when you mold it into a saddle."

16. **B. acceptance.**

    Resignation is a noun that means a reluctant agreement.

    "In the famous movie, William Wallace accepted his terrible fate with resignation."

17. C. destroy.

Obliterate is a verb that means to demolish or annihilate.

"The goal is to obliterate the enemy's communication abilities so they can't conduct military operations."

18. B. abide.

Heed is a verb meaning to take warning or advice in earnest.

"Pilar told Beto to heed her warning about the cat's aggression because she didn't want him to get scratched."

19. A. massive

Immense is an adjective meaning very large or colossal.

20. A. follow

Pursue is a verb meaning to go after something or someone.

21. C. sensitive

Tactful is an adjective that means being thoughtful or delicate.

22. A. tolerate

Endure is a verb that means to bear with patience or tolerate, or to hold out against.

23. D. endurance

In this sentence, *longevity* is a noun meaning a prolonged ability. It can also refer to length of service or tenure, or the length or duration of life.

24. B. comfort

Console is a verb that means to alleviate or lessen grief, sorrow, or disappointment.

25. C. scatter

Disperse is a verb that means to move in different directions.

26. D. covered.

Enshrouded is a verb meaning to encompass or obscure something.

"The sun went down, and soon we were enshrouded in darkness."

27. A. disown.

Repudiate is a verb that means to reject as having no authority or strongly deny something or someone.

"The judge knew he would have to repudiate the man's claim."

28. C. indirect.

Oblique is an adjective meaning not straight or not straightforward.

"The candidate made only oblique references to the scandal."

29. **A. agree with.**

Acquiesce is a verb meaning to consent by way of giving in.

"Two of the six partners had to acquiesce because the other four (the majority) had already agreed on the plan."

30. **B. flimsy.**

Tenuous is an adjective describing something weak or lacking substance.

"The man's adult stepson had a tenuous claim to the inheritance, so the court would have to decide one way or the other."

31. **C. rampant**

Unbridled is an adjective meaning unrestrained.

32. **C. exclude**

Ostracize is a verb meaning to leave out intentionally.

33. **A. full.**

Replete is an adjective that means ample or fully supplied.

"The book was replete with detail, describing every character and scene so readers could really envision them."

34. **B. mystery.**

Enigma is a noun that means something puzzling, not clear, or not understandable.

"The private millionaire, who rarely leaves his house, is an enigma to everyone in town."

35. **A. pacify**

Assuage is a verb meaning to pacify or lessen the intensity of something.

Part 3: Paragraph Comprehension

The Paragraph Comprehension subtest can be a bit tricky, but you need to get a good score on this subtest if you want to ace the AFQT. Pay special attention to your reading skills if you missed more than a couple of these answers — you need some study time (see Chapter 6 and 7). Remember that rereading the paragraph several times to make sure that you have the right answer is perfectly fine. The best method of improving your reading comprehension skills is simply to read more. You can find additional practice questions in Chapter 7.

1. **D. Trainers should avoid becoming emotional.**

The first sentence states the point: "Dog training isn't for the faint of heart." In other words, sometimes you have to discipline the dog without becoming an emotional wreck.

2. **A. determination.**

The last sentence of the passage lets you know that your *resolve* will be tested because you may feel guilty for training your dog. You have to be very determined to train your pet because pity could make you want to drop everything and play.

3. C. 1

A scan of the passage shows you that it clearly says "including one Daytona 500 race." You can answer questions like these quickly on the ASVAB, so read the question thoroughly, find your answer, and move on.

4. B. severe.

The description of the mood swings states that moods range from a heightened place to an extreme state of depression. *Severe* is the only word that describes the large range experienced.

5. C. 4

The passage states that rugby has been added and dropped three times but was added back in 2016. The first three times plus the most recent equals four times rugby has been added to the Olympic Games.

6. D. Brazil

The passage lists many locations, but careful scanning shows you that the 2016 Olympics were in Rio de Janeiro, Brazil.

7. C. Breadmaking is more exact than cooking.

The paragraph gives examples of how making bread, unlike cooking, uses exact measurements and ratios to get the desired result. The last sentence also states the answer in different terms.

8. B. outlawed.

The paragraph states that the number of bald eagles continued to decline despite trapping and killing having been barred. The term *despite* tells you that *barred* signifies an action against trapping and killing. In fact, the act banned, or outlawed, those practices against the eagle.

9. A. 1972

The passage indicates that DDT was responsible for the decline of the species. Thus, the banning of DDT in 1972 would be the beginning of the repopulation of the bald eagle. You may have been tempted by 1940, but the congressional act didn't contribute to the population regrowth. When an ASVAB question asks you for a specific date, scan the paragraph quickly for numbers; you'll be able to find the answer easily.

10. C. Joining the Joffrey Ballet is Jill's life's goal.

Although many of these things could be true about Jill, the question asks for the main point of the passage. The passage stresses the importance of her audition and how being accepted by the Joffrey Ballet would be "a dream come true," so the main point is that she has been eagerly anticipating this moment for some time.

11. B. have opportunities to make a lot of money.

The paragraph describes the popularity of quilting and mentions contests with best in show prizes reaching $10,000. Therefore, you can assume quilters today can make a good amount of money.

12. D. None of the above

Although areas of the other answers may have depths of less than 4 feet, they can all have deeper areas. Because the seller clearly says the lifeboat should not be used by people who cannot swim, it shouldn't be used in open water.

13. D. preventing a child from becoming overweight before the age of 5

The information states that children obese at age 5 were more likely to be obese in adolescence. Although the passage doesn't explicitly state that weight management before the age of 5 is desirable, you can reason that from the information provided. The other three answers aren't stated in the passage, so you can quickly rule them out as possible answers.

14. A. one-third

The passage states that approximately two-thirds of the children involved in the study remained obese in their later years, so you can reason that one-third became thinner.

15. A. version.

The movie is based on the TV show, so an *adaptation* is another version of the show.

Part 4: Mathematics Knowledge

Some folks find math to be a breeze and can't understand why the rest of us approach math problems with all the enthusiasm of a trip to the dentist. However, the military considers math skills to be important, and it's right. If you miss more than four or five questions, you should consider brushing up on your basic math skills — Chapters 8 and 9 can help with this. As with the Arithmetic Reasoning subtest, the following *For Dummies* books may also be of some help: *Algebra I For Dummies* and *Algebra II For Dummies*, both by Mary Jane Sterling; *Basic Math & Pre-Algebra For Dummies* by Mark Zegarelli; *Geometry For Dummies* by Mark Ryan; and *SAT II Math For Dummies* by Scott Hatch, JD, and Lisa Zimmer Hatch, MA (all published by John Wiley & Sons, Inc.). Chapter 10 also has some additional practice questions.

1. B. 2

A prime number is a number that is bigger than 1 and has only itself and 1 as factors. The number 2 is the only choice that fits the definition of a prime number.

2. C. 0.011

Eleven thousandths is the same as $\frac{11}{1,000}$. To divide a number by 1,000, move the decimal point 3 places to the left: $\frac{11}{1,000} = 0.011$.

3. C. 1.281

When adding decimals, arrange the numbers in an addition column with the decimal points lined up:

$$\begin{array}{r} \overset{1}{1.091} \\ +0.19 \\ \hline 1.281 \end{array}$$

When adding the 9s in the hundredths column, remember to carry the 1 to the tenths column.

4. A. 18 ft

An equilateral triangle has three equal sides. The perimeter is the sum of all three sides. To find the length of one side, divide the perimeter by 3: $54 \div 3 = 18$ ft.

5. D. 88

Write 40 percent as a decimal: 40 percent $= 0.4$. Multiply 0.4 by 220: $0.4(220) = 88$.

6. D. 3.25

Divide 26 by 8 using long division.

$$
\begin{array}{r}
3.25 \\
8\overline{)26.00} \\
-24 \\
\hline
20 \\
-16 \\
\hline
40 \\
-40 \\
\hline
0
\end{array}
$$

7. A. p^2

To multiply terms with the same base, add the exponents: $p^{3+(-1)} = p^{3-1} = p^2$.

8. B. $\dfrac{1}{5}$

To subtract fractions with the same denominator, subtract the numerators but keep the denominators the same. You can then simplify the difference $\dfrac{5}{25}$ to $\dfrac{1}{5}$.

$$\frac{8}{25} - \frac{3}{25} = \frac{8-3}{25} = \frac{5}{25} = \frac{1}{5}$$

9. A. −9

Get y alone on one side of the inequality symbol by subtracting 2 from both sides:

$$
\begin{aligned}
y + 2 &< -6 \\
y + 2 - 2 &< -6 - 2 \\
y &< -8
\end{aligned}
$$

So y can be any number less than -8. The only answer choice that is less than -8 is -9.

10. B. $7x - 15$

Use the distributive property to remove the parentheses. Then add the like terms $3x$ and $4x$.

$$
\begin{aligned}
3(x-5) + 4x &= 3x - 15 + 4x \\
&= 7x - 15
\end{aligned}
$$

11. **C. 15 ft**

Use the Pythagorean theorem $a^2 + b^2 = c^2$ to find the length of the remaining side. Remember that the hypotenuse, c, is always the longest side of a right triangle. Let a represent the length of the remaining side.

$$a^2 + 8^2 = 17^2$$
$$a^2 + 64 = 289$$
$$a^2 + 64 - 64 = 289 - 64$$
$$a^2 = 225$$
$$a = \pm\sqrt{225} = \pm 15$$

Use the positive answer because length is always positive.

12. **D. −4**

The quotient of 40 and 20 is $40 \div 20 = 2$. The sum of 1 and 5 is 6. Decrease 2 by 6 using subtraction: $2 - 6 = -4$.

13. **C. 3**

Use the order of operations, which says to simplify inside the parentheses first, compute all exponents, multiply and/or divide from left to right, and then add and/or subtract from left to right. (You might know this order of operations as PEMDAS.) This equation has no parentheses (or other grouping symbols), so start with the exponents:

$$15 - 3 \times 2^2 = 15 - 3 \times 4$$
$$= 15 - 12$$
$$= 3$$

14. **B. 60**

To find the least common multiple (LCM) of two numbers, write out the multiples of each number and find the smallest number that they have in common.

Multiples of 12: 12, 24, 36, 48, 60

Multiples of 20: 20, 40, 60

The LCM is 60.

Another way (and one that could save you precious time on the ASVAB) to tackle this problem is to check which answer choices are divisible by both 12 and 20. Start with the smallest answer choice and you'll find that you can toss Choice (A) right out the window. Try choice (B), and you'll see that it's the correct answer.

15. **A. $\frac{6}{7}$**

Product means multiplication. When multiplying two fractions, multiply the numerators by each other and multiply the denominators by each other.

$$\frac{3}{4} \times \frac{8}{7} = \frac{3 \times 8}{4 \times 7} = \frac{24}{28}$$

Remember to simplify all fractions. Simplify this fraction by dividing the numerator and denominator by the greatest common divisor, 4:

$$\frac{24 \div 4}{28 \div 4} = \frac{6}{7}$$

16. D. 24

This question asks for the product of four numbers. You can multiply two numbers at a time. Remember that the product of two numbers with the same sign is positive, and the product of two numbers with different signs is negative.

$$3(-4)(1)(-2) = (-12)(1)(-2)$$
$$= (-12)(-2)$$
$$= 24$$

17. D. 4 only

A cube root is a number that when multiplied by itself three times equals the number under the radical sign. Because $4(4)(4) = 64$, 4 is the cube root of 64.

18. C. $\frac{11}{15}$

You need to find the common denominator for these two fractions. The common denominator is the least common multiple of 5 and 3.

Multiples of 5: 5, 10, 15

Multiples of 3: 3, 6, 9, 12, 15

The common denominator for these two fractions is 15. Multiply the numerator and denominator of each fraction by the number that makes each denominator 15.

$$\frac{2}{5} + \frac{1}{3} = \frac{2 \cdot 3}{5 \cdot 3} + \frac{1 \cdot 5}{3 \cdot 5}$$
$$= \frac{6}{15} + \frac{5}{15}$$
$$= \frac{6+5}{15}$$
$$= \frac{11}{15}$$

19. B. 86 m²

First, find the area of the square by using the formula $A = s^2$, where s is the length of one side of the square. Because $s = 20$ meters, the area of the square is $20^2 = 400$ m².

Next, find the area of the circle by using the formula $A = \pi r^2$, where r is the radius of the circle. Because the diameter of the circle runs the length of one side of the square, the radius is half the length of one side of the square, so $r = 10$ meters. The area of the circle is $A = \pi(10^2) = 3.14(100) = 314$ m².

To find the area of the region inside the square but outside the circle, subtract the area of the circle from the area of the square: $400 - 314 = 86$ m².

20. A. 21

Let x represent the middle number. Next, add and subtract 2 (to represent the other odd numbers), written as $(x + 2)$ and $(x - 2)$.

$$(x+2) + x + (x-2) = 63$$
$$3x = 63$$
$$\frac{3x}{3} = \frac{63}{3}$$
$$x = 21$$

If you're not big on algebra (surprisingly, it's not everyone's favorite subject), you may not need to use it on questions like this one. When you're adding three consecutive odd numbers, you can reason that each number is going to be close to one-third of the sum, 63:

$$\frac{63}{3} = 21$$

Check 21 as your middle number to see if it works:

$$19 + 21 + 23 = 63$$

It does, so Choice (A) is correct.

21. D. 4 and −4

This equation is a quadratic equation because the unknown quantity *(x)* has an exponent of 2. To solve it, first isolate the variable by subtracting 4 from both sides:

$$x^2 + 4 = 20$$
$$x^2 + 4 - 4 = 20 - 4$$
$$x^2 = 16$$

Next, take the square root of both sides. (With any positive real number, you'll get a positive and negative answer to the square-root problem, because when you multiply a negative number by a negative number, you get a positive number.)

$$x = \pm\sqrt{16}$$
$$x = \pm 4$$

22. A. 60°

If two angles are supplementary, the sum of their measures is 180°. Label the angle you're trying to find as *x* and the supplement as 2*x*. You can then set up an equation:

$$x + 2x = 180$$
$$3x = 180$$
$$\frac{x}{3} = \frac{180}{3}$$
$$x = 60$$

23. B. $1\frac{1}{9}$

To solve for *x*, cross-multiply and isolate the variable:

$$\frac{9}{x} = \frac{81}{10}$$
$$81x = 9(10)$$
$$81x = 90$$
$$\frac{81x}{81} = \frac{90}{81}$$
$$x = \frac{90}{81}$$

Use long division to write the answer as a mixed number.

$$\begin{array}{r} 1 \\ 81\overline{)90} \\ -81 \\ \hline 9 \end{array}$$

The quotient forms the whole number; the remainder, 9, is the numerator of the fraction, and the divisor, 81, is the denominator: $1\frac{9}{81}$. You can simplify this number to $1\frac{1}{9}$.

24. **C.** $x+4$

The numerator is a difference of two squares. Use the formula $x^2 - a^2 = (x-a)(x+a)$ to factor the numerator. The factor $(x-4)$ cancels out in the numerator and in the denominator.

$$\frac{x^2-16}{x-4} = \frac{(x-4)(x+4)}{x-4}$$
$$= \frac{(\cancel{x-4})(x+4)}{\cancel{x-4}}$$
$$= x+4$$

25. **D.** 52°

The sum of the angles in a quadrilateral always equals 360°. Write an equation to find the value of n: $55 + 90 + 111 + 2n = 360$.

To solve this equation, isolate the variable:

$$256 + 2n = 360$$
$$256 + 2n - 256 = 360 - 256$$
$$2n = 104$$
$$n = 52$$

Answer Key

Part 1: Arithmetic Reasoning

1.	C	9.	D	17.	D	25.	B
2.	A	10.	C	18.	B	26.	C
3.	C	11.	D	19.	A	27.	D
4.	B	12.	B	20.	A	28.	C
5.	C	13.	B	21.	B	29.	A
6.	A	14.	C	22.	B	30.	C
7.	A	15.	A	23.	B		
8.	D	16.	C	24.	A		

Part 2: Word Knowledge

1.	C	10.	B	19.	A	28.	C
2.	C	11.	C	20.	A	29.	A
3.	A	12.	A	21.	C	30.	B
4.	B	13.	D	22.	A	31.	C
5.	D	14.	C	23.	D	32.	C
6.	B	15.	B	24.	B	33.	A
7.	B	16.	B	25.	C	34.	B
8.	D	17.	C	26.	D	35.	A
9.	C	18.	B	27.	A		

Part 3: Paragraph Comprehension

1.	D	5.	C	9.	A	13.	D
2.	A	6.	D	10.	C	14.	A
3.	C	7.	C	11.	B	15.	A
4.	B	8.	B	12.	D		

Part 4: Mathematics Knowledge

1.	B	8.	B	15.	A	22.	A
2.	C	9.	A	16.	D	23.	B
3.	C	10.	B	17.	D	24.	C
4.	A	11.	C	18.	C	25.	D
5.	D	12.	D	19.	B		
6.	D	13.	C	20.	A		
7.	A	14.	B	21.	D		

Chapter 16

Practice Exam 3

▌n the sections that follow, you find the four subtests of the Armed Services Vocational Aptitude Battery (ASVAB), which make up the Armed Forces Qualification Test (AFQT) score: Arithmetic Reasoning, Word Knowledge, Paragraph Comprehension, and Mathematics Knowledge.

I note in Chapter 1 that the military services use the scores derived from these four subtests to determine your overall AFQT score and that the AFQT score is the primary factor that decides whether you're qualified to enlist in the military branch of your choice. Remember to use the results of the following practice exam to decide which areas you should dedicate more study to.

Use the answer key and explanations in Chapter 17 to score your practice exam. Remember not to be too concerned with how many you get right and how many you get wrong. Some of the questions on the practice exam are hard, and others are very easy. When you take the actual subtests as part of the ASVAB, harder questions are awarded more points than easier questions.

Consider taking this practice exam about a week before you're scheduled to take the actual ASVAB. Use the results to determine which AFQT subjects need a little extra attention.

Answer Sheet for Practice Exam 3

Part 1: Arithmetic Reasoning

1. Ⓐ Ⓑ Ⓒ Ⓓ
2. Ⓐ Ⓑ Ⓒ Ⓓ
3. Ⓐ Ⓑ Ⓒ Ⓓ
4. Ⓐ Ⓑ Ⓒ Ⓓ
5. Ⓐ Ⓑ Ⓒ Ⓓ
6. Ⓐ Ⓑ Ⓒ Ⓓ

7. Ⓐ Ⓑ Ⓒ Ⓓ
8. Ⓐ Ⓑ Ⓒ Ⓓ
9. Ⓐ Ⓑ Ⓒ Ⓓ
10. Ⓐ Ⓑ Ⓒ Ⓓ
11. Ⓐ Ⓑ Ⓒ Ⓓ
12. Ⓐ Ⓑ Ⓒ Ⓓ

13. Ⓐ Ⓑ Ⓒ Ⓓ
14. Ⓐ Ⓑ Ⓒ Ⓓ
15. Ⓐ Ⓑ Ⓒ Ⓓ
16. Ⓐ Ⓑ Ⓒ Ⓓ
17. Ⓐ Ⓑ Ⓒ Ⓓ
18. Ⓐ Ⓑ Ⓒ Ⓓ

19. Ⓐ Ⓑ Ⓒ Ⓓ
20. Ⓐ Ⓑ Ⓒ Ⓓ
21. Ⓐ Ⓑ Ⓒ Ⓓ
22. Ⓐ Ⓑ Ⓒ Ⓓ
23. Ⓐ Ⓑ Ⓒ Ⓓ
24. Ⓐ Ⓑ Ⓒ Ⓓ

25. Ⓐ Ⓑ Ⓒ Ⓓ
26. Ⓐ Ⓑ Ⓒ Ⓓ
27. Ⓐ Ⓑ Ⓒ Ⓓ
28. Ⓐ Ⓑ Ⓒ Ⓓ
29. Ⓐ Ⓑ Ⓒ Ⓓ
30. Ⓐ Ⓑ Ⓒ Ⓓ

Part 2: Word Knowledge

1. Ⓐ Ⓑ Ⓒ Ⓓ
2. Ⓐ Ⓑ Ⓒ Ⓓ
3. Ⓐ Ⓑ Ⓒ Ⓓ
4. Ⓐ Ⓑ Ⓒ Ⓓ
5. Ⓐ Ⓑ Ⓒ Ⓓ
6. Ⓐ Ⓑ Ⓒ Ⓓ
7. Ⓐ Ⓑ Ⓒ Ⓓ

8. Ⓐ Ⓑ Ⓒ Ⓓ
9. Ⓐ Ⓑ Ⓒ Ⓓ
10. Ⓐ Ⓑ Ⓒ Ⓓ
11. Ⓐ Ⓑ Ⓒ Ⓓ
12. Ⓐ Ⓑ Ⓒ Ⓓ
13. Ⓐ Ⓑ Ⓒ Ⓓ
14. Ⓐ Ⓑ Ⓒ Ⓓ

15. Ⓐ Ⓑ Ⓒ Ⓓ
16. Ⓐ Ⓑ Ⓒ Ⓓ
17. Ⓐ Ⓑ Ⓒ Ⓓ
18. Ⓐ Ⓑ Ⓒ Ⓓ
19. Ⓐ Ⓑ Ⓒ Ⓓ
20. Ⓐ Ⓑ Ⓒ Ⓓ
21. Ⓐ Ⓑ Ⓒ Ⓓ

22. Ⓐ Ⓑ Ⓒ Ⓓ
23. Ⓐ Ⓑ Ⓒ Ⓓ
24. Ⓐ Ⓑ Ⓒ Ⓓ
25. Ⓐ Ⓑ Ⓒ Ⓓ
26. Ⓐ Ⓑ Ⓒ Ⓓ
27. Ⓐ Ⓑ Ⓒ Ⓓ
28. Ⓐ Ⓑ Ⓒ Ⓓ

29. Ⓐ Ⓑ Ⓒ Ⓓ
30. Ⓐ Ⓑ Ⓒ Ⓓ
31. Ⓐ Ⓑ Ⓒ Ⓓ
32. Ⓐ Ⓑ Ⓒ Ⓓ
33. Ⓐ Ⓑ Ⓒ Ⓓ
34. Ⓐ Ⓑ Ⓒ Ⓓ
35. Ⓐ Ⓑ Ⓒ Ⓓ

Part 3: Paragraph Comprehension

1. Ⓐ Ⓑ Ⓒ Ⓓ   4. Ⓐ Ⓑ Ⓒ Ⓓ   7. Ⓐ Ⓑ Ⓒ Ⓓ   10. Ⓐ Ⓑ Ⓒ Ⓓ   13. Ⓐ Ⓑ Ⓒ Ⓓ
2. Ⓐ Ⓑ Ⓒ Ⓓ   5. Ⓐ Ⓑ Ⓒ Ⓓ   8. Ⓐ Ⓑ Ⓒ Ⓓ   11. Ⓐ Ⓑ Ⓒ Ⓓ   14. Ⓐ Ⓑ Ⓒ Ⓓ
3. Ⓐ Ⓑ Ⓒ Ⓓ   6. Ⓐ Ⓑ Ⓒ Ⓓ   9. Ⓐ Ⓑ Ⓒ Ⓓ   12. Ⓐ Ⓑ Ⓒ Ⓓ   15. Ⓐ Ⓑ Ⓒ Ⓓ

Part 4: Mathematics Knowledge

1. Ⓐ Ⓑ Ⓒ Ⓓ   6. Ⓐ Ⓑ Ⓒ Ⓓ   11. Ⓐ Ⓑ Ⓒ Ⓓ   16. Ⓐ Ⓑ Ⓒ Ⓓ   21. Ⓐ Ⓑ Ⓒ Ⓓ
2. Ⓐ Ⓑ Ⓒ Ⓓ   7. Ⓐ Ⓑ Ⓒ Ⓓ   12. Ⓐ Ⓑ Ⓒ Ⓓ   17. Ⓐ Ⓑ Ⓒ Ⓓ   22. Ⓐ Ⓑ Ⓒ Ⓓ
3. Ⓐ Ⓑ Ⓒ Ⓓ   8. Ⓐ Ⓑ Ⓒ Ⓓ   13. Ⓐ Ⓑ Ⓒ Ⓓ   18. Ⓐ Ⓑ Ⓒ Ⓓ   23. Ⓐ Ⓑ Ⓒ Ⓓ
4. Ⓐ Ⓑ Ⓒ Ⓓ   9. Ⓐ Ⓑ Ⓒ Ⓓ   14. Ⓐ Ⓑ Ⓒ Ⓓ   19. Ⓐ Ⓑ Ⓒ Ⓓ   24. Ⓐ Ⓑ Ⓒ Ⓓ
5. Ⓐ Ⓑ Ⓒ Ⓓ   10. Ⓐ Ⓑ Ⓒ Ⓓ   15. Ⓐ Ⓑ Ⓒ Ⓓ   20. Ⓐ Ⓑ Ⓒ Ⓓ   25. Ⓐ Ⓑ Ⓒ Ⓓ

Part 1: Arithmetic Reasoning

TIME: 36 minutes for 30 questions

DIRECTIONS: Arithmetic Reasoning is the second subtest of the ASVAB; it follows General Science. These questions are designed to test your ability to use mathematics to solve various problems that may be found in real life — in other words, math word problems.

Each question is followed by four possible answers. Decide which answer is correct, and then mark the corresponding space on your answer sheet. Use your scratch paper for any figuring you want to do. You may *not* use a calculator.

1. Luis has 15 quarters and 22 dimes. What is the dollar value of these coins?

   (A) $4.95
   (B) $5.95
   (C) $5.85
   (D) $6.05

2. A pool has 4,856 gallons of water. How many gallons of water remain after 919 gallons are drained from the pool?

   (A) 3,917 gallons
   (B) 5,775 gallons
   (C) 3,937 gallons
   (D) 4,937 gallons

3. One mile is equal to 5,280 ft. Use this relationship to estimate the number of feet in 50 miles.

   (A) about 250,000 ft
   (B) about 350,000 ft
   (C) about 25,000 ft
   (D) about 300,000 ft

4. Cooking one package of noodles requires 3 cups of water. How many cups of water do you need to cook one and a half dozen packages of noodles?

   (A) 18 cups
   (B) 20 cups
   (C) 54 cups
   (D) 64 cups

5. A boat is carrying 40 passengers, 18 of whom are men. What is the ratio of men to women passengers?

   (A) $\frac{11}{9}$
   (B) $\frac{9}{11}$
   (C) $\frac{9}{20}$
   (D) $\frac{1}{2}$

6. Minnie earned $175 for 14 hours of work. What is her hourly pay rate?

   (A) $12.00
   (B) $9.50
   (C) $12.50
   (D) $13.25

7. Dominique made 42 phone calls during the fundraiser. Cheng made 6 fewer calls than Dominique. How many calls did Cheng make?

   (A) 36
   (B) 48
   (C) 7
   (D) 38

8. A bicycle wheel has a diameter of 32 inches. When the bicycle is upright, how far is the center of the wheel from the ground?

   (A) 8 in.
   (B) 24 in.
   (C) 64 in.
   (D) 16 in.

9. A builder needs 420 nails to build a garage. The nails he wants come in boxes of 50. How many boxes of nails must he buy to build the garage?

(A) 8 boxes

(B) 42 boxes

(C) 9 boxes

(D) 5 boxes

10. Ricardo bought a bottle of flavored water for $2.25. He gave the cashier a $5 bill and got $3.25 in change. Which choice describes this transaction?

(A) Ricardo got $0.50 more change than he should have.

(B) Ricardo got $0.75 more change than he should have.

(C) Ricardo got the right amount of change.

(D) Ricardo got $0.50 less change than he should have.

11. Carl has a day job and a night job. He earns $9.50 an hour at the day job and $12 an hour at the night job. Last week, he worked 8 hours at each job. How much more did he earn from his night job than his day job?

(A) $40

(B) $20

(C) $22

(D) $36

12. One hour into the potluck, there were $9\frac{1}{3}$ pies on the dessert table. Throughout the rest of the lunch, the guests ate $2\frac{1}{6}$ pies. How many pies were left on the table at the end of the potluck?

(A) $7\frac{1}{6}$

(B) $6\frac{1}{6}$

(C) $7\frac{1}{3}$

(D) $6\frac{1}{7}$

13. A sheet of construction paper is three-eightieths of an inch thick. A ream of this paper has 240 sheets. How thick is a ream of paper?

(A) 6 in.

(B) 4.5 in.

(C) 9 in.

(D) 18 in.

14. Mr. Franklin invests $4,000 into a savings account. After one year, he earns $200 in interest. What is the annual interest rate for the account?

(A) 5.5 percent

(B) 4.5 percent

(C) 5 percent

(D) 20 percent

15. How far will a car travel in 90 minutes if it is traveling at a constant speed of 70 miles per hour?

(A) 115 miles

(B) 95 miles

(C) 100 miles

(D) 105 miles

16. The weight in pounds of five different rocks is 8.1, 7.2, 6.5, 4.4, and 10.3. What is the average of the weights of these rocks?

(A) 7.6 pounds

(B) 6.5 pounds

(C) 7 pounds

(D) 7.3 pounds

17. At 3:30 p.m., the outside temperature was −12° Fahrenheit. By 4:45 p.m., the temperature had dropped another 8° Fahrenheit. What was the temperature at 4:45 p.m.?

(A) −20° Fahrenheit

(B) −4° Fahrenheit

(C) −10° Fahrenheit

(D) 4° Fahrenheit

18. One ounce is equal to about 28 grams. Roughly how many grams are in $1\frac{1}{5}$ ounces?

(A) $29\frac{3}{5}$

(B) $33\frac{1}{5}$

(C) $33\frac{3}{5}$

(D) $35\frac{4}{5}$

19. To ride the roller coaster, a person's height (x) in inches must satisfy the inequality $2x - 84 > 0$. A person with which height cannot ride the roller coaster?

(A) 43 in.

(B) 42 in.

(C) 46 in.

(D) Both A and B.

20. The bed of a flatbed truck is in the shape of a rectangle and has an area of 72 square feet. What is the perimeter of the flatbed if the width is 6 feet?

(A) 42 ft

(B) 36 ft

(C) 18 ft

(D) 60 ft

21. Patrick charges $1.25 for every square foot of wall that he paints. A rectangular wall has a length of 25 feet and a height of 10 feet. How much will Patrick charge to paint this wall?

(A) $325.50

(B) $315.00

(C) $312.50

(D) $316.75

22. A coat that originally sold for $80 is on sale at a 20-percent discount. What is the discount price of the coat?

(A) $60.00

(B) $64.00

(C) $72.00

(D) $56.00

23. James is twice as old as Kiki. In 5 years, the sum of their ages will be 28. How old is James now?

(A) 14

(B) 6

(C) 16

(D) 12

24. A rectangular playground is 5 yards longer than it is wide. Its area is 300 square yards. What is the length of the playground?

(A) 15 yd

(B) 20 yd

(C) 14 yd

(D) 25 yd

25. A car lot has 140 new vehicles for sale. The graph shows the percent of the cars that are available in blue, yellow, green, and red. How many more blue cars are available than red cars?

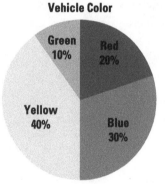

Vehicle Color

Illustration by Thomson Digital

(A) 42

(B) 28

(C) 14

(D) 40

26. Convert $-15°$C to degrees Fahrenheit. Use the formula $\frac{9}{5}C + 32°$.

(A) $5°$ Fahrenheit

(B) $10°$ Fahrenheit

(C) $-10°$ Fahrenheit

(D) $59°$ Fahrenheit

GO ON TO NEXT PAGE

27. At a grocery store, hot dogs come in packages of 8; hot dog buns come in packages of 6; and small bags of chips come in packages of 16. How many packages of each do you need to buy so you have an equal number of hot dogs, hot dog buns, and bags of chips?

(A) 8 packages of hot dogs, 6 packages of buns, and 3 packages of chips

(B) 6 packages of hot dogs, 8 packages of buns, and 4 packages of chips

(C) 6 packages of hot dogs, 8 packages of buns, and 3 packages of chips

(D) 8 packages of hot dogs, 8 packages of buns, and 12 packages of chips

28. Each wheel on Adnan's bicycle has a diameter of 20 inches. When riding down his driveway, Adnan moved approximately 6,280 inches. About how many full revolutions did each wheel make during his trip?

(A) 50 revolutions

(B) 100 revolutions

(C) 1,000 revolutions

(D) 500 revolutions

29. Alexa is selling carnival tickets. Each adult ticket costs 40 percent more than a child's ticket. She's sold 10 child tickets and 12 adult tickets for $134. How much does a single adult ticket cost?

(A) $12

(B) $8

(C) $5

(D) $7

30. A parking meter contains $3.40 in quarters, dimes, and nickels. There are 8 nickels and twice as many quarters as dimes. How many quarters are in the parking meter?

(A) 10 quarters

(B) 5 quarters

(C) 15 quarters

(D) 8 quarters

Part 2: Word Knowledge

TIME: 11 minutes for 35 questions

DIRECTIONS: The Word Knowledge subtest is the third subtest of the ASVAB; it follows Arithmetic Reasoning. The questions are designed to measure your vocabulary knowledge. You'll see three types of questions on this subtest. The first type simply asks you to choose a word or words that most nearly mean the same as the underlined word in the question. The second type includes an underlined word used in a sentence, and you are to choose the word or words that most nearly mean the same as the underlined word, as used in the context of the sentence. The third type of question asks you to choose the word that has the opposite or nearly opposite meaning as the underlined word. Each question is followed by four possible answers. Decide which answer is correct, and then mark the corresponding space on your answer sheet.

1. Perjury most nearly means
   (A) order.
   (B) remark.
   (C) oath.
   (D) lie.

2. Dynamic most nearly means
   (A) special.
   (B) vibrant.
   (C) ordinary.
   (D) dull.

3. The word most opposite in meaning to abandon is
   (A) discard.
   (B) maintain.
   (C) remove.
   (D) become.

4. Momentous most nearly means
   (A) major.
   (B) minute.
   (C) heavy.
   (D) brief.

5. Vital most nearly means
   (A) perfect.
   (B) intentional.
   (C) critical.
   (D) deep.

6. Drone most nearly means
   (A) shout.
   (B) hum.
   (C) cackle.
   (D) engage.

7. Stifle most nearly means
   (A) regurgitate.
   (B) reward.
   (C) release.
   (D) restrain.

8. Prisha's new apartment was small but very quaint.
   (A) grand
   (B) charming
   (C) boring
   (D) outlandish

9. Trying to teach the old dog new tricks is futile.
   (A) worthy
   (B) robust
   (C) pointless
   (D) doomed

10. The student's essay about Martians at Thanksgiving was pure drivel.
    (A) poetry
    (B) nonsense
    (C) logic
    (D) fantasy

11. The chef tried to change the negative stereotype against vegetarian cooks.

    (A) label
    (B) identity
    (C) lie
    (D) characteristic

12. The word most opposite in meaning to betray is

    (A) protect.
    (B) deceive.
    (C) annoy.
    (D) rely.

13. Amble most nearly means

    (A) stroll.
    (B) navigate.
    (C) accelerate.
    (D) rush.

14. The skier wanted to garner a few more medals at this year's event.

    (A) cherish
    (B) generate
    (C) gain
    (D) display

15. The flat, monotonous section of the cross-country course challenged even the most enthusiastic runners.

    (A) varied
    (B) manic
    (C) exciting
    (D) dull

16. The politician's promises were dubious because of his checkered past.

    (A) honest
    (B) questionable
    (C) forthright
    (D) manipulative

17. Quarantine most nearly means

    (A) gather.
    (B) reunite.
    (C) isolate.
    (D) dispel.

18. The word most opposite in meaning to endorse is

    (A) condemn.
    (B) approve.
    (C) promote.
    (D) quibble.

19. Mitigate most nearly means

    (A) concede.
    (B) enhance.
    (C) reduce.
    (D) support.

20. Faith was so complacent with her life that she frequently passed up new opportunities.

    (A) content
    (B) unsatisfied
    (C) daring
    (D) concerned

21. The word most opposite in meaning to dominate is

    (A) control.
    (B) govern.
    (C) surrender.
    (D) ignore.

22. The police officer had to commandeer Julie's bike during a foot chase.

    (A) portray
    (B) seize
    (C) divide
    (D) return

23. Vindicate most nearly means

    (A) succeed.
    (B) blame.
    (C) win.
    (D) justify.

24. They are staunch advocates for animal rights.

    (A) smelly
    (B) grotesque
    (C) devoted
    (D) bloated

25. The professor took off points for the <u>colloquial</u> content in the student's midterm paper.

   (A) unique
   (B) commonplace
   (C) avant garde
   (D) intellectual

26. <u>Atrophy</u> most nearly means

   (A) shrivel.
   (B) explode.
   (C) tire.
   (D) awaken.

27. The authorities were on the hunt for the <u>insurgent</u> behind the uprising.

   (A) scout
   (B) partner
   (C) scapegoat
   (D) rebel

28. The choreographer requested they <u>augment</u> the music with a longer section to fit the routine.

   (A) replace
   (B) enlarge
   (C) trade
   (D) diminish

29. <u>Intermittent</u> most nearly means

   (A) regular.
   (B) variable.
   (C) uniform.
   (D) abnormal.

30. The residents were in a <u>quandary</u> after the only bridge accessing their town was destroyed.

   (A) solution
   (B) puzzle
   (C) resolution
   (D) predicament

31. The doctor gave the diagnosis with a <u>stoic</u> demeanor.

   (A) intelligent
   (B) anxious
   (C) unemotional
   (D) overwrought

32. <u>Aversion</u> most nearly means

   (A) distracter.
   (B) dislike.
   (C) goal.
   (D) element.

33. <u>Garish</u> most nearly means

   (A) gaudy.
   (B) frightening.
   (C) boisterous.
   (D) inappropriate.

34. <u>Intrepid</u> most nearly means

   (A) random.
   (B) nervous.
   (C) brave.
   (D) fearful.

35. The word most opposite in meaning to <u>vanquish</u> is

   (A) bemoan.
   (B) conquer.
   (C) crush.
   (D) yield.

Part 3: Paragraph Comprehension

TIME: 13 minutes for 15 questions

DIRECTIONS: Paragraph Comprehension is the fourth subtest on the ASVAB; it comes after Word Knowledge. The questions are designed to measure your ability to understand what you read. In this part of the test, you see one or more paragraphs of reading material, followed by incomplete statements or questions. Read the paragraph and select the choice that best completes the statement or answers the question. Then mark the corresponding space on your answer sheet.

Questions 1 and 2 refer to the following passage.

People are often confused about the difference between the fiddle and the violin. The truth is that there's no difference except for the way they're played. Violins are often part of orchestras, and the music tends more toward classical and composed pieces. The sounds are played fluidly and in long notes. On the other hand, the fiddle is often played in country or bluegrass bands. The notes are more melodic and tend to be shorter and repetitive. Although they sound like separate instruments, the fiddle and violin are the same and can be played in both styles.

1. What is the main point of the passage?

    (A) The violin is not as popular as the fiddle.

    (B) Country music is more entertaining than classical music.

    (C) Violins are used only in orchestras.

    (D) Fiddles and violins are the same instrument.

2. In the passage, the term <u>fluidly</u> most nearly means

    (A) smoothly.

    (B) roughly.

    (C) staccato.

    (D) broken.

Acupuncture is becoming more accepted in modern society as a form of healing; however, the practice of acupuncture has been used for healing in the Eastern world for centuries. The Chinese first began the art of moving *qi* by applying pressure or creating a release in a *chakra*, or energy zone in the body, more than 2,000 years ago. Although acupuncture treatments have taken on a boutique quality, becoming popular features at full-service spas, the ideas behind this ancient form of healing have remained: Moving the stagnant or blocked *qi* in the body allows the life force to move freely and heal the body of physical ailments and medical conditions.

3. What is the author trying to convey with the phrase "boutique quality"?

    (A) Acupuncture is not done properly.

    (B) Acupuncture is done in hair salons.

    (C) Acupuncture has become trendy in spa settings.

    (D) Acupuncture is different in America.

Questions 4 and 5 refer to the following passage.

Researchers from two leading universities in the United States have discovered what may be the answer to the prayers of many parents. Findings reveal that ingesting negligible amounts of peanuts or peanut proteins may help reduce the sensitivity of allergic reactions through contact. The number of children who suffer from peanut allergies in America is in the hundreds of thousands, and many parents live in fear of their children being exposed to peanut oil or other byproducts that could cause severe and sometimes deadly reactions. Researchers say that in order for this treatment to work, daily to weekly doses of peanut products may be required for up to four to five years.

4. How many children in America have peanut allergies?

    (A) less than 1,000

    (B) about 10,000

    (C) hundreds of thousands

    (D) just under a million

5. How could this research help parents of children with peanut allergies?

   (A) It means their children could eat peanuts again.

   (B) It could reduce their anxiety about exposure.

   (C) It could help pay for the medical treatment.

   (D) None of the above.

Residents of suburban communities throughout the western United States are becoming increasingly concerned about coming face-to-face with a mountain lion in their backyards. In the last year, mountain lions have been found prowling neighborhoods in Colorado, Utah, California, and other areas where urban and rural communities rest at the base or within mountainous regions. The main concern for these owners, according to a recent poll, is that their small pets will become prey for the wild animals. Although officials from the Department of Wildlife and Fisheries have provided strategies to protect households, such as clearing the ground of bushes and vegetation to remove possible hiding spots, they say the main cause of the problem is urban sprawl, which continues to displace mountain lions from their natural habitat.

6. According to the passage, why are mountain lions appearing in residential neighborhoods?

   (A) to hide in low bushes

   (B) to eat small pets

   (C) because of urban sprawl

   (D) to access better vegetation

Despite hailing from Chicago, Illinois, in 1927, the Harlem Globetrotters took the name of the Manhattan neighborhood to represent the Black community that was large and prevalent in Harlem, New York. However, the team known for its outlandish antics and moves on the basketball court didn't play in its namesake city until the late 1960s.

7. As used in this paragraph, <u>outlandish</u> most nearly means

   (A) run of the mill.

   (B) perfect.

   (C) bizarre.

   (D) illegal.

Lou Gehrig was known in major league baseball as "The Iron Horse" for his strength and prowess in the batter's box. Gehrig played first base for the New York Yankees from 1923 to 1938. He set many major-league baseball records, including most consecutive games played (2,130), that stood the test of time until the second half of the 20th century. The famed Yankee was diagnosed with a debilitating and fatal disease (now referred to as Lou Gehrig's disease) that attacks the central nervous system. The disease all but shuts down motor function, though the sufferer's mind remains coherent. The greatest first baseman in the history of baseball died in 1941, two years after his diagnosis.

8. How many years did Lou Gehrig play major league baseball?

   (A) 2,130

   (B) 15

   (C) 38

   (D) 20

Questions 9 and 10 refer to the following passage.

Learning to ski is much different for children than for adults. First, adults have farther to fall, so the fear factor is greater. Second, children are still learning about their coordination and can adjust their body positions more quickly than adults can. Third, children follow directions better than adults do. Fourth, adults have a lifetime of injuries that make them afraid of getting hurt, and they heal more slowly than children do. Fifth, children don't worry about health insurance and hefty medical bills if they get hurt.

9. What is the author saying about children in this passage?

   (A) They are more talented.

   (B) They are better skiers.

   (C) They learn to ski more easily.

   (D) They are better at sports.

GO ON TO NEXT PAGE

10. According to the passage, what would make learning to ski easier for adults?

(A) being less fearful

(B) better directions

(C) lessons

(D) better equipment

The drive-in movie theater industry was once a booming pastime, but since its heyday in the late 1950s, the number of drive-ins has been reduced by almost 90 percent. Once a fun weekend activity with the family or a hangout for teens, the drive-in has been reduced to only 500 viable theaters around the country. Experts say that one of the main causes of drive-in decline is growing real estate prices. Perhaps if landowners appreciated the piece of history they had on their property, they would help keep these relics alive for families and teens to enjoy forever.

11. The author is using the word heyday to mean

(A) end.

(B) prime.

(C) country.

(D) farm.

Fidgety children lined in front of the building, eager parents pacing by their sides. Some of the kids were talking to themselves, and some were counting on their fingers or being quizzed by their parents. But on everyone's face was the anticipation of greatness. The national spelling bee was only moments away.

12. According to the passage, some of the children waiting to compete in the spelling bee seemed

(A) bored.

(B) calm.

(C) nervous.

(D) spoiled.

Questions 13 and 14 refer to the following passage.

Perhaps the most famous gymnast of all time is Romanian Nadia Comaneci, who was the first female gymnast to receive a perfect ten score in an Olympic gymnastics competition. She did so at the 1976 Olympic Games in Montreal, Quebec, where she achieved the feat seven times. Her strong suits were the uneven bars and the balance beam, but she often won the top place in the vault and, less often, the floor routine. After her coaches defected during a tour in the United States in 1981, Comaneci, seen as a Romanian national treasure, was heavily guarded and forbidden to travel. She finally found her freedom in 1989 when she defected to the United States. She eventually found a new home in Canada, but she will always be remembered as the 14-year-old phenomenon at the Summer Olympics.

13. Why was Nadia Comaneci considered a phenomenon at the Summer Olympic Games?

(A) She was from Romania.

(B) She excelled at the vault.

(C) She was the youngest gymnast to compete.

(D) She achieved the highest score given in Olympic gymnastics.

14. In what year did Nadia Comaneci defect from Romania?

(A) 1989

(B) 1976

(C) 1980

(D) 1981

Natural gas vehicles (NGVs) are good not only for the environment but also for drivers' wallets. They offer cleaner emissions and better gas mileage than gasoline-burning vehicles, and the price of a gallon of compressed natural gas is more than $1 cheaper than a gallon of gasoline. However, only slightly more than 100,000 NGVs are on the roads in the United States. If Americans knew about these savings, they would likely purchase more NGVs.

15. According to the passage, why do most Americans drive gasoline-burning vehicles?

(A) lack of knowledge about prices

(B) preference for fossil fuel emissions

(C) inability to drive them

(D) high cost of natural gas

DO NOT TURN THE PAGE UNTIL TOLD TO DO SO **STOP** DO NOT RETURN TO A PREVIOUS TEST

Part 4: Mathematics Knowledge

TIME: 24 minutes for 25 questions

DIRECTIONS: Mathematics Knowledge is the fifth subtest on the ASVAB; it follows Paragraph Comprehension. The questions are designed to test your ability to solve general mathematical problems. Each question is followed by four possible answers. Decide which answer is correct, and then mark the corresponding space on your answer sheet. Use your scratch paper for any figuring you want to do. You may *not* use a calculator.

1. $45 - 6 + 15 =$

(A) 24

(B) 54

(C) 35

(D) 0

2. What is 30 percent of 720?

(A) 216

(B) 310

(C) 240

(D) 220

3. In the number 4.5972, which decimal place does the nine occupy?

(A) tenths

(B) hundredths

(C) thousandths

(D) millionths

4. Express the decimal 0.026 as a percent.

(A) 2.6 percent

(B) 0.26 percent

(C) 26 percent

(D) 260 percent

5. What is 234,678 rounded to the nearest thousand?

(A) 234,700

(B) 230,000

(C) 235,000

(D) 200,000

6. In the decimal 845.721, which digit is in the hundredths place?

(A) 8

(B) 4

(C) 7

(D) 2

7. $4! =$

(A) 12

(B) 24

(C) 120

(D) 9

8. Evaluate $\frac{m}{-7}$ if $m = 28$.

(A) -4

(B) 4

(C) 21

(D) -21

9. Solve for m: $-55 = m - 17$

(A) -38

(B) 38

(C) -72

(D) 935

10. What is the percent increase when 20 is increased to 23?

(A) 3 percent

(B) 17 percent

(C) 15 percent

(D) 7.5 percent

11. Write 0.00000436 using scientific notation.

(A) 4.36×10^6

(B) 4.36×10^{-5}

(C) 436×10^{-6}

(D) 4.36×10^{-6}

12. Which point has coordinates $(-3, 2)$?

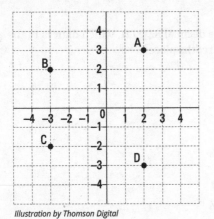

Illustration by Thomson Digital

(A) Point A

(B) Point B

(C) Point C

(D) Point D

13. $5\frac{1}{3} - 4\frac{1}{2} =$

(A) $\frac{1}{6}$

(B) $1\frac{1}{6}$

(C) $\frac{5}{6}$

(D) $1\frac{1}{5}$

14. Simplify: $7(-3m)$

(A) $4m$

(B) $-3 + 7m$

(C) $21m$

(D) $-21m$

15. The lengths of the three sides of a triangle are 14, y, and 6. Which choice could be a value of y?

(A) 19

(B) 21

(C) 25

(D) 31

16. $10 + 2(5 - 3)^2 =$

(A) 48

(B) 18

(C) 26

(D) 36

17. What is 12 divided by $\frac{3}{4}$?

(A) $12\frac{3}{4}$

(B) 9

(C) 16

(D) $\frac{1}{16}$

18. Given $p^4 = \sqrt{x}$, what is x?

(A) p^{16}

(B) p^2

(C) p^8

(D) p^4

19. A number is equal to 12 less than the product of 4 and -2.5. What is the number?

(A) -2

(B) -22

(C) 2

(D) 22

20. What are the measures of the three angles of the triangle?

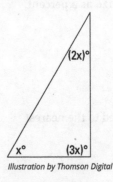

Illustration by Thomson Digital

(A) $30°, 75°, 75°$

(B) $36°, 72°, 108°$

(C) $36°, 54°, 90°$

(D) $30°, 60°, 90°$

21. $\left(3x^2 - 4x + y\right) - \left(2y - 6x^2\right) =$

    (A) $9x^x - 4x - y$

    (B) $-3x^2 - 4x - y$

    (C) $9x^2 - 4x + y$

    (D) $-3x^2 - 4x + y$

22. What is the quotient of 4.8×10^{-4} and 1.2×10^{-9}?

    (A) 2.5×10^{-3}

    (B) 4×10^5

    (C) 4×10^{-5}

    (D) 4×10^{-13}

23. $\sqrt{66 - 2 \cdot 5^2} =$

    (A) $2\sqrt{11}$

    (B) 10

    (C) 4

    (D) 40

24. Evaluate $\dfrac{45}{x} - \dfrac{39}{y}$ if $x = -5$ and $y = 3$.

    (A) 4

    (B) -4

    (C) 22

    (D) -22

25. The radius of a circle is m centimeters. The radius of another circle is $3 + m$ centimeters. What is the difference of the areas of the two circles?

    (A) $(9m\pi + 6\pi)$ cm^2

    (B) 9π cm^2

    (C) $(9\pi + 6m\pi)$ cm^2

    (D) $54m^2\pi$ cm^2

Chapter 17

Practice Exam 3: Answers and Explanations

A re you getting tired of math and English yet? I certainly hope not. If you still want more practice after finishing the exams in this book, I recommend you head to your favorite book seller and pick up a copy of *1,001 ASVAB AFQT Practice Questions For Dummies*, written by Angie Papple Johnston (published by John Wiley & Sons, Inc.).

Use the answers in the following sections to find out how you did on the AFQT practice exam in Chapter 16. The accompanying explanations tell you how you can get to the correct answer if you got somewhat lost along the way.

Part 1: Arithmetic Reasoning

If you already took three practice AFQT exams, and the temperature is a steady 87 degrees, what is the probability that you got most of the questions right on all four subtests? Okay, that's not a real arithmetic reasoning question (insufficient data, as my computer friends say), but I'm betting you've done pretty well. Now it's time to see how you did on this Arithmetic Reasoning practice subtest.

REMEMBER

If you need more practice doing arithmetic reasoning–type problems, Chapters 10 and 11 are a good place to start. You can also check out *Math Word Problems For Dummies, Algebra I For Dummies,* and *Algebra II For Dummies,* all by Mary Jane Sterling; *Geometry For Dummies* and *Calculus For Dummies* both by Mark Ryan; and *Basic Math & Pre-Algebra For Dummies* by Mark Zegarelli — all published by John Wiley & Sons, Inc.

1. B. $5.95

Because you want dollar values, write the value of a quarter as $0.25 and the value of a dime as $0.10. The value of the quarters is $15(\$0.25) = \$3.75$, and the value of the dimes is $22(\$0.10) = \$2.20$. Add to find the answer: $\$3.75 + \$2.20 = \$5.95$.

2. C. 3,937 gallons

This problem just uses simple subtraction. However, remember that this subtraction involves borrowing:

$$
\begin{array}{r}
\overset{3}{\cancel{4}}\overset{18}{\cancel{8}}\overset{4}{\cancel{5}}\overset{16}{\cancel{6}} \\
-9\,1\,9 \\
\hline
3\,9\,3\,7
\end{array}
$$

3. A. 250,000 ft

Because you're estimating, you don't actually need to multiply 5,280 by 50. Instead, round 5,280 down to 5,000 and then multiply: $50(5,000) = 250,000$.

4. C. 54 cups

One dozen is equal to 12 packages, and half of a dozen is 6 packages. You want to find out how much water you need for $12 + 6 = 18$ packages of noodles. Multiply to find the answer: $3(18) = 54$.

5. B. $\dfrac{9}{11}$

To find this ratio, you need to find the number of women passengers by subtracting the number of men from the total number of passengers: $40 - 18 = 22$ women passengers. Write the ratio of men to women passengers by using a fraction. Simplify by dividing the numerator and denominator by their greatest common factor (GCF, the largest number that will go into both), which is 2:

$$
\frac{\text{men}}{\text{women}} = \frac{18}{22} = \frac{18 \div 2}{22 \div 2} = \frac{9}{11}
$$

6. C. $12.50

To find her hourly pay rate, divide 175 by 14:

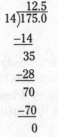

Her pay rate is $12.50 an hour.

7. A. 36

If Cheng made 6 fewer calls than Dominique, you subtract 6 from 42 to find out how many calls Cheng made: $42 - 6 = 36$.

8. D. 16 in.

The distance between the center of the wheel and the outside of the wheel (where the wheel touches the ground) is the radius. A circle's radius equals half its diameter, so the center is $32 \div 2 = 16$ inches from the ground.

9. C. 9 boxes

Divide 420 by 50 to find out how many whole boxes of nails the builder needs: $420 \div 50 = 8$ with a remainder of 20. Eight boxes aren't enough for the project because the builder still needs 20 more nails. The builder needs 9 boxes.

10. A. Ricardo got $0.50 more change than he should have.

Subtract $2.25 from $5 to find the amount of change Ricardo should have received: $5 - \$2.25 = \$2.75$. Compare this amount to the change Ricardo actually received ($3.25) to see that he received too much in change. Subtract $2.75 from $3.25 to find the amount of the discrepancy: $\$3.25 - \$2.75 = \$0.50$.

Another approach is to add the cost of the water to the amount of change he received:

$\$2.25 + \$3.25 = \$5.50$ That's $0.50 too high, which shows that Ricardo received $0.50 more than he should have.

11. B. $20

Multiply to find out how much Carl earned at his day job: $8(\$9.50) = \$76$. Multiply again to find out how much he earned at his night job: $8(\$12) = \$96$. He earned $\$96 - \$76 = \$20$ more at his night job last week.

You can also reason that Carl worked the same number of hours at each job. That means you can find the difference in pay, then multiply it by 8 (the number of hours he worked) to solve this problem:

$$\$12 - \$9.50 = \$2.50$$
$$\$2.50(8) = \$20$$

12. A. $7\frac{1}{6}$

This problem is easiest to solve if you treat whole numbers and fractions as separate parts:

$$9 \text{ pies} - 2 \text{ pies} = 7 \text{ pies}$$
$$\frac{1}{3} - \frac{1}{6} = \frac{2}{6} - \frac{1}{6} = \frac{1}{6} \text{ pie}$$

That tells you that you have $7\frac{1}{6}$ pies left.

13. C. 9 in.

A fraction written in words isn't much help, so make it into a fraction: three-eightieths $= \frac{3}{80}$. Set up an equation to multiply this fraction by 240, and cross-cancel to save time:

$$\frac{3}{80} \cdot 240 = \frac{3}{80} \cdot \frac{240}{1} = \frac{3}{\cancel{80}_1} \cdot \frac{\cancel{240}^3}{1} = \frac{3}{1} \cdot \frac{3}{1} = \frac{9}{1} = 9$$

14. C. 5 percent

Use the interest formula, $I = prt$, where I is the interest, p is the principal, r is the interest rate (as a decimal), and t is the time in years. Substitute the known values into the formula and solve for r:

$$200 = 4{,}000(r)(1)$$
$$200 = 4{,}000r$$
$$\frac{200}{4{,}000} = r$$
$$r = \frac{1}{20} = 0.05$$

Write 0.05 as a percent by moving the decimal point two places to the right: $0.05 = 5$ percent.

15. D. 105 miles

The first thing you should notice about this problem is that the speed is in miles per hour but the time traveled is in minutes. You can't solve the problem until you convert the minutes to hours. Fortunately, doing so for this problem is pretty simple: 90 minutes = 1.5 hours. Now you can plug the numbers into the distance formula, $d = rt$ (where d equals distance, r equals rate, and t equals time), using 1.5 for t: $d = 70(1.5) = 105$ miles

Another way to look at this problem (especially if you don't remember the distance formula) is to note that the car traveled 70 miles in the first hour and half that distance, or 35 miles, in the next half-hour:

$$70 + \frac{70}{2} = 70 + 35 = 105$$

When you take the ASVAB, find the shortest path to the correct answer and take it.

16. D. 7.3 pounds

To find the average, add up all the weights and then divide by 5.

$$\frac{8.1 + 7.2 + 6.5 + 4.4 + 10.3}{5} = \frac{36.5}{5}$$

You can use long division to find the answer.

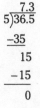

The average weight is 7.3 pounds.

17. A. –20° Fahrenheit

When the temperature drops, you have to subtract. In this case, you want to subtract 8° Fahrenheit from –12° Fahrenheit. If you find subtracting negatives a little confusing, think of it this way: Subtracting 8 from the point labeled –12 means moving 8 units below –12. So $-12 - 8 = -20$.

18. **C.** $33\frac{3}{5}$ **grams**

Address the whole numbers and fractions separately to make solving this problem simpler.

You know that the whole number (1 ounce) equals about 28 grams, so find out what $\frac{1}{5}$ of 28 grams is:

$$\left(\frac{1}{5}\right)(28 \text{ grams}) = \frac{28}{5} = 5\frac{3}{5} \text{ grams}$$

Add the whole numbers, and then add the fraction to that sum:

$$28 + 5 = 33$$
$$33 + \frac{3}{5} = 33\frac{3}{5}$$

Conversely, you could write $1\frac{1}{5}$ as an improper fraction and multiply it by 28 to arrive at the correct answer:

$$1\frac{1}{5} = \frac{5(1)+1}{5} = \frac{6}{5}$$

Now you can multiply to get the answer: $\frac{6}{5} \times 28 = \frac{6}{5} \times \frac{28}{1} = \frac{168}{5} = 33\frac{3}{5}$

19. **B.** 42 in.

Based on the problem, you may be able to reason that the shortest person in the answer choices can't ride the roller coaster. You can also solve the inequality by isolating x:

$$2x - 84 > 0$$
$$2x > 84$$
$$x > 42$$

If a person's height x must be greater than 42, a person with a height of 42 inches can't ride the roller coaster.

REMEMBER

Make sure you read the questions carefully because the folks who write ASVAB questions construct them so you can get hung up on the details. Sometimes you'll need to go back and read the question one more time, after you work out the math, to make sure you're giving the appropriate answer.

20. **B.** 36 ft

This problem uses two formulas. First, use the area formula, $A = lw$, to find the length l of the flatbed. Substitute known values into the formula and solve for l:

$$A = lw$$
$$72 = l(6)$$
$$\frac{72}{6} = \frac{6l}{6}$$
$$12 = l$$

Now substitute $w = 6$ and $l = 12$ into the perimeter formula, $P = 2l + 2w$:

$$P = 2(12) + 2(6) = 24 + 12 = 36 \text{ feet}$$

21. **C. $312.50**

The formula to determine the area of a rectangle is $A = lw$. Substitute known values to find the area:

$$A = 10 \times 25 = 250 \text{ square feet}$$

Patrick charges $1.25 per square foot, so he'd require a total of $250(\$1.25) = \$312.50$ to paint the wall.

22. **B. $64.00**

If the coat is 20 percent off, you're paying 80 percent of the original price ($100\% - 20\% = 80\%$). You can multiply:

$$\$80 \times 0.8 = \$64$$

You can also solve this problem by first finding the amount of the discount: $0.2(80) = \$16$. Then subtract that amount from the original price to find the current cost: $\$80 - \$16 = \$64$. (Both of these approaches work, even when you have to deal with more complicated figures, but the best idea is to find which method is easiest for you — and that you'll be able to remember — on test day.)

23. **D. 12**

Let x = Kiki's age. James is twice as old as Kiki, so his age is $2x$. Kiki's age in 5 years is $x + 5$, and James's age in 5 years is $2x + 5$. In 5 years, the sum of their ages will be 28. Use these expressions to make an equation:

$$x + 5 + 2x + 5 = 28$$
$$3x + 10 = 28$$
$$3x = 18$$
$$x = 6$$

Because Kiki is 6 years old, James's age is $2(6) = 12$.

24. **B. 20 yd**

Let w = the width of the playground. This means that the length is $w + 5$. The formula for the area of a rectangle is $A = lw$. Substitute all known values into the formula and simplify:

$$300 = w(w + 5)$$
$$300 = w^2 + 5w$$
$$0 = w^2 + 5w - 300$$

This is a quadratic equation because it's in the form $ax^2 + bx + c = 0$. You can solve it by factoring. To factor $w^2 + 5w - 300$, or any quadratic equation, you need to think of two numbers that multiply to equal the value of c, or -300 in this case, and add to equal b, which is 5. The only two numbers that fit this description are 20 and -15.

$$0 = w^2 + 5w - 300$$
$$0 = (w + 20)(w - 15)$$

Now set each factor equal to 0 and solve for w:

$$w + 20 = 0$$
$$w = -20$$

$$w - 15 = 0$$
$$w = 15$$

Solving a quadratic equation by factoring produces two solutions. Next, decide which one is correct for this situation. Because a distance can't be negative, the width is 15 yards. The length is $15 + 5 = 20$ yards.

25. **C. 14**

Find the difference in percentages and multiply by the total number of cars:

30% blue $-$ 20% red $=$ 10% more blue cars than red cars
$$(10\%)(140) = 14 \text{ cars}$$

You can also solve this problem by reasoning the number of blue cars in the parking lot is equal to $0.3(140) = 42$ and the number of red cars in the parking lot is equal to $0.2(140) = 28$. Subtract the number of red cars from the number of blue cars: $42 - 28 = 14$ more blue cars.

26. **A. 5° Fahrenheit**

Plug the numbers into the formula:

$$F = \frac{9}{5}C + 32°$$
$$= \frac{9}{5}(-15) + 32$$
$$= \frac{9(-15)}{5} + 32$$

First, divide -15 by 5. Remember that a negative number divided by a positive number is negative:

$$F = 9(-3) + 32$$

Next, multiply the result by 9. Remember that a negative number multiplied by a positive number is negative:

$$F = -27 + 32$$

For the final step, add 32 to -27. Remember that adding a negative is the same as subtracting a positive: $32 + (-27) = 32 - 27 = 5°F$.

27. **C. 6 packages of hot dogs, 8 packages of buns, and 3 packages of chips**

This problem involves finding the least common multiple, or LCM, of three numbers. To find the LCM, write out multiples of each number and find the first multiple that they all have in common:

Hot dogs: 8, 16, 24, 43, 40, 48

Buns: 6, 12, 18, 24, 30, 36, 42, 48

Chips: 16, 32, 48

The LCM of 8, 6, and 16 is 48, so you need 48 of each item. For each item, count how many multiples it took to get to 48:

Hot dogs: 8, 16, 24, 43, 40, 48 (6 packages)

Buns: 6, 12, 18, 24, 30, 36, 42, 48 (8 packages)

Chips: 16, 32, 48 (3 packages)

You can take a shortcut in this problem if you noticed that the packages of chips (16) are twice as large as the packages of hot dogs (8). The number of packages of chips must be double the number of packages of hot dogs — and the only answer choice that meets that requirement is Choice (C), which has 6 packages of hot dogs to 3 packages of chips.

Multiply the numbers in Choice (C) by the numbers of items in each package to check:

$6(8) = 48$ hot dogs

$8(6) = 48$ buns

$3(16) = 48$ chips

28. B. 100 revolutions

First, find the circumference of each wheel. The formula for the circumference of a circle is $C = \pi d$. Remember when approximating π, round to 3.14. The circumference of a wheel is $C = 3.14(20) = 62.8$ inches. Every time a wheel makes a full revolution, the bicycle moves approximately 62.8 inches. Divide the total distance traveled by the circumference to find the total number of revolutions: $\frac{6,280}{62.8} = 100$. Each wheel made about 100 full revolutions.

29. D. $7

Let x = the cost of a child's ticket. Alexa has sold a total of $10x$ dollars in children's tickets. An adult ticket costs 40 percent more, which is $0.4x$, so the cost of an adult ticket is $x + 0.4x = 1.4x$. Alexa has sold $12(1.4x)$ dollars in adult tickets. Make an equation and solve for x:

$$10x + 12(1.4x) = 134$$
$$10x + 16.8x = 134$$
$$26.8x = 134$$
$$\frac{26.8x}{26.8} = \frac{134}{26.8}$$
$$x = 5$$

Children's tickets sell for $5, so each adult ticket sells for $1.4(\$5) = \$7$.

30. A. 10 quarters

Let q = the number of quarters and d = the number of dimes. The value of the quarters is $0.25q$, and value of the dimes is $0.10d$. Because you know there are 8 nickels, you know the value of the nickels is $0.5(8)$. The sum of the values of the quarters, dimes, and nickels is equal to 3.40. Start by multiplying the entire equation by 100 to clear the decimals:

$$(0.25q + 0.10d + 0.5(8)) \cdot 100 = 3.40 \cdot 100$$
$$25q + 10d + 5(8) = 340$$

Because there are twice as many quarters as there are dimes, you can substitute $q = 2d$ into the equation and solve for d:

$$25(2d) + 10d + 5(8) = 340$$
$$50d + 10d + 40 = 340$$
$$60d + 40 = 340$$
$$60d = 300$$
$$d = 5$$

There are 5 dimes, so there are $2(5) = 10$ quarters.

Part 2: Word Knowledge

Scoring well on the Word Knowledge subtest is crucial to scoring high on the AFQT and getting into the military branch of your choice. If your score is weak in this area, spend time reviewing the material and improving your vocabulary (see Chapter 4).

Other great references that can help you improve your score in this area are *Vocabulary For Dummies* by Laurie E. Rozakis and *SAT Vocabulary For Dummies* by Suzee Vlk (both published by John Wiley & Sons, Inc.). Plus, see Chapter 5 for more practice questions.

1. D. lie.

Perjury is a noun that means a lie told after taking an oath.

"The man committed perjury by telling the judge he had nothing to do with the crime, despite video evidence to the contrary."

2. B. vibrant.

Used as an adjective, *dynamic* means full of energy and vigorous activity. It's also a noun that means a force that stimulates change or progress.

"The dynamic toddlers ran around the room, laughing and playing."

3. B. maintain.

Used as a verb, *abandon* means to cease or to leave behind.

"The neighbor was afraid the family would abandon their dog."

4. A. major.

Momentous is an adjective that means extremely important or significant.

"The wedding will be a momentous occasion."

5. C. critical.

Vital is an adjective that describes something crucial or very important.

"The commander had the vital task of determining whether to give the 'all clear' signal to her troops."

6. B. hum.

Used as a verb, *drone* means to make a low-pitched humming noise. It's also a noun that means a low, continuous humming sound.

"You can hear the drone of the machinery a mile away from the factory."

7. D. restrain.

Stifle is a verb that means to repress or prevent.

"Ellie had to stifle her laughter during the four-star general's briefing."

8. B. charming

Quaint is an adjective that means having an old-fashioned or pleasant quality.

9. C. pointless

Futile is an adjective that describes something useless or fruitless.

10. B. nonsense

Drivel is a noun that means something foolish or without sense.

11. A. label

Used as a noun, *stereotype* means an oversimplified categorization of a person or group.

12. A. protect.

Betray is a verb that means to harm or to be disloyal.

"A good friend would never betray you by talking about you behind your back."

13. A. stroll.

Amble is a verb that means a leisurely walk for pleasure.

"The parents watched their children amble along the boardwalk, pointing at all the attractions."

14. C. gain

Garner is a verb that means to acquire or gather.

15. D. dull

Monotonous is an adjective that means repetitive or dull.

16. B. questionable

As used in this sentence, *dubious* is an adjective that describes something suspect or untrustworthy.

17. C. isolate.

Used as a verb, *quarantine* means to detain someone from the public or away from others.

"In order to stop the spread of the virus, the CDC had to quarantine the people who had already contracted it."

18. A. condemn.

Endorse is a verb that means to give support to.

"Very few politicians wanted to endorse the presidential candidate."

19. C. reduce.

Mitigate is a verb meaning to lessen or decrease.

"Your platoon sergeant's job is to mitigate the risks you'll face when you're training."

20. A. content

Complacent is an adjective that means unworried or self-satisfied.

21. C. surrender.

Dominate is a verb that means to take over or dictate.

"The king's goal was to dominate all of Europe, so he started to plan for war."

22. B. seize

Commandeer is a verb that means to take or confiscate something by force.

23. D. justify.

Vindicate is a verb that means to prove that something is correct or justified.

"The evidence will vindicate the suspect when it comes out in court."

24. C. devoted

Staunch is an adjective that means loyal or steadfast.

25. B. commonplace

Colloquial is an adjective that describes something usual or informal.

26. A. shrivel.

Atrophy is a verb that means to waste away or deteriorate.

"If you don't exercise, your muscles will atrophy."

27. D. rebel

Insurgent is a noun that represents somebody who rebels against authority.

"An armed insurgent tried to take over the compound, but the local police stopped him."

28. B. enlarge

Augment is a verb that means to add to something or to expand.

29. B. variable.

Intermittent is an adjective that means occurring at sporadic times.

"If you live in Tampa, expect intermittent rain each day during the summer."

30. D. predicament

Quandary is a noun that represents a dilemma or difficult situation.

31. C. unemotional

Stoic is an adjective that describes someone patient or impassive.

32. B. dislike.

Aversion is a noun that means a distaste for something.

"Try to get over your aversion to running before you report to Basic Combat Training." (Seriously.)

33. A. gaudy.

Garish is an adjective that means overly ornate or bright.

"I can't take someone seriously when he's wearing such a garish outfit."

34. C. brave.

Intrepid is an adjective that means courageous or fearless.

"The intrepid storm chasers saw more than five tornadoes that day."

35. D. yield.

Vanquish is a verb that means to overcome or defeat.

"Union soldiers tried hard to vanquish the Confederate artillery unit at Charleston, but they failed."

Part 3: Paragraph Comprehension

Those ASVAB folks sure don't give you much time to read all those paragraphs, do they? But with a little practice, anyone can improve his or her reading speed and comprehension skills. The material in Chapter 6 can be helpful in these endeavors. There are also more practice questions in Chapter 7.

1. D. Fiddles and violins are the same instrument.

Both the opening and closing sentences in this paragraph state the main point. The different styles of music are secondary information.

2. A. smoothly

Fluidly is an adjective that means gracefully or flowingly.

3. C. Acupuncture has become trendy in spa settings.

Although the passage doesn't directly define *boutique*, the use of the term "popular" indicates that Choice (C) is the only choice that makes sense.

4. C. hundreds of thousands

The passage says that the number of children with peanut allergies is in the "hundreds of thousands."

5. B. It could reduce their anxiety about exposure.

The research mentioned in the passage indicates that reduced sensitivity is the possible outcome of the treatment. This reduced sensitivity helps decrease the risk of a negative reaction, which could relieve parents' concerns about a reaction from secondary sources of peanuts.

6. C. because of urban sprawl

The last sentence in the passage specifically states that the main cause is urban sprawl, which refers to the uncontrolled expansion of urban areas into more rural areas, so you can quickly scan and find the answer if you don't remember it from reading.

7. C. bizarre.

Outlandish is an adjective that means peculiar or unusual.

8. **B. 15**

The passage states that he played with the Yankees from 1923 to 1938. Simple subtraction finds you the correct answer.

9. **C. They learn to ski more easily.**

The passage provides examples of why children learn to ski more quickly than adults do, but it makes no other judgments about their abilities.

10. **A. being less fearful**

In the passage, many of the factors that make skiing more difficult for adults involve some kind of fear (fear of falling, fear of injury, fear of medical bills). None of the other answer choices fit the information in the passage.

11. **B. prime**

Heyday is a noun that means at the height or top of a situation or timeline.

12. **C. nervous**

The passage describes the fidgety behavior or last-minute preparation of the children as they wait in line. These are signs of nervousness.

13. **D. She achieved the highest score given in Olympic gymnastics.**

The passage states that Comaneci was the first female gymnast to receive a perfect ten for her performance, which she did seven times at the Montreal games. Choice (D) provides this answer.

14. **A. 1989**

You can find the answer to this question at the end of the passage, where it specifically states she "found her freedom in 1989 when she defected to the United States."

15. **A. lack of knowledge about prices**

The passage states that more Americans would likely drive NGVs if they knew about the savings, so their lack of knowledge must be what's keeping them from getting on the NGV bandwagon.

Part 4: Mathematics Knowledge

Many people find the Mathematics Knowledge subtest to be more difficult than the Arithmetic Reasoning subtest, but doing well on this subtest is just as important. If you missed more than a few answers, or you ran out of time before you finished, you have a date with the books (Chapter 8 is a great place to start). Getting in touch with a math teacher at your high school or a local community college (or at least finding a good basic-algebra textbook) can help. You can also try out the following *For Dummies* books: *Algebra I For Dummies* and *Algebra II For Dummies*, both by Mary Jane Sterling; *Geometry For Dummies* by Mark Ryan; *Basic Math & Pre-Algebra For Dummies* by Mark Zegarelli; and *SAT II Math For Dummies* by Scott Hatch, JD, and Lisa Zimmer Hatch, MA (all published by John Wiley & Sons, Inc.). Chapter 9 also has some additional practice questions.

1. **B. 54**

When a numerical expression just has addition and subtraction, the order of operations is flexible. You can work from left to right, like this: $45 - 6 + 15 = 39 + 15 = 54$, or you can add 45 and 15 before you subtract 6. You can use the method you're most comfortable with to find the answer when you encounter a problem like this one.

2. A. 216

Write 30 percent as a decimal: 30 percent = 0.3. The word *of* in a word problem means *multiply*, so multiply 0.3 by 720: 0.3(720) = 216.

3. B. hundredths

The numbers in the decimal system increase as you move from left to right when reading a number. In this case, the number is 4.5972, where the 4 is in the ones place, the 5 is in the tenths place, the 9 is in the hundredths place, the 7 is in the thousandths place, and the 2 is in the ten-thousandths place.

4. A. 2.6 percent

To turn a decimal into a percent, simply move the decimal point two places to the right (which is the same thing as multiplying by 100).

5. C. 235,000

For the given number, 8 is in the ones place, 7 is in the tens place, 6 is in the hundreds place, and 4 is in the thousands place. You round 4 up to 5 because the digit one place to the right of it (6) is 5 or greater. You can round 234,678 to 235,000.

6. D. 2

The first digit after the decimal point is in the tenths place, and the second digit is in the hundredths place. In this problem, the 2 is in the hundredths place.

7. B. 24

4! means the factorial of 4. You find it by multiplying all the whole numbers from 4 down to 1:

$4 \times 3 \times 2 \times 1 = 24$

8. A. −4

Evaluate means to substitute the given value of m into the expression and then simplify the result. Remember that a positive number divided by a negative number results in a negative number.

$$\frac{28}{-7} = 28 \div (-7) = -4$$

9. A. −38

Isolate the variable, m, by adding 17 to each side of the equation.

$$-55 = m - 17$$
$$-55 + 17 = m - 17 + 17$$
$$-38 = m$$

10. C. 15 percent

Subtract the original number from the new number to get the difference: $23 - 20 = 3$.

To find what percent of 20 is 3, divide the difference (3) by the original number (20). This is the percent increase: $3 \div 20 = 0.15 = 15$ percent.

You can also create a fraction and then increase its terms so the denominator is 100 (in this instance, you have to multiply the 20 by 5 to reach 100). Then apply the same multiplier to the numerator to get the right answer:

$$\frac{3}{20} = \frac{x}{100}$$

$$\frac{3(5)}{20(5)} = \frac{15}{100}$$

11. **D. 4.36×10^{-6}**

A number written in scientific notation is a number between 1 and 10 multiplied by a power of 10. To make a number between 1 and 10, move the decimal point six places to the right to get 4.36. You find the power of 10 by taking the number of spaces you moved the decimal and determining whether it should be positive or negative based on which direction you moved it. Because you moved it to the right (that is, the given number is less than 1), the power of 10 must be negative: 10^{-6}.

12. **B. Point B**

First, notice that the x-coordinate is -3. This means that from the origin (0, 0), you move to the left three units. The y-coordinate is 2, so you then move up two units. That puts you at Point B.

13. **C. $\frac{5}{6}$**

Write each mixed number as an improper fraction:

$$5\frac{1}{3} = \frac{3(5)+1}{3} = \frac{15+1}{3} = \frac{16}{3}$$

$$4\frac{1}{2} = \frac{2(4)+1}{2} = \frac{8+1}{2} = \frac{9}{2}$$

The common denominator is 6. Rewrite each fraction with the common denominator:

$$\frac{16}{3} - \frac{9}{2} = \frac{16 \cdot 2}{3 \cdot 2} - \frac{9 \cdot 3}{2 \cdot 3}$$

$$= \frac{32}{6} - \frac{27}{6}$$

$$= \frac{5}{6}$$

14. **D. $-21m$**

This is basically just three values being multiplied together: 7, -3, and m. However, because you don't know the value of m, you only need to multiply 7 and -3. Remember that a positive number times a negative number is a negative number:

$$7(-3m) = 7(-3)m = -21m$$

15. **A. 19**

In any triangle, any side length must be less than the sum of the other two side lengths. So that means y has to be less than $14 + 6 = 20$. All the answer choices are greater than 20 except 19.

16. B. 18

Use the order of operations (PEMDAS), which says to simplify inside the parentheses first, compute all exponents next, multiply and divide from left to right after that, and then add and subtract from left to right:

$$10 + 2(5-3)^2 = 10 + 2(2)^2$$
$$= 10 + 2(4)$$
$$= 10 + 8$$
$$= 18$$

17. C. 16

Remember that dividing by a fraction is the same as multiplying by the reciprocal of the fraction. Dividing 12 by $\frac{3}{4}$ is the same as multiplying 12 by $\frac{4}{3}$.

$$12 \div \frac{3}{4} = 12 \times \frac{4}{3}$$
$$= \frac{12}{1} \times \frac{4}{3}$$
$$= \frac{48}{3}$$
$$= 16$$

Tip: Sometimes you can skip all the calculations and find the most logical answer choice. In this problem, you're dividing by a number that's less than 1, so the answer must be greater than 12. Choices (B) and (D) are out of the question, and Choice (A) is too close to 12 to be correct. The most likely answer is Choice (C).

18. C. p^8

A square root is a number that when multiplied by itself equals the number under the radical sign. Square both sides of the equation to clear the square root. When the base is the same, you add the exponents to multiply, so

$$p^4 = \sqrt{x}$$
$$\left(p^4\right)^2 = \left(\sqrt{x}\right)^2$$
$$\left(p^4\right)\left(p^4\right) = x$$
$$p^{4+4} = x$$
$$p^8 = x$$

19. B. −22

Let x = the number you want to find. Remembering that "12 less than the product" means to subtract 12 from the product, write an equation:

$$x = 4(-2.5) - 12$$

Now, solve the equation, following the order of operations by multiplying first and then subtracting:

$$x = 4(-2.5) - 12$$
$$x = -10 - 12$$
$$x = -22$$

20. D. 30°, 60°, 90°

Remember that for any triangle, the sum of the three angle measures is always 180°. You can make an equation by adding the three expressions shown in the diagram and setting the sum equal to 180°. Then solve the equation.

$$x + 2x + 3x = 180$$
$$6x = 180$$
$$x = 30$$

The measures of the angles are

$$x = 30°$$
$$2x = 2(30°) = 60°$$
$$3x = 3(30°) = 90°$$

21. A. $9x^2 - 4x - y$

For problems like this one, the first thing you want to do is remove the parentheses. Remember that when you have a subtraction sign in front of a set of parentheses, you need to change the sign of all the terms inside the parentheses. Then combine like terms and simplify:

$$(3x^2 - 4x + y) - (2y - 6x^2) = 3x^2 - 4x + y - 2y + 6x^2$$
$$= 9x^2 - 4x - y$$

22. B. 4×10^5

Quotient means division, so first, write this problem as a fraction:

$$\frac{4.8 \times 10^{-4}}{1.2 \times 10^{-9}}$$

Now, separate that fraction into a product of two fractions:

$$\frac{4.8}{1.2} \times \frac{10^{-4}}{10^{-9}}$$

The first fraction simplifies to 4, because $\frac{4.8}{1.2} = 4$. Because the bases are the same in the second fraction, subtract the exponents:

$$\frac{4.8 \times 10^{-4}}{1.2 \times 10^{-9}} = 4 \times 10^{-4 - (-9)} = 4 \times 10^{-4+9} = 4 \times 10^5$$

23. C. 4

Simplify everything under the radical sign first, using the order of operations. For this problem, that means computing the exponent first, multiplying next, and then subtracting:

$$\sqrt{66 - 2 \cdot 5^2} = \sqrt{66 - 2 \cdot 25}$$
$$= \sqrt{66 - 50}$$
$$= \sqrt{16}$$

Then find the square root of the result: $\sqrt{16} = 4$

24. D. −22

First, substitute the given values of x and y into the expression: $\dfrac{45}{-5} - \dfrac{39}{3}$. Then use the order of operations to simplify. Remember that you have to divide the fractions before you subtract. Also remember that a positive number divided by a negative number produces a negative number:

$$\frac{45}{-5} - \frac{39}{3} = -9 - 13$$
$$= -22$$

25. C. $(9\pi + 6m\pi)\,cm^2$

A good strategy for this problem is to find the area of each circle and then subtract. Use formula for the area of a circle, $A = \pi r^2$.

Area of smaller circle:

$$A_1 = \pi \cdot m^2 = m^2\pi$$

Area of larger circle:

$$A_2 = \pi(3 + m)^2$$
$$= \pi(3 + m)(3 + m)$$
$$= \pi\left(9 + 6m + m^2\right)$$
$$= 9\pi + \pi(6m) + \pi\left(m^2\right)$$
$$= 9\pi + 6m\pi + m^2\pi$$

Now subtract the area of the smaller circle from the area of the larger circle:

$$9\pi + 6m\pi + m^2\pi - m^2\pi = 9\pi + 6m\pi$$

The answer choices didn't factor out pi, so you can stop your work there. When you see an opportunity to save yourself time on the ASVAB, take it!

Answer Key

Part 1: Arithmetic Reasoning

1.	B	9.	C	17.	A	25.	C
2.	C	10.	A	18.	C	26.	A
3.	A	11.	B	19.	B	27.	C
4.	C	12.	A	20.	B	28.	B
5.	B	13.	C	21.	C	29.	D
6.	C	14.	C	22.	B	30.	A
7.	A	15.	D	23.	D		
8.	D	16.	D	24.	B		

Part 2: Word Knowledge

1.	D	10.	B	19.	C	28.	B
2.	B	11.	A	20.	A	29.	B
3.	B	12.	A	21.	C	30.	D
4.	A	13.	A	22.	B	31.	C
5.	C	14.	C	23.	D	32.	B
6.	B	15.	D	24.	C	33.	A
7.	D	16.	B	25.	B	34.	C
8.	B	17.	C	26.	A	35.	D
9.	C	18.	A	27.	D		

Part 3: Paragraph Comprehension

1.	D	5.	B	9.	C	13.	D
2.	A	6.	C	10.	A	14.	A
3.	C	7.	C	11.	B	15.	A
4.	C	8.	B	12.	C		

Part 4: Mathematics Knowledge

1.	B	8.	A	15.	A	22.	B
2.	A	9.	A	16.	B	23.	C
3.	D	10.	C	17.	C	24.	D
4.	A	11.	D	18.	C	25.	C
5.	C	12.	B	19.	B		
6.	D	13.	C	20.	D		
7.	B	14.	D	21.	A		

Chapter 18

Practice Exam 4

When you've taken all four practice AFQT exams in this book, you should be ready to tackle the actual Armed Services Vocational Aptitude Battery (ASVAB) and impress all those military recruiters by acing the four subtests that make up the AFQT. If you still want some more practice after this exam, or you want to study for the other ASVAB subtests as well, might I humbly suggest *ASVAB For Dummies* (John Wiley & Sons, Inc.)?

The four sections that follow represent the four subtests of the ASVAB that make up your all-important AFQT score. This is the score that determines whether you're qualified to join the military branch of your choice (see Chapter 1). The four subtests are Arithmetic Reasoning, Word Knowledge, Paragraph Comprehension, and Mathematics Knowledge.

Use the answer key and explanations in Chapter 19 to score the following sections. *Remember:* On the actual ASVAB, harder questions are worth more points than easier questions when you determine your AFQT score.

Consider taking this final practice exam a day or two before the ASVAB to make sure you're ready and to boost your confidence. If you don't score well, you may want to consider asking your recruiter to reschedule your ASVAB test for a later date to give you more time to study.

Ready, set, go!

Answer Sheet for Practice Exam 4

Part 1: Arithmetic Reasoning

1. Ⓐ Ⓑ Ⓒ Ⓓ	7. Ⓐ Ⓑ Ⓒ Ⓓ	13. Ⓐ Ⓑ Ⓒ Ⓓ	19. Ⓐ Ⓑ Ⓒ Ⓓ	25. Ⓐ Ⓑ Ⓒ Ⓓ
2. Ⓐ Ⓑ Ⓒ Ⓓ	8. Ⓐ Ⓑ Ⓒ Ⓓ	14. Ⓐ Ⓑ Ⓒ Ⓓ	20. Ⓐ Ⓑ Ⓒ Ⓓ	26. Ⓐ Ⓑ Ⓒ Ⓓ
3. Ⓐ Ⓑ Ⓒ Ⓓ	9. Ⓐ Ⓑ Ⓒ Ⓓ	15. Ⓐ Ⓑ Ⓒ Ⓓ	21. Ⓐ Ⓑ Ⓒ Ⓓ	27. Ⓐ Ⓑ Ⓒ Ⓓ
4. Ⓐ Ⓑ Ⓒ Ⓓ	10. Ⓐ Ⓑ Ⓒ Ⓓ	16. Ⓐ Ⓑ Ⓒ Ⓓ	22. Ⓐ Ⓑ Ⓒ Ⓓ	28. Ⓐ Ⓑ Ⓒ Ⓓ
5. Ⓐ Ⓑ Ⓒ Ⓓ	11. Ⓐ Ⓑ Ⓒ Ⓓ	17. Ⓐ Ⓑ Ⓒ Ⓓ	23. Ⓐ Ⓑ Ⓒ Ⓓ	29. Ⓐ Ⓑ Ⓒ Ⓓ
6. Ⓐ Ⓑ Ⓒ Ⓓ	12. Ⓐ Ⓑ Ⓒ Ⓓ	18. Ⓐ Ⓑ Ⓒ Ⓓ	24. Ⓐ Ⓑ Ⓒ Ⓓ	30. Ⓐ Ⓑ Ⓒ Ⓓ

Part 2: Word Knowledge

1. Ⓐ Ⓑ Ⓒ Ⓓ	8. Ⓐ Ⓑ Ⓒ Ⓓ	15. Ⓐ Ⓑ Ⓒ Ⓓ	22. Ⓐ Ⓑ Ⓒ Ⓓ	29. Ⓐ Ⓑ Ⓒ Ⓓ
2. Ⓐ Ⓑ Ⓒ Ⓓ	9. Ⓐ Ⓑ Ⓒ Ⓓ	16. Ⓐ Ⓑ Ⓒ Ⓓ	23. Ⓐ Ⓑ Ⓒ Ⓓ	30. Ⓐ Ⓑ Ⓒ Ⓓ
3. Ⓐ Ⓑ Ⓒ Ⓓ	10. Ⓐ Ⓑ Ⓒ Ⓓ	17. Ⓐ Ⓑ Ⓒ Ⓓ	24. Ⓐ Ⓑ Ⓒ Ⓓ	31. Ⓐ Ⓑ Ⓒ Ⓓ
4. Ⓐ Ⓑ Ⓒ Ⓓ	11. Ⓐ Ⓑ Ⓒ Ⓓ	18. Ⓐ Ⓑ Ⓒ Ⓓ	25. Ⓐ Ⓑ Ⓒ Ⓓ	32. Ⓐ Ⓑ Ⓒ Ⓓ
5. Ⓐ Ⓑ Ⓒ Ⓓ	12. Ⓐ Ⓑ Ⓒ Ⓓ	19. Ⓐ Ⓑ Ⓒ Ⓓ	26. Ⓐ Ⓑ Ⓒ Ⓓ	33. Ⓐ Ⓑ Ⓒ Ⓓ
6. Ⓐ Ⓑ Ⓒ Ⓓ	13. Ⓐ Ⓑ Ⓒ Ⓓ	20. Ⓐ Ⓑ Ⓒ Ⓓ	27. Ⓐ Ⓑ Ⓒ Ⓓ	34. Ⓐ Ⓑ Ⓒ Ⓓ
7. Ⓐ Ⓑ Ⓒ Ⓓ	14. Ⓐ Ⓑ Ⓒ Ⓓ	21. Ⓐ Ⓑ Ⓒ Ⓓ	28. Ⓐ Ⓑ Ⓒ Ⓓ	35. Ⓐ Ⓑ Ⓒ Ⓓ

Part 3: Paragraph Comprehension

1. Ⓐ Ⓑ Ⓒ Ⓓ   4. Ⓐ Ⓑ Ⓒ Ⓓ   7. Ⓐ Ⓑ Ⓒ Ⓓ   10. Ⓐ Ⓑ Ⓒ Ⓓ   13. Ⓐ Ⓑ Ⓒ Ⓓ

2. Ⓐ Ⓑ Ⓒ Ⓓ   5. Ⓐ Ⓑ Ⓒ Ⓓ   8. Ⓐ Ⓑ Ⓒ Ⓓ   11. Ⓐ Ⓑ Ⓒ Ⓓ   14. Ⓐ Ⓑ Ⓒ Ⓓ

3. Ⓐ Ⓑ Ⓒ Ⓓ   6. Ⓐ Ⓑ Ⓒ Ⓓ   9. Ⓐ Ⓑ Ⓒ Ⓓ   12. Ⓐ Ⓑ Ⓒ Ⓓ   15. Ⓐ Ⓑ Ⓒ Ⓓ

Part 4: Mathematics Knowledge

1. Ⓐ Ⓑ Ⓒ Ⓓ   6. Ⓐ Ⓑ Ⓒ Ⓓ   11. Ⓐ Ⓑ Ⓒ Ⓓ   16. Ⓐ Ⓑ Ⓒ Ⓓ   21. Ⓐ Ⓑ Ⓒ Ⓓ

2. Ⓐ Ⓑ Ⓒ Ⓓ   7. Ⓐ Ⓑ Ⓒ Ⓓ   12. Ⓐ Ⓑ Ⓒ Ⓓ   17. Ⓐ Ⓑ Ⓒ Ⓓ   22. Ⓐ Ⓑ Ⓒ Ⓓ

3. Ⓐ Ⓑ Ⓒ Ⓓ   8. Ⓐ Ⓑ Ⓒ Ⓓ   13. Ⓐ Ⓑ Ⓒ Ⓓ   18. Ⓐ Ⓑ Ⓒ Ⓓ   23. Ⓐ Ⓑ Ⓒ Ⓓ

4. Ⓐ Ⓑ Ⓒ Ⓓ   9. Ⓐ Ⓑ Ⓒ Ⓓ   14. Ⓐ Ⓑ Ⓒ Ⓓ   19. Ⓐ Ⓑ Ⓒ Ⓓ   24. Ⓐ Ⓑ Ⓒ Ⓓ

5. Ⓐ Ⓑ Ⓒ Ⓓ   10. Ⓐ Ⓑ Ⓒ Ⓓ   15. Ⓐ Ⓑ Ⓒ Ⓓ   20. Ⓐ Ⓑ Ⓒ Ⓓ   25. Ⓐ Ⓑ Ⓒ Ⓓ

Part 1: Arithmetic Reasoning

1. One pound is equal to 16 ounces. How many ounces are in 5 pounds?

   (A) 21 ounces

   (B) 3.2 ounces

   (C) 80 ounces

   (D) 64 ounces

2. Ishaan is reading a book that is 180 pages long. He is 40 percent of the way through the book. What page is he on?

   (A) page 40

   (B) page 72

   (C) page 45

   (D) page 76

3. If you toss two coins, what is the probability that both coins show tails?

   (A) 33 percent

   (B) 30 percent

   (C) 25 percent

   (D) 50 percent

4. In a triangle, one angle has a measure of 40°, and the other two angles have measures equal to each other. What is the measure of one of the two other angles?

   (A) 30°

   (B) 40°

   (C) 80°

   (D) 70°

5. A truck gets 22 miles per gallon on the highway. How many miles on the highway can it travel on 4 gallons of gasoline?

   (A) 88 miles

   (B) 44 miles

   (C) 22 miles

   (D) 26 miles

6. Sergeant Williams cut a 24-foot rope into smaller ropes, each with a length of 4 feet. How many times did they cut the rope?

   (A) 4

   (B) 6

   (C) 3

   (D) 5

7. The refrigerator's temperature dropped from 32° Fahrenheit to 28° Fahrenheit. What is the percent decrease in temperature?

   (A) 15 percent

   (B) 4 percent

   (C) 25 percent

   (D) 12.5 percent

8. Carter has $6.70. Dirk has 4 times as much money as Carter. Xiomara has half as much money as Dirk. How much money does Xiomara have?

   (A) $26.80

   (B) $13.40

   (C) $5.35

   (D) $10.70

9. The ages of a group of adults are 24, 26, 37, 23, and 40. What is the average age for this group?

(A) 26

(B) 32

(C) 30

(D) 28

10. A pitcher has 2.5 gallons of juice. Twenty-five people share all the juice equally. How much juice does each person get?

(A) 0.1 gallon

(B) 0.25 gallon

(C) 0.01 gallon

(D) 0.2 gallon

11. Timothy's age in years is one more than twice Sam's age. The sum of their ages is 31. What is Sam's age?

(A) 21

(B) 10

(C) 11

(D) 16

12. The value of a new car depreciates 10 percent each year after it was purchased. What is the car's value two years after it is purchased new if the initial value is $14,000?

(A) $11,340

(B) $11,200

(C) $11,034

(D) $10,955

13. The formula $W = 0.5n + 47$ gives the percent of women (W) in a certain country who owned a laptop computer n years after the year 2000. In what year did 50 percent of women in this country own a laptop computer?

(A) 2004

(B) 2006

(C) 2011

(D) 2008

14. A rhombus has two interior angle measurements of 87° and 93°. Which of the following can be a measure of one of the remaining angles?

(A) 6°

(B) 90°

(C) 93°

(D) 180°

15. To make a certain type of juice, the ratio of water to juice concentrate is 8 to 1. How much concentrate should be added to 6 gallons of water?

(A) $\frac{2}{3}$ gallon

(B) 2 gallons

(C) $1\frac{1}{3}$ gallons

(D) $\frac{3}{4}$ gallon

16. Lillian invests $5,000 into a savings account. After one year, she had earned $100 in interest. What is the annual interest rate for the account?

(A) 0.2 percent

(B) 0.5 percent

(C) 2 percent

(D) 5 percent

17. The number of members in a club has doubled every 2 years. The club started in 2002 with 42 members. How many members were in the club in 2008?

(A) 672

(B) 1,344

(C) 336

(D) 168

18. The high temperature (H) was ten degrees less than twice the low temperature (L). Which equation shows this relationship?

(A) $H = 2L - 10$

(B) $H = 10 - 2L$

(C) $2H = L - 10$

(D) $2H + L = 10$

19. What is the area of the triangle?

Illustration by Thomson Digital

(A) 136 cm²

(B) 96 cm²

(C) 102 cm²

(D) 45 cm²

20. The table shows how many men and women live in different regions of a town. How many more women live in the West region than men?

	East region	West region	South region
Men	320	110	421
Women	120	262	338

Illustration by Thomson Digital

(A) 110

(B) 372

(C) 262

(D) 152

21. You have two jobs. Last week, you earned a total of $314 from both jobs, working 16 hours at the first job and 14 hours at the second job. You earn $10 an hour at your first job. What is your hourly rate at your second job?

(A) $12

(B) $11

(C) $9

(D) $8

22. A bag has a total of 270 red, blue, and green marbles. The ratio of red to blue to green marbles is 1:3:5. How many blue marbles are in the bag?

(A) 30

(B) 90

(C) 150

(D) 50

23. A truck and a car leave from the same place at the same time. The truck takes a road that goes directly north, and the car takes a road that goes directly east. The truck travels at an average speed of 30 miles per hour, and the car travels at an average speed of 40 miles per hour. How far apart are the vehicles 2 hours after departure?

(A) 10 miles

(B) 1,000 miles

(C) 100 miles

(D) 70 miles

24. Evan is twice as old as Joe. In two years, the sum of their ages will be 85. How old is Evan now?

(A) 27

(B) 29

(C) 54

(D) 56

25. Gregory started the day with $45.10 in his wallet. The first thing he did was buy breakfast for himself, which cost $8.50. He left a 20-percent tip. How much did Gregory have left after he paid for breakfast?

(A) $10.20

(B) $34.80

(C) $34.90

(D) $36.60

26. Kendra's first three quiz scores were 7, 6, and 10. On the fourth quiz, she earned twice as much as she did on the fifth quiz. Her average score on the first five quizzes was 7. What was her score on the fourth quiz?

(A) 6.5

(B) 7.5

(C) 4

(D) 8

GO ON TO NEXT PAGE

27. The floor plan of a laboratory is shown. Its area is 126 square meters. What is the length of *x*?

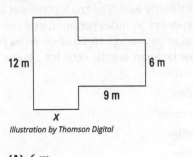

12 m   6 m

9 m

x

Illustration by Thomson Digital

(A) 6 m

(B) 4 m

(C) 5 m

(D) 10 m

28. The company truck weighs 3.5 tons when carrying forty 20-pound cylinder blocks. What is the weight of the truck when it isn't carrying a load?

(A) $3\frac{1}{5}$ tons

(B) $3\frac{7}{10}$ tons

(C) $3\frac{1}{10}$ tons

(D) 4 tons

29. Carla has $4 in quarters and dimes. She has 5 fewer quarters than dimes. How many quarters does she have?

(A) 8

(B) 10

(C) 15

(D) 20

30. A secret building has a front and a rear entrance. The front entrance requires a three-character code, where the first character must be an odd number but the next two characters can be any number 0 through 9. The rear entrance requires a two-character code, where the first character is a letter and the second character can be any number 0 through 9. How many possible entrance codes are there for the rear entrance?

(A) 260

(B) 361

(C) 760

(D) 500

STOP

DO NOT TURN THE PAGE UNTIL TOLD TO DO SO   DO NOT RETURN TO A PREVIOUS TEST

Part 2: Word Knowledge

TIME: 11 minutes for 35 questions

DIRECTIONS: The Word Knowledge subtest is the third subtest of the ASVAB; it follows Arithmetic Reasoning. The questions are designed to measure your vocabulary knowledge. You'll see three types of questions on this subtest. The first type simply asks you to choose a word or words that most nearly mean the same as the underlined word in the question. The second type includes an underlined word used in a sentence, and you are to choose the word or words that most nearly mean the same as the underlined word, as used in the context of the sentence. The third type of question asks you to choose the word that has the opposite or nearly opposite meaning as the underlined word. Each question is followed by four possible answers. Decide which answer is correct, and then mark the corresponding space on your answer sheet.

1. Condescend most nearly means
   - (A) share.
   - (B) conjoin.
   - (C) belittle.
   - (D) soften.

2. He's a legend in the bluegrass community, with a career spanning 35 years.
   - (A) star
   - (B) fairytale
   - (C) myth
   - (D) antagonist

3. Lavish most nearly means
   - (A) soapy.
   - (B) thick.
   - (C) meek.
   - (D) extravagant.

4. Retraction most nearly means
   - (A) withdrawal.
   - (B) application.
   - (C) memory.
   - (D) solitude.

5. Decoy most nearly means
   - (A) message.
   - (B) trap.
   - (C) plan.
   - (D) scheme.

6. Obsession most nearly means
   - (A) pastime.
   - (B) piece.
   - (C) fixation.
   - (D) apathy.

7. Brawny most nearly means
   - (A) obese.
   - (B) scrawny.
   - (C) meager.
   - (D) hefty.

8. The word most opposite in meaning to relocate is
   - (A) rearrange.
   - (B) move.
   - (C) continue.
   - (D) remain.

9. Lisa found power-washing her driveway therapeutic because it allowed her to free her mind.
   - (A) astounding
   - (B) healing
   - (C) obstructing
   - (D) injurious

10. Ji-Yeon was poised to take over as captain this year.
    - (A) perched
    - (B) proper
    - (C) ready
    - (D) unqualified

GO ON TO NEXT PAGE

11. The meaning of the poem was <u>obscure</u> and created a lot of debate.

(A) clear

(B) vague

(C) obvious

(D) pointed

12. Paolo wasn't ready to deal with the <u>ramifications</u> of his car accident.

(A) consequences

(B) prizes

(C) presentations

(D) rewards

13. The <u>eccentric</u> minister made the ceremony more enjoyable than your average church wedding.

(A) foolish

(B) conventional

(C) peculiar

(D) standard

14. The word most opposite in meaning to <u>meander</u> is

(A) wander.

(B) hurry.

(C) dawdle.

(D) discourage.

15. <u>Volatile</u> most nearly means

(A) speedy.

(B) steady.

(C) unlawful.

(D) unpredictable.

16. The skaters had obviously done the work to <u>hone</u> their jumps since the last competition.

(A) tarnish

(B) maintain

(C) polish

(D) contain

17. Cary wanted to <u>broach</u> the topic, but Jeffrey wasn't paying attention.

(A) mention

(B) conclude

(C) kill

(D) belabor

18. The family was worried when the dog's behavior became <u>erratic</u>.

(A) irrational

(B) random

(C) constant

(D) even

19. <u>Obsolete</u> most nearly means

(A) absent.

(B) old.

(C) prominent.

(D) innovative.

20. <u>Decorum</u> most nearly means

(A) design.

(B) festivities.

(C) servitude.

(D) respectability.

21. My editing style tends to favor <u>brevity</u> over long-winded explanations.

(A) rudeness

(B) briefness

(C) lengthy

(D) continuous

22. The word most opposite in meaning to <u>mayhem</u> is

(A) gathering.

(B) confusion.

(C) havoc.

(D) stability.

23. <u>Hiatus</u> most nearly means

(A) gap.

(B) inequality.

(C) mismatch.

(D) shift.

24. Cynical most nearly means
   (A) friendly.
   (B) hopeful.
   (C) pessimistic.
   (D) depressed.

25. Riddled most nearly means
   (A) mysterious.
   (B) inquisitive.
   (C) full of.
   (D) covered with.

26. Sean was finally released after his larceny conviction four years ago.
   (A) gift
   (B) theft
   (C) help
   (D) skill

27. The word most opposite in meaning to proposition is
   (A) demand.
   (B) suggestion.
   (C) offer.
   (D) plan.

28. The movie gave a poignant portrayal of the fallen soldier.
   (A) lackluster
   (B) traumatic
   (C) moving
   (D) composed

29. I had to take a respite from work or I was never going to rest.
   (A) interval
   (B) start
   (C) end
   (D) continuation

30. The celebrity had to debunk the rumors of his death.
   (A) chide
   (B) shoot down
   (C) alarm
   (D) conceal

31. Adamant most nearly means
   (A) erratic.
   (B) flexible.
   (C) fickle.
   (D) resolute.

32. The word most opposite in meaning to malarkey is
   (A) drivel.
   (B) nonsense.
   (C) justification.
   (D) wisdom.

33. The bobsledding team won the bronze medal despite the adversity they had to overcome.
   (A) hardship
   (B) strength
   (C) death
   (D) fortune

34. The defunct band still sold records years after its split.
   (A) rising
   (B) extinct
   (C) promising
   (D) useless

35. Origin most nearly means
   (A) section.
   (B) closure.
   (C) beginning.
   (D) new.

Part 3: Paragraph Comprehension

TIME: 13 minutes for 15 questions

DIRECTIONS: Paragraph Comprehension is the fourth subtest on the ASVAB; it comes after Word Knowledge. The questions are designed to measure your ability to understand what you read. In this part of the test, you see one or more paragraphs of reading material, followed by incomplete statements or questions. Read the paragraph and select the choice that best completes the statement or answers the question. Then mark the corresponding space on your answer sheet.

Questions 1 through 3 refer to the following passage.

"November had come; the crops were in, and barn, buttery, and bin were overflowing with the harvest that rewarded the summer's hard work. The big kitchen was a jolly place just now, for in the great fireplace roared a cheerful fire; on the walls hung garlands of dried apples, onions, and corn; up aloft from the beams shone crook-necked squashes, juicy hams, and dried venison — for in those days deer still haunted the deep forests, and hunters flourished. Savory smells were in the air; on the crane hung steaming kettles, and down among the red embers copper saucepans simmered, all suggestive of some approaching feast."

—Louisa May Alcott

1. In this passage, <u>flourished</u> most nearly means
   (A) failed.
   (B) prospered.
   (C) congregated.
   (D) killed.

2. Where is the scene described in the passage taking place?
   (A) the kitchen
   (B) the forest
   (C) the barn
   (D) at a feast

3. What is happening in the passage?
   (A) The season is changing.
   (B) Hunters are looking for deer.
   (C) Farmers are harvesting their crops.
   (D) A feast is being prepared.

The topic of creating a high-speed rail system in the United States is the focus of the annual High-Speed Rail Summit in Washington, D.C. The purpose of this summit is to determine the most optimal and logical maneuvers that would allow a rail system to succeed on American soil. Critics have long contested the system as an expensive endeavor lacking the appropriate ridership numbers. Regardless, the summit participants will spend two full days hashing out the details to work toward a high-speed rail system in the future.

4. What is the main point of the passage?
   (A) to define what a high-speed rail system is
   (B) to explain why critics are against a high-speed rail system
   (C) to explain the purpose of the High-Speed Rail Summit
   (D) to suggest ways to improve ridership on a high-speed rail system

Questions 5 and 6 refer to the following passage.

California is often the location for devastating natural events, such as earthquakes or droughts. However, the aftermath of those events can often be worse than the events themselves. For instance, the near-record drought in 2013 led to a wildfire season that began in May and continued until the end of the year. Fire season typically lasts from September to October, but in 2013, a fire in central California burned thousands of acres of land right before the Christmas holiday. Without rain, the number and severity of wildfires increased in 2013.

5. According to the passage, which of the following is a true statement?

   (A) California gets an average amount of rain.

   (B) Forest fires are rare.

   (C) Firefighters are often able to reduce the damage caused by forest fires.

   (D) The 2013 fire season was much longer than normal.

6. What caused the increase in forest fires in 2013?

   (A) careless campers

   (B) a lack of rain

   (C) lightning

   (D) heavily vegetated areas

Richard had never had rhythm and didn't enjoy dancing. He only went to the ballroom dance class to watch his wife perform. Then the instructor grabbed Richard's hands, pulling him onto the floor and showing him exactly what to do and how to do it. After that, Richard was dancing like a pro. He realized the secret to dancing wasn't rhythm; it was enjoying moving and being free.

7. According to this passage, Richard's lack of rhythm is

   (A) unimportant.

   (B) his downfall.

   (C) an embarrassment.

   (D) hilarious.

Making a good war movie is a tricky business. The subject matter is very dear to the hearts of many people, and accuracy is key. The combat scenes, soldiers, accommodations, and relationships among and throughout the different ranks must all be portrayed well to avoid negative backlash and ensure a profitable film.

8. According to the passage, which of the following is likely to make a war movie profitable?

   (A) length

   (B) emotional acting

   (C) historical accuracy

   (D) violence

Anyone can be a world-record holder if they have the wits and determination to do so. Guinness World Records has been making record-holders out of ordinary citizens since 1955. All that's required is filling out an application stating which record you want to break or make and sending in the evidence of your achievement. If the judges approve of your evidence, you become a world-record holder, and the sky is now the limit.

9. According to the passage, what do you have to do to be recognized by Guinness World Records?

   (A) break a record in front of a Guinness judge

   (B) file an application and ask to be accepted

   (C) prove that you have broken a record

   (D) both B and C

Questions 10 and 11 refer to the following passage.

The fervor that each side brings to the Mac versus PC debate is so extreme that you'd think people had a personal stake in the matter. Despite the obvious popularity of Apple products, recent studies have shown that only a small fraction (about 15 percent) of the computers sold each year are Macs. Of course, there's only one Apple company and a multitude of PC manufacturers. Perhaps that's why many feel the Mac operating system is superior to Microsoft Windows. So how do you choose? Price and need are usually the best factors to consider. Why spend a lot of money if all you need is a word processor?

10. As used in this passage, the word fervor most nearly means

   (A) passion.

   (B) illness.

   (C) cruelty.

   (D) refreshments.

11. According to the passage, when choosing a new computer, you should consider

   (A) a brand's popularity and reliability.

   (B) price and need.

   (C) popularity and price.

   (D) None of the above

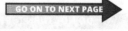
GO ON TO NEXT PAGE

If you get a flat tire while driving, stay calm. As long as you have a spare that's full of air, you can fix the problem in no time. The most important thing is to pull off the road to a safe location away from passing cars and with the flat side away from the road, if possible. Use a tire iron to loosen the lug nuts before jacking the car up. Next, place the jack under the vehicle in the appropriate spot and crank it so the car is just a foot or two off the ground. Remove the lug nuts, replace the flat tire with the spare, and put the nuts back on. After you've released the car to the ground, tighten the lug nuts. If you try to tighten the nuts while the wheel is suspended, you won't have the proper resistance to get them as tight as you want. Now you're ready to drive off into the sunset.

12. The author is giving advice on

(A) jack safety.

(B) proper lug nut resistance.

(C) appropriate places to pull off the road.

(D) changing a flat tire.

Questions 13 and 14 refer to the following passage.

The face of tennis was never the same after 14-year-old Venus Williams hit the scene in 1994. After she claimed the distinction of being the first African American woman to rank number one in the world, she and her sister Serena took over. Between the two of them, they dominated the Grand Slam circuit between 2000 and 2012, with 24 Grand Slam singles titles between them and doubles gold medals as a team in the 2000, 2008, and 2012 Summer Olympics. Their athleticism and aggressive playing style have been credited for changing the way women play tennis. They will forever be considered two of the greatest tennis players in history.

13. What year did the Williams sisters *not* win an Olympic gold medal?

(A) 2004

(B) 2000

(C) 2008

(D) 2012

14. How did the Williams sisters change the way women's tennis is played?

(A) by ranking number one

(B) with their uniforms

(C) by being sisters

(D) with their aggressive style

The work of cobblers is very time-consuming. They have to not only find the perfect materials but also size them perfectly, soften the leather for shaping, and attach the leather to the sole. Cobblers use more than 15 techniques when making shoes by hand. Most shoe shoppers have no idea how hard a cobbler's job is.

15. What is the main point of the passage?

(A) Cobblers use many techniques to make shoes.

(B) More people should become cobblers.

(C) Being a cobbler is hard work.

(D) Leather is the only material used to make shoes.

Part 4: Mathematics Knowledge

TIME: 24 minutes for 25 questions

DIRECTIONS: Mathematics Knowledge is the fifth subtest on the ASVAB; it follows Paragraph Comprehension. The questions are designed to test your ability to solve general mathematical problems. Each question is followed by four possible answers. Decide which answer is correct, and then mark the corresponding space on your answer sheet. Use your scratch paper for any figuring you want to do. You may *not* use a calculator.

1. A circle has a diameter of 15 inches. What is its approximate circumference?

   (A) 47.1 inches

   (B) 30 inches

   (C) 55.3 inches

   (D) 64.7 inches

2. $4x + 7xy + 6x =$

   (A) $17xy$

   (B) $10x + 7xy$

   (C) $17x + y$

   (D) $24x + 7xy$

3. Which is 8 inches less than 3 feet?

   (A) 28 in.

   (B) 3.5 ft

   (C) 32 in.

   (D) 2.8 ft

4. Which inequality represents all numbers m that are at least 14?

   (A) $m > 14$

   (B) $m < 14$

   (C) $m \geq 14$

   (D) $m \leq 14$

5. An angle has a measure of 37°. What is the measure of its complementary angle?

   (A) 63°

   (B) 53°

   (C) 143°

   (D) 163°

6. Round 120,459 to the nearest hundred.

   (A) 120,400

   (B) 120,460

   (C) 120,000

   (D) 120,500

7. One possible equality to $\sqrt{16} + \sqrt{100} =$ is?

   (A) $\sqrt{116}$

   (B) 14

   (C) $\sqrt{14}$

   (D) 58

8. What is the least common multiple (LCM) of 12 and 14?

   (A) 26

   (B) 168

   (C) 2

   (D) 84

9. $\left(\dfrac{2x}{4}\right)^3 =$

   (A) $\dfrac{3x^3}{4}$

   (B) $\dfrac{x^3}{2}$

   (C) $2x^3$

   (D) $\dfrac{x^3}{8}$

10. $\dfrac{1}{5} + \dfrac{2}{7} =$

   (A) $\dfrac{1}{4}$

   (B) $\dfrac{2}{35}$

   (C) $\dfrac{3}{12}$

   (D) $\dfrac{17}{35}$

11. Solve the equation for x: $\dfrac{x^2}{2} = 8$.

(A) 4 only

(B) 4 and −4

(C) 32 only

(D) 8 and −8

12. Fifteen is what percent of 75?

(A) 20 percent

(B) 15 percent

(C) 25 percent

(D) 5 percent

13. $4(x+1)+x$

(A) $x+4$

(B) $5x+4$

(C) $5x+1$

(D) $6x$

14. Eighty-five percent of 320 is

(A) 85

(B) 262

(C) 305

(D) 272

15. Given that $6m = 7n$, what is the ratio of n to m?

(A) $\dfrac{7}{6}$

(B) $\dfrac{6}{7}$

(C) $\dfrac{1}{42}$

(D) $\dfrac{13}{1}$

16. Two angles of a triangle measure 40° and 100°. What is the name of this kind of triangle?

(A) isosceles

(B) obtuse

(C) equilateral

(D) right

17. What is the length a in the right triangle?

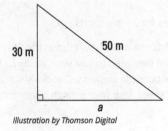

Illustration by Thomson Digital

(A) 48.6 cm

(B) 41.5 cm

(C) 35 m

(D) 40 m

18. Which fraction has the greatest value?

(A) $\dfrac{1}{4}$

(B) $\dfrac{7}{12}$

(C) $\dfrac{2}{3}$

(D) $\dfrac{5}{9}$

19. What is a positive product of $\sqrt{81}$ and $\sqrt{121}$?

(A) 9,801

(B) 40

(C) 20

(D) 99

20. What is the value of $(1-x)^3$ if $4x - 1 = 19$?

(A) 64

(B) 125

(C) −124

(D) −64

21. The height of a right cylinder is $8x$, and the cylinder's radius is $\dfrac{x}{2}$. What is the volume of the cylinder?

(A) $2\pi x^3$

(B) $2\pi x^2$

(C) $4\pi x^3$

(D) $4\pi x$

22. If $2p + x + 5q = 14p + 15q$, then $x =$

    (A) $12p + 10q$

    (B) $12p - 3q$

    (C) $7p + 3q$

    (D) $10p + 12q$

23. Square A has a perimeter of 8 feet. Square B has an area of 64 square feet. What is the ratio of the area of square A to the area of square B?

    (A) $\dfrac{1}{4}$

    (B) $\dfrac{1}{8}$

    (C) $\dfrac{1}{16}$

    (D) $\dfrac{3}{8}$

24. If $\left(x^9\right)\left(x^3\right) = x^{12}$, then $\left(x^{12}\right) \div \left(x^3\right) =$

    (A) x^4

    (B) x^{15}

    (C) x^9

    (D) x^6

25. What is the value of m?

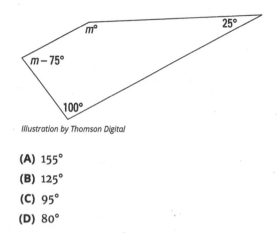

Illustration by Thomson Digital

    (A) $155°$

    (B) $125°$

    (C) $95°$

    (D) $80°$

DO NOT TURN THE PAGE UNTIL TOLD TO DO SO **STOP** DO NOT RETURN TO A PREVIOUS TEST

Chapter **19**

Practice Exam 4: Answers and Explanations

Are you ready to take the actual ASVAB yet and max out the AFQT score? I sure hope so. I hope you're feeling confident as well. If you still don't feel ready, you may want to look over the practice exams again, until you're comfortable with the types of questions that will be presented on the real test. You may also want to consider reading *ASVAB For Dummies* (John Wiley & Sons, Inc.) for two more full-length AFQT practice exams, as well as three full-length ASVAB practice tests.

The answer keys in the following sections tell you how well you did on the final AFQT practice exam. *Remember:* Don't be too concerned about the percent right or wrong. On the actual test, harder questions are worth more points than easier questions when computing your AFQT score, so it's entirely possible to miss a few questions and still max out your AFQT score.

Part 1: **Arithmetic Reasoning**

How'd you do on this subtest? If you don't feel so good about the results, you may want to postpone taking the real ASVAB until you've gotten some more study time under your belt, and perhaps taken a math course or two at your neighborhood community college. You may also want to take another look at Chapters 10 and 11.

Other great resources to improve your math skills are *Math Word Problems For Dummies*, *Algebra I For Dummies*, and *Algebra II For Dummies*, all by Mary Jane Sterling; *Geometry For Dummies* by Mark Ryan; *SAT II Math For Dummies* by Scott Hatch, JD, and Lisa Zimmer Hatch, MA; and *Basic Math & Pre-Algebra For Dummies* by Mark Zegarelli — all published by John Wiley & Sons, Inc.

1. C. 80 ounces

Because 1 pound = 16 ounces, you can convert 5 pounds to ounces by multiplying 5 pounds by the conversion factor $\frac{16 \text{ ounces}}{1 \text{ pound}}$. A *conversion factor* is a ratio that represents the relationship between two different units, and in this case, multiplying 5 pounds by the pounds-to-ounces conversion factor looks like this:

$$5 \text{ pounds} \times \frac{16 \text{ ounces}}{1 \text{ pound}} = 5 \times 16 \text{ ounces}$$
$$= 80 \text{ ounces}$$

2. B. page 72

In order to find the page Ishaan is on, you need to find 40 percent of 180. Write 40 percent as a decimal and multiply by 180: $0.4(180) = 72$. Ishaan is on page 72.

3. C. 25 percent

There are four possible outcomes: two heads (HH), heads on the first coin and tails on the second (HT), tails on the first coin and heads on the second (TH), and two tails (TT). The desired outcome is TT. The probability is $\frac{1}{4} = 25$ percent.

4. D. 70°

The sum of the angles of any triangle is 180°. You know one of the angles is 40°, so the sum of the remaining two angles is 140° ($180° - 40° = 140°$). Because the remaining two angles have equal measures, divide 140° by 2 to find the measure of one of the angles:

$$\frac{140°}{2} = 70°$$

5. A. 88 miles

If the truck gets 22 miles per gallon on the highway, that means it can go 22 miles on a gallon of gasoline. Multiply the mileage by 4 to find out how far it can travel using 4 gallons of gasoline: $4(22) = 88$ miles.

6. D. 5

After cutting the 24-foot rope into 4-foot lengths, Sergeant Williams would have six smaller ropes. To get these smaller ropes, he'd have to cut the rope five times. The following figure illustrates each of the cuts Sergeant Williams had to make at 4-foot increments. Sometimes drawing a picture can help you solve a problem.

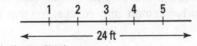

Illustration by Thomson Digital

7. D. 12.5 percent

To calculate percent decrease, divide the change in temperature (4° Fahrenheit) by the original temperature. Then convert the result to a percent:

$$\frac{4}{32} = \frac{1}{8} = 0.125 = 12.5\%$$

8. B. $13.40

First, multiply 4 times $6.70 to find out how much money Dirk has: $4(\$6.70) = \$26.80$. Xiomara has half this amount:

$$\frac{1}{2}(\$26.80) = \frac{\$26.80}{2} = \$13.40$$

Tip: Sometimes you can skip the calculations and reason your way to the correct answer. In this case, you know Dirk has 4 times as much money as Carter has, and Xiomara has half as much as Dirk does. That means Xiomara has twice as much money as Carter has. To find out how much money Xiomara has, double Carter's money: $\$6.70 \cdot 2 = \$13.40$.

9. C. 30

To find the average age, add up all the ages and then divide by the number of adults in the group.

$$\frac{24 + 26 + 37 + 23 + 40}{5} = \frac{150}{5} = 30$$

Tip: You can save a little time during the addition step if you pair up numbers with ones digits that add up to 10 or with tens digits that add up to 100. That's the associative property, and here's what it looks like in practice:

$$\frac{(24 + 26) + (37 + 23) + 40}{5} = \frac{50 + (60 + 40)}{5}$$
$$= \frac{150}{5}$$
$$= 30$$

10. A. 0.1 gallon

The word *share* is a clue that this problem uses division, so you need to divide 2.5 by 25.

$$\frac{2.5}{25} = \frac{25}{250} = \frac{1}{10} = 0.1$$

11. B. 10

If x is Sam's age, then Timothy's age is $2x + 1$. Use the fact that the sum of their ages is 31 to set up an equation and solve for x:

$$x + 2x + 1 = 31$$
$$3x + 1 = 31$$
$$3x = 30$$
$$x = 10$$

Sam is 10 years old.

12. A. $11,340

If the car depreciates 10 percent in a year, the car's value after one year is 90 percent of what it was a year earlier. You can multiply the two percentages (0.9 and 0.9) by the car's initial value ($14,000) to figure out how much it's worth two years after purchase:

$$(0.9)(0.9)(\$14,000) = 0.81(\$14,000)$$
$$= \$11,340$$

The value of the car after two years is $11,340.

13. B. 2006

Because you're given a formula, you can substitute the known values and solve for n:

$$W = 0.5n + 47$$
$$50 = 0.5n + 47$$
$$3 = 0.5n$$
$$6 = n$$

The problem states that n represents the number of years after the year 2000, so 50 percent of the women owned a laptop in the year 2006.

14. C. 93°

A rhombus is a quadrilateral, a geometric shape with four sides with interior angles totaling 360°. A rhombus has equal opposite interior angles, so two angles are 93°, and the other two are 87°, totaling 360°.

15. D. $\frac{3}{4}$ gallon

The ratio is 8:1, which means for every 8 gallons of water, you need 1 gallon of concentrate. In this problem, you have only 6 gallons of water, so the amount of concentrate must be less than 1 gallon, which means you can eliminate Choices (B) and (C) right away. (Any time you can rule out incorrect answer choices on the ASVAB, take the opportunity!)

Let x = the amount of concentrate that should be added. Write a proportion using the two ratios and then cross-multiply to solve for x:

$$\frac{8}{1} = \frac{6}{x}$$
$$8x = 6(1)$$
$$x = \frac{6}{8}$$
$$x = \frac{3}{4}$$

16. C. 2 percent

Use the interest formula ($I = prt$), where I is the interest, p is the principal, r is the interest rate (as a decimal), and t is the time in years. Substitute the known values into the formula and solve for r:

$$100 = 5,000(r)(1)$$
$$100 = 5,000r$$
$$\frac{100}{5,000} = r$$
$$\frac{1}{50} = r$$
$$0.02 = r$$

Write 0.02 as a percent by moving the decimal point two places to the right (which is the same as multiplying by 100): $0.02 = 2$ percent.

17. C. 336

To determine club membership over this six-year period, it's best to work in increments. In 2004, after the first two years, the club's membership of 42 had doubled to 84. In 2006, the previous number of members doubled: $2(84) = 168$. Finally, in 2008, membership doubled again: $2(168) = 336$.

You can organize your work in a table:

Year	Number of members
2002	42
2004	2(42) = 84
2006	2(84) = 168
2008	2(168) = 336

Illustration by Thomson Digital

The club had 336 members in 2008.

If you're not a big fan of using tables to organize, try this: The problem tells you that the number of members doubled in 2004, 2006, and 2008. That describes three years in which membership doubled, so multiply the club's membership by 2 three times:

$$42(2)(2)(2) = 42(8) = 336$$

18. **A.** $H = 2L - 10$

First, write twice the low temperature as $2L$. You know that **H** is 10 less than this amount, or $2L - 10$, so now you have your equation: $H = 2L - 10$.

19. **B. 96 cm²**

The formula for the area of a triangle is $A = \frac{1}{2}bh$, where b is the base and h is the height. The height is drawn perpendicular to the bottom side of the triangle (with a measure of 16 cm), so use the bottom as the base. Substitute $b = 16$ and $h = 12$ into the formula to find the area:

$$A = \frac{1}{2}bh = \frac{1}{2}(16)(12) = 8(12) = 96$$

20. **D. 152**

Looking at the table, you see that 262 women and 110 men live in the West region. To find how many more women there are than men, you need to subtract: $262 - 110 = 152$.

21. **B. $11**

Use your hourly rate and the number of hours worked to find how much you earned at your first job: $16(\$10) = \$160$. Subtract that amount from the total pay to find how much you earned at your second job last week: $\$314 - \$160 = \$154$. Finally, divide $154 by 14 to find the hourly pay at your second job: $\$154 \div 14 = \$11$.

22. **B. 90**

If the ratio of red to blue to green marbles is 1:3:5, then there are x red marbles, $3x$ blue marbles, and $5x$ green marbles (x is some common multiple). Write an equation and solve for x:

$$x + 3x + 5x = 270$$
$$9x = 270$$
$$x = 30$$

This solution tells you there are 30 red marbles, which means that there are $3x = 3(30) = 90$ blue marbles.

23. C. 100 miles

First, use the distance formula, $d = rt$ (where d is the distance traveled, r is the rate of speed, and t is the time elapsed), to find how far each vehicle traveled in 2 hours:

Truck: $d = 30(2) = 60$ miles

Car: $d = 40(2) = 80$ miles

Now draw a diagram showing the paths of the two vehicles.

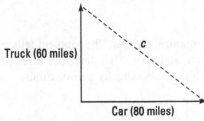

Looking at the diagram, you see a right triangle with the hypotenuse (c) missing, so it's Pythagorean theorem time:

$$c^2 = 60^2 + 80^2$$
$$c^2 = 3,600 + 6,400$$
$$c^2 = 10,000$$
$$c = \pm\sqrt{10,000} = \pm 100$$

Because distance is never negative, you use the positive answer. After 2 hours, the vehicles are 100 miles apart.

24. C. 54

Let Joe's age $= x$. Because Evan is twice as old as Joe, his age can be represented as $2x$. In two years, Joe's age will be $x + 2$, and Evan's age will be $2x + 2$. The sum of their ages together will equal 85.

Write your equation like this and solve for x:

$$(x + 2) + (2x + 2) = 85$$
$$3x + 4 = 85$$
$$3x + 4 - 4 = 85 - 4$$
$$3x = 81$$
$$\frac{3x}{3} = \frac{81}{3}$$
$$x = 27$$

Now that you know Joe's age, you can figure out Evan's:

$$27 \times 2 = 54$$

Check by plugging into the formula:

$$(27 + 2) + (2 \times 27 + 2) = 85$$
$$29 + 56 = 85$$

25. C. $34.90

First, find out how much of a tip Gregory left by finding 20 percent of $8.50: $0.2(\$8.50) = \$1.70$. The total cost of breakfast after the tip was $\$8.50 + \$1.70 = \$10.20$. Now, subtract the total amount paid from the amount in Gregory's wallet at the start of the day: $\$45.10 - \$10.20 = \$34.90$ left over after breakfast.

26. D. 8

Let x equal Kendra's score on the fifth quiz. Her score on the fourth quiz was twice that amount, so let $2x$ represent the fourth score. To find the average score, add up all the scores, and then divide by the number of quizzes taken:

$$\frac{7 + 6 + 10 + 2x + x}{5} = 7$$
$$\frac{23 + 3x}{5} = 7$$
$$23 + 3x = 35$$
$$3x = 12$$
$$x = 4$$

Her score on the fourth quiz was $2(4) = 8$.

27. A. 6 m

For problems like this one, your best bet is to break the odd-shaped figure down into rectangles. You can break this figure into two rectangles and find their areas separately:

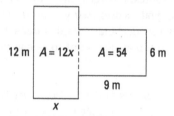

Illustration by Thomson Digital

Because the sum of the two areas is 126, you can write and solve an equation to find x:

$$12x + 54 = 126$$
$$12x = 72$$
$$x = 6$$

28. C. $3\frac{1}{10}$ tons

If you remember that 1 ton equals 2,000 pounds, you can work with tons (they're more manageable than pounds in this problem).

Find the total weight of all the cylinder blocks: $20(40) = 800$.

Convert that to tons:

$$\frac{800 \text{ pounds}}{2,000 \frac{\text{pounds}}{\text{ton}}} = \frac{8}{20} = \frac{2}{5} = 0.4 \text{ ton}$$

Subtract the weight of the cylinder blocks from the total weight:

$$3.5 - 0.4 = 3.1 = 3\frac{1}{10} \text{ tons}$$

29. B. 10

Let d equal the number of dimes Carla has; the number of quarters she has is $d-5$. The values of the dimes and quarters are 10 cents and 25 cents, respectively, and the coins add up to \$4 (or 400 cents). Write an equation and solve for d:

$$10d + 25(d-5) = 400$$
$$10d + 25d - 125 = 400$$
$$35d = 525$$
$$d = 15$$

Carla has 15 dimes, which means she has $15 - 5 = 10$ quarters.

30. A. 260

Ignore the information in the problem for the front entrance; the question asks you to find out how many entrance codes there are for the rear entrance. To find the number of possible codes for the rear entrance, multiply the number of possibilities for each character of the code:

26 possible letters × 10 possible numbers = 260 possible combinations

Part 2: Word Knowledge

The Word Knowledge subtest, as with all the AFQT subtests, determines whether you qualify for enlistment. If you're not seeing the improvement in your scores that you need to see, work with a partner who can quiz you on vocabulary. Review your vocabulary words intensely, even several times a day, to ensure your success on this subtest. You may also want to reread the information in Chapter 4.

Also check out *Vocabulary For Dummies* by Laurie E. Rozakis and *SAT Vocabulary For Dummies* by Suzee Vlk (both published by John Wiley & Sons, Inc.). Finally, see Chapter 5 for more practice questions.

1. C. belittle.

Condescend is a verb that means to talk down to someone.

"Even if you're teaching toddlers, it's important not to condescend to them."

2. A. star

As used in this sentence, *legend* is a noun that refers to someone famous or popular in a certain field.

3. D. extravagant.

Lavish is an adjective that means in abundance.

"The lavish décor made us feel as if we were at a luxury resort."

4. A. withdrawal.

Retraction is a noun that means the taking back of a statement.

"The newspaper printed a retraction when the editors found out the entire story was based on a lie."

5. B. trap.

Decoy is a noun that means a distraction or trick.

"Hunters who use a decoy duck tend to have more success than those who don't."

6. C. fixation.

Obsession is a noun that means a preoccupation with something or someone.

"Bryan's obsession with cleaning the house drove Tina crazy."

7. D. hefty.

Brawny is an adjective that means muscular or appearing strong.

"The brawny weightlifter picked up the 400-pound barbell easily."

8. D. remain.

Relocate is a verb that means to change places.

"Many retirees relocate from Michigan to Florida to escape the cold."

9. B. healing

Therapeutic is an adjective that describes something relating to good health or beneficial.

10. C. ready

As used in this sentence, *poised* is an adjective that means to be in position or prepared.

11. B. vague

As used in this sentence, *obscure* is an adjective that means unclear or ambiguous.

12. A. consequences

Ramification is a noun that means a result or an outcome.

13. C. peculiar

Eccentric is an adjective that describes something or someone unusual or odd.

14. B. hurry.

Meander is a verb that means to roam or stroll leisurely, or to follow a winding course (as in a road or river).

"A lot of teenagers meander around the mall for hours without buying anything."

15. D. unpredictable.

Volatile is an adjective that means something unstable or explosive.

"The situation became more volatile as the protesters refused to leave, so the police began putting on riot gear."

16. C. polish

As used in this sentence, *hone* is a verb that means to improve or perfect something.

17. A. mention

Broach is a verb that means to bring up or raise.

18. **B. random**

Erratic is an adjective that describes something inconsistent or frequently changing.

19. **B. old.**

Obsolete is an adjective that means something outdated or no longer in use.

"The version of software you're using is obsolete, so you should upgrade as soon as you can."

20. **D. respectability.**

Decorum is a noun that means appropriate behavior.

"Although the runner-up was unhappy with her position, she maintained decorum and offered the winner her congratulations."

21. **B. briefness**

Brevity is a noun that means conciseness or shortness.

22. **D. stability.**

Mayhem is a noun that means disruption or chaos.

"The fans quickly got out of control, and the entire concert descended into mayhem."

23. **A. gap.**

Hiatus is a noun that means a break or pause in something continuous.

"The professor is taking a short hiatus from teaching after this semester because he needs a break."

24. **C. pessimistic.**

Cynical is an adjective that means distrusting or having a negative outlook.

"Robert's cynical attitude led him to spread negativity through the entire office."

25. **C. full of.**

Riddled is an adjective that means containing a lot of something.

"Some of the old buildings on Schofield Barracks are riddled with bullet holes from World War II."

26. **B. theft**

Larceny is a noun that describes the illegal removal of another's possessions.

27. **A. demand.**

Used as a noun, *proposition* means an idea or a proposal.

"The team made their proposition to the company president, who agreed that it was a great idea to hold an annual picnic for employees and their families."

28. **C. moving**

Poignant is an adjective that describes something understanding and emotional.

29. **A. interval**

Respite is a noun that means a brief break in something or a period of rest.

30. **B. shoot down**

Debunk is a verb that means to expose false or exaggerated claims.

31. **D. resolute.**

Adamant is an adjective that means having an unyielding or unwavering opinion.

"The little boy was adamant that the other kids put away the toys when they were finished playing."

32. **D. wisdom.**

Malarkey is a noun that means rubbish or insincere talk.

"Everything the candidate said was malarkey; he didn't mean any of it."

33. **A. hardship**

Adversity is a noun that represents a difficulty or misfortune.

34. **B. extinct**

Defunct is an adjective that means no longer in existence.

35. **C. beginning.**

Origin is a noun that indicates where something started.

"Historians have traced the Roman Empire to its origin during the eighth century BCE."

Part 3: Paragraph Comprehension

If you're struggling with this subtest, remember to take your time when you read the passages. And after you read each question, you can quickly reread the passage just to make sure you're on the money. The information is in the paragraph; you just have to concentrate to pull it out. Turn to Chapter 6 if you still need additional help to pull off a good score on this subtest. You can also find more practice questions in Chapter 7.

1. **B. prospered.**

Flourished is a verb that means to thrive or do well.

2. **A. the kitchen**

Although many things are being described in the passage, the scene remains the same: in the "big kitchen."

3. **D. A feast is being prepared.**

Although Alcott is talking about the harvest and hunting, the only action taking place is the cooking of the feast, as stated in the last sentence: "all suggestive of some approaching feast." Sometimes reading through the answers and eliminating those that are obviously wrong is the best way to answer questions on the ASVAB.

4. **C. to explain the purpose of the High-Speed Rail Summit**

Although the passage touches on many of the other answers, the focus remains on the summit.

5. **D. The 2013 fire season was much longer than normal.**

The passage compares the typical fire season (September to October) to the 2013 fire season (May to December). None of the other choices are addressed.

6. **B. a lack of rain**

The passage states that wildfire season started early due to a drought and later reinforces that the number of fires increased because of a lack of rain.

7. **A. unimportant.**

The last sentence states that the secret to dancing isn't rhythm, so the fact that Richard doesn't have any doesn't matter. The passage never says that Richard is embarrassed by his lack of rhythm or that it has harmed him in any way. Although watching Richard dance may be funny, the passage clearly says that the secret to dancing isn't rhythm; it's "enjoying moving and being free." That means Richard's lack of rhythm is unimportant.

8. **C. historical accuracy**

The passage discusses the aspects that make a good and profitable war movie. It indicates that an accurate portrayal of war is important to "ensure a profitable film," so Choice (C) is the best answer.

9. **D. both B and C**

The passage says aspiring record-holders have to do only two things: complete an application and submit evidence that they have broken the record. Breaking the record in front of a judge isn't required.

10. **A. passion.**

Even if you didn't know what *fervor* meant, the context in which the passage uses it can help you eliminate the incorrect choices. By reading the next part of the sentence, which says, "you'd think people had a personal stake in the matter," you can tell that people take it very seriously. That signifies that each side is passionate about its beliefs.

11. **B. price and need.**

The passage poses the question "So how do you choose?" and then answers it: "Price and need are usually the best factors to consider."

12. **D. changing a flat tire**

This passage gives step-by-step instructions for changing a flat tire. Some of the other answer choices are mentioned, but they're part of the advice given about Choice (D).

13. **A. 2004**

The Summer Olympics occur every four years. The passage lists every Summer Olympic year between 2000 and 2012 except for 2004, so the Williams sisters didn't win that year. When the ASVAB asks you for specific dates, scan the paragraph for them instead of rereading the entire passage.

14. **D. with their aggressive style**

   The end of the passage clearly tells you that the Williams sisters' "athleticism and aggressive playing style have been credited for changing the way women play tennis," which is exactly what the question asked.

15. **C. Being a cobbler is hard work.**

   The first and last sentences both mention the laborious and difficult nature of shoemaking. Choice (A) is a fact mentioned in the passage, but it's in support of the idea that shoemaking is a tough job.

   On the ASVAB, many questions are easier than they look. By reading through your answer options, you can see that the passage doesn't say anything about the need for more people to take up cobbling, Choice (B). You can also see that Choice (D) probably isn't correct because the passage doesn't say that leather is the only material used. Though Choice (A) may have tempted you, the passage as a whole is about how tough it is to be a cobbler, making Choice (C) the correct answer.

Part 4: Mathematics Knowledge

If you're missing too many math questions, you may need to take more drastic measures like enrolling in a basic-algebra class at a local community college. If your scores are improving, keep hitting the books and testing yourself up until the day of the ASVAB. Chapter 8 will also be a good review.

If you want to increase your math skills, the following *For Dummies* books will help: *Basic Math & Pre-Algebra For Dummies* by Mark Zegarelli; *Algebra I For Dummies* and *Algebra II For Dummies* by Mary Jane Sterling; *Geometry For Dummies* by Mark Ryan; and *SAT II Math For Dummies* by Scott Hatch (all published by John Wiley & Sons, Inc.). Chapter 9 also has some additional practice questions.

1. **A. 47.1 inches**

   Using the circumference formula $C = \pi d$, plug in the known values and solve. Remember to round pi to 3.14 when a problem uses the term *approximate*:

   $$
   \begin{aligned}
   C &= \pi d \\
   &= (3.14)(15) \\
   &= 47.1
   \end{aligned}
   $$

2. **B. $10x + 7xy$**

   This expression has two like terms: $4x$ and $6x$. Combine them by adding their coefficients:

   $$
   \begin{aligned}
   4x + 7xy + 6x &= 4x + 6x + 7xy \\
   &= (4 + 6)x + 7xy \\
   &= 10x + 7xy
   \end{aligned}
   $$

3. **A. 28 in.**

   Convert the 3 feet to inches by multiplying by 12: $3(12) = 36$ inches. Now subtract 8 inches to get the answer: $36 - 8 = 28$.

4. C. $m \geq 14$

"All numbers that are at least 14" means all numbers greater than or equal to 14, which is represented by the symbol $\geq$. The answer is $m \geq 14$.

5. B. 53°

Complementary angles have a sum of 90°. To find the measure of the complement of 37°, subtract from 90°: $90° - 37° = 53°$.

6. D. 120,500

Determine what your rounding digit is; you're rounding to the hundreds place, so you want the hundreds digit. Now look at the number immediately to the right of it. If that number is 4 or less, don't change the rounding digit. If the digit is 5 or more, the rounding digit rounds up by one number. Here, the number in the hundreds place is 4 and the number to the right is 5, so you round up.

7. B. 14

Here, you solve the square roots and then add. The real, principal square root of 16 is 4, and the real, principal square root of 100 is 10. So $\sqrt{16} + \sqrt{100} = 4 + 10 = 14$.

8. D. 84

One way to find the LCM of two numbers is to list all the multiples of each number and find the smallest number that is common to both:

12: 12, 24, 36, 48, 60, 72, 84

14: 14, 28, 42, 56, 70, 84

The LCM of 12 and 14 is 84.

Another way is to check the answer choices to find the smallest one that's divisible by 12 and 14. That rules out Choice (C), because it's *too* small, and Choice (A), which isn't a multiple of 14. The next-smallest number is Choice (D), which happens to be the correct answer. If you find it easier to reduce fractions than to use long division, your work will look something like this:

$$\frac{84}{12} = \frac{21}{3} = 7$$

$$\frac{84}{14} = \frac{42}{7} = 6$$

9. D. $\frac{x^3}{8}$

First, reduce the fraction inside the parentheses:

$$\left(\frac{2x}{4}\right)^3 = \left(\frac{x}{2}\right)^3$$

Whenever you raise a fraction to a power, the exponent applies to the numerator and the denominator:

$$\left(\frac{x}{2}\right)^3 = \frac{x^3}{2^3} = \frac{x^3}{8}$$

10. D. $\frac{17}{35}$

You can solve this problem by multiplying the denominators by each other: $5 \times 7 = 35$.

(Most of the answer choices use 35 as the denominator, so that's a clue that 35 is a good choice.)

Now apply 35 as the common denominator and solve:

$$\frac{1}{5} + \frac{2}{7} = \frac{7}{35} + \frac{10}{35} = \frac{17}{35}$$

If fractions don't come easily to you, find the common denominator, which is the least common multiple of 5 and 7.

Multiples of 5: 5, 10, 15, 20, 25, 30, 35

Multiples of 7: 7, 14, 21, 28, 35

The common denominator for these two fractions is 35. Multiply the numerator and denominator of each fraction by the number that makes each denominator 35; then add:

$$\frac{1}{5} + \frac{2}{7} = \frac{1 \cdot 7}{5 \cdot 7} + \frac{2 \cdot 5}{7 \cdot 5}$$
$$= \frac{7}{35} + \frac{10}{35}$$
$$= \frac{7 + 10}{35}$$
$$= \frac{17}{35}$$

11. **B. 4 and −4**

First, isolate the variable by multiplying both sides of the equation by 2:

$$\frac{x^2}{2} = 8$$
$$2 \cdot \frac{x^2}{2} = 2 \cdot 8$$
$$x^2 = 16$$

Next, take the square root of both sides of the equation. The *square-root rule* says that if $x^2 = k$, then $x = \pm\sqrt{k}$, where k is a number. The $\pm$ symbol indicates that when you take the square root of a number, you get two answers — one positive and one negative. That's because when you square a negative number, you get a positive result; for example, $(-4)^2 = (-4)(-4) = 16$; when you square a positive number, you also get a positive result.

$$x = \pm\sqrt{16}$$
$$x = \pm 4$$

12. **A. 20 percent**

Begin by writing the problem as a fraction: $\frac{15}{75}$. You can also write an equation if you can't remember how to arrange the fraction. Remember *is* means "equals" and *of* means "multiply," so $15 = x(75)$. Divide both sides by 75 to create the correct fraction. Then divide the numerator by the denominator (you can reduce the fraction to $\frac{3}{15}$ or even $\frac{1}{5}$ first if that makes the division easier): $15 \div 75 = 0.2$. Finally, move the decimal point two spaces to the right, which is the same as multiplying by 100, to express the number as a percent: 20 percent.

13. **B. $5x + 4$**

To simplify an expression like this one, first use the distributive property to remove the parentheses:

$$4(x + 1) + x = 4x + 4 + x$$

This expression has two like terms: $4x$ and x. Combine the like terms by adding their coefficients:

$$4x + 4 + x = (4+1)x + 4$$
$$= 5x + 4$$

14. **D. 272**

First, write 85 percent as a decimal: $\frac{85}{100} = 0.85$. Next, multiply 0.85 by 320: $0.85(320) = 272$.

15. **B.** $\frac{6}{7}$

The goal here is to use the given equation to find the ratio $\frac{n}{m}$. Start by dividing both sides of the equation by m:

$$6m = 7n$$
$$6 = \frac{7n}{m}$$

To get $\frac{n}{m}$ alone, get rid of the 7 by multiplying both sides by $\frac{1}{7}$ (which is the same as dividing both sides by 7):

$$\frac{1}{7} \cdot \frac{6}{1} = \frac{1}{7} \cdot \frac{7n}{m}$$
$$\frac{6}{7} = \frac{1}{7} \cdot \frac{7n}{m}$$
$$\frac{6}{7} = \frac{n}{m}$$

16. **A. isosceles**

The sum of the angles of a triangle is always 180°. To find the measure of the third angle, subtract the known angles from 180°: $180° - 100° - 40° = 40°$. Because two of the angles of the triangle have the same measure, the sides opposite them are the same length. A triangle with two equal sides is an isosceles triangle.

17. **D. 40 m**

Use the Pythagorean theorem $\left(a^2 + b^2 = c^2\right)$ and the known values to find a. Remember, a and b are always the side lengths in the formula, and c is always the hypotenuse:

$$a^2 + 30^2 = 50^2$$
$$a^2 + 900 = 2{,}500$$
$$a^2 = 1{,}600$$
$$\sqrt{a^2} = \pm\sqrt{1{,}600}$$
$$a = \pm 40$$

Use the positive answer because a length is never negative.

18. **C.** $\frac{2}{3}$

On the ASVAB, it pays to rule out obviously wrong answer choices before you start your work. Choice (A) is obviously less than $\frac{1}{2}$, so it can't be correct. Move forward comparing Choices (B), (C), and (D).

Find the least common denominator by taking the least common multiple of all the denominators; in this case, that's 36. Rewrite the fractions with the common denominator, multiplying the numerators and denominators by the number that makes each denominator 36:

$$\frac{7}{12} = \frac{7 \cdot 3}{12 \cdot 3} = \frac{21}{36}$$

$$\frac{2 \cdot 12}{3 \cdot 12} = \frac{24}{36}$$

$$\frac{5}{9} = \frac{5 \cdot 4}{9 \cdot 4} = \frac{20}{36}$$

The greatest fraction is the one with the greatest numerator: $\frac{24}{36} = \frac{2}{3}$.

19. **D. 99**

The real, principal square root of 81 is 9 and the square root of 121 is 11, because $9 \times 9 = 81$ and $11 \times 11 = 121$. The real, principal product of those two numbers (9×11) is 99.

20. **D. −64**

The first thing you need to do is find the value of x by solving the given equation:

$$4x - 1 = 19$$
$$4x = 20$$
$$x = 5$$

Now you can substitute 5 for x in the expression $(1-x)^3$ and simplify to find the answer. Remember to simplify inside the parentheses before applying exponents.

$$(1-5)^3 = (-4)^3$$
$$= (-4)(-4)(-4)$$
$$= -64$$

21. **A. $2\pi x^3$**

This problem uses the formula for the volume of a right cylinder: $V = \pi r^2 h$. You're given the values of h and r in terms of x, so you can just substitute those values in place of r and h in the formula:

$$V = \pi r^2 h$$
$$= \pi \left(\frac{x}{2}\right)^2 (8x)$$
$$= \pi \left(\frac{x^2}{4}\right)(8x)$$
$$= \frac{\pi \cdot x^2 \cdot 8x}{4}$$
$$= \frac{8\pi x^3}{4}$$
$$= 2\pi x^3$$

22. A. 12p + 10q

Work through the equation, remembering that you can only combine like terms:

$$2p + x + 5q = 14p + 15q$$
$$(2p - 2p) + x + (5q - 5q) = (14p - 2p) + (15q - 5q)$$
$$x = 12p + 10q$$

23. C. $\dfrac{1}{16}$

You already know the area of square B, so you need to find the area of square A. To do that, you need to find the side length of square A based on what you know about the square's perimeter. The formula for the perimeter of a square is $P = 4s$. Substitute the known values for square A and then solve for s:

$$P = 4s$$
$$8 = 4s$$
$$2 = s$$

Now you can use the area formula for a square, $A = s^2$:

$$A = s^2$$
$$= (2)^2$$
$$= 4$$

Finally, you can express the ratio of the area of square A to the area of square B with a fraction:

$$\frac{\text{Area of square A}}{\text{Area of square B}} = \frac{4}{64} = \frac{1}{16}$$

24. C. x^9

When multiplying exponents, you add. When dividing exponents, you subtract:

$$\left(x^{12}\right) \div \left(x^3\right) = x^{12-3}$$
$$= x^9$$

25. A. 155°

This figure is a quadrilateral, which means the sum of its angles is 360°. Because m is equal to is 360° minus the other three angles, plug in the values and solve:

$$m = 360 - 25 - 100 - (m - 75)$$
$$m = 360 - 25 - 100 - m + 75$$
$$m = 360 - 25 - 25 - m$$
$$m = 360 - 50 - m$$
$$2m = 310$$
$$\frac{2m}{2} = \frac{310}{2}$$
$$m = 155$$

Answer Key

Part 1: Arithmetic Reasoning

1.	C	9.	C	17.	C	25.	C
2.	B	10.	A	18.	A	26.	D
3.	C	11.	B	19.	B	27.	A
4.	D	12.	A	20.	D	28.	C
5.	A	13.	B	21.	B	29.	B
6.	D	14.	C	22.	B	30.	A
7.	D	15.	D	23.	C		
8.	B	16.	C	24.	C		

Part 2: Word Knowledge

1.	C	10.	C	19.	B	28.	C
2.	A	11.	B	20.	D	29.	A
3.	D	12.	A	21.	B	30.	B
4.	A	13.	C	22.	D	31.	D
5.	B	14.	B	23.	A	32.	D
6.	C	15.	D	24.	C	33.	A
7.	D	16.	C	25.	C	34.	B
8.	D	17.	A	26.	B	35.	C
9.	B	18.	B	27.	A		

Part 3: Paragraph Comprehension

1.	B	5.	D	9.	D	13.	A
2.	A	6.	B	10.	A	14.	D
3.	D	7.	A	11.	B	15.	C
4.	C	8.	C	12.	D		

Part 4: Mathematics Knowledge

1.	A	8.	D	15.	B	22.	A
2.	B	9.	D	16.	A	23.	C
3.	A	10.	D	17.	D	24.	C
4.	C	11.	B	18.	C	25.	A
5.	B	12.	A	19.	D		
6.	D	13.	B	20.	D		
7.	B	14.	D	21.	A		

5
The Part of Tens

IN THIS PART . . .

Check out ten tips for getting a better score on the AFQT.

Discover ten math concepts that may prove handy when you take the ASVAB, one of the most important exams of your life.

De-stress with ten tried-and-true strategies for relaxing and easing tension before you take the test.

Chapter **20**

Ten Tips for a Better AFQT Score

The U.S. military enlists around 250,000 new troops every year, counting the active and reserve components. And all those people share one thing in common: They all earned a qualifying score on the AFQT. (See Chapter 1 for qualifying AFQT scores for each branch of service.)

Many people score very high, which makes their families proud and their recruiters smile. A high score also opens up a new world of special enlistment programs and enlistment incentives that are available only to those who score well on the AFQT.

I'm sure you want to be counted among that group; otherwise, why would you be reading this book? If so, this chapter will be a big help. Here, I list ten surefire ways to maximize your AFQT score and get you on your way to a satisfying and successful military career.

Take Your Time Studying

Don't cram. Study after study has shown that it doesn't work. For example, a 2007 study conducted by University of South Florida psychologist Doug Rohrer determined that last-minute studying reduces retention of material and may hinder the learning process. If you don't plan for adequate study time, your test scores will suffer the consequences.

REMEMBER

Rome wasn't built in a day, but it took only hours for the city to crash and burn. If you develop a solid study plan and stick with it for six to eight weeks, you'll score much higher on the AFQT than if you try to pack four subjects' worth of knowledge into your brain in one or two days. Plus, you won't walk into the testing center with your eyes red and your brain fried.

Make a Study Plan

You wouldn't expect the U.S. military to fight a war without a plan, would you? It would be chaos, and probably nothing would be achieved. The same is true when you're studying for the AFQT (or doing anything else, for that matter). If you try to study without a plan, you'll wind up wandering here and there, reading this and that, but you won't really accomplish anything. Check out Chapter 2 for help developing your individual study plan.

TIP

Start by studying the subjects you find the hardest, and spend extra time on those areas. You're only as strong as your weakest subject. When you focus on the areas where you need the most improvement, you increase your entire score. After you feel confident in your weakest areas, start perfecting and reviewing the areas you consider less problematic.

Use the Practice Exams to Your Advantage

If you bought this book expecting the practice exams to include the exact same questions you'll see on the ASVAB, I'm afraid I have bad news: You won't see the same questions on the ASVAB that I include in this book (or any other ASVAB/AFQT preparation guide). Giving you the actual questions and answers in advance would be cheating — and illegal. The military classifies ASVAB tests as "for official use only." That means only those with an official "need to know" have access to the test questions and answers, and that certainly doesn't include authors of ASVAB AFQT prep books.

The best I can do is to provide you with practice questions that are very similar to the ones you'll see on the ASVAB. In short, don't waste your time trying to memorize the questions and answers on the practice exams.

Even so, the practice exams are a very valuable study tool. They give you an idea about the types of questions you'll see and the test's format. They're also useful in determining what AFQT subject areas you need to spend the most time on.

REMEMBER

If you've already taken some or all of the exams and you didn't follow a schedule, that's okay, too. The key is to take the exams and learn from them. You may even find repeating each test and comparing your scores helpful. It's a good way to show personal progress.

Memorize Basic Math Formulas

The Arithmetic Reasoning and Mathematics Knowledge subtests require you to know many standard mathematical formulas used in geometry and algebra. As a minimum, you should have the following committed to memory by the time you sit down to take the ASVAB:

- » **Perimeter of a square:** $P = 4s$, where s = one side of the square
- » **Area of a square:** $A = s^2$
- » **Diagonal of a square:** $d = s\sqrt{2}$
- » **Perimeter of a rectangle:** $P = 2l + 2w$, where l = the length and w = the width of the rectangle; you can also write this formula as $P = 2(l + w)$. (Here's a tip: You can find the perimeter of a shape by adding all its sides.)

>> **Area of a rectangle:** $A = lw$

>> **Diagonal of a rectangle:** $d = \sqrt{l^2 + w^2}$, where d = the diagonal, l = the length, and w = the width of the rectangle. This formula is the Pythagorean theorem solved for the hypotenuse (c) — it just uses different letters.

>> **Perimeter of a triangle:** $P = s_1 + s_2 + s_3$, where s = the length of each side of the triangle

>> **Area of a triangle:** $A = \frac{1}{2}bh$, where b = the length of the triangle's base (bottom) and h = the height of the triangle

>> **Pythagorean theorem:** $a^2 + b^2 = c^2$

>> **Radius of a circle:** $r = \frac{1}{2}d$, where d = the diameter of the circle

>> **Diameter of a circle:** $d = 2r$

>> **Circumference of a circle:** $C = 2\pi r$ or $C = \pi d$

>> **Area of a circle:** $A = \pi r^2$

>> **Volume of a cube:** $V = s^3$, where s = the length of one side of the cube

>> **Volume of a rectangular prism or box:** $V = lwh$, where l = the length, w = the width, and h = the height of the box. This formula is the area of a rectangle (the base of the box) multiplied by the height.

>> **Volume of a cylinder:** $V = \pi r^2 h$, where r = the radius of the cylinder and h = the height of the cylinder; it's really the area of a circle (the base of the cylinder) multiplied by the height.

>> **Surface area of a cube:** $SA = 6s^2$

>> **Surface area of a rectangular box:** $SA = 2lw + 2wh + 2lh$; you can also write this as $SA = 2(lw + wh + lh)$

>> **Distance formula:** $d = rt$, where d = distance, r = rate, and t = time

>> **Interest formula:** $I = prt$, where I = interest, p = principal, r = rate, and t = time

Know the Math Order of Operations

When a math problem asks you to perform more than one operation, you need to perform the operations in the correct order:

1. **Start with calculations in brackets or parentheses.**

   Note: When you have *nested* parentheses or brackets — parentheses or brackets inside other parentheses or brackets — do the inner ones first and work your way out.

2. **Work on terms with exponents and roots.**

3. **Do all the multiplication and division, in order from left to right.**

4. **Finish up with addition and subtraction, also in order from left to right.**

TIP

A helpful memory device for the order of operations is "Please Excuse My Dear Aunt Sally" or the acronym PEMDAS. It stands for parentheses, exponents, multiplication and division, and addition and subtraction. Remembering one or both of these will ensure you follow the proper steps in math problems that require you to perform calculations in a certain order.

TIP

There are exceptions to the order of operations; sometimes you can juggle the order around to make calculations easier, such as when parentheses appear in a string of numbers you're adding (you can ignore the parentheses in that case). Try to figure out when and why you're allowed to make such exceptions. Chapter 8 fills you in on some properties that may let you choose an order that makes numbers smaller and easier to work with while still giving you the right answer.

Boost Your Vocabulary

The Word Knowledge subtest is nothing more than a vocabulary test. This subtest contains questions that usually ask you to find the word that is "closest in meaning" to a given word. You may also have to find the *antonym*, or opposite, of a given word. The more words you know, the better you'll do on this subtest. It's that simple. (For details on how to increase your vocabulary, check out Chapter 4.)

Comprehend What You Read

To do well on the Paragraph Comprehension subtest, you must be able to read a paragraph, understand the information, and then correctly answer questions about the material. Generally, paragraph comprehension questions fall into four categories: inferring the main point or idea, analyzing the data, finding specific information, and identifying vocabulary in context. Understanding how to pick apart this information from your reading material is vital to a successful AFQT score.

TIP

Sharpen your comprehension daily by reading a paragraph in a book, newspaper, or magazine and then asking a friend to question you about information included in that paragraph.

Arrive at the Test Site Refreshed and Prepared

Don't let the recruiter schedule you to take the ASVAB until you're sure you're ready. Your recruiter may want to test you as soon as possible so he or she can fill recruiting goals. However, if you don't achieve a qualifying AFQT score, you waste your time, your recruiter's time, and the military's time. *Remember:* You may have to wait for up to six months for a retest. Make sure you're ready. (For more on retesting, turn to Chapter 1.)

The ASVAB test day can be drawn out and overwhelming, especially if nerves and stomach butterflies come out of nowhere or you struggle to use brainpower for an extended period of time. Give yourself a head start against the fatigue factor by arriving well-rested and motivated. Get a good night's sleep on the night before the test. If you're traveling to the test site in a bus or car, get a quick nap during the journey — as long as you're not the one driving, of course!

Try to eat a light meal or snack just before the test, and drink enough water. You don't want to become dehydrated or have your grumbling stomach distract you from solving a quadratic equation.

Watch the Clock

You have a limited amount of time to complete each subtest, but don't worry about it. The more you panic, the more likely you are to make mistakes. Just work at a steady pace, and you'll do fine. Chapter 1 breaks down how much time you have for the number of questions on each subtest (for both the paper and computerized tests).

If you're taking the computerized version of the ASVAB (CAT-ASVAB), you'll see a counter on the screen, counting down the time remaining on the subtest. If you're taking the paper version of the ASVAB, a clock will be clearly visible on the wall, and the test proctor will post the start and stop times of the subtest where you can easily see them.

Most people have plenty of time to complete all the subtests on the computerized and paper versions.

TIP

Don't spend too much time on one question. If you're drawing a blank, make a guess and move on. Keep in mind that if you're taking the CAT-ASVAB, you can't go back to change your answers or review any questions if you finish early, so make your guess a good one! (I explain how to do that in the next section.)

Guess Smart

Despite your extensive study, you may stumble on a question that has you stumped. Prepare Plan B by knowing how to use the process of elimination. If you're stuck on a question, try to eliminate any answers that you know to be wrong instead of making a wild guess. If you can eliminate even one wrong answer, you increase your chances of guessing the right answer from one in four to one in three. If you can eliminate two wrong answers, your chances increase to 50/50. (For more tips on intelligent guessing, see Chapter 3.)

Chapter **21**

Ten Math Concepts to Memorize

'll be the first to admit that the newest edition of *ASVAB AFQT For Dummies* is a great book — quite possibly the greatest book ever published (my well-known modesty aside). However, I can't pack everything you need to know about math, vocabulary, reading, and joining the military into all these pages. But what I *can* do is provide you with a tip that may help you perform better on the mathematics sections of the test: Memorize the concepts in this chapter because there's a good chance you'll see questions that ask you to use them.

First, though, you need to know that your mileage will vary if you, like most people, take the computerized version of the ASVAB. The test adapts to your ability to test your knowledge as quickly as possible, which means it presents a medium-difficulty question first. If you get the answer right, you'll likely see a hard question next; get it wrong and you're in for an easier question. Some people take the entire ASVAB without seeing a hard question, while others power through one tough question after another. (If most of your questions feel pretty easy, you're either a math whiz or you keep getting medium-difficulty questions wrong.)

With all that said, check out the following ten math concepts. If you don't already have them down, now's the time to get to work. And remember: A better score on the ASVAB's math subtests can translate into more desirable job choices.

Averages

Plenty of ASVAB questions deal with averages. If Amanda sells 13 popsicles on Monday, 17 on Tuesday, and 36 on Wednesday, what's her daily average? If Miguel records 26 videos in February, 18 in March, 10 in April, and 33 in May, what's his monthly average? If Dante scores a 97, 94, and 83 on his exams, what's his average score?

Averages require some addition and division — and that's it. You simply add the group of numbers (such as Amanda's 13, 17, and 36 popsicles) and then divide them by the count of those numbers (in Amanda's case, it's three). Her average is 22 popsicles a day, even though there weren't any days she actually sold 22 popsicles.

Miguel's monthly average is 29. Here's how you reach that conclusion: $26 + 18 + 10 + 33 = 87$; $87 \div 3 = 29$. Finally, Dante's average score is 91.33 because $97 + 94 + 83 = 274$; $274 \div 3 = 91.33$.

Percentages

You can calculate percentages by using a formula that looks like this: $\frac{\text{value}}{\text{total value}} \times 100$. If you encounter a problem that asks you to find a discount, turn a fraction into a percentage, or something similar, this formula will come in handy.

For example, if a question says that 9 out of 10 students saw a popular movie this weekend and wants to know what percentage that is, plug in your numbers: $\frac{9}{10} \times 100 = 90\%$.

Perimeter Formulas

Perimeter is the distance around a two-dimensional shape — and the best news about this formula is that it's one of the simplest that you'll ever use. All you do is add the length of each side and you're good to go.

For example, if you need to know your yard's perimeter so you can build a fence around it, measure each side and add them all together. It doesn't matter whether your yard is a square, a rectangle, a pentagon or some other shape.

But what about circles? Things get a little more complicated, but the perimeter of a circle is called its *circumference*. Check out the section "Circumference of a Circle" later in this chapter to get the scoop on solving a problem like that.

Area of a Rectangle

The formula to calculate the area of a rectangle is $A = lw$, where A represents area, l represents length, and w represents width. It's pretty straightforward; two of these three variables are usually included in questions about the area of a rectangle. If you have two variables, you can solve for the third.

For example, if Sgt. Maj. of the Army Weimer's swimming pool measures 15 feet long and 10 feet wide, you plug in the l and w variables to determine that its area is 150 square feet. Plenty of space for water PT! Keep this in mind, too: You can calculate the area of a square in the same way.

Area of a Triangle

You can figure out the area of a triangle — that is, the space between all three points and all three lines — with the formula $A = \frac{1}{2}bh$, where A represents area, b represents the length of the triangle's base, and h represents the triangle's height.

Here's a simple example. If you need to determine how much sod you need for a triangular patch of your yard, and that patch is 3 feet wide at its base and 4 feet high, replace the variables b and h, then do a little dividing, like so:

$$A = \frac{1}{2}(3 \times 4)$$
$$A = \frac{1}{2}(12)$$
$$A = 6$$

Area of a Circle

Figuring out the area of a circle requires you to know the formula $A = \pi r^2$ — and that A represents area while r represents the circle's radius. A question may ask you directly to find a circle's area or it may say something like "What's the area of a New York-style pizza with a radius of 8 inches?"

In either case, plug in what you know, like this:

$$A = \pi(8^2)$$
$$A = 3.14 \times 64$$
$$A \approx 200.96$$

TIP

When you see a pi-related question on the ASVAB, use 3.14. And if you see a pie-related question, focus until you're done with the test; then ask your recruiter to take you to the nearest pizza or pie shop to celebrate your great score.

Circumference of a Circle

Need to find the distance across a pizza, a pie, a round swimming pool or any other type of circle? You need circumference, which you can represent as C. Then, stick that into the following equation: $C = 2\pi r$. In this equation, r represents the circle's radius. (If you know only the circle's diameter, that's okay, too; just cut it in half and it becomes its radius.)

For example, if you need the circumference of a circle with a radius of 10, your equation will look like this:

$$C = 2 \times 3.14 \times 10$$
$$C = 62.83$$

The Pythagorean Theorem

You may not see any questions involving the Pythagorean theorem on the ASVAB. But if you're powering through the test, getting plenty right, you just may — so it doesn't hurt to commit it to memory. It tells you the length of one side of a right-sided triangle if you know the lengths of the other two sides. In real life, you'd bust out a measuring tape — but on the ASVAB, you'll use this formula: $c = \sqrt{a^2 + b^2}$. In this case, c represents the missing length, a represents the length of one side, and b represents the length of the other.

For example, if one side of a right triangle is 3 feet long and another is 5 feet long, put those figures into the formula to find the missing length:

$$c = \sqrt{3^2 + 4^2}$$
$$c = \sqrt{9 + 16}$$
$$c = \sqrt{25}$$
$$c = 5$$

Volume of a Rectangular Solid

A rectangular solid — like a prism, a shoebox, or even a cabinet — has *volume*, which refers to the amount of space in a 3D object. You may see a question or two asking you how many cubic feet of sand can fit into a sandbox, how many 1-cubic-foot concrete blocks can fit into a storage container, or something similar. To figure out these answers, you need to know that the necessary formula is $V = lwh$, where V represents volume, l represents length, w represents width, and h represents height.

If you need to know the volume of a shoebox that's 12 inches long, 8 inches wide, and 6 inches high, your equation will look like this:

$$V = 12 \times 8 \times 5$$
$$V = 576$$

TIP

Volume is measured in cubes of whatever unit you're using. In this case, it's cubic inches, but you may encounter problems that require you to use feet, meters, or some other unit. You mark a cubic measurement with a superscript 3, so 20 cubic inches is the same as 20 in.^{3}.

Volume of a Right Cylinder

The volume of a right cylinder — like a can, silo, or toilet paper roll — is best determined by solving $V = \pi r^2 h$, where V represents volume, r represents radius, and h represents height. Like some of the other more complex formulas, you may not see this on the ASVAB at all; it depends on how well you're performing. If you're not getting medium or hard questions right, you won't see tough ones like this.

However, if you do find a question that asks you to figure out the volume of a toilet paper roll with a radius of 1 inch and a length of 4 inches, here's what to scrawl out on your scratch paper:

$$V = \pi(1^2)4$$
$$V = 3.14 \times 1 \times 4$$
$$V = 12.56$$

Chapter **22**

Ten Pre-Test Tension Busters

Being a little nervous before you take a test is normal. In fact, those pre-test jitters can help you get a laser-focus on the questions and reach into your brain's depths to get the right answers. But because the ASVAB is a big deal — after all, it helps determine what kind of training you'll receive and what job you'll be doing for at least the next few years — your test-anxiety may threaten to get the best of you.

This chapter helps you dodge overwhelming stress so you can walk confidently into your testing location. You may still have butterflies (I know I did), but armed with all the knowledge you've picked up from this book and pre-test tension busters in this chapter, you'll be in better shape than most. The best part? You can use these techniques before any test — or any other stressful event — to calm your nerves so you can drive on.

Breathing Your Way to Zen

Your body comes pre-loaded with a pair of powerful tools to help you deal with acute and chronic anxiety and stress: Your lungs. Though breathing is automatic, you can control it; the amount of oxygen you take in, as well as the speed with which you inhale and exhale, can help calm your nervous system before and during a stressful event.

TECHNICAL STUFF

You're more likely to breathe in short, shallow bursts when you're stressed, which makes you feel tense and more anxious. It can even push your brain into producing a fight-or-flight response.

Several breathing exercises can help with anxiety, and here are some of the most popular:

» **Belly breathing:** Belly breathing, sometimes called *diaphragmatic breathing,* requires you to put one hand on your stomach and one on your chest. When you breathe in, imagine you're filling a balloon in your stomach; when you breathe out, imagine you're deflating it. Do this by slowly counting to two while breathing in through your nose and counting to three while you slowly exhale through your mouth. So why's your hand on your chest? It's there to make sure you're breathing deeply; that hand should remain mostly still while the one on your stomach rises and falls with each breath.

>> **Humming breath:** Humming as you exhale can help you focus on controlling your breath. Get comfortable in a sitting or standing position and keep your spine straight. Breathe in through your nose, taking at least five seconds to fill your lungs. Then, with your mouth closed, hum (like saying "hmmm") until you're completely out of breath. I don't recommend using this technique during the test — you'll get some dirty looks and may even be tossed out — but it's a good one to try while you're sitting in the car, alone in your room, or in a busy public restroom. (I'm kidding . . . mostly.)

>> **Pursed lips breathing:** If you feel short of breath, pursed lips breathing can help you slow things down and regain control. Breathe in through your nose. Then, breathe out with pursed lips; try to look like you're going to blow out a candle. Try to breathe out slower than you breathed in. Repeat this at least five times — more if you need to — and stop if you feel lightheaded.

TECHNICAL STUFF

Breathing exercises that require controlled, extended exhalation activate your parasympathetic nervous system, which counteracts your stress response by stimulating your vagus nerve, which lowers your heart rate and drops your blood pressure. When you regularly use deep-breathing techniques, your body rewards you with calm, relaxed feelings.

Eating Right Before (and On) Test Day

Your brain, like the rest of your body, needs fuel to function properly. Drink plenty of water the day before the test to make sure you're hydrated and eat a well-balanced dinner the night before. Foods rich in zinc, like cashews, beef, and egg yolks, have been linked with lowered anxiety; so have those with omega-3 fatty acids, such as salmon. According to Harvard scientists, foods like avocado, almonds, asparagus, and pickles can help your brain release serotonin and dopamine, which can help manage anxiety.

If you're already anxious, steer clear of coffee and energy drinks on test day. Highly caffeinated beverages can amp up your nervous system and make things worse. Go easy on sugar, too, which can give you a burst of energy that leads to a crash.

Working Out Your Stress at the Gym

Exercise boosts your overall health and wellbeing, but what you may not know is that working out is also a stress-buster. When you get moving, your body pumps out endorphins, which are feel-good chemicals that interact with receptors in your brain, triggering positive feelings in your body. And if you exercise regularly — not just when you're stressed or anxious — scientists say you'll experience less stress overall.

If you haven't already, start a regular exercise routine now. During military training, you exercise five to seven days a week; you can prep your body and work out all your stress at the same time.

Catching All the Zs

I've always said that I'll catch up on sleep when I'm dead — but realistically, that's not a healthy attitude. (I'm a work in progress, okay?) The harsh reality is that there's no such thing as "catching up" on sleep; after you've missed an opportunity to sleep, it's gone forever.

Adequate rest, on the other hand, gives your body all kinds of benefits that help you enjoy your life more when you're awake, which includes lowering feelings of stress and anxiety.

The average adult needs between seven and nine hours of shut-eye each night. You can improve your *sleep hygiene* by creating a bedroom environment and routines that promote uninterrupted, consistent sleep. Keep a stable sleep schedule (including consistent bedtimes and wake-up times), make your bedroom cool and comfortable, and follow a relaxing pre-bed routine that doesn't involve any electronics. Give yourself at least 30 minutes to wind down from your day, and fill it with anything that makes you calm, like soft music, stretching, reading, or the deep-breathing exercises from the section, "Breathing Your Way to Zen" earlier in this chapter. Dim the lights and go device-free so your brain gets the idea that it's okay to relax.

TIP

If you don't fall asleep after 20 minutes in bed, get up and do something else that calms you before heading back for round two.

TECHNICAL STUFF

Sleep gives your brain a chance to reset and go into a self-cleaning mode. Researchers believe that cerebrospinal fluid flushes toxic waste from your brain as you sleep, whisking it away so your brain is clean and clear for the next day.

Keeping an Eye on the Big Picture

Sometimes giving yourself a little perspective helps put pre-test stress in its place. Try to shift your focus from the test itself to what happens next: You get into the military, which is why you're taking the ASVAB in the first place. Whatever your reasons for joining, know that after the test is over, you'll be one step closer to your new job, the opportunity to serve your country, a steady paycheck, complimentary (and pretty darn good) health insurance for your spouse and kids, a new set of military-issued friends, world travel, retirement benefits, and everything else that motivates you.

Soaking Up Some Sun

Exposing yourself to sunlight can elevate your mood by boosting serotonin, which is sometimes called the happiness hormone, in your body. Sunshine also helps improve your sleep. The brighter exposure you get during the day, the more melatonin your body produces at night, improving your sleep and lowering your stress. Experts say that if you can manage to get between 5 and 15 minutes of sunlight on your arms, hands, and face a few times a week, your body can properly use its vitamin D stores.

WARNING

Though getting some sun is beneficial, don't overdo it — the risks may outweigh the benefits. You're more likely to get sunburned between the hours of 10 a.m. and 4 p.m., when ultraviolet rays are at their strongest. Even when the sun's not shining brightly, your body can still absorb its radiation. Unprotected exposure to ultraviolet rays can damage your skin, eyes, and immune system. It can also cause cancer, so use sunblock if you spend more than a short while outdoors.

Tuning In to Your Favorite Music

Your playlist can help you de-stress before you take the ASVAB or head toward any other anxiety-inducing event. Scientists have studied music therapy for several years, and the consensus is that binaural beats and 432 Hz-tuned music can help reduce anxiety. Your favorite music streaming app most likely has a collection of music that falls into both these categories, and you can take a few songs for a test drive to see what helps you most.

TECHNICAL STUFF

Binaural beats are auditory illusions that rely on different frequencies in each ear, so you need surround-sound speakers or earbuds to "hear" them. For example, if you listen to a sound at a frequency of 135 Hz in your left ear and a sound at a frequency of 125 Hz in your right ear, your brain makes you hear the two tones in each ear and invents your perception of a 10 Hz tone — the difference between the two tones coming in through your ears. The tone doesn't exist in the music; it's literally all in your head. Different frequency ranges for this tone produce different effects: A 30-Hz difference can improve memory, cognition, and mood, while a difference of 13 to 30 Hz can make you more alert and perform memory tasks better. An 8-Hz to 13-Hz difference can enhance creativity, and a 4-Hz to 8-Hz difference can induce a meditative state.

Practicing Mindfulness

Mindfulness — the practice of being conscious or aware of something by focusing on the present moment — can help dial down your body's response to stress. According to the American Psychological Association, mindfulness works because it influences two stress pathways in your brain: those related to attention and emotion regulation.

Learning to practice mindfulness is easy. You can take classes, watch videos online, download an app, or read about it online. You can also try one of the following methods:

» **Sitting mindfulness.** Sit comfortably with your back straight, feet flat on the floor, and hands resting in your lap. Breathe through your nose, focusing on the way air moves through your body. If you feel physical sensations, acknowledge them and return your focus to the air in your body.

» **Body scan mindfulness.** Lie on your back, keeping your legs straight and your arms at your sides with your palms facing up. Focus your attention on each part of your body, going in order from your head to your toes or vice versa; repeat in the opposite direction. Stay aware of sensations, emotions, or even thoughts you experience as you focus on each part of your body.

» **Walking mindfulness.** Find a quiet place you can pace 10 to 20 feet. Walk slowly and focus on your entire experience; be aware of the movements that help you keep your balance while you move. When you reach the end of your path, turn around and pace again.

» **The name game.** Re-center yourself in the moment by sitting quietly, with a straight but relaxed posture and naming three things you can hear, two things you can see, and one sensation you feel.

» **Gratitude listing.** Write down 5 to 10 very specific things you're grateful for. Rather than making broad statements, such as "I'm grateful for my family," zero in on something like "I'm grateful for the phone call with my parents last week."

Writing Down Your Worries

Journaling can be a very effective way to relieve stress. A 2011 study by Gerardo Ramirez and Sian L. Beilock showed that writing specifically about testing anxieties helped people perform better on exams. And in general, many people find that writing down (or typing) their thoughts and feelings helps alleviate tension and anxiety. If sitting down to write paragraphs about what's going on in your brain doesn't work for you, try one of the following methods:

>> **Bullet point journaling.** Forget complete sentences, grammar, and punctuation — simply jot down a bulleted list of what's on your mind.

>> **Art journaling.** Like creating a vision board, collage, or scrapbook, art journaling lets you create visually appealing pages that reflect your thoughts. If you're artistically inclined, you can even draw your journal entries.

>> **Gratitude journaling.** Some people thrive when they write down the good things that they're thankful for each day. Aim for three to five points each day and switch them up; don't use the same ones all week.

>> **Voice journaling.** If you're not much for sitting down with a notebook or keyboard, try voice journaling; it's stream-of-consciousness talking to your phone or computer using a dictation or voice journaling app.

Affirming the Positives

If positive affirmations are your jam, you can use them to alleviate pre-test stress. There are all kinds of things you can say to yourself to relieve anxiety and reduce stress (ASVAB-related and in general). The key to making affirmations powerful tools that work for you is to repeat them to yourself regularly.

If you have to line your bathroom mirror or laptop screen with sticky notes, set reminders on your phone, or put affirmation time on your calendar, do it! Can't think of what to say to yourself? Try some of the following affirmations on for size:

>> "I choose to feel calm."

>> "I am right where I need to be."

>> "I look forward to starting my military career."

>> "I'm getting better every day."

>> "I am unstoppable."

Affirmations can help you authentically encourage yourself by using words consistent with your truth. The idea is to build up your sense of self so you improve your ability to cope with stressful situations (like taking the ASVAB).

Writing Down Your Worries

Affirming the Positives

Index

C

capitulate, defined, 57

CAST (Computer Adaptive Screening Test), 13

CAT-ASVAB

  about, 11–12

  choosing random answers, 33

celestial, defined, 56

characteristic, 112

choosing answers, 163–164

circles

  about, 120–121

  area of, 122, 335, 341

  circumference of, 122, 335, 341

  diameter of, 122, 335

  formulas for, 122, 148

  radius of, 122, 335

circular, defined, 57

circumference of a circle, 120–121, 122, 335, 341

clemency, defined, 56

Coast Guard

  minimum qualifying scores for, 15

  retests for, 17

Coast Guard Reserves, minimum qualifying scores for, 15

coaxial, defined, 55

coefficient, defined, 92

coin problems, 148–149

colossal, defined, 57

combined questions, 130, 131

combining like terms, 113

common denominators, finding, 103–104

common multiple, 97

commutative property, 94–95

comparing fractions, 103–104

complementary angle, 119

completion, defined, 57

composite number, 92

comprehending, 336

Computer Adaptive Screening Test (CAST), 13

conclusions, drawing, 76–77

context

  defining words from their, 51–52

  exercise answers and explanations, 57–58

convene, defined, 54

converting

decimals, 107–108

decimals to fractions, 105, 124

fractions to decimals, 102–103, 124

creating

  strategies for Arithmetic Reasoning subtest, 162–165

  study plan, 334

  vocabulary, 72

  words from scratch, 41–44

  your vocabulary, 37–58

cross-product method, 104

crosswords, 39

cube roots, 111–112

cubes

  formulas for, 148

  surface area of, 335

  volume of, 335

cylinders

  formulas for, 148

  volume of, 335

D

day before, 32

decimals

  about, 104–105

  adding, 105

  converting fractions to, 102–103, 124

  converting to fractions, 105

  dividing, 106–108

  multiplying, 106

  percents, 108

  rounding, 108

  subtracting, 105

deep thinking questions, 81–82

defining words from their context, 51–52

Delayed Entry Program (DEP), 17

deleterious, defined, 57

denominators

  about, 99

  adding fractions with different, 101–102

  adding fractions with like, 101

  finding common, 103–104

  subtracting fractions with different, 101–102

  subtracting fractions with like, 101

DEP (Delayed Entry Program), 17

devalue, defined, 55

About the Author

Angie Papple Johnston joined the U.S. Army in 2006 as a Chemical, Biological, Radiological, and Nuclear specialist, ready to tackle chemical weapons in a Level-A HAZMAT suit. During her second deployment as part of Operation Iraqi Freedom, Angie became her battalion's public affairs representative, writing press releases and photographing historic moments from Tikrit to Kirkuk. She also served as the Lead Cadre for the Texas Army National Guard's Recruit Sustainment Program, teaching brand-new privates how to survive Basic Combat Training, Advanced Individual Training, and the Army, as well as the CBRN noncommissioned officer-in-charge of an aviation battalion in Washington, D.C. Angie currently serves as the senior writer/editor and speechwriter of a federal agency.

Author's Acknowledgments

Lindsay Berg, thank you so much for all the opportunities you've given me over the years. I really appreciate the chances you've taken on my books and the patience you've had with my math skills . . . and so much more.

Chad Sievers, I appreciate the tremendous amount of work you've put into this book. Thank you for having such a good feel for what goes where, your brilliant editing skills, and for just being you.

A very special thanks to Jonathan Kralick for helping make this book the best AFQT resource available.

Publisher's Acknowledgments

Executive Editor: Lindsay Berg

Project Editor and Copy Editor: Chad R. Sievers

Technical Editors: Jonathan Kralick

Production Editor: Saikarthick Kumarasamy

Cover Photos: © LuVo/Getty Images

Leverage the power

Dummies is the global leader in the reference category and one of the most trusted and highly regarded brands in the world. No longer just focused on books, customers now have access to the dummies content they need in the format they want. Together we'll craft a solution that engages your customers, stands out from the competition, and helps you meet your goals.

Advertising & Sponsorships

Connect with an engaged audience on a powerful multimedia site, and position your message alongside expert how-to content. Dummies.com is a one-stop shop for free, online information and know-how curated by a team of experts.

- Targeted ads
- Video
- Email Marketing
- Microsites
- Sweepstakes sponsorship

20 MILLION PAGE VIEWS EVERY SINGLE MONTH

15 MILLION UNIQUE VISITORS PER MONTH

43% OF ALL VISITORS ACCESS THE SITE VIA THEIR MOBILE DEVICES

700,000 NEWSLETTER SUBSCRIPTIONS TO THE INBOXES OF

300,000 UNIQUE INDIVIDUALS EVERY WEEK

# of dummies

Custom Publishing

Reach a global audience in any language by creating a solution that will differentiate you from competitors, amplify your message, and encourage customers to make a buying decision.

- Apps
- Books
- eBooks
- Video
- Audio
- Webinars

Brand Licensing & Content

Leverage the strength of the world's most popular reference brand to reach new audiences and channels of distribution.

For more information, visit dummies.com/biz

PERSONAL ENRICHMENT

Staying Sharp dummies	**Facebook** dummies	**Guitar** dummies	**Investing** dummies	**Beekeeping** dummies	**Digital Photography** dummies
9781119187790 USA $26.00 CAN $31.99 UK £19.99	9781119179030 USA $21.99 CAN $25.99 UK £16.99	9781119293354 USA $24.99 CAN $29.99 UK £17.99	9781119293347 USA $22.99 CAN $27.99 UK £16.99	9781119310068 USA $22.99 CAN $27.99 UK £16.99	9781119235606 USA $24.99 CAN $29.99 UK £17.99
Meditation dummies	**Pregnancy** ALL-IN-ONE dummies	**Samsung Galaxy S7** dummies	**iPhone** dummies	**Crocheting** dummies	**Nutrition** dummies
9781119251163 USA $24.99 CAN $29.99 UK £17.99	9781119235491 USA $26.99 CAN $31.99 UK £19.99	9781119279952 USA $24.99 CAN $29.99 UK £17.99	9781119283133 USA $24.99 CAN $29.99 UK £17.99	9781119287117 USA $24.99 CAN $29.99 UK £16.99	9781119130246 USA $22.99 CAN $27.99 UK £16.99

PROFESSIONAL DEVELOPMENT

Windows 10 dummies	**AutoCAD** dummies	**Excel 2016** dummies	**QuickBooks 2017** dummies	**macOS Sierra** dummies	**LinkedIn** dummies	**Windows 10** ALL-IN-ONE dummies
9781119311041 USA $24.99 CAN $29.99 UK £17.99	9781119255796 USA $39.99 CAN $47.99 UK £27.99	9781119293439 USA $26.99 CAN $31.99 UK £19.99	9781119281467 USA $26.99 CAN $31.99 UK £19.99	9781119280651 USA $29.99 CAN $35.99 UK £21.99	9781119251132 USA $24.99 CAN $29.99 UK £17.99	9781119310563 USA $34.00 CAN $41.99 UK £24.99
SharePoint 2016 dummies	**Fundamental Analysis** dummies	**Networking** dummies	**Office 2016** dummies	**Office 365** dummies	**Salesforce.com** dummies	**Coding** dummies
9781119181705 USA $29.99 CAN $35.99 UK £21.99	9781119263593 USA $26.99 CAN $31.99 UK £19.99	9781119257769 USA $29.99 CAN $35.99 UK £21.99	9781119293477 USA $26.99 CAN $31.99 UK £19.99	9781119265313 USA $24.99 CAN $29.99 UK £17.99	9781119239314 USA $29.99 CAN $35.99 UK £21.99	9781119293323 USA $29.99 CAN $35.99 UK £21.99

dummies.com

A Wiley Brand